Tradition, Treaties, and Trade

Qing Imperialism and Chosŏn Korea, 1850–1910

Harvard East Asian Monographs 295

Tradition, Treaties, and Trade

Qing Imperialism and Chosŏn Korea, 1850–1910

Kirk W. Larsen

Published by the Harvard University Asia Center
Distributed by Harvard University Press
Cambridge (Massachusetts) and London 2008

Printed in the United States of America

The Harvard University Asia Center publishes a monograph series and, in coordination with the Fairbank Center for East Asian Research, the Korea Institute, the Reischauer Institute of Japanese Studies, and other faculties and institutes, administers research projects designed to further scholarly understanding of China, Japan, Vietnam, Korea, and other Asian countries. The Center also sponsors projects addressing multidisciplinary and regional issues in Asia.

Library of Congress Cataloging-in-Publication Data

Larsen, Kirk W.

Tradition, treaties, and trade : Qing imperialism and Choson Korea, 1850–1910 / Kirk W. Larsen.

p. cm. -- (Harvard East Asian monographs ; 295)

Includes bibliographical references and index.

ISBN 978-0-674-02807-4 (cl : alk. paper)

ISBN 978-0-674-06073-9 (pbk : alk. paper)

1. Korea--Foreign relations--China. 2. China--Foreign relations--Korea. 3. Korea--Foreign relations--1864–1910. 4. China--Foreign relations--1644–1912. I. Title.

DS910.2.C5L37 2008

3048'251905109034--dc22

2007038579

Index by the author

Printed on acid-free paper

Acknowledgments

This book is a revision of my Ph.D. dissertation. It can, therefore, be seen as the culmination of more years of reading, research, thinking, and writing than I care to remember. What has made the long years more bearable and, it is hoped, the final result more coherent and compelling is the advice, expertise, and support of friends, colleagues, and institutions along the way.

Mark Peterson is largely responsible for my decision to explore the history of East Asia in the first place. It was also from one of his engaging lectures that my interest in Yuan Shikai's presence in Korea was first piqued. Carter Eckert, Bill Kirby, and Philip Kuhn provided invaluable guidance and advice during the interminable process of converting a vague idea into a coherent dissertation. Their support and encouragement has continued long after their mentoring duties had officially ended. The Fulbright program, the Korea Foundation, the Harvard ROC Club, and the Harvard History Department all provided financial support for research travel to Asia. Friends and colleagues at Harvard, both during and long after my graduate studies there, have offered helpful criticism, friendly listening ears, and examples of first-rate scholarship to emulate. Special thanks are due to Matt Christensen, Caroline Elkins, Karl Gerth, Kyung Moon Hwang, Christine Kim, Michael Kim, Hyung Gu Lynn, Eugene Park, and Chiho Sawada.

Numerous individuals and institutions in the Republic of Korea and the Republic of China gave generously of their time and resources to facilitate my research in Asia. Special thanks goes to Lin Man-houng, Zhang Cunwu, and the staff of the Institute of Modern History at the Academia Sinica. I am also indebted to the staff of the Kyujanggak, Seoul National University Library, National Central Library, and Korean Customs Museum in Korea. South Korean scholars including Yi T'ae-jin, Young-ick Lew, the late Kim

Key-hiuk, and Eun Kyung Park spent far more time giving advice, access to materials, and encouragement than my status as a Ph.D candidate/ young scholar warranted. Members of the Overseas Chinese community in Korea including Sun Shuyi, Wang Jingpeng, David Wi, and Patricia Hsiao shared their stories and extremely useful historical materials.

The Department of History at The George Washington University and the Sigur Center for Asian Studies have given financial and other support during the revision process. Friends and colleagues at both the University of Texas–Austin and GWU have read portions (or all) of various versions of the manuscript, discussed issues large and small, and have offered invaluable advice and encouragement. Special thanks goes to Tyler Anbinder, Muriel Atkin, Ed Berkowitz, Gregg Brazinsky, Harry Harding, Dane Kennedy, Ed McCord, Shawn McHale, Mike Mochizuki, Marcia Norton, Ed Rhoads, Daqing Yang, Margherita Zanasi, and Andrew Zimmerman. I have also benefited from the assistance of Alexandra Chwat, Jiyoung Lee, and Ji-yeong Rhim.

As I presented parts of the book and its arguments in various conferences and forums, I have greatly benefited from the questions and feedback I received from a number of scholars, including Paul Cohen, John Duncan, Alexis Dudden, David Kang, JaHyun Kim-Haboush, Gari Ledyard, Dennis McNamara, Jim Millward, Bonnie Oh, the late James Palais, and Ned Shultz. In addition, the two anonymous readers for the Harvard University Asia Center Publications Program provided extremely useful advice. The staff at the Harvard University Asia Center Publications Office has invariably been patient, professional, and supportive.

Given the high intellectual caliber of the many friends and colleagues who have influenced the writing of this book, one could reasonably expect nothing but brilliant perfection in the final product. Alas, this book is also a reflection of my own abilities, proclivities, and characteristics. All errors, mistakes, and omissions are, therefore, entirely my own.

Last but most definitely not least, I wish to acknowledge and thank my wife, Kathy, and my children, Julia and Jon, for their love, patience, and support. Writing a book is fun. Living with the three of you is joy.

K.W.L.

Contents

Conventions and Abbreviations

Chinese terms are romanized according to the *pinyin* system; Korean, the McCune-Reischauer system; Japanese, the Hepburn system. The dates of primary source documents are listed according to date indicated in the document; this usually means using the lunar calendar and the reign title of the polity in which the document was written. For example GX 5.1.18 indicates the eighteenth day of the first month of the fifth year of the reign of the Qing Guangxu Emperor (r. 1875–1907). An asterisk (*) after the month indicates an intercalary month. The Western (solar) calendar equivalent is also listed. These dates were derived via the Academia Sinica's on-line generator (http://www.sinica.edu.tw/~tdbproj/sinocal/luso.html).

Abbreviations Used in Notes

For complete publication information, see the Works Cited, pp. 297–318.

ACDM	Il-keun Park, ed., *Anglo-American and Chinese Diplomatic Materials Relating to Korea*
British Consular Reports	British Foreign Office, *Diplomatic and Consular Reports on Trade and Finance*, 1884–1910
British Documents	Ian Nish, ed., "Korea, the Ryukyu Islands, and North-East Asia, 1875–1888"
Ch'ŏngan	Koryŏ taehakkyo, ed., *Ku-Han'guk oegyo munsŏ: Ch'ŏngan*
CC	Ch'ŏlchong (r. 1849–64)

CS	Kuksa p'yonch'an wiwŏnhoe, ed., *Ch'ŏlchong sillok*. Unless otherwise indicated, all references are to the Classical Chinese original (*wŏnmun*).
CSR	"Korean Customs Service Reports," in China, Imperial Maritime Customs, *Returns of Trade and Trade Reports*. Year cited is that in the title of the report, not the year the report was published.
Diangao	Li Hongzhang, *Li wenzhong gong quanshu, Diangao*
GX	Guangxu era (1875–1907)
Haegwanan	Koryŏ taehakkyo, ed., *Ku-Han'guk oegyo kwan'gye pusok munsŏ: Haegwanan*
JDZH	Zhang Cunwu, ed., *Jindai Zhong-Han guanxishi ziliao huibian*
JSSL	Gugong bowuyuan, ed., *Qing Guangxu chao Zhong-Ri jiaoshe shiliao*
KAR	Spencer J. Palmer, ed., *Korean-American Relations: Documents Pertaining to the Far Eastern Diplomacy of the United States*. Vol. 1: *The Initial Period, 1883–1886*. Vol. 2: *The Period of Growing Influence, 1887–1895*
KJ	Kojong (r. 1864–1907)
KM	Kwangmu era (1897–1907)
KS	Kuksa p'yŏnch'an wiwŏnhoe, ed., *Kojong sillok*. Unless otherwise indicated, all references are to the Classical Chinese original (*wŏnmun*).
NGB	*Nihon gaikō bunsho*
SS	Kuksa p'yonch'an wiwŏnhoe, ed., *Sunjong sillok*. Unless otherwise indicated, all references are to the Classical Chinese original (*wŏnmun*).
Togan	Koryŏ taehakkyo, ed., *Ku-Han'guk oegyo munsŏ: Togan*
Treaties, Regulations, etc.	China, Imperial Maritime Customs, *Treaties, Regulations, etc., Between Corea and Other Powers. 1876–1889*

TSIS	Kim Kyŏng-t'ae, ed., *T'ongsang hwich'an: Han'guk p'yŏn*
TZ	Tongzhi era (1862–74)
WJSL	Wang Liang and Wang Yanwei, eds., *Qingji wai-jiao shiliao*
YH	Yunghŭi era (1907–10)
YHWN	Korean Customs Service, *Yunghŭi wŏnnyŏn Han'guk oeguk muyŏk yollam*
YSHG	Li Hongzhang, *Li wenzhong gong quanshu: Yishu han'gao*
ZRHGX	Academia Sinica, Institute of Modern History, ed., *Qingji Zhong-Ri-Han guanxi shiliao*

Tradition, Treaties, and Trade

Qing Imperialism and Chosŏn Korea,

1850–1910

Introduction

In December 1882, a steamship filled with foreign imperialists dropped anchor off the Korean port of Inch'ŏn.[1] Observers of Korea had long noted that ships approaching Inch'ŏn were forced to navigate a course made treacherous by myriad islands, tidal mudflats, and seasonal fog and ice. One observer concluded that it was "probable that these natural conditions . . . have had a large share in pre-determining the exclusive policy of the Korean people. It is certain that they have powerfully aided that policy."[2] In addition to the barriers presented by Korea's geography, many in the Chosŏn Kingdom (1392–1910) were less than sanguine about the prospect of opening up the "Hermit Nation" to foreign goods and ideas.[3] But the passengers of the steamship were determined to do just that for their own geopolitical and commercial ends. The advent of the steamship itself, with its unprecedented ability to project military power and distribute manufactured goods even in the face of geographical and political barriers, lent inexorable momentum to the wave of imperialism that was washing on Korea's shores.

---

1. The port the ship approached was at the time known as Chemulp'o. In the ensuing years, the town of Chemulp'o rapidly grew and quickly merged with the nearby village of Inch'ŏn, keeping the latter's name.

2. Hall, "A Visit to the West Coast and Capital of Korea," 148.

3. The English appellation "Hermit" was first applied to Korea by William Elliot Griffis, an American educator and preacher who lived in Japan in the 1870s and, while never actually visiting Korea or reading Korean-language materials, wrote *Corea, the Hermit Nation*, a history of Korea widely read in the late nineteenth century. An isolationist foreign policy was hardly an immutable fixture of Korean history. It is, however, a fairly apt description of the Chosŏn Kingdom's attitude toward Westerners for much of the nineteenth century.

Eighteen eighty-two was a busy if not always good year for imperialists throughout the world. After years of increasing involvement and entanglement in Egypt's tortured finances, Great Britain sent troops to that country to protect the Suez Canal Zone and impose stronger controls over the nominally autonomous Egyptian government. France fought against Black Flag pirates and Qing Chinese troops to increase its stranglehold on Indochina. The Russian government announced its intention to fund the annual migration of 2,500 families to settle the Russian Far East. The United States Congress, fearing competition within its recently settled western territories, signed the Chinese Exclusion Act. Only dimly perceptible at the time, the world stood on the threshold of a transition to the era of so-called high imperialism, with its attendant fierce competition for land and resources. Before it would end, some 85 percent of the earth's land area would be occupied or at least officially claimed by one imperial power or another.[4]

Off the coast of Inch'ŏn, the passengers of the steamship had to wait for hours before the tide changed and small Korean boats could, for a fee, ferry them to shore. Like most imperialists of the nineteenth century, their ambitions were complex and often contradictory; their motivations were influenced by their own worldviews and proclivities, not to mention the possibility of personal profit. Over the course of the next three decades, their activities and those of their superiors and compatriots would transform Korea and the whole of East Asia.

Those with a passing familiarity with the history of nineteenth-century East Asia might posit several possible nationalities for the imperialists arriving on the Korean coast. Surprisingly, however, the steamship and its passengers were not Japanese, British, French, Russian, or American. Rather, they hailed from the Qing Empire (1644–1912). The arrival of the China Merchants Steamship Company steamer, the *Xingxin*, and its passengers Ma Jianchang, Tang Tingshu, Chen Shutang, and Paul Georg Moellendorf reflected the ongoing transformation of the imperial strategies and tactics utilized by the Qing Empire to project and promote its interests in Chosŏn Korea.[5]

Our difficulties with recognizing Qing imperialism in the nineteenth century for what it was probably owe much to influential and widely

---

4. Fieldhouse, *Economics and Empire*, 3.

5. For Korean acknowledgment of the arrival of Tang Tingshu, Chen Shutang, Moellendorff, and others, see *KS*, Dec. 14, 1882 (KJ 19.11.5).

shared notions of Chinese exceptionalism. First is the idea that China was neither an imperialist power nor an empire but, rather, a victim of foreign imperialism. Some Westerners categorically deny that China ever has been an empire.[6] Others, while granting the possibility that ancient dynasties such as the Han, Tang, or even the Ming may have been empires, have emphasized that a Chinese decline in recent centuries resulted in the disappearance of China from the ranks of imperialist powers by the nineteenth century at the very latest.[7] This is due in part to an assumption that imperialism, especially in its modern guises, is largely a Western enterprise. Thus, as Emma Jinhua Teng aptly puts it, "The presumption that colonizers were European and the colonized non-European is deeply entrenched both inside and outside the academy. The very notion of studying 'Chinese colonialism' thus seems alien to many."[8]

For their part, contemporary Chinese, academics and officials alike, have done little to challenge this prevailing wisdom. In part, this arises from the unavoidable reality that China in the nineteenth and twentieth centuries *was* a victim of the imperialism of others. The Opium War (1839–1842), the sacking of the Qing Summer Palace (1860), the ill-fated Boxer Rebellion (1900), the "carving of the Chinese melon," and the foreign diplomats, merchants, missionaries, and adventurers who appeared in China in ever increasing numbers all combine to create a powerful narrative of more

---

6. "China has never been a great Empire or had any strong national existence in a European sense" (Hobson, *Imperialism*, 319). Cf. Stephen Howe's (*Empire*, 56) statement: "China is rarely considered among the great modern empires."

7. For example, Paul Kennedy (*Rise and Fall of Great Powers*, 7–9), in his sweeping analysis of Great Power politics over the course of the last five centuries, briefly mentions Ming China at the outset, but argues that "China had decided to turn its back on the world" in the early Ming, ushering in an era of "steady relative decline" that continued through the subsequent Qing dynasty. Following this brief mention, China virtually disappears from consideration as a "Great Power" in the book until the period after 1949. See also Stephen Howe's (*Empire*, 56) acknowledgment that although "for centuries it had been not only a vast, multi-ethnic polity—clearly fitting most historians' definitions of an imperial system—but the world's most populous, prosperous, and by many measures most sophisticated society," China's "story in the 19th and earlier 20th centuries was largely one of decline." In "Imperialism in East Asia," Akira Iriye makes a strong and eloquent case for considering Japan alongside the Western powers as an imperialist power in Asia but, curiously, sees no need to make a similar case for China. See also Abernathy, *Dynamics of Global Dominance*, 9–10; and Meyer, *Dust of Empire*, 12.

8. Emma Teng, *Taiwan's Imagined Geography*, 7.

than a century of "national humiliation" (*guochi*).[9] Resisting and eliminating foreign imperialism was a central element of both Guomindang (Nationalist) and Chinese Communist (CCP) policy. Mao Zedong's 1949 declaration that China had "stood up" was a sign of how central anti-imperialism was to the CCP agenda. The widespread celebration of the return of Hong Kong to the PRC in 1997 signaled the continuing resonance of the anti-imperialist struggle.[10]

In addition to emphasizing China's status as a victim of foreign imperialism, many PRC scholars, for whom "talk of 'Chinese imperialism' is heresy," characterize the Qing Empire's acquisition of significant amounts of territory not as expansionism but as "national unification" (*tongyi*). In contrast to the depredations that China suffered at the hands of outsiders, the Qing territorial enlargement is often depicted in terms of a process in which the Empire's diverse peoples came together (*tuanjie*) to result in today's China.[11] This particular view of the past plays an influential role not only in the general conception of history and identity held by many Chinese today but also in the PRC's efforts to maintain its claims to far-flung territories such as Xinjiang and Tibet.[12]

---

9. For a discussion of the role of "humiliation" in Chinese historical memory, see Paul Cohen, *China Unbound*, 148–67. Cohen notes that in the 1990s, more than four decades after the PRC had ostensibly "stood up," calls not to forget (*wuwang*) the humiliations of the past were still prevalent (ibid., 149). See also Callahan, "National Insecurities." Memories of humiliation have been linked to contemporary discourses of resurgent Chinese nationalism; see Garver, "More from the 'Say No Club,'" 151–53.

10. See, e.g., Wang Jianlang, *Zhongguo feichu bupingdeng tiaoyue de licheng.*

11. Emma Teng, *Taiwan's Imagined Geography*, 6, 250–51. Teng also notes that official PRC orthodoxy insists that "Qing expansionism be studied under the rubric of 'frontier studies' (*bianjiangxue*) and not 'imperial studies' or 'colonial studies'" (ibid., 251). The decision of PRC scholars to emphasize a narrative of benign Chinese "national unification" juxtaposed with tales of national humiliation has resulted in some surprising omissions within the national humiliation literature. Callahan ("National Insecurities," 205) notes that works such as the *Record of National Humiliation* (*Guochi lu*) "and other such texts" literally ignore "the key event of the nineteenth century: the Taiping Rebellion (1851–1864), which has been called 'the most destructive civil war in the history of the world (at least in terms of lives lost)' and was 'the most serious threat to the survival of the last imperial dynasty in China.' That pivotal event is not included in such books because it does not fit in with the moral narrative of national humiliation: foreign imperialism encouraged by domestic corruption."

12. Hostetler, *Qing Colonial Enterprise*, 25.

A second aspect of Chinese exceptionalism is traditional China's purported means of interacting with other powers and peoples. Central to this is the image of a "Chinese World Order," a tendency to portray all of China's relations with the outside world as being delimited by a "tribute system" predicated on Confucian ritual.[13] This contrasts dramatically with Western-style international relations, which are presumed to be motivated by and predicated on more substantive principles and concerns. The failure of the 1792–93 Macartney Mission to secure the establishment of substantive diplomatic and commercial relations between the British and Qing empires has been taken by many as emblematic of the gap between East and West in this regard. Obsessed with ritual protocol, the Qing Qianlong emperor (r. 1736–95) blithely dismissed Macartney for not adhering to the rules of the tribute system.[14] Thus, the Qing Empire has been regarded not only as a victim of foreign imperialism but also as a polity behind the times, and one obsessed by ritual at that.[15]

Third, and related to the second, is the notion that Confucian China seldom if ever took commercial considerations into account when formulating foreign policies. Again, the contrast with the aggressive resource- and market-seeking Westerners (and later Japanese) is seen as dramatic and obvious.[16]

---

13. Fairbank, ed., *The Chinese World Order.*

14. For a comprehensive account of the Macartney Mission, see Peyrefitte, *The Immobile Empire.*

15. See, e.g., Peyrefitte, *The Collision of Two Civilisations,* xvii; Bickers, "Introduction," 8; and Shunhong Zhang, "Historical Anachronism," 39.

16. For example, Tseng-Tsai Wang ("The Macartney Mission," 45) writes: "To worsen matters further, the formal policy of China was hostile to commerce until recent times, and the mercantile calling was not regarded as honorable. For this reason, it has been a misfortune to Great Britain and the West generally that they were brought into contact to China through commerce." Although many historians of China disagree and are well aware of the importance and even the centrality of commerce to the ostensibly Confucian polity and society of late imperial China, the idea that China's Confucian elite disdained commerce still holds considerable currency among many nonspecialists. Cf., e.g., David Landes's (*The Wealth and Poverty of Nations,* 95) statement that "a new Confucian crowd competed for influence, mandarins who scorned and distrusted commerce (for them, the only true source of wealth was agriculture)." Cf. also Francis Fukayama's ("Asian Values and the Asian Crisis," 23) statement that "to put it another way, economic growth was contingent on the rejection by Asians of important elements of their own cultural heritage, including the Mandarin disdain for commerce and physical labor." See also Paul Kennedy, *Rise and Fall of Great Powers,* 8.

All three of these notions of Chinese exceptionalism have been challenged by recent scholarship on the Qing Empire and on China more generally. If one accepts Chinese claims that "China" has enjoyed millennia of continuous existence, then it is patently obvious that China constitutes one of the largest and most successful empires in human history. Beginning with the consolidation of the so-called Warring States in northern China in the third century B.C., Chinese dynasties have expanded their reach to include vast swathes of territory, much of it beyond the imagination of the First Emperor of the Qin (Qinshihuangdi), who is said to have "unified China" in 221 B.C. Over the centuries, China has ruled over and often incorporated a myriad of peoples of varying ethnicities, a development sometimes masked by an emphasis on the continuous existence of a single, unitary Han Chinese ethnic group.[17]

Whatever one might conclude about Chinese imperial expansion in earlier eras, the Qing Empire (although its ruling house was Manchu not Han Chinese) constitutes the apex of Chinese imperial expansion. In the seventeenth and eighteenth centuries, the Qing expanded its territory to incorporate Taiwan, Mongolia, Tibet, and parts of Central Asia.[18] Moreover, Qing rulers also claimed suzerainty over a much wider area, including Korea, the Liuqiu (Ryūkyū) Islands, Annam (Indochina), and Burma. The PRC has relinquished claims to some of these imperial possessions and vassals, but the present-day borders of the PRC display a remarkable correspondence with those of the Qing Empire in the late nineteenth century,

---

17. The notion of "China" as a continuous entity, imperial or otherwise, is more a product of historiography and memory than an accurate reflection of the vagaries of millennia of history. Many of the dynasties that ruled "China" were not ethnically Han Chinese in origin. Moreover, emphasis on continuity masks important periods of division and fragmentation. Still, the larger point is that the political entity often written of and remembered as "China" has often behaved in ways that can be seen only as imperialistic. For acknowledgment of China as an empire and of the perceived continuity of modes of Chinese imperial rule, see Lieven, *Empire*, 27–40.

18. Emma Teng (*Taiwan's Imagined Geography*, 5) summarizes: "By 1760, the Qing had achieved the incredible feat of doubling the size of the empire's territory, bringing various non-Chinese frontier peoples under its rule. The impact of Qing expansionism was thus tremendous, as the Qing not only redefined the territorial boundaries of China, but also refashioned China as a multiethnic realm—shifting the traditional border between Chinese (*Hua*) and barbarian (*yi*). In doing so, the Qing created an image of 'China' that differed vastly from that of the Ming."

a fact that clearly demonstrates the continuities of the Chinese imperial tradition.[19]

Scholars studying the Qing Empire have not been content with merely noting the dramatic expansion of territory under Manchu rule. They have also made a compelling case for considering the Qing as an empire worthy of comparison with other empires across the world.[20] Far from being isolated from the broader streams of world history, the Qing Empire was, in the words of Laura Hostetler, "an active participant in a shared world order."[21] Like its counterparts in other places in the world, the Qing used a variety of sophisticated ideologies and practices to manage its large multiethnic empire. Officials utilized modern cartography to demarcate the boundaries of the empire,[22] observed and classified a wide range of subject peoples both within and beyond the empire's borders,[23] and actively encouraged migration and colonization to solidify the Qing's control of its hard-won territories.[24] These and a myriad of other practices have attracted increased scholarly attention and have served to narrow the conceptual gap between East and West; they have also prompted a reassessment of Qing China and its place in the early modern world.

The notion of a unitary Chinese World Order has come under growing scrutiny and criticism as it has become increasingly clear that the Qing

---

19. For a map comparing Qing and PRC borders, see Hostetler, *Qing Colonial Enterprise*, 34.

20. Adas, "Imperialism and Colonialism in Comparative Perspective"; Perdue, "Comparing Empires"; Emma Teng, *Taiwan's Imagined Geography*, 3.

21. Hostetler, *Qing Colonial Enterprise*, 1.

22. For examples of the role of maps and cartography in Western imperialism, see Edney, *Mapping an Empire*; and Abernathy, *Dynamics of Global Dominance*, 8. For a cogent summary of the ways in which maps served to inscribe Western notions of space, boundaries, and territories on the peoples and lands they depicted, see Anderson, "Census, Map, Museum," 247–52. See also Thongchai, *Siam Mapped*. For Qing analogues, see Hostetler, *Qing Colonial Enterprise*, 51–80; and Teng, *Taiwan's Imagined Geography*, 34–59.

. 23. For examples of how classification and the production of knowledge played a role in Western imperialism, see Said, *Orientalism*. See also Hevia, *English Lessons*, 119–55. For Qing analogues, see Hostetler, *Qing Colonial Enterprise*, 81–100, 127–204; and Emma Teng, *Taiwan's Imagined Geography*, esp. 122–72.

24. For examples of the role of settlers in Western and Japanese imperialism, see Elkins and Pedersen, *Settler Colonialism in the Twentieth Century*. For Qing analogues, see Millward, *Beyond the Pass*; Perdue, *China Marches West*; and Giersch, "'A Motley Throng.'"

Empire, not to mention its predecessors, dealt with the myriad groups, states, and peoples both within the empire itself and beyond in a variety of ways, many of which do not easily fit within the mold of a Sinocentric tribute system.[25] Moreover, the idea that an emphasis on ritual in diplomatic relations is somehow a uniquely Chinese proclivity has also been questioned. In *Cherishing Men from Afar*, James Hevia makes a strong case for arguing that the oft-cited Macartney Mission to the Qing Empire does not represent a clash between the pragmatic, substantive British and the ritual-obsessed Qing. Rather, it marks an encounter between competing imperial systems, both of which exhibited a mixture of ritual and matters of substance. The gap between the Chinese kowtow (*ketou*) and the British formal bow is not nearly as great as many once had thought.[26]

In addition to similarities in imperial impulses and practices, scholars have also noted a surprising parity between the most developed areas of Western Europe and their counterparts in China in terms of demography, agricultural productivity, per capita consumption of food and goods, land use, and a variety of other indices of development.[27] These comparisons have eroded the easy confidence with which observers and scholars used to invoke Weberian platitudes to explain the "Rise of the West" and the concomitant decline of the East.[28] Asia in general and China in particular appear to have been far more significant, even central, to the functioning of the world economy than was once imagined. The "great divergence" of the nineteenth century now appears to owe more to a small array of contingent and often almost capricious factors than to fundamental civilizational differences. In many respects, China has rejoined the stream of world history as an equal.[29]

Relations between the Qing Empire and Chosŏn Korea, however, remain a calm backwater largely undisturbed by these wider currents of

----

25. See Rossabi, *China Among Equals*. For a more general overview of East Asian international relations, see Warren Cohen, *East Asia at the Center*.

26. Hevia, *Cherishing Men from Afar*.

27. Pomeranz, *The Great Divergence*.

28. For a rich and compelling account of how the city of Hankow displayed commercially oriented tendencies not recognized by Weber et al., see Rowe, *Hankow: Commerce and Society in a Chinese City*. For a more general treatment of Chinese commercial activities, see Hao, *The Commercial Revolution in Nineteenth-Century China*. See also von Glahn, *Fountain of Fortune*; and Brook, *Confusions of Pleasure*.

29. Pomeranz, *The Great Divergence*; Frank, *ReOrient*; Wong, *China Transformed*.

historiography. Although growing numbers recognize seventeenth- and eighteenth-century Qing colonialism in many other parts of the empire as a phenomenon on par with the expansionist activities of other world empires, when it comes to Korea, the historical literature tends to portray a yawning chasm between the nations of the West (and Japan), who are thought to have been seeking new forms of relations with Korea, and the Qing Empire, which merely sought to maintain or, as is more often described, reassert an old policy. Descriptions of these efforts often use a similar array of terms—"reassert," "restore," "recover"—to portray what the Qing Empire was trying to do with its traditional "suzerainty" in Korea.[30]

This type of portrayal results in the sometimes explicit, but more often implied, contrast between Japanese imperialism and Qing suzerainty in Korea. Policy makers in Meiji Japan unequivocally included expansion as an integral part of their quest to develop a "rich country and a strong army" (*fukoku kyōhei*). Observers of the day were quick to presume that this

---

30. See Ki-baik Lee, *A New History of Korea*, 274; Han U-gŭn, *The History of Korea*, 201; Deuchler, *Confucian Gentlemen and Barbarian Envoys*, 142–43; Hak-chun Kim, *Korea's Relations with Her Neighbors in a Changing World*, 584; Duus, *Abacus and the Sword*, 50; Jung, *Nation Building*, 155–65; Gold, *State and Society in the Taiwan Miracle*, 33; Kim Chŏng-gi, "Ch'ŏng ŭi Chosŏn chŏngch'aek (1876–1894)"; and Pak Su-i, "Kaehanggi Han'guk muyŏk chabon e kwanhan yŏn'gu," 134. For a general overview of previous Japanese-, Korean-, and Chinese-language works on nineteenth-century Qing-Chosŏn relations, see Ku Sŏn-hŭi, *Han'guk kŭndae daeQing chŏngch'aeksa yŏn'gu*, 12–15. The vast majority of these works depict Qing policy in Korea as a reassertion or strengthening of Qing suzerainty. One notable exception to this trend is the scholarship of Key-hiuk Kim. In his magisterial work, *The Last Phase of the East Asian World Order*, Kim concludes that by 1882, "the traditional suzerain-vassal relationship between China and Korea gave way to a new type of relationship between imperialist power and colonial dependent" (348). Sadly, this conclusion seems to have been lost on many if not most considerations of both late imperial Chinese and late Chosŏn Korean history. Moreover, Kim tantalizingly ends his work just as the "new" Qing imperialism began, leaving unexplored and unanswered what happened next. See also Key-hiuk Kim, "The Aims of Li Hung-Chang's Policies Toward Japan and Korea, 1870–1882." This is not to say that studies of Qing-Chosŏn relations never use the word "imperialism" to describe these relations. Indeed, many do so. For examples, see Dalchoong Kim, "Chinese Imperialism in Korea"; Il-keun Park, "China's Policy Toward Korea, 1880–1884"; Yur-bok Lee, *West Goes East*, 32–40, *passim*; Young Ick Lew, "Yuan Shih-K'ai's Residency"; and Kim Chŏng-gi, "Ch'ŏng ŭi Chosŏn chŏngch'aek (1876–1894)." However, in many of these cases, the term "imperialism" is juxtaposed with the more frequently seen "reassertion of suzerainty," with an emphasis on the latter.

remarkable development was a function of Japan's wholesale abandonment of the past in favor of a Western-style modernity. As one contemporary American concluded:

This has taken Japan out of the ranks of the non-progressive nations to place it, if not in the van of modern improvement, at least not very far in the rear. It has taken it out of the stagnant life of Asia, to infuse into its veins the life of Europe and America. In a word, it has, as it were, unmoored Japan from the coast of Asia, and towed it across the Pacific to place it alongside the New World, to have the same course of life and progress.[31]

The indubitable reality of Japan's imperial expansion in the late nineteenth and early twentieth centuries has prompted acknowledgment of Japan's place among the ranks of imperialist powers, but a strong strand of writing on imperialism concludes that "Japan's rise as a colonial power stands as an anomaly in the history of modern imperialism" and retains an emphasis on imperialism as defined and practiced by Western powers.[32] In such a conceptual universe, there appears to be little room for considering other Asian powers such as the Qing Empire as modern imperialists like the West or Japan. Qing policy makers were thought to have focused primarily on the past and been motivated and constrained by traditional modes of relations.

This work contends that the motivations, strategies, and successes (and failures) of the imperialists of the Qing Empire engaged in Chosŏn Korea should not be seen as exceptional or separated from the broader streams of regional and world history. The passengers of the *Xingxin* were certainly interested in maintaining the notion that the Qing-Chosŏn relationship was but the latest in a long line of benevolent relations between a Chinese suzerain and a Korean vassal. But they were also interested in an array of other matters ranging from security to commercial interests. The actions of the Qing Empire in Korea mirrored in many ways those taken by other imperialists in the region. Indeed, in some cases the Qing Empire blazed new trails for other would-be imperialists to follow and played a fundamental

---

31. Henry M. Field, quoted in Duus, *The Japanese Discovery of America*, 38.

32. Peattie, "The Japanese Colonial Empire," 217. Peattie (ibid.) continues, "As the only non-Western imperium of modern times, Japan's overseas empire stood apart from its European counterparts, its circumstances scarcely duplicated elsewhere." For a comprehensive survey of scholarly works on the Japanese Empire, particularly with regard to Korea, see Schmid, "Colonialism and the 'Korea Problem.'"

role in Korea's integration into regional and global political and economic systems. And although the Qing Empire certainly did not accomplish all its aims, it demonstrated a degree of flexibility and aptitude not often granted to Qing leaders in the Empire's dying days.

Describing the Qing Empire as practicing "imperialism" in Korea necessarily requires a precise definition of the term. Unfortunately, "imperialism," along with its cousin "colonialism," has been used to describe such a diverse range of relationships, events, and processes as to make any comprehensive, all-inclusive definition virtually meaningless.[33] It is, however, important to acknowledge several salient characteristics of imperial theory and practice that inform my understanding of Qing imperialism in Chosŏn Korea.

First is the concept of informal empire. Initially articulated by John Gallagher and Ronald Robinson,[34] the idea that imperialism can exist even in the absence of direct annexation of territory is of obvious significance to the study of imperialism in East Asia in the nineteenth century. Although most of the century saw little direct territorial acquisition by foreign powers (with the exception of Hong Kong, Macao, and, after 1895, Taiwan), few would be persuaded that the absence of direct seizure of territory allows us to conclude that there was no imperialism in East Asia. The parameters of informal empire in East Asia are clearly and succinctly expressed by Jürgen Osterhammel: "'Informal empire' is defined here as a historical situation of some stability and permanence in which overt foreign rule is avoided while economic advantages are secured by 'unequal' legal and institutional arrangements, and also by the constant threat of political meddling and military coercion that would be intolerable in relations between fully sovereign states."[35] Informal empire (or semi-colonialism) stands in contrast to the

---

33. For a brief, accessible introduction to various theories and conceptions of empire, see Howe, *Empire*. See also Fieldhouse, *Economics and Empire*; idem, *Colonialism*; Maier, *Among Empires*, 1–143; Lieven, *Empire*, 3–88; and Doyle, *Empires*, 19–50. Seminal but still influential works on imperialism include Seeley, *The Expansion of England*; Hobson, *Imperialism*; and Lenin, *Imperialism*. For a good overview of relatively recent post-colonial approaches to imperialism, see Dane Kennedy, "Imperial History and Post-Colonial Theory."

34. Gallagher and Robinson, "The Imperialism of Free Trade."

35. Osterhammel ("Britain and China," 148–49) continues, "It is crucial to see that 'informal empire' implies more than economic asymmetry, cultural dependency, or the sporadic use of preponderant influence by a Great Power towards a weaker neighbor. 'Informal empire' rests on the three pillars of: (1) legal privilege for foreigners; (2) a free

entanglements and expense of formal colonial rule; the latter was, in the words of D. K. Fieldhouse, "not a preference but a last resort."[36]

"Informal empire" has direct relevance to the understanding of Qing-Chosŏn relations at the end of the nineteenth century. The Qing and many of its Chinese predecessors claimed some sort of suzerain-vassal relationship with Korea. Yet, this seldom if ever meant direct Chinese intervention in Korean domestic affairs, let alone Chinese occupation or control of Korean territory. In the nineteenth century, the Qing Empire dramatically transformed its relations with Chosŏn Korea and became much more interventionist, but Qing policy makers assiduously avoided direct annexation of the peninsula (despite calls from some domestic and foreign circles to do so). This was due in part to the tradition of suzerainty yet noninterference that had long characterized Sino-Korean relations and in part to Qing statesmen's pragmatic assessment of contemporary geopolitics as well as a strategic ordering of priorities.

Second is the importance of commercial interests in motivating imperialism and its implementation in the nineteenth century. Some Western powers certainly had noncommercial reasons for expanding their empires, competition with other powers and the promotion of Christianity being two of the more significant. But the perceived need to impose informal or even formal control over an ever-greater area of the world's surface was stimulated primarily by the expectation of greater access to resources and markets that such control would provide.

Many of the imperialistic enterprises of the period do not fit easily into the Leninist "monopoly stage of capitalism" or other Marxist structural theories, and some scholars posit that the role of industrial interests in motivating imperialist expansion has been exaggerated.[37] It is, however, often

---

trade regime imposed from outside; and (3) the deployment of instruments of intervention such as the gunboat and the 'imperial' consul."

36. Fieldhouse, *Economics and Empire*, 476–77. For other considerations of informal empire and comparisons to formal colonial rule, see Lieven, *Empire*, 29; Maier, *Among Empires*, 35; and Horowitz, "International Law and State Transformation," 447.

37. Lenin, *Imperialism*; for a more recent re-evaluation of Marxist theories of imperialism, see Chilcote, *Political Economy of Imperialism*. For a critique of Lenin's theories, see Fieldhouse, *Economics and Empire*, 1–9, 38–62. The need to export surplus capital was clearly not a motivation for Japanese imperial expansion, since Meiji Japan, in the words of Kimura Mitsuhiko ("Japanese Imperialism and Colonial Economy in Korea and Taiwan," 2), "suffered from capital shortage rather than capital surplus" during its early expansion. For the argument that financial, not industrial, interests were the pri-

quite clear that the potential for profit motivated many a would-be imperialist. This is particularly evident in Asia, where the demands for additional open ports on the Chinese, Japanese, and Korean coasts and rivers were predicated primarily on those ports' potential commercial significance. Writing in 1905, one of the earliest theoreticians of imperialism, J. A. Hobson, concluded that imperialism in the Far East is "stripped nearly bare of all motives and methods save those of distinctively commercial origin."[38]

In the case of Qing-Chosŏn relations, influential merchants and members of what Louis Sigel describes as the "treaty-port community" in China played a prominent role in the formulation and execution of Qing "commercial warfare" in Korea.[39] Moreover, Chinese merchants constituted an important vanguard of Qing imperialism as they traveled to Korea and did a surprisingly prosperous business there.

A third characteristic is the use of treaties and international law to advance the interests of would-be imperialists. The nineteenth century saw the increasingly aggressive and uncompromising insistence that all peoples of the world must adhere to largely Western standards of international relations, standards that emphasized diplomatic and commercial relations between sovereign and equal nation-states as defined by treaty and implemented and enforced by diplomatic representation. Virtually all these relations were bilateral, but they assumed a multilateral if not universal adherence to the Westphalian norms thought to have held sway in Europe for some time.

The Qing Empire is sometimes portrayed as being either ignorant of or fiercely resistant to the imperatives of the new system of Western-style international law. However, in the case of Korea, Qing policy makers saw treaties and international law as a useful tool for promoting their own security and commercial interests in Korea. Far from misunderstanding Western

---

mary drivers of British imperialism, see Cain and Hopkins, *British Imperialism, Innovation and Expansion.*

38. Hobson, *Imperialism*, 307. It should be noted that Hobson's treatise on imperialism was not actually the first of its kind. In the West, Hobson was preceded by H. Gaylord Wilshire, a Los Angeles real estate developer whose writings apparently influenced Hobson (Maier, *Among Empires*, 49). In Japan, according to Alexis Dudden (*Japan's Colonization of Korea*, 24), the "Japanese anarchist Kotoku Shusui predated Hobson by a year with his own scathing condemnation of colonizing politics, entitled *Imperialism: Monstrosity of the Twentieth Century.*"

39. Sigel, "The Role of Korea in Late Qing Foreign Policy"; idem, "Foreign Policy Interests and Activities of the Treaty-Port Chinese Community."

law, Qing statesmen used it to protect their interests in Korea and to pave the way toward bringing about treaty revision back home. Moreover, no matter how much Qing officials resented the blatantly unequal aspects of the legal imposition of Western imperialism in China itself—foreign concessions, extraterritoriality, and lack of tariff autonomy being among the most offensive—they were more than willing to assert the same unequal privileges for the Qing Empire in Korea.

Fourth, advances in technology—military, transportation, communications—greatly facilitated the ability of the advanced industrial powers to project their influence across the globe. The steamship, the telegraph line, improvements in artillery, and, somewhat later, the repeating gun and railroad allowed would-be imperialists to utilize an astonishingly small number of soldiers, sailors, and diplomats to establish informal control often at great distances.[40] Despite the still lingering image of the Qing Empire as premodern and unable or unwilling to fully utilize modern technology and institutions,[41] in the case of Korea, the Qing aggressively and forcefully used gunboats, telegraph lines, and other modern accoutrements of empire to project and defend its interests on the Korean peninsula.

Finally, it is important to note that the type of informal empire imposed on East Asia was generally what Akira Iriye calls "multilateral imperial-

---

40. An iconic case of how asymmetry in technology can dictate outcomes in imperial expansion is the 1898 battle between British forces led by Lord Kitchener and the Mahdi army in the Sudan. Armed with Maxim guns, the British and their Egyptian allies killed some 18,000 Mahdi dervishes while experiencing only 28 British and 20 non-British deaths. The awesome power of the Maxim gun prompted the Anglo-Catholic poet Hilaire Belloc to write, "Whatever happens, we have got / The Maxim Gun, and they have not" (Meyer, *Dust of Empire*, 9–10).

41. Summarizing scholarship on the so-called period of self-strengthening in China, Charles Desnoyers ("Toward 'One Enlightened and Progressive Civilization,'" 138) writes: "Until recently, regardless of the ideological context in which the period was examined, the emphasis was usually on the shortcomings of 'modernization' in a 'traditional' Confucian society. Many scholars viewed modern technology, capitalism, and representative or constitutional political institutions as fundamentally incompatible with the preservation of Confucianism. Any attempt at synthesis, such as that expressed in the famous formula *zhongxue wei ti, xixue wei yong* (Chinese studies for the essentials, Western studies for practical application), was bound to fail, as Joseph Levenson and Mary Wright eloquently argued, because the relationship between Chinese *ti* (essentials) and Western *yong* (practical application) pitted irresistibly dynamic Western forces against social structures requiring stability."

ism."[42] Although no single outside power conquered and colonized the Qing Empire, Chosŏn Korea, or Tokugawa-Meiji Japan, outside powers *did* make considerable inroads into the sovereignty and autonomy of all three states. The vigorous application of the most-favored-nation principle guaranteed that any privilege secured by one outside power was available to all. At the same time, the territorial integrity and autonomy of the victims of this multilateral imperialism were protected, albeit in an all-too-often truncated fashion.

All these characteristics will be quite familiar to the observer of Western imperialism in East Asia. Less often recognized is the fact that they also aptly describe relations between the Qing Empire and Chosŏn Korea.[43] Motivated in part by geopolitical and security concerns, but also in part by the potential for commercial profits, the Qing Empire embarked on an aggressive and interventionist course in Chosŏn Korea. Yet, Qing policy makers steadfastly resisted calls for the direct annexation of Korea. Qing statesmen, such as Li Hongzhang and his assistant Ma Jianzhong, used treaties and international law not only to resist the inroads of Japanese and Russian imperialists in Korea but also to advance Chinese commercial interests on the peninsula. Qing troops occupied Seoul in the early 1880s,

---

42. Iriye, "Imperialism in East Asia," 129.

43. An extensive and detailed list of the characteristics of semi-colonialism in China can be found in Osterhammel, "Semi-Colonialism and Informal Empire in Twentieth-Century China," 290–91. A significant number of these characteristics of foreign imperialism in China also describe Qing imperialism in Korea.

It is interesting to note that whereas David Abernathy (*Dynamics of Global Dominance*, 20) rejects the concept of informal empire as "unacceptably vague," his own definition and conception of imperialism would still appear to describe Qing-Chosŏn relations during the last part of the nineteenth century. Abernathy notes that "a dominant state is an imperial metropole and a weaker territory a colony when:

—the dominant state formally claims the right to make authoritative decisions affecting the weaker territory's domestic affairs and external relations;

—the weaker territory is not recognized as a sovereign state by major actors in the interstate system; and

—the dominant state establishes and staffs administrative structures that extract resources, allocate resources, and enforce regulations within some economically or strategically significant portion of the weaker territory. Administrative control might be exercised over a port and its hinterland, for example, or over a coastal zone or transport networks linking a port to zones of mineral and agricultural wealth."

As will become evident, all these characteristics are present in the nineteenth-century Qing-Chosŏn relationship.

and Qing steam-powered gunboats prowled near Korean ports throughout the 1880s and early 1890s. Qing diplomats stationed in Korea established, defended, and expanded Chinese concessions in Korean treaty ports in which Qing subjects enjoyed extraterritorial and other unequal privileges. The Qing Empire played a prominent role in the establishment and management of key communications infrastructures such as overland telegraph lines, as well as in important government institutions such as the Korean Maritime Customs Service. Much of this was done in the name of a traditional ritual suzerainty, but it is patently clear that other motivations—chiefly geopolitical and commercial—weighed heavily in the minds of Qing decision makers.

To argue that the Qing Empire's imperialism in Korea was part of wider regional and global trends is not to say that the Qing-Chosŏn relationship was indistinguishable from other contemporary instances of imperialism. Indeed, one key difference was the fact that Sino-Korean relations had a long history that influenced how both the Qing Empire and Chosŏn Korea negotiated new forms of relations. The notion of a tradition of amicable relations based on proper Confucian ritual as well as the general tendency of China not to interfere in Korean domestic affairs shaped how the Qing Empire and Chosŏn Korea understood their relations and the boundaries beyond which neither side wished to go.

Although the general trajectory of Qing-Chosŏn relations during the period 1850–1910 was the transformation of customary, ritual-based relations into relations based on Western-style treaties and animated by treaty-port concessions, diplomatic representation, and all the other accoutrements of the most "modern" imperialism, this work will resist the temptation to describe this shift in terms of a change from premodern (or traditional) to modern forms of relations. In some respects, such a description may be accurate. On the other hand, ritual is not exclusively a premodern phenomenon; even the most modern of relations are suffused with a healthy dose of ritual. It is in many respects more accurate to describe the dramatic shift in relations not in terms of an artificial and arbitrary dichotomy between tradition and modernity but in terms of the flexible adaptation of one of the world's major empires in response to new challenges.

It is also important to emphasize that the new modes of Qing imperialism were not exclusively Western. Rather, they amounted to a hybrid of East Asian and Western mechanisms and institutions, the most significant of which has often been labeled the "treaty-port system." Moreover, as Korea became the object of attention and competition of a number of regional and global powers, it also became a site for a number of competing imperial strategies and systems. It was not the Qing Empire or the nations of the West that first introduced the treaty-port system to Korea but Meiji Japan. But although the forms—treaties, ports, and concessions—appeared to be similar to those found in both China and Japan, Japanese policy makers and diplomats were clear in the pursuit of unilateral and exclusive privileges in Korea. Meiji Japan attempted to implement a unilateral but informal imperial rule in Korea during the period 1876–82, again in 1894–95 during the Sino-Japanese War and its immediate aftermath, and yet again in 1905 after its victory in the Russo-Japanese War. Challenging this unilateral imperialism was the multilateral imperialism introduced to Korea by the Qing Empire. After the dramatic Qing intervention in Korean affairs in 1882, Korea became open to all foreign imperialist powers rather than merely to Japan. Paradoxically, even as the Qing Empire utilized treaties and international law to entice a number of powers to become interested and involved in Korea, it also sought to maintain some semblance of exclusive privileges in Korea based on its traditional suzerainty. Proponents of Western-style relations between sovereign and equal nation-states scoffed at these Qing attempts and dismissed them as relics of an antiquated and hopeless past. Western diplomats on the ground in Korea as well as many of their superiors in their home governments, however, often tacitly acknowledged Qing claims to a special position in Korea while asserting that the Chosŏn Kingdom was sovereign and independent.

The question of Qing claims to a special status in Korea was settled, more or less, by the dramatic Qing defeat in the Sino-Japanese War. However, the system of multilateral imperialism introduced to Korea by the Qing withstood most Japanese attempts to reassert exclusive and unilateral privileges. Even in the absence of Qing officials on the ground in Korea, foreign, particularly British, diplomats went to great lengths to uphold the system predicated on equal access by all foreign powers and anchored by most-favored-nation privileges. Thus, the system of multilateral but informal empire continued for a decade after the Sino-Japanese War, and Chinese officials, merchants, and migrants continued to enjoy many privileges within it. It was only with the Japanese victory in the Russo-Japanese War and the subsequent establishment of Korea as a Japanese protectorate that the system of multilateral imperialism began to unravel. Even though many of the forms of the treaty-port system remained intact, the sheer weight of the growing Japanese colonial presence served to crowd out other, especially Chinese, competitors in Korea.

This transition was part of a larger regional and even global pattern. By the end of the nineteenth century, an increasing number of imperialist powers were abandoning the equal-access prerogatives of multilateral imperialism in favor of direct territorial acquisition. The case of Korea was no exception. In the age of "high imperialism" and the scramble for colonies in which nearly every significant power on earth participated, treaties and traders proved to be no match for raw military power and a concerted attempt to establish formal colonial rule.

Two issues need to be clarified. The first is the conceptual and semantic issue of whether "China" and "the Qing Empire" are interchangeable terms. Those in present-day China who wish to regard their history as one of millennia of continuous existence must of necessity regard the period of Qing rule as part of Chinese history. And yet many leading Chinese revolutionaries such as Sun Yat-sen clearly regarded the Qing's Manchu rulers as alien oppressors whose overthrow and eradication were necessary for China to recover its national greatness. A recent wave of scholarship has emphasized the fact that the Qing Empire may have ruled over a territory and people we now recognize as "Chinese," but it was more than just another Chinese dynasty. Rather, it was a multi-ethnic, multi-lingual empire that drew not only on Chinese historical and cultural precedents but also on a variety of other sources in its attempts to administer and rule its territory. Compounding the complexity of Qing-Chosŏn relations, however, is that, aside from the extremely important strategic decision to focus resources on shoring up Qing rule in Central Asia at the expense of the Chinese maritime littoral, there is very little that is identifiably Manchu (or non-Chinese) about the Qing approach to relations with Korea in the nineteenth century. Rather, both the Qing Empire and Chosŏn Korea appear to have preferred to regard and describe their relationship as merely the latest instance in a long line of Sino-Korean relations. For purposes of rhetorical consistency, this work will generally prefer the term "the Qing Empire" or "Qing" to "China." But there are cases in which the protagonists' appeals to pre-Qing precedents or simple felicity of expression seem to require the use of "China" or the prefix "sino-." In addition, this work will generally refer to the people who came from the Qing Empire to Korea as "Chinese." The historical record does not include references to any cases of ethnic Manchus (or Mongols, Uighurs, or Tibetans for that matter) in Korea in the late nineteenth or early twentieth centuries. The designation "Chinese" is merely shorthand for a person from the Qing Empire rather than an irrevocable judgment concerning the ethnicity of said person.

The second issue concerns the agency of Korea and Koreans during the period under consideration. The very selection of the Qing Empire as the focus of investigation and the designation of Qing activities in Korea as "imperialism" would seem to privilege the Qing Empire as the prime mover in the transformation of Qing-Chosŏn relations, relegating Korea to the status of a passive victim. To be sure, Korea's options were extremely limited by the demographic, geographic, economic, and military realities of the day. Korea and Korean leaders were, however, more than "puck[s] on the shuffleboard controlled by the big powers," to quote the characterization of one historian.[44] The direction, trajectory, and ultimate outcome of Chosŏn Korea's relations with its neighbors owe much to Korean agency and to Korean domestic political decisions and configurations. This is not to say that there necessarily was a counterfactual past in which Chosŏn Korea could have avoided being colonized by an outside power. To expect such is to expect Korea to have been truly exceptional in the age of high imperialism. The decision to focus on Qing imperial strategies and tactics in Korea should not, however, detract from the fact that decisions and actions taken on the Korean "periphery" were often as significant and influential as those taken by the Qing Empire itself.

The organization of this work is chronological. However, in many chapters, issues of particular historical or historiographical significance whose relevance transcends the narrow temporal delimitation of the individual chapter are highlighted and discussed in some depth. Chapter 1 provides an overview of the long history of relations between the peoples and states on the Chinese mainland and those on the Korean peninsula. It highlights the diversity of those relations, a diversity that is masked by those who choose to describe them as fitting within a Chinese World Order predicated on amicable relations and tribute missions. It emphasizes the significance and importance for Korean states of the non-Chinese "barbarians" on their northern frontier, the last of which would become the founders and rulers of the Qing Empire. However, it also calls attention to the fact that by the nineteenth century, Chosŏn Korea did indeed in many important ways function as a Qing tributary state, perhaps the best (and only) example of such.

Chapter 2 explores the empires and imperial systems that competed in East Asia in the nineteenth century. It notes both internal and external events that changed the way the Qing Empire interacted with its myriad

---

44. Cumings, *Korea's Place in the Sun*, 110–11.

constituencies and neighbors. It also highlights the diverse range of actors that had an impact on the Qing Empire's policies toward Korea. Like most empires, the Qing seldom spoke with one voice on important matters of the day. Li Hongzhang's "mainstream approach" had to contend with the criticism of the so-called Purist Party (*qingliudang*), on the one hand, and the demands of China's treaty-port elite on the other. In the case of Chosŏn Korea, the Qing Empire's customary suzerainty was challenged by Meiji Japan, which, after 1876, sought to impose a unilateral informal imperialism on the Korean peninsula.

Chapter 3 focuses on the critical year of 1882. Motivated by a desire on the part of both Koreans and Chinese to counter the growing Japanese presence and power in Korea, the Qing Empire took the unprecedented step of mediating Chosŏn Korea's first treaties with Western Powers. This effort to counter Japanese unilateral imperialism with a system of multilateral imperialism experienced a sharp challenge when a soldiers' mutiny in Korea threatened to derail the carefully laid plans of the Qing. The Qing Empire responded with alacrity by sending 3,000 troops to Korea to quell the mutiny, a manifestation of heretofore extremely rare direct intervention in Korean affairs. Subsequently, the Qing also negotiated its first-ever commercial treaty with Korea, a treaty whose provisions were filled with the same set of unequal privileges and prerogatives that characterized the treaties between Western powers and China, Japan, and Korea. The Qing Empire's activities of 1882 demonstrate a concern for and a facility with treaties and international law that is often neglected in depictions of the Empire in the late nineteenth century. Its efforts bore fruit when most of the international community accepted the Qing claims that even as Chosŏn Korea was becoming a member of the international "family of nations," it simultaneously remained a Qing dependency or vassal.

Chapter 4 chronicles the efforts of the Qing Empire to facilitate Korean "self-strengthening," particularly in the military arena. These efforts were somewhat successful, at least from the perspective of the Korean King Kojong (r. 1864–1907), as Qing and Qing-trained Korean soldiers were instrumental in putting down a coup attempt in 1884. The chapter also recounts how Qing diplomats established a permanent diplomatic and consular presence in Korea. For the first time in its history, the Qing Empire sought not only to establish legations and concessions abroad but also to actively encourage Chinese merchants and migrants to reside and do business in Korea. The oft-overlooked official Chen Shutang played a prominent role in these efforts, assisting Chinese commerce and resisting Japanese attempts to maintain exclusive Japanese privileges in Korea.

The next three chapters investigate the "Residency" of Yuan Shikai in Korea (1885–94). Chapter 5 examines how the Qing Empire established and operated Korea's first overland telegraph lines, set up the Korean Customs Service, and played a prominent role in the successes and failures of Korea's attempts to borrow money from abroad. It notes that in all these cases, the aims and tactics of different groups within the Qing Empire itself were not always harmonious. In addition, the emphasis on the Qing Empire's use of arguably "modern" tools and techniques of imperialism (not to mention the earlier Qing efforts to facilitate Korean "self-strengthening" reforms) necessitates a reassessment of a prominent strand of Korean historiography that argues that Qing intervention, by virtue of its intrinsically "anachronistic" and "illogical" nature, was an immutable impediment to Korean reform and modernization.

Chapter 6 explores the ways in which the Qing Empire in general and Yuan Shikai in particular are thought to have challenged Korean independence and autonomy. It notes that excessive emphasis on the Qing Empire's "man on the spot" distracts from the fact that many if not most of Yuan Shikai's oppressive and interventionist schemes and intrigues were failures, often because his superiors in China countermanded them. In the arena of diplomacy and foreign relations, the Qing Empire was generally successful in upholding the Chosŏn Kingdom's status as both an autonomous member of the family of nations and a Qing vassal. Those who highlight Qing resistance to Chosŏn Korea's attempts to establish legations abroad exaggerate both the Chosŏn government's actual desire to sever all customary relations with the Qing Empire and the promised benefits that such a course would bring to Korea. In the end, most foreign powers active in Korea were much more interested in maintaining unequal access and privileges in Korea than they were with promoting Korea's full independence.

Chapter 7 recounts the ways in which the Qing Empire continued to support and promote Chinese commerce in Korea during the Residency of Yuan Shikai. These efforts are often downplayed or neglected by scholars who overemphasize the Qing concern with maintaining ritual suzerainty and with other political matters. Qing officials sought to expand and protect the Chinese presence in the Korean capital and in the treaty ports, promote Chinese shipping ventures, and attempt (not always successfully) to bypass the treaty-port system and the Korean Customs Service. Chinese merchants proved to be worthy competitors to their Japanese counterparts in a variety of trades and sectors, both old and new. They enjoyed an array of geographical, organizational, and other advantages that helps explain their rise to commercial prominence. Equally significant, however, was the backdrop of treaty-guaranteed privilege and prerogative afforded by the Qing-introduced and -supported system of multilateral but informal empire in Korea.

Chapter 8 explores the Sino-Japanese War and its aftermath. The dramatic Japanese victory brought about the end of Korean tribute missions to Beijing and, therefore, signaled the end of Qing traditional ritual suzerainty. Taking advantage of its preponderance of military might on the peninsula, Meiji Japan sought to reintroduce the practices and prerogatives of unilateral, monopolistic (but still informal) imperialism in Korea. Leading the resistance to this effort were British diplomats in Korea, who skillfully invoked Korea's treaties with foreign powers to defend the system of multilateral imperialism. Their efforts bore fruit and maintained a space in which Chinese merchants could return to Korea and continue to compete successfully with the Japanese for control of key sectors of Korea's foreign trade. In short, despite a widely held view that China and the Chinese vanish as significant actors on the Korean stage after 1894, the Chinese presence and activities in Korea continued to flourish for another decade within the comforting confines of the treaty-port system.

Chapter 9 chronicles the end of multilateral imperialism in Korea because of Japan's victory in the Russo-Japanese War, Japan's 1905 declaration of a protectorate in Korea, and the ultimate formal annexation of Korea in 1910. In an era of high imperialism, treaties and international law proved to be no match for a concerted attempt, backed by military force, to annex territory. The growing formal Japanese colonial presence in Korea was a boon to Japanese commerce on the peninsula as both Chinese and Western competitors were gradually crowded out. This chapter also explores how the idea of Chinese suzerainty and the purported baleful impact of Chinese culture on Korea played a prominent role in reimagining Korean history and identity. Finally, it concludes with some general observations about the significance and legacies of the Qing imperialist turn in Korea.

ONE

Pre-Nineteenth-Century Sino-Korean Relations

When Western powers sought to engage in commercial or diplomatic relations with Korea in the nineteenth century, they often asked the Qing Empire to explain the nature of its relations with Chosŏn Korea. The response of the Zongli yamen, the Qing foreign policy organization created in 1861, to one such inquiry read: "Chosŏn is a tributary of China; but as for said country's autonomy in its own politics, religion, prohibitions, and orders, China has never interfered with it."[1] Japanese diplomats received a similar reply: "That Korea is a dependent state of China is known by all; that it is an autonomous country is also known by all."[2] Such statements caused no small amount of confusion to foreign, particularly Western, observers. Owen Denny, an American judge who served as an adviser to King Kojong in the 1880s, concluded that the relationship between the Qing Empire and Chosŏn Korea was based on principles that "such well-known expounders as Grotius, Vattell, and Wheaton never comprehended."[3] John Russell Young, the American minister to Beijing, dismissed the Qing claims as merely part of the "romance and hyperbole which surrounds these Oriental claims to sovereignty."[4]

---

1. Zongli yamen to Rutherford Alcock, Mar. 10, 1868 (TZ 7.2.17), *ZRHGX*, 96. For a similar declaration, see Zongli yamen to Frederick Low, Dec. 23, 1871 (TZ 10.11.12), *ZRHGX*, 243–44.

2. Zongli yamen memorial, Feb. 8, 1879 (GX 5.1.18), *ZRHGX*, 353–54.

3. Denny, *China and Korea*, 24.

4. M. F. Nelson, *Korea and the Old Orders in Eastern Asia*, 162.

However difficult representatives of Western powers may have found it to fit the Sino-Korean relationship into categories comprehensible to them, they had little trouble accepting Chinese claims that nineteenth-century Sino-Korean relations were a continuation of centuries if not millennia of tradition. Qing officials did little to disabuse them of the notion that relations between China and Korea had been and always would be the same. This notion was based on two assumptions that have significantly influenced generations of historians both Asian and Western. The first is the existence of an essential, easily defined and observed nation—"China" or "Korea"— whose history can be traced from the present back to antiquity. Historians have engaged in considerable mental gymnastics to craft a narrative of un- broken continuity, often by either ignoring or incorporating periods of "for- eign" presence, influence, or even domination into the story of the nation. The idea that both China and Korea can claim an unbroken existence of some millennia remains powerful to this day.[5] The second assumption is that most if not all of premodern China's foreign relations were conducted with- in a Sinocentric order that China's neighbors recognized through periodic offerings of tribute. Yet, even a cursory examination of relations between the inhabitants and states of the Chinese mainland and the Korean peninsula reveals a wide variety of interactions, ranging from harmonious alliances to open warfare. The seductive simplicity of the tribute system and John King Fairbank's Chinese World Order does little justice to the multiplicity of rela- tions between China and Korea over the centuries.[6] Nevertheless, some as- pects of the ideal-type tribute system do approximate the Sino-Korean rela- tionship that so confused nineteenth-century Western observers.

Beginnings

Determining precisely when relations between China and Korea began de- pends largely on one's definition of "China" and "Korea" and one's trust in ancient documents. The legend of the "Viscount of Ji" (C. Jizi; K. Kija),

---

5. For a critique, see Duara, *Rescuing History from the Nation*.

6. Fairbank, ed., *The Chinese World Order*. Fairbank and others have been vigorously criticized for (among other things) their apparent acceptance of Chinese claims of cen- trality in their use of the "tribute system" to describe Chinese relations with foreign powers. For a recent example of such criticism, see Schmid, "Constructing Indepen- dence," 25–30. For a general survey of Chinese foreign policy over the past three centu- ries, see Mancall, *China at the Center*; see also Warren Cohen, *East Asia at the Center*.

who was said to have left the emerging Zhou Kingdom in 1122 B.C. to found his own realm on the Korean peninsula centered around the "willow capital" of P'yŏngyang, is mentioned in various Confucian classics and was widely known in Korea at least as early as the Koryŏ period (A.D. 918–1392). However, archaeological evidence such as oracle bones or bronzes that would point to a Shang presence in Korea in the twelfth century B.C. has yet to be unearthed. The story of Wei Man (K. Wiman), a refugee from the border state of Yan who fled to Korea and set up a kingdom known in Korea as Wiman Chosŏn in 194 B.C., is mentioned in numerous Chinese historical texts. Whether Wei Man / Wiman should be considered "Chinese," "Yan," or even "Korean," is still a matter of considerable debate. Whatever the case, the kingdom that Wei Man and his successors ruled was destroyed by armies of the Chinese Han dynasty in 108 B.C.

The subsequent establishment of Chinese commanderies (C. *jun*; K. *kun*) in Korea is thought by many to be the first unequivocal case of Chinese imperialism in Korea. If maps are any indication, many if not most histories of China include at least the northern half of the Korean peninsula as an unproblematic part of the Han Empire (206 B.C.–A.D. 220).[7] Some Koreans respond with the not terribly convincing argument that Han commanderies such as Lelang (K. Nangnang), Lintun (K. Imdun), Xuantu (K. Hyŏndo), and Chenfan (K. Chinbŏn) were located not on the Korean peninsula but in Liaodong or other areas to the north and west.[8] Others portray the Han commanderies as mere outposts whose existence and influence were fiercely resisted by local Koreans.[9] The archaeological record, however, attests to an undeniable and influential Han presence in much of the Korean peninsula.[10] Whatever degree of political or administrative control the Chinese commanderies actually represented, it is clear that many inhabitants of

––––––

7. See, e.g., Warren Cohen, *East Asia at the Center*, 20, 23; Cottrell, *East Asia*, 24; Ebrey et al., *East Asia*, 44, 62; and Fairbank, *China: A New History*, 61.

8. For a recent articulation of this argument, see Hyun-hee Lee et al., *New History of Korea*, 92–102.

9. South Korean historians have often focused on the "Three Han" (Samhan), a group of tribal confederations located in the southern part of the Korean peninsula that was thought to have been less influenced by the Chinese presence. The "Han" in the name of the Republic of Korea, Taehan min'guk, harks back to the Samhan (Hyun-hee Lee et al., *New History of Korea*, 135–41).

10. Pai, *Constructing "Korean" Origins*, 127–236, 291–409; Sarah Nelson, *Archaeology of Korea*, 164–205.

the Korean peninsula were willing and eager to adopt systems of writing, thought, political organization, and statecraft as well as artistic styles and techniques that originated in China and were introduced to the peninsula via the Han commanderies.

The Chinese commanderies outlasted the Han dynasty, but the growing political and military power of the kingdom of Koguryŏ (trad. 37 B.C.–A.D. 668) made their presence increasingly untenable. The last commandery, Lelang, fell to Koguryŏ armies in A.D. 313. The following centuries, known in Korea as the "Three Kingdoms Period," were marked by growing competition among the states of Koguryŏ, Paekche (trad. 18 B.C.–A.D. 660), and Silla (trad. 57 B.C.–A.D. 936). At times, all three sought alliances with various powers on the Chinese mainland in their struggle for survival and supremacy on the peninsula. The Korean kingdoms also clashed with their erstwhile allies. The most dramatic of the military confrontations was between the Sui dynasty (589–618) and the kingdom of Koguryŏ. Massive Sui assaults in the early seventh century were repulsed by Koguryŏ armies whose leaders, particularly General Ŭlchimundŏk, are regarded as Korean heroes to this day.[11] Due in part to its defeats at the hands of Koguryŏ, the Sui collapsed in A.D. 618. Its successor, the Tang (618–907), formed an alliance with the southeastern kingdom of Silla. Silla-Tang armies destroyed the Paekche and then Koguryŏ kingdoms in the 660s. The subsequent Tang attempt to establish commanderies and puppet kingdoms on Korean territory was fiercely resisted by the Silla King Munmu (r. 661–81), whose defeat of Tang forces resulted in the Chinese acknowledgment of Silla's independence by A.D. 676.

Despite their sometimes conflict-ridden beginnings, Silla-Tang relations were often quite amicable. Official Silla diplomatic and commercial missions, invariably recorded in Chinese annals as tribute missions, facilitated a thriving trade between China and Korea. Korean merchants and migrants flocked to the Tang Empire, appearing in large numbers in "Silla towns"

---

11. Although most histories of Korea, China, and East Asia more generally have accepted the Korean claim that Koguryŏ was "Korean," the Northeast Project, a mammoth scholarly and archaeological projected promoted by the People's Republic of China, has highlighted Chinese claims that Koguryŏ "was a regime established by ethnic groups in northern China some 2,000 years ago, representing an important part of Chinese culture" ("China's Ancient Koguryŏ Kingdom Site Added to World Heritage List"). For more on this dispute, see Ahn, "Competing Nationalisms."

in Shandong and elsewhere.[12] Korean scholars, such as Ch'oe Ch'i-wŏn, served in the Tang bureaucracy.[13] Korean monks traveled to Chinese monasteries. Korean soldiers served and even led Tang armies.[14] The cosmopolitan Tang generally appeared willing to embrace good relations with both Silla and its northern neighbor Parhae (698–926) as long as the Korean kingdoms accepted their roles as Tang tributaries and did not cause too much trouble.

The collapse of the Tang roughly corresponded with the dissolution of Silla. After a period of division and disunion, the Song (960–1279) and Koryŏ (918–1392) dynasties established unified and central rule in China and Korea, respectively. The attitude and approach of early Koryŏ kings toward China were in many respects emblematic of the more general Korean attitude toward China at the time. Like its predecessors, Koryŏ paid tribute to China, but Korean officials made it clear that, rather than expressing Korean subjection, participation in tribute missions was intended to *limit* relations with China. In the late tenth century, the prominent Koryŏ statesman Ch'oe Sŭng-no advocated that "from now on we combine tribute missions with trade and strictly forbid all other contacts [with China]."[15] The founder of Koryŏ, Wang Kŏn (King T'aejo, r. 918–43), acknowledged the significant cultural debt Korea owed to China but cautioned that "our country occupies a different geographical location and our people's character is different from that of the Chinese. Hence, there is no reason to strain ourselves unreasonably to copy the Chinese way."[16] Cognizant of its own uniqueness, Koryŏ Korea used tribute missions not only to maintain friendly relations with Song China but also to keep the Chinese at arm's length.

Another way in which Koryŏ did not always "copy the Chinese way" was in its dealings with its neighbors to its immediate north. Cases of "barbarian" incursions into Korea abound. Khitan forces sacked the Koryŏ capital of Kaesŏng in 1010. A century later, the Jurchen Jin threatened

---

12. Reischauer, *Ennin's Travels in Tang China,* 272–94.

13. Peter H. Lee and de Bary, *Sources of Korean Tradition,* 1: 67, 71–73.

14. Gao Xianzhi, the commander of several Tang campaigns in Central Asia, was of Korean origin. He is most famous for commanding Tang forces when they were defeated by Arab armies at the Battle of Talas (A.D. 751) (Holcombe, *The Genesis of East Asia,* 24).

15. Ch'oe Sŭngno, "Ch'oe Sŭngno: On Current Affairs," 1: 283.

16. Wang Kŏn, "Wang Kŏn: Ten Injunctions," 1: 155.

invasion if their demands were not met. Still later, as the Mongols established their rule over most of East Asia and beyond, Koryŏ became a vassal state of the Mongol Empire in the 1250s. For over a century, the Koryŏ crown prince was held hostage in the Mongol capital, was married to a Mongol princess, and returned to Korea only after the death of the previous king. By the end of the Mongol Yuan dynasty in 1368, Koryŏ royalty was, by blood, more Mongol than Korean.[17] Unlike the Tang or Song Chinese, who were generally satisfied with ritual declarations of Korean vassalage and periodic tribute missions, the Mongols stationed "resident commissioners" (*darughachi*) on Korean soil. They also demanded extensive Korean support for two abortive invasions of Japan.[18]

In many cases, Koryŏ leaders simultaneously offered tribute to Song China and to various "barbarian" powers to the north. Subsequent generations of Koreans would remember this strategy as a pragmatic effort to guarantee the survival of the kingdom. Describing this Koryŏ strategy, a 1554 entry in the *Annals of the Chosŏn Kingdom* (*Chosŏn wangjo sillok*) reads:

Mencius said that when the small serves the big it is because of fear of heaven. What is meant by fear is nothing other than fearing the power of a big nation in order to preserve one's own country's people, so serving the big nations is only to serve the people. When perchance there is someone who serves a large nation, but brings destruction on his own people it is because he has not carefully thought about how to deal with it [the situation]. In the era of Koryŏ they served Sung [Song] in the south and served Chin [Jin] in the north. When they paid tribute to the Sung, they hid this fact from Chin. When they paid tribute to Chin, they hid this fact from Sung. If you consider this from an ethical point of view it might not be correct, but seen from the point of power it was the means to preserve the people. If it were not like this, if they served Sung and broke off with Chin, then people of the whole nation would become fish and meat [they would perish and die]. Koryŏ would not have to wait five hundred years more to be destroyed [in this way Koryŏ could survive such long years], so officials at that time knew the welfare of the country.[19]

An oft-repeated proverb describes Korea as a shrimp among whales. That an identifiably Korean people and polity have managed to survive for

---

17. Some present-day Koreans attribute the popular dish *pulgogi* ("fire meat") to the period of Mongol rule in Korea. However, the connection between *pulgogi* and actual thirteenth-century Mongol culinary practices is dubious at best.

18. The best English-language treatment of the Mongol subjugation of Koryŏ remains Henthorn, *Korea: The Mongol Invasions*.

19. Quoted in Etsuko Hai-Jin Kang, *Diplomacy and Ideology in Japanese-Korean Relations*, 169.

nearly two millennia testifies to the tenacity and ability of the inhabitants of the Korean peninsula. Skillfully utilizing a combination of armed resistance, diplomatic accommodation, and submission, the Korean shrimp has managed to outlast a succession of whales.

Chosŏn-China Relations

By the time the Korean Chosŏn Kingdom (1392–1910) was established, Sino-Korean relations had for centuries been predicated on Korea's acceptance of Chinese claims to suzerainty as expressed through tribute missions. The ebb and flow of inner Asian "barbarian" empires often interrupted this mode of relations and imposed much more direct and harsh demands on both Korea and China. With the advent of the Ming in 1368 and its assertion of centrality in East Asia, Koreans were required to seek some sort of accommodation with the most powerful realm in the region.[20]

Korea's relationship with the ruling powers in Asia was a primary reason for the establishment of a Chosŏn Kingdom in the first place. In 1388, King U (r. 1374–88), one of the last monarchs of the Koryŏ Kingdom, sent an army north to contest Ming Chinese claims to territory in Manchuria. Incensed at Ming encroachments on what he perceived to be Korean lands and seeking to placate the still-powerful Mongols, who occupied much of the territory directly north and northwest of the Korean peninsula, King U ordered Yi Sŏng-gye (1335–1408), one of the leading generals of the Koryŏ army, to join the Mongols in an assault on the Ming. Yi marched as far north as the Yalu River, but then turned back and took control of the Koryŏ capital of Kaesŏng in a bloodless coup. After four years of appropriate

----

20. Korean accommodation with the Ming was hardly exceptional at the time. David Kang ("Hierarchy, Balancing, and Empirical Puzzles," 174) writes that "accommodation of China was the norm in East Asia during the Ming (1368–1644) and Qing (1644–1911) eras. This did not, however, involve a significant loss of national independence, as nearby states were largely free to conduct their domestic and foreign policy independent of China." It should be noted that Kang's (ibid., 175) contention that this China-centered "international system" "functioned in essentially the same manner," "from Japan to Siam . . . for more than six centuries" ignores the diversity of relations the Qing Empire had with its neighbors. His observations are most appropriate for some members of Fairbank's "Sinic zone" such as Korea, Liuqiu (Ryūkyū), Annam, and, to a lesser extent, Japan. They fit far less well for relations between the Ming and Qing and various powers in Central Asia (including Russia) and beyond. For articulation of the "Sinic zone," see Fairbank, "A Preliminary Framework," 2, 13.

Confucian procrastination and rule through figurehead Koryŏ kings, Yi Sŏng-gye declared a new dynasty, the Chosŏn, with himself as the first king (known to posterity as King T'aejo, r. 1392–98).

One of Yi's first acts was to seek acknowledgment of his legitimacy from the Ming. Donald Clark notes that "fealty to the Ming was a cardinal point of Yi Sŏng-gye's political program and he sent an embassy to Nanking immediately to make this point and to request investiture and approval of the new government."[21] The Ming Hongwu emperor (r. 1368–98) granted recognition to the new dynasty and even selected its name: Chosŏn (C. Chaoxian).[22] The emperor was less eager to grant legitimacy to the new kingdom's first ruler. Concerned about possible Korean-Jurchen cooperation against the Ming and uncomfortable with the parallels with his own rise to power, the Hongwu emperor always referred to Yi Sŏng-gye by temporary titles.[23] This imperial reluctance did not, however, discourage Korean missions to China or reduce their numbers. The Hongwu emperor's successors, experiencing challenges to their authority at home, were more appreciative of Korean offers of fealty. They welcomed Korean tribute missions and quickly granted full recognition and investiture to King T'aejo's successors.[24] In Korea, the Chosŏn-Ming relationship came to be known as "serving the great" (*sadae*; C. *shida*), and the periodic tribute mis-

———

21. Clark, "The Ming Connection," 82.

22. The Hongwu emperor was given two suggestions for the name of the new dynasty. The other name was Hwanyŏng, one name of Yi Sŏng-gye's birthplace (Keith Pratt et al., *Korea: A Historical and Cultural Dictionary*, 232). Chaoxian/Chosŏn was the name of one or more ancient Korean kingdoms. Tan'gun Chosŏn (2333–1122 B.C.) and Old Chosŏn (first millennium B.C.) occupy prominent places in contemporary Korean historical narratives, but proof of their existence, not to mention their Koreanness, rests on rather dubious archaeological foundations. A misreading of the characters for "Chosŏn" is the source of the popular nickname "Land of the Morning Calm" for Korea. Although written the same (and pronounced the same in Korean), the *cho* (朝) in Chosŏn means "dynasty" or "court" rather than "morning" (and is pronounced *chao* rather than *zhao* in modern standard Chinese). Whatever the case, the characters are most likely a transliteration of an ancient term whose original meaning is now lost. For an early English-language invocation of "morning calm," see Lowell, *Choson: Land of Morning Calm.*

23. Clark ("The Ming Connection," 82) observes "the emperor lost no opportunity to criticize and humiliate King T'aejo [Yi Sŏng-gye]—whether over his ancestry, his policies, the quality of the tribute he offered up, the literary quality of his petitions, or the honesty of his ambassadors."

24. Clark, "Sino-Korean Tributary Relations Under the Ming," 276–79.

sions sent to China as the "dispatch of envoys of submission" (*sadae sa-haeng*; C. *shida shixing*).[25] Two basic principles would animate Sino-Korean relations for the next five centuries: hierarchy and distance.

HIERARCHY

After the solidification of Ming-Chosŏn relations, the powers that ruled Korea and China reached an understanding on the basic principles that would govern their dealings. The first principle was the mutual acceptance of a hierarchical order in which China was the superior and Korea the inferior. A variety of terms was used to describe this relationship, ranging from the very simple "superior country" (*shangguo*; K. *sangguk*) and "inferior country" (*xiaguo*; K. *haguk*) to "suzerain" (*zong*; K. *chong*) and "vassal" (*shubang*, K. *sokbang*). Both sides, however, appeared to favor the use of Confucian familial terms and characterized the Chinese empire as the father or older brother and the Korean kingdom as the son or younger brother.[26]

Korean acceptance of Chinese suzerainty was ritually expressed through participation in the so-called tribute system. Three or four times a year, envoys from the Chosŏn kingdom traveled to China to declare Korean loyalty to the Ming and present goods, congratulations, or other ritual niceties to the Ming emperor and his house. The goods offered as tribute varied according to the demands of the Chinese imperial throne, but generally included furs, paper, silk, and grass-cloth and other textiles. During the early Ming, demands for human tribute—girls to serve in the imperial harem and household, and boys to serve as eunuchs—were frequent and resented. After presenting the tribute goods and declaring loyalty to the emperor, the Chosŏn tribute emissaries returned home with gifts from the emperor.

The Chosŏn court also expressed its acceptance of the suzerain-vassal relationship by using the official Chinese calendar and by accepting and entertaining the occasional visits of Chinese envoys. These usually came to Korea to grant investiture to Chosŏn kings. When the Chinese envoy neared Seoul, the Korean king would leave his palace and travel to the Welcoming Imperial Grace Gate (Yŏngŭnmun) on the outskirts to meet

---

25. Tu-ki Min, "The Jehol Diary and the Character of Ch'ing Rule," 1.

26. Chŏn In-yŏng, "Chung-Il kabo chŏnjaeng chŏnhu," 41*n*; Key-hiuk Kim, *The Last Phase of the East Asian World Order*, 7–8; M. F. Nelson, *Korea and the Old Orders in Eastern Asia*, 86–91.

the envoy. There he would prostrate himself as the message from the emperor was read aloud.[27] The sight of the Chosŏn king bowing to a relatively low-ranking Chinese official provided seemingly irrefutable evidence for the claim that "never did a country make herself more abject in her acceptance of a vassal's position."[28] These envoys were also lavishly treated despite the often-considerable drain on the Chosŏn government's treasury.

The tendency of Chinese records to characterize nearly every contact with outside powers as "tribute" clearly did not reflect geopolitical or cultural realities in many instances. However, Chosŏn Korea was as close to a model tributary state as China ever found. Korean willingness to accept vassal status was motivated in part by a clear-eyed assessment of Ming China's power and the dangerous consequences of a conflict between China and Korea. For many of Chosŏn Korea's *yangban* elite, however, acceptance of Korea's place in the Sinocentric Asian order was not only pragmatic but also proper. Korean envoys reveled in their status as model tributaries; they looked down on the clumsy attempts of the ruler of the Liuqiu (Ryūkyū) Islands to follow proper ritual protocol in memorials to China; they swelled with pride when they discovered that some Korean authors, poets, and thinkers were known in China or when they recorded the statement of the Ming Grand Secretariat that "Korea, a land of decorum and righteousness, has for generations been a screen to China. How could we treat Koreans as foreigners?"[29]

This is not to say that the Koreans were blind to the difficulties and challenges of the tributary relationship. Korean resentment of Ming demands for human tribute has already been noted. Korean tributary envoys also complained of the abuses of Ming protocol officers, who often extorted large sums of silver from them before allowing them to return to Korea; they chafed at Ming restrictions on their freedom of movement within Beijing.[30] Still, it is clear that for many elites in the Chosŏn Kingdom, proper conduct in tributary relations with Ming China was part of the larger project of creating a state and society governed by Neo-Confucian principles.[31]

———

27. Wright, "The Adaptability of Ch'ing Diplomacy," 366; Key-hiuk Kim, *The Last Phase of the East Asian World Order*, 6–7.

28. Hulbert, *History of Korea*, 2: 132.

29. Peter Lee, *A Korean Storyteller's Miscellany*, 80–81, 93, 133, *passim*.

30. Ibid., 74–76.

31. For an examination of this process of the "Neo-Confucianization" of Korea, see Deuchler, *The Confucian Transformation of Korea*.

DISTANCE

The Korean practice of "serving the great" was roundly criticized by late nineteenth-century Korean reformers who saw the Chosŏn Kingdom's relations with China as unwarranted dependence on an outside power. Indeed, the very term *sadaejuŭi* (*sadae*-ism) is now synonymous with toadyism or flunkeyism. However, Korea's decision to accept vassal status vis-à-vis China did not reflect the obsequious servility these terms connote. Rather, the decision was motivated by a quite pragmatic assessment of the best way to guarantee both security and autonomy for Korea.

Moreover, an exclusive focus on ritual declarations of servility distracts attention from the second major principle that animated Ming-Chosŏn relations: distance and separation. Participation in the tribute system can be understood as Korea's best means for limiting contact with China. As noted earlier, a Korean desire to do just this can be seen at least as early as the late tenth century. As long as the Korean court declared fealty to China, it was left alone to do virtually as it pleased.[32] In addition, Korea's willing participation in a Sinocentric tribute system did not mean abject dependence. Koreans have often displayed a strong sense of cultural uniqueness if not superiority vis-à-vis their neighbors.[33] For example, advances in printing technology achieved under the reign of King Sejong (r. 1418–50) were the cause of some not so subtle self-congratulation:

The purpose of the invention was to supply the state with books and a better means of gaining knowledge. . . . We are prepared now to print any book there is and all men will have the means of study. Literature will increase and grow, and religion flourish in the earth. The kings of T'ang and Han spent their strength in the

---

32. Chŏn In-yŏng, "Chung-Il kabo chŏnjaeng chŏnhu," 82.

33. Acceptance of Chinese suzerainty did not negate the assertion of a putative vassal's own superior status vis-à-vis other countries and peoples in the region. For example, David Marr writes the following concerning the Vietnamese Le dynasty (1427–1787): "This reality [China's overwhelming size], together with sincere cultural admiration, led Vietnam's rulers to accept the tributary system. Providing China did not meddle in Vietnam's internal affairs . . . Vietnamese monarchs were quite willing to declare themselves vassals of the Celestial Emperor. The subtlety of this relationship was evident from the way in which Vietnamese monarchs styled themselves 'king' (*vuong*) when communicating with China's rulers, but 'emperor' (*hoang dê*) when addressing their own subjects or sending messages to other Southeast Asian rulers" (quoted in David Kang, "Hierarchy, Balancing, and Empirical Puzzles," 174–75).

training and equipment of armies; how much better is the work of our good king. As high as heaven overtops the earth so does this deed outshine theirs. Endless blessing for Korea.[34]

Chosŏn rulers were fastidious in their dispatch of tribute missions to Ming China, but they were equally determined to limit the number of Ming envoys visiting Korea. They repeatedly expressed their desire to conduct any necessary diplomatic business via tribute missions sent to the Ming capital. This was particularly the case in the early years of the Chosŏn Kingdom when Ming envoys were often ethnic Korean eunuchs (a legacy of Ming demands for human tribute) whose haughty behavior earned them little affection in the land of their nativity. The desire of both Chosŏn Korea and Ming China to limit interaction was amplified by the Ming proclamation and Korean acceptance of a ban on maritime travel, trade, and communications between the two countries and by the fact that trade and travel via the overland route to China was hampered by the extremely rugged terrain of northern Korea.

The limiting of relations to tribute missions had the perhaps unintended consequence of amplifying the commercial significance of these missions for Korea. By virtue of functioning as the only legal medium of trade between Korea and China, tribute missions became extremely lucrative for those officials fortunate enough to participate in them. As a result, many officials and even merchants sought to accompany official tribute missions to the Ming capital. They brought Korean products such as ginseng, furs, horses, and silver (much of which originated in Japan) and exchanged them for Chinese luxuries including silks, books, medicines, and porcelain. Confucian orthodoxy may have proclaimed disdain for profit seeking, but it is clear that Korean officials were more than willing to benefit from the opportunities afforded by the tribute trade, a tendency that, in the words of Key-hiuk Kim, "developed networks of vested bureaucratic and commercial interest in both countries" and helped to maintain the stability of relations between Korea and China.[35]

––––

34. Gale and Rutt, *James Scarth Gale and His History of the Korean People*, 234–35. Another example can be found in the preface to the Korean literature anthology, the *Tongmunsŏn*. It reads: "The literature of the East is neither the literature of the Song or Yuan, nor the literature of the Han and Tang. It is the literature of our country" (Schmid, "Constructing Independence," 37).

35. Key-hiuk Kim, *The Last Phase of the East Asian World Order*, 11. Chiefly through the tribute missions but also through trade along Korea's northern border and a clan-

The mutually agreeable system of noninterference experienced a significant shock at the end of the sixteenth century. The Japanese invasions of Korea of the 1590s led by Hideyoshi Toyotomi devastated the peninsula and prompted the dispatch of a large Ming army to Korea to repulse the Japanese invaders. The Ming decision to send troops to Korea may have been motivated as much by a concern that the Japanese subjugation of Korea might lead to a direct Japanese assault on China as by a need to fulfill China's obligation as suzerain to give aid to its vassal in times of trouble. Nevertheless, the dispatch of troops was described purely in terms of upholding the traditional obligations between suzerain and vassal, and generations of grateful Koreans clearly saw it as such.[36] The price paid by the Ming for such behavior was a heavy one; some speculate that fighting Hideyoshi irrevocably weakened the Ming and paved the way for its fall four decades later.

The "Barbarian" Challenge

The ascent of the Manchus, their conquest of the Ming, and their subjugation of Korea illustrate one of the primary dynamics of Northeast Asian geopolitics and history. For many, particularly in Korea, the nomadic or semi-nomadic "barbarians" of present-day Manchuria, Mongolia, and Central Asia constituted a more immediate and threatening presence than did the ruling power in China.

From the perspective of early Ming rulers, a troubling issue was the reputed close connection between the founder of the Chosŏn Kingdom, Yi Sŏng-gye, and groups of Jurchen, who were to be found on both sides of the Yalu. For Koreans, dealing with Jurchen still living south of the Yalu who were opposed to the new Chosŏn state was a significant challenge for

---

destine trade, Korea was an active participant in a Northeast Asian commerce that saw, among other things, Japanese silver going to China in return for Chinese silks, textiles, medicines, and other products. However, beginning in the sixteenth century, competition from Spanish silver coming through Manila, structural changes in the Japanese economy, and Korea's increasing isolation served to gradually reduce the amount of goods traded among the three countries. For an overview of this phenomenon, see John Lee, "Trade and Economy in Preindustrial East Asia."

36. King Sŏnjo (r. 1568–1608) felt that, even during this time of crisis, the approval of Ming China was a vital prerequisite to his rule (Ledyard, "Confucianism and War"). For an entertaining overview of the Hideyoshi invasions, see Turnbull, *Samurai Invasion*.

much of the fifteenth century.[37] Disagreements over how to respond to the growing Jurchen threat across the Yalu in the early sixteenth century was one of the causes of the second and third "literary purges" (sahwa) in the Chosŏn government.[38] When the Jurchen/Manchus decided to invade the Chosŏn Kingdom in 1627, they were aided by a group of Korean yangban literati who had fled north and offered to lead the Jurchen back into Korea in order to avenge perceived offenses.[39] The Chosŏn Kingdom proved unable to repel the invasion and grudgingly acceded to the Jurchen offer of "brotherly relations." However, Korean intransigence and the growing ambition of the Jurchen-cum-Manchu kingdom brought new demands on Korea, including the 1636 ultimatum: "You break off relations with them [the Ming], stop using the era name of [the Ming], and all the documents will treat us as the suzerain state."[40] Korean resistance resulted in a devastating invasion and complete Korean submission in the same year.[41]

The Manchu invasions and the subsequent overthrow of the Ming in 1644 convinced most in Chosŏn Korea of the necessity of doing business with the new "barbarians." There was, naturally, much resentment of the Manchu invasions and the Qing claims of suzerainty. King Hyojong (r. 1649–59) actually began preparations for a "northern expedition" (pukbŏl undong) against the Manchus but did not act on his designs.[42] After an initial transition period in which the Manchus kept members of the Chosŏn court hostage at their capital and, like the Ming in its early years, demanded human tribute, the rulers of the newly founded Qing dynasty did

---

37. Apparently not all Jurchen in Korea were seen as fit only for immediate expulsion. In fact, Mongke Temur cooperated with Chosŏn forces in an attempt to oust other groups of Jurchen from Korea. While his immediate clan left Korea after his death in 1434, the fate of other Jurchen in Korea is less clear (Crossley, The Manchus, 39; Robinson, "From Raiders to Traders").

38. Wagner, The Literati Purges, 51–120.

39. Han Yŏng-u, Tasi ch'annŭn uri yŏksa, 323–24.

40. Etsuko Hai-Jin Kang, Diplomacy and Ideology in Japanese-Korean Relations, 180.

41. To commemorate the submission of the Chosŏn King Injo (r. 1623–49), the Manchus erected the Three Ferry Fields Stone of Shame (Samjŏn-do hanbi) in 1638 near the Han River. The stele was inscribed in both Chinese and Manchu. In the early years of the Republic of Korea, Syngman Rhee ordered it destroyed, but the Ministry of Culture had it buried instead. It has since been unearthed (Keith Pratt et al., Korea: A Historical and Cultural Dictionary, 401).

42. Han Yŏng-u, Tasi ch'annŭn uri yŏksa, 327. In 1654, the Chosŏn Kingdom was forced to send soldiers to fight alongside Qing troops against the Russians in the Amur River region; see Lee Keun-yeup, "Glory of Ancestors, Contemptible Descendants."

little to modify the structure of China's relations with Korea. They demanded tribute missions (although the number of regular missions sent each year was soon reduced from three or four to one) and sent occasional envoys to grant investiture to Korean kings. Other forms of interaction—trade, travel, and migration—were strictly limited or prohibited outright. And, like the Ming, the Qing virtually never interfered with Korean domestic affairs.

The willingness of the Qing to grant Korea dependent-yet-autonomous status is rather remarkable, given the fact that the Qing was an expansionistic empire. Under the rule of vigorous monarchs such as Kangxi (r. 1662–1722), Yongzheng (r. 1722–1735), and Qianlong (r. 1736–1795), the Qing Empire expanded its borders to include areas of Mongolia, Central Asia, Turkestan, and Tibet. Yet, once Korean fealty was secured, the Qing appears never to have seriously considered subjugating and ruling outright the territory so close to the southern border of the Manchu homeland.[43]

For their part, the Koreans were more than happy to limit relations with the barbarians who happened to be occupying the Chinese mainland. The devastation of the Hideyoshi and Manchu invasions prompted the gradually increasing isolation of Korea, as the Chosŏn court sought to limit its ties not only with the Qing but also with Tokugawa Japan. Nevertheless, tributary relations with the Qing continued to be predicated on the ceremonial expression of Qing suzerainty, on one hand, and distance and noninterference, on the other. Korea generally headed the Qing lists of tributaries, and the number of tribute missions from Korea dwarfed those coming from other places. Judging by the frequency and consistency of these tribute missions, Korea continued to be China's most faithful tributary state.[44] The trade conducted by Korean tributary envoys continued

---

43. Ming loyalists and others who resisted the Qing conquest of China had other ideas. Wu Sangui, the leader of the Rebellion of the Three Feudatories (1673–81), gave the young Kangxi emperor two choices, commit suicide or retreat to his ancestral homelands in Manchuria "where he would be 'allowed' to take Korea" (Wakeman, *The Great Enterprise*, 1108). A similar proposal was made well over a century later by Hwang Sa-yong, a Korean adherent to Catholicism, in the famous "silk manuscript," which led to widespread persecution of Catholics within Korea (Hara, "Korea, China and Western Barbarians," 397–99).

44. Tu-ki Min, "The Jehol Diary and the Character of Ch'ing Rule," 2. Hae-jong Chun ("Sino-Korean Tributary Relations in the Ch'ing Period," 99) has concluded that Korea sent 474 tribute missions to China during the period 1637–1894, an average of nearly two missions per year. When one considers Mark Mancall's (*China at the Center*, 15) estimation that the total number of tribute missions sent by 62 countries over the

unabated, with one embassy in 1787 bringing at least 80,000 taels' worth of goods to trade.[45]

Trade was also permitted at designated periodic trade fairs along the Sino-Korean border at Chunggang (C. Zhongjiang), Hoeryŏng (C. Huining), and Kyŏngwŏn (C. Qingyuan). This exchange was heavily regulated by both governments. Korean merchants sometimes grumbled that the border trade amounted to little more than a means of subsidizing poor Manchu families, who exchanged animal skins and shoddy blue cotton cloth for cattle, paper, salt, and other necessities.[46]

Although complying with Qing demands for tribute and faithfully participating in the required ceremonial exchanges, many Korean officials kept the Ming flame alive, albeit not in sight of Qing envoys. They offered sacrifices to shrines dedicated to Ming rulers and often used the reign-dates of the last Ming emperor, Chongzhen (r. 1628–44), rather than the reigning Qing emperor, or even the Korean king, to date their documents.[47] Some

---

course of nearly the same period was somewhere in the neighborhood of 500, the extent to which China's relations with Korea constitute the classic, and perhaps the only legitimate, example of a Sinocentric tributary relationship becomes clear. For Korea's pre-eminent position in the Qing *Illustrations of Tributaries*, see Hostetler, *Qing Colonial Enterprise*, 42.

45. Pak Chi-wŏn estimated the amount of silver brought by annual tribute missions to be 100,000 ounces (Ledyard, "Hong Taeyong and his 'Peking Memoir,'" 88). For a description of Sino-Korean tribute trade during the Qing period, see Zhang Cunwu, *Qing-Han zongfan maoyi*; and Hae-jong Chun, "Sino-Korean Tributary Relations in the Ch'ing Period." It is clear that the Korean tribute emissaries' desires for trade and profit often transcended the bounds and limitations of the rules of the tributary relationship. According to Mary Wright ("The Adaptability of Ch'ing Diplomacy," 366*n*9), there is evidence of Korean tribute emissaries "selling copper and ginseng in Tientsin [Tianjin], Anhwei [Anhui], and other points remote from their supposed route."

46. Hae-jong Chun. "Sino-Korean Tributary Relations in the Ch'ing Period," 108. See also Key-hiuk Kim, *The Last Phase of the East Asian World Order*, 10–11. The tribute trade, the border trade, the trade with Japan, and a difficult to quantify but not insignificant amount of smuggling combined to create a situation in which Chosŏn Korea was connected to a number of regional trading networks; see Hamashita, "Tribute and Treaties," 19.

47. For Ming loyalism in Korea, see Chai-sik Chung, *A Korean Confucian Encounter with the Modern World*, 7–13; and Palais, *Politics and Policy in Traditional Korea*, 120–24, 190–91. See also Ledyard, "Hong Taeyong and His 'Peking Memoir,'" 72. For examples of dating according to the reign of Chongzhen, see Keith Pratt et al., *Korea: A Historical and Cultural Dictionary*, 291. Disdain for the Qing was such that leading *silhak* (practical learning) scholars such as Pak Che-ga (b. 1750) noted that if "someone suggests that the

Korean tributary envoys enjoyed flaunting their Ming costumes and hair-styles in Beijing and sometimes discomfited their Chinese hosts by making pointed pro-Ming statements. Many cheered the anti-Qing revolt of the Three Feudatories (1673–81) and were disappointed at its failure. Koreans also sought to clearly demarcate the Qing-Chosŏn border in the early eighteenth century; the officials tasked with the project suffered generations of criticism for giving up Korean claims to land north of the Tumen River.[48] Yet, as time wore on, a growing number of Koreans became resigned to the reality of Qing rule.[49] Some even had grudging praise for the Manchus.[50]

The alternative to public acceptance of Qing suzerainty was confrontation, and Korea was sure to lose any prolonged military conflict with the Qing. Ritual declarations of submission were a small price to pay for peace and autonomy. This is not to say that Koreans during the Chosŏn period lacked a strong sense of identity or confidence in the value of Korean

---

ways of China be studied, people rise and laugh at him." Furthermore, most Koreans "do not want to learn a single Chinese way and have contact with a single Chinese scholar." The call of Pak and other *silhak* scholars to learn from Qing commercial and political innovations fell largely on deaf ears (see Pak Che-ga, "On Revering China," 103–4).

48. See Schmid, *Korea Between Empires*, 206–8.

49. For some, the reality of China under "barbarian rule" highlighted the urgency with which Koreans had to defend their Confucian civilization. JaHyun Kim Haboush (*The Confucian Kingship in Korea*, 24) writes: "What emerged from the Korean recognition of Ch'ing [Qing] China as a permanent, not temporary, reality was the perception that Korea was now the only bastion of Confucian civilization and that, as the sole carrier of the civilized tradition which was lost in China, the Yi monarchy had to be guarded with even greater zeal."

50. For Korean tribute emissaries and their opinions of the Manchus and the Chinese, see Ledyard, "Hong Taeyong and His 'Peking Memoir'"; and Tu-ki Min, "The Jehol Diary and the Character of Ch'ing Rule." For Korean views on the Revolt of the Three Feudatories, see Etsuko Hai-Jin Kang, *Diplomacy and Ideology in Japanese-Korean Relations*, 190–91. Mary Wright ("The Adaptability of Ch'ing Diplomacy," 367) writes: "Yet in spite of the striking differences between China and Korea and the very limited contact that was allowed, each country treated the other with a remarkably affectionate decorum. The Korean expressions of loyalty to China seem to me to have a quality lacking in the protestations of other tributary states. China on her part constantly pointed out that Korea's relation was uniquely close, that she was 'not the same as other tributary states.' Concessions to Korean pride were frequent, and numerous Chinese historical works were corrected by edict on points Korea found offensive." The "not the same as other tributary states" quote is from the *Da-Qing huidian shili* (Guangxu ed.) 504.1b–2a.

culture. In terms of international relations, however, accepting the tribute system was the most effective way to ensure harmony between China and Korea.

The bottom line for both Korea and China was that this system of relations guaranteed security for both parties with a minimum of commitment and entanglement. Aside from the two invasions just before and after the turn of the seventeenth century, this peace lasted for nearly five centuries in Korea. Compared to the analogous figures for any state in Europe during the same period, two major conflicts in five hundred years is an enviable figure.[51] The system also allowed Korea the privilege of being an active participant in the Sinocentric world order without compromising Korean autonomy.

Although it is clear that adhering to the tenets of the tribute system brought tangible benefits for Korea and the Koreans, it might be less clear at first glance what benefits the system of relations brought to China. Why didn't Ming China ever seek to subjugate and occupy Chosŏn Korea? And if not the Ming, why not the expansionistic Qing? After all, Korea bordered directly on the Jurchen-Manchu homelands, and the Manchus had subjugated Korea even before conquering most of China proper.

The answer is not entirely clear, but a few possibilities strike me as worthy of consideration. First, it is apparent that for many in China, particularly among the Confucian scholar-bureaucrats, there was a recognition that Korean civilization was only slightly below if not on par with Chinese civilization, particularly in terms of adherence to Confucian principles. Since one of the stated purposes or dynamics of the putative Sinocentric world order was the pacifying, ordering, and ultimately civilizing of all who

---

51. David Kang ("Getting Asia Wrong," 66–67) writes: "Until the intrusion of the Western powers in the nineteenth century, East Asian interstate relations were remarkably stable, punctuated only occasionally by conflict between countries. The system was based on Chinese military and economic power but was reinforced through centuries of cultural exchange, and the units in the system were sovereign states that had political control over recognized geographic areas. East Asian international relations emphasized formal hierarchy among nations while allowing considerable informal equality. With China as the dominant state and surrounding countries as peripheral or secondary states, as long as hierarchy was observed there was little need for interstate war. This contrasts sharply with the Western tradition of international relations, which has consisted of formal equality between nation-states, informal hierarchy, and near-constant interstate conflict." See also Hamashita, "Tribute and Treaties," 20.

approached the Son of Heaven, it would appear that Korea and the Koreans had essentially accomplished the task of becoming civilized. There was, from the standpoint of Confucian morality, no real reason to insist on more direct Chinese power or control in Korea.[52] And since the Qing emperors appear to have cultivated the image of model Confucian monarch in their relations with Korea (as contrasted with their interactions with other peoples both within and outside the imperium), there was little within the rhetorical and conceptual confines of Confucian familial relations that would permit invasion, subjugation, and annexation.[53] Second, in terms of security and geopolitics, as long as Korea pledged its loyalty to China, it constituted an important buffer zone between China and any enemies who might approach from the sea (as Japan attempted to do in the late sixteenth century). Third, the tribute system provided an important conduit for Sino-Korean and indeed Sino-Japanese trade, a conduit that enriched many Chinese as well as Korean officials and merchants. The aggregate significance of this commercial exchange declined as a Japanese turn toward autarchy and the ready availability of New World silver via Manila reduced the Chinese demand for Japanese silver and other goods. But the tribute system remained a steady and reliable source of desired goods and specie.

In the end, however, it is clear that whatever the underlying motivations of Ming and Qing emperors and officials, the system worked. Described in classical Confucian terms, the power and influence of the ultimate

---

52. The Kangxi emperor declared, "Among the outer vassals only Chosŏn is close to China in its 'reputation and civilization, legal and political system'" (Wei Yuan, *Shengwuji*, 35, cited in Nan-Tsung Kim, "Neighbour as Mirror," 56–57). A 1599 encyclopedia "depicts Koreans as 'civilized barbarians,' considered closest to the Chinese cultural world because of their incessant importation of Chinese customs and books since antiquity. Next to a drawing of a Korean man dressed impeccably in Ming-style literati robe and shoes, a description reads: 'In governmental buildings, bureaucracy, poetry, writing, rituals, music, medicine, divination, *cap and gown*, they follow Chinese institutions in their entirety'" (Yu Xiangdou, *Santai wanyong zhengzong*, 5.1a., quoted in Dorothy Ko, "The Body as Attire," 12–13; emphasis in Ko).

53. For a concurring view, see Key-hiuk Kim, *The Last Phase of the East Asian World Order*, 11–12. For the Qing efforts to highlight continuity with Ming ritual and practice, see Crossley, *A Translucent Mirror*, 306, 333. To be sure, not all Chinese shared the lofty opinions of the Koreans declared by the Qing Emperors. Some Europeans recounted hearing from Southern Chinese denunciations of the "filthy Coreans" who "are stupid, they look at all things but observe nothing" (Fairbank, *Trade and Diplomacy on the China Coast*, 68n, 72n).

Confucian gentleman who occupied the throne in Beijing effortlessly flowed throughout the world, and the common folk of Korea bent like grass. Put in more contemporary terms, both the Ming and the Qing were able to maintain their geopolitical and commercial interests vis-à-vis Korea while devoting a relatively small amount of resources to cultivating the relationship. In short, the result was the best outcome of indirect or informal rule that the Ming and Qing could wish for.[54]

---

54. Some may object to describing pre-nineteenth century Sino-Korean relations as Chinese informal rule. Although I am far more confident about the relevance and applicability of the concept of informal empire to nineteenth-century Qing-Chosŏn relations, I am struck by how closely Charles Maier's (*Among Empires*, 33) more general description of some of the attributes of empires resonates in may ways with the relations Chosŏn Korea had with Ming and Qing China: "Empires are a particular form of state organization in which the elites of differing ethnic or national units defer to and acquiesce in the political leadership of the dominant power. Whether out of constraint, convenience, or conviction, they accept the values of those who govern the dominant center or metropole, although they often seek to implant or influence those very values. Having achieved status within their own societies, they can now play a role on a transnational stage. The influential classes in each national or regional capital defer to the projects of the imperial capital. They usually enlist against common enemies. They take satisfaction in visits to the imperial center."

T W O

Nineteenth-Century Challenges
and Changes

The system of stable and mutually beneficial relations between the Qing Empire and Chosŏn Korea was challenged and ultimately transformed by the combination of internal challenges and outside threats that affected all of East Asia in the nineteenth century. The Qing Empire started down the path toward the ever-increasing direct involvement in Korea decades before the critical milestone year of 1882. But the Qing Empire was not alone in changing its relationship with Chosŏn Korea. Western powers and Japan also sought new relations. The combination of increasing outside pressure and domestic developments brought the introduction of the treaty-port system to Korea. Simultaneously an amplification of previous modes of foreign relations and a transformation of them, the treaty-port system in Korea dramatically increased the amount of interaction Korea and Koreans had with the outside world. Some of the biggest questions hanging over the entire system were issues of control. Chosŏn Korea sought to manipulate, resist, or otherwise use the system to keep unwanted foreigners at arm's length. Meiji Japan attempted to utilize it to secure monopolistic privileges in Korea. Others, including the Qing Empire, responded to the Japanese challenge by seeking to transfer to Korea the norms of foreign relations that held sway in China (and Japan), including most-favored-nation privileges and equal access for all outsiders.

As the nineteenth century dawned, the Qing Empire was among the largest and most prosperous empires in the world. Under the aggressively expansionist rule of a succession of able emperors, the Qing had expanded its territory to nearly double the size of that ruled by the Ming. It exerted informal but powerful sway and influence over an even larger area.[1] In terms of economic size and prosperity, the Qing was a major force. Those who perpetuate the common image of the Qing Empire as increasingly backwards in a rapidly modernizing world fail to consider why the European powers had, for centuries, been trying to obtain greater commercial access to China: China produced goods others wanted and needed in copious quantities.[2]

The nineteenth century would, however, present the Qing with a series of changes and challenges that would shake the empire to its core, eventually bringing its demise in the early twentieth century. Territories that were seized or claimed needed to be consolidated and controlled.[3] A burgeoning population, the result of the considerable prosperity of the realm accelerated by the adoption and expansion of New World crops, presented ever-greater challenges to an all-too-limited number of bureaucrats and officials.[4] Rebellions large and small wracked the empire, leaving destruction in their wake. The largest of these, the Taiping (1850–64), devastated the prosperous Yangzi River Basin and left at least twenty million dead. The Taiping Rebellion also set into motion a significant shift in the balance of power within the Qing Empire, as powerful provincial and local officials such as Zeng Guofan and Li Hongzhang raised and trained their own armies to put it down. These officials, while loyal to the Qing imperial house,

---

1. For an illuminating map of Qing territory and influence, see Warren Cohen, *East Asia at the Center*, 224–25.

2. Many Westerners were also motivated by the prospect of tapping the large China market, a desire that was often rooted more in their hopes and aspirations than in any commercial reality; see, e.g., Varg, "The Myth of the China Market."

3. The tipping point between vigorous expansion and inevitable decline was described by the novelist Italo Calvino, who put the following words in the mouth of Mongol emperor Khublai Khan: "In the lives of emperors there is a moment that follows upon the pride in the unbounded breadth of the territories that we have conquered. . . . This is the desperate moment in which we discover that this empire which seemed to us to be the sum of all wonders is a defeat without end or form, that the rot is already too gangrenous for our scepter to be able to repair it, that our triumph over our enemy sovereigns has made us heirs to their long ruination" (quoted in Maier, *Among Empires*, 13).

4. One of the best studies on Chinese population growth remains Ping-ti Ho, *Studies on the Population of China, 1368–1953*. For population pressures and their impact on Chinese agriculture and administration, see Perdue, *Exhausting the Earth*.

proved reluctant to relinquish their newfound powers once the immediate crisis had passed.[5]

In addition to the daunting internal problems, the Qing also faced a growing number of challenges from without, as other imperialist and would-be imperialist powers contested Qing claims to regional hegemony and sought geopolitical, commercial, and other interests in East Asia. Russian migration and expansion meant that another primarily land empire was bumping up against the Qing along an extremely long northern border. The increasing Russian presence also prompted British-led reactions, an extension of the "Great Game" into East Asia.[6] European maritime powers also began to push in earnest for access and advantage in East Asia. The French established and expanded a colonial presence in Indochina, challenging Qing claims to suzerainty in the region; French diplomats, merchants, and adventurers also had an eye on expanding French power into the Qing Empire proper, particularly Yunnan province.[7] The British became increasingly insistent that the terms and conditions of relations between the Qing and British empires be modified to suit British interests. What diplomacy could not achieve was secured by military force, as a series of conflicts led to the annexation of Hong Kong and an unprecedented degree of British diplomatic and commercial access to the Qing Empire.[8] Other powers, particularly the United States and, later, Germany, were more than willing to follow where the British and French led, securing

---

5. Kuhn, *Rebellion and Its Enemies in Late Imperial China.*

6. Ch'oe Mun-hyŏng, *Han'guk ŭl tullŏssan chegukchuŭi yŏlgang ŭi kakch'uk,* 14–16; Chŏn In-yŏng, "Chungil kabo chŏnjaeng chŏnhu," 42; for more general treatments of Russian imperial expansion and the Great Game, see Lieven, *Empire,* and Hopkirk, *The Great Game.* Russian expansion into the Far East was not merely geopolitical in intent. Throughout much of the eighteenth century, Russians also conducted a thriving overland trade with the Qing Empire, the combined worth of which may have amounted to twice that of the trade between Britain and the Qing Empire conducted at Guangzhou (Canton) at mid-century (Edmund Clubb, *China and Russia: The 'Great Game,'* 71, quoted in Warren Cohen, *East Asia at the Center,* 267).

7. Warren Cohen, *East Asia at the Center,* 265–67. One French adventurer concluded that if France could solidify its hold on Indochina up to and including the border with the Qing Empire, "Yunnan could provide a rich outlet for French trade and Saigon would eventually rival Shanghai as the great commercial entrepôt for eastern Asia" (Cady, *The Roots of French Imperialism in Eastern Asia,* 281).

8. Osterhammel, "Britain and China, 1842–1914"; Fairbank, *Trade and Diplomacy on the China Coast.*

similar degrees of access through treaties of their own. Finally, Japan, a growing maritime empire with a desire to become a continental power as well, presented yet another competitor and potential threat to Qing power and interests in the region.[9]

Although this work uses the phrase "the Qing Empire," the Qing, like any of its contemporary counterparts, was far from unitary or monolithic. Indeed, one of the hallmarks of the Qing was its lack of a single, all-encompassing foreign ministry, or foreign policy for that matter. Rather, the Qing Empire used different institutions and different approaches to deal with its many neighbors and borders. The Board of Rites (Libu) mediated Qing relations with tributary states (including Korea) in East and Southeast Asia. The Office of Border Affairs (Lifanyuan) handled relations with the Mongols, Zunghars, and others groups (including Russia) along the northern border. European missionaries (before their expulsion from Beijing) were dealt with by the Imperial Household. Before 1842, Western merchants were forced to approach China via the so-called Canton System, which kept virtually all Westerners in or near the southern port of Canton (Guangzhou) and made direct contact between Western diplomats or merchants and Qing central officials difficult if not impossible.[10]

This diversity belies the ease with which some have described a "Chinese World Order" predicated on a tribute system. The Qing Empire proved willing to abandon its insistence on portraying all interactions with outsiders as a meeting of unequals; the 1689 Treaty of Nerchinsk, for example, refers to the Qing and Russian empires in terms of equality.[11] Within the confines of the empire itself, the Qing approaches to various areas was equally diverse, with policies and practices in Tibet, Central Asia, the southwest, and northeast all demonstrating a flexible appreciation of the needs, challenges, and interests that each region posed.[12] This simulta-

---

9. Beasley, *Japanese Imperialism 1894–1945*; Myers and Peattie, *The Japanese Colonial Empire*.

10. Kirby, "Traditions of Centrality," 16–17; Sigel, "The Role of Korea in Late Qing Foreign Policy," 77–78.

11. Kirby, "Traditions of Centrality," 16.

12. For a discussion of Qing imperial policies toward Xinjiang, see Millward, *Beyond the Pass*. See also Perdue, *China Marches West*. For an examination of some issues relating to the Southwest frontier, see Giersch, "A Motley Throng." For an overview of Qing Imperial ideology and practice, see Crossley, *A Translucent Mirror*; see also Hostetler, *Qing Colonial Enterprise*.

neous utilization of different ideologies and institutions to appeal to different "constituencies" in the Qing imperium is, according to Pamela Crossley, an important hallmark of Qing imperial ideology and practice.[13]

The notion that the arrival in force of the Western imperialist powers shattered a single, monolithic Chinese World Order, is, therefore, a problematic one that masks as much as it reveals about the complexity of the Qing Empire's relations with the outside world. This is not to say, however, that the Western impact on the Qing Empire was inconsequential. Although the results and implications of this intensification were far more multivalent and complex than those described by the "impact-response paradigm" articulated by John King Fairbank and Teng Ssu-yu, it remains clear that the Qing Empire was indeed a rather different place for having interacted with the West.[14] Several developments are worthy of brief notice.

First, the nineteenth century saw the globalization of the Qing Empire's international relations. Diplomats representing peoples who were, for many Chinese, vague and distant rumors demanded and eventually obtained the right to reside in Beijing and interact directly with the Qing imperial court. Foreign merchants, missionaries, and adventurers also appeared in an ever-growing number of Chinese treaty ports. Chinese laborers, so-called coolies, traversed the globe to work in places as distant as Cuba and Peru.[15] In part in response to the pressing need to represent and protect Chinese workers overseas, the Qing also took the unprecedented step of establishing legations in a number of nations in Europe and

---

13. See Crossley, *A Translucent Mirror*. Although the nineteenth century is by no means the focus of her study, Crossley observes a conflation and abandonment of this multivalent rule in favor of one that, in her words, "had become particularistically 'Confucian' in the aftermath of the Taiping War" (ibid., 285). She continues, "As with many other developments of the earlier Qing, the imperial trajectory went from consolidations for purposes of conquest to archetypes for purposes of expressing imperial universality to collapse, conflation, and fusion of court representation in the period of disintegrating imperial rule and increasing influence from civilian elites, progressive military leaders, and anxious aristocrats" (ibid.).

14. For the seminal articulation of the "impact-response paradigm," see Teng Ssu-yü and Fairbank, *China's Response to the West*; for a trenchant critique of this approach, see Paul Cohen, *Discovering History in China*, 9–55. See also Cohen's more recent ruminations on "China-centered" history in his *China Unbound*, 185–99.

15. Yen, *Coolies and Mandarins*. The demand for Chinese "coolie" workers grew dramatically after the abolition of the slave trade (Van de Ven, "The Onrush of Modern Globalization in China," 173).

the Western Hemisphere. The first Qing official stationed in Europe arrived in Britain in 1877. By 1880, the Qing had legations and/or representatives in Britain, Japan, the United States, France, and Russia (with Qing
diplomats also visiting Spain, Peru, and elsewhere). Enterprising Chinese
merchants encouraged the establishment of diplomatic and consular representation overseas in the hope of expanding their activities abroad and
profiting thereby.[16] All this intensification was facilitated by technological
and organizational advances ranging from steamships and telegraphs to increasingly sophisticated banking and financial institutions.[17]

Second, the conduits of the treaty ports and the shipping lines and lanes
that connected them began to compete seriously with the traditional tributary and junk trades for primacy in the Qing Empire's commercial relations
with the outside world. This is not to say that the tribute and junk trade
routes completely vanished. Indeed, a growing body of scholarship points
to the fact that the new treaty-port system and older networks and patterns
of trade coexisted, with the same technological factors that spurred the
new system also boosting the growth and intensification of traditional
forms of commerce.[18]

Third, the growth of foreign trade had a generally deleterious impact on
the Qing Empire's overall balance of payments. Western powers had
traded with China for centuries, purchasing large amounts of Chinese tea,
silk, porcelain, and other goods. However, until the nineteenth century,
few were able to supply Western-produced products that generated much
commercial interest in China. The result was a fairly consistent pattern of
foreign silver being exchanged for Chinese goods and, thus, a favorable
balance of payments for China. However, after centuries of fruitless
searching for products that would gain them access to the long-fabled but

---

16. In an 1874 essay advocating the establishment of diplomatic and consular representation abroad, Fujian Governor Wang Kaitai wrote that when wealthy Chinese merchants "learn that there are Chinese officials abroad who will protect them, the great tea
and silk firms will be encouraged to take their merchandise thither themselves" (Biggerstaff, "The Establishment of Permanent Chinese Diplomatic Missions Abroad," 23–24).
See also Desnoyers, "Toward 'One Enlightened and Progressive Civilization,'" 147–48.

17. Hans Van de Ven ("The Onrush of Modern Globalization in China," 167) argues
that these technological and institutional advances "all testified to the acceleration in
the 'velocity of exchanges' in China's trade with the outside world and the resulting
'time-space compression.'"

18. See Van de Ven, "The Onrush of Modern Globalization in China," 168–69. See
also Hamashita, "Tribute and Treaties."

seldom tapped "China market," British merchants hit upon the ingenious if opprobrious solution of illegal and addicting drugs. As the trickle of opium, "foreign mud," became a flood, Qing officials observed to their dismay the favorable balance of payments turn against them. This process only intensified as the fruits of the industrial revolution, particularly machine-woven cotton textiles, began to find markets in Asia.

The changes in relations between the Qing Empire and Western maritime powers also led to the establishment of new systems and institutions designed to mediate interactions between the Qing Empire and other powers. The most significant of these for purposes of understanding of both Qing-Western and Qing-Chosŏn relations are the treaty-port system as a whole, the Chinese Imperial Maritime Customs Service, and the Zongli yamen.

The treaty-port system was established as a result of Western insistence that the Qing Empire grant Western diplomats, merchants, missionaries, and others greater access to the Empire. The Qing was reluctant to do so, but a series of military defeats left it little choice. Elements of this system included the restriction of trade to designated areas, usually known as treaty ports; the establishment of foreign settlements, sometimes known as concessions, within those ports; extraterritorial privileges for foreigners; the establishment of a uniform tariff code, usually quite favorable to foreign merchants; and the enforcement of that code by a Maritime Customs Service run largely by foreigners. Systems with similar characteristics were subsequently established in Japan and, later, Korea.[19]

It is tempting to view the treaty-port system as an entirely foreign entity forced upon unwilling Asian victims. Difficult as it is to imagine the Qing Empire willingly agreeing to grant the right of foreign diplomatic residence in Beijing or to allow missionary work to be carried out in China, it is misleading to characterize the system as entirely foreign. The idea of restricting foreign trade to a limited number of locations, usually coastal ports, was hardly a new one in Asia. Canton has often been the place where powerful Chinese regimes insisted that foreign maritime trade take place. During much of the Qing period, foreigners were not only restricted to Canton but also required to conduct their diplomatic and commercial business

---

19. For an examination of the development of this system, see Son Chŏng-mok, *Han'guk kaehanggi tosi pyŏnhwa kwajŏng yŏn'gu*, 11–53; see also Fairbank, *Trade and Diplomacy on the China Coast*; and idem, "The Creation of the Treaty System," 213–63.

through state-sanctioned merchants (hongs). Similarly, Tokugawa Japan confined foreign trade to a handful of Dutch and Chinese merchants in or near Nagasaki. Chosŏn Korea followed the same pattern, limiting Japanese merchants' access to Korea to three ports on the southeastern coast and further reducing access to the sole conduit of the Japan House (Waegwan) near the port of Pusan after the Hideyoshi invasions of the late sixteenth century. Moreover, the practice of granting foreigners some degree of autonomy (e.g., "concessions") within designated treaty ports and even the practice of extraterritoriality have Asian precedents that long predate the "unequal treaties" of the mid-nineteenth century.[20]

The function of the treaty-port system has been a matter of considerable debate. Some emphasize that the system facilitated the inflow of goods, people, and ideas into Asian nations that were often initially reluctant to accept them. Others argue that the treaty ports actually served to *limit* foreign influence by restricting the foreigners to a confined space, thus allowing indigenous merchants and, later, industries to grow and flourish.[21]

As the number of treaty ports and the concomitant amount of Sino-foreign trade grew, Western powers called for the establishment and operation of an institution that would regulate trade on the basis of treaty-

---

20. Cassel, "Excavating Extraterritoriality"; Fairbank, "The Early Treaty System in the Chinese World Order." Hara Takemichi ("Korea, China, and Western Barbarians," 395–96) notes that Chinese envoys to Korea also enjoyed a status that closely resembles extraterritoriality. "Something like an extraterritorial jurisdiction operated under the tributary relationship with China: a Chinese national found on Korean soil had to be extradited to China; he could be punished or executed only if the Korean government had an explicit permission from the Chinese government." See also Wright, "The Adaptability of Ch'ing Diplomacy," 367. Some have also noted precedents in extraterritorial rights granted by the Ottoman Empire; but as Richard Horowitz ("International Law and State Transformation," 459–60) notes, "the inscription of extraterritoriality into treaties changed the situation in important ways. This was a formalized system, which foreigners blatantly used to their own advantage in pursuing both commercial enterprises and carrying on private lives. Most importantly, within the treaty system extraterritorial rights could not simply be revoked by the host government without fear of serious reprisals."

21. Osterhammel, "Semi-Colonialism and Informal Empire in Twentieth-Century China," 293–94; Grove and Sugiyama, "Introduction," 5–6. That the treaty-port system may have actually isolated foreigners rather than facilitated foreign commercial penetration was due in part to cultural proclivities on the part of the foreigners themselves. For an analysis of the case of Americans in Japan, see Murphy, *The American Merchant Experience in 19th Century Japan.*

stipulated equality. Thus, the Imperial Maritime Customs Service was created. Largely managed by foreigners, the Customs Service catalogued goods flowing in and out of China's treaty ports, assessed tariffs and other duties, assumed a wide variety of roles including harbor maintenance and map-making, and even sought to reform and stabilize China's currency. One scholar notes that the Imperial Maritime Customs Service "facilitated China's globalization, in good Victorian fashion, by drawing up rules applicable to goods which were to be obeyed by all regardless of status and connections and which were enforced through an efficient and centralized bureaucracy differentiated from local society."[22]

Another innovation that significantly influenced the course of Qing-Chosŏn relations was the establishment of the Zongli yamen. The appellation Zongli yamen is a shortened version of Zongli geguo shiwu yamen, the Office for the Management of the Business of All Foreign Countries. The institution was established in 1861 in recognition of the fact that the Western powers, led by the British, refused to adhere to the confines of the Canton System. Although descriptions of the Zongli yamen as being equivalent to a foreign ministry neglect the other institutions and actors that mediated the Qing Empire's interactions with its neighbors, it did become the first institution to which most Western powers would go to resolve issues with the Qing Empire. In addition, its functions went well beyond diplomatic mediation, as it also became a center for Qing self-strengthening efforts.[23]

The combination of internal challenges and external threats prompted the Qing Empire to re-examine and reconsider its relations with its Korean neighbor and vassal. Given the Chosŏn Kingdom's relative military weakness, Qing decision makers feared that Korea would experience the same military defeats and diplomatic setbacks at the hands of Western powers that the Qing itself had suffered since 1839. Moreover, although the Westerners' collective approach to China meant that the danger of outright annexation of Qing territory (with the exceptions of Hong Kong and Macao) was fairly low, such was not the case for Korea. Described as the lips that protected the Chinese teeth, the loss of Korea to France, Britain, Russia, or Japan was perceived as a significant threat to the security and prestige of the Qing Empire itself.

---

22. Van de Ven, "The Onrush of Modern Globalization in China," 177. See also Horowitz, "International Law and State Transformation," 456–57.

23. Meng, *The Tsungli Yamen.*

The task of crafting and executing a policy designed to meet these challenges fell largely to the Zongli yamen. As such, it was the Zongli yamen that was approached by inquiring Westerners and Japanese for clarification concerning the relationship between the Qing Empire and Chosŏn Korea. And it was the Zongli yamen that repeatedly issued the paradoxical declarations that Korea was simultaneously a dependency of China and an autonomous nation. However, at the same time as it was confusing foreign diplomats with its apparently obtuse language, officials within the Zongli yamen sought to harmonize Korea's relations with foreigners by advising Chosŏn Korea how best to deal with the growing foreign threat. Utilizing the tribute system and Chinese envoys sent to Korea to pass on informal advice and "information," the Zongli yamen attempted to encourage a softening of Korea's stance toward foreigners in general and toward border issues and Christianity in particular.[24]

Korean Isolationism: The Rule of the Taewŏn'gun

These initial attempts failed, since Chosŏn Korea in the mid-nineteenth century demonstrated little interest in modifying its relations with the outside world. As noted previously, Chosŏn Korea generally sought to limit rather than encourage contact and interaction with foreigners. This determination to keep foreigners at arm's length only intensified after the Hideyoshi (1592–98) and the Manchu invasions (1627, 1636). The occasional shipwrecked foreigner was generally treated well but hurried off to China or Japan.[25] Even relations with the Qing Empire were restricted to little more than the annual tribute missions.

The typical explanation offered by Chosŏn officials for the kingdom's reluctance to engage in commercial or diplomatic relations was that Korea was poor and lacking in resources. There was, therefore, no conceivable benefit to commercial exchanges with the outside world.[26] Moreover, Chosŏn Korea had a long and well-known tradition of eschewing relations with

---

24. For a discussion of the Zongli yamen's attempts to modify Korean foreign policy, see Wright, "The Adaptability of Ch'ing Diplomacy"; and Key-hiuk Kim, *The Last Phase of the East Asian World Order*, 62–76.

25. An exception was the case of the Dutch crew of the *Sperwer* (*Sparrowhawk*), who were kept as prisoners in Korea for many years; see Ledyard, *The Dutch Come to Korea*.

26. For an official prohibition on trading Western goods, see *KS*, Nov. 24, 1866 (KJ 3.10.18).

outsiders. Finally, Chosŏn officials often invoked the fact that, absent permission from Korea's suzerain, it was impossible to modify its system of relations with the outside world.[27]

Korean concern about the threats and challenges posed by the new foreigners appearing in Asia was heightened as news of the depredations of Western powers in China and the forced opening of Tokugawa Japan trickled into Korea. Of particular concern was the news of the joint British and French assault on Beijing in 1860. Reports from tribute emissaries concerning events in China led to a widespread panic in Korea, with many officials fleeing to the mountains in anticipation that the foreigners would come for Korea next.[28]

Of equal concern was the influence of Christianity, particularly Catholicism, in Korea. Introduced to the Chosŏn Kingdom in the late eighteenth century through books brought from Beijing by tribute envoys, Catholicism quickly gained adherents at both the elite and the popular levels. Fear of what was regarded by the Neo-Confucian scholar-elite as a subversive creed led to anti-Catholic purges in 1801, 1839, and 1866. Many of Korea's Confucian elite were troubled about the new doctrine and the potential mass appeal of its egalitarian claims. The 1866 purge was particularly

---

27. See, e.g., *KS*, Dec. 11, 1866 (KJ 3.11.5), and Apr. 10, 1871 (KJ 8.2.21). See also Key-hiuk Kim, *The Last Phase of the East Asian World Order*, 40–41; and Wright, "The Adaptability of Ch'ing Diplomacy," 364–73. Although the Koreans often expressed their opinion that the true responsibility for Korea's foreign relations resided with the suzerain, Qing officials were not always quick to agree. After encountering the British warship *Samarang* in 1845, Chosŏn officials reported the incident to the Qing and requested that the Qing "instruct" the British to leave Korea alone. According to Key-hiuk Kim, Qiying, "the imperial commissioner in charge of relations with Westerners at the Chinese trade ports," explained Korea's unique position to the British: "It [Korea] could not be opened to trade by China, for it was not part of China; it could not open itself for trade, for it was not independent" (Key-hiuk Kim, *The Last Phase of the East Asian World Order*, 40). Whether Qiying's statement was intended to be a logically consistent declaration of Korea's actual status or an attempt to discourage the British from seeking relations with Korea is not clear.

28. For the reports of Chosŏn tribute emissaries on the conditions in China, see *CS*, vol. 13, May 6, 1861 (CC 12.3.27), and vol. 13, July 26, 1861 (CC 12.6.19). One of the major fears of many in Korea was that the Qing imperial court might flee to Manchuria or even to Korea itself, thus attracting unwanted foreign attention to Korea (Hulbert, *History of Korea*, 2: 200–202). This fear is consistent with the cases of Wu Sangui and Hwang Sa-yong recommending or predicting a greater Manchu presence in Korea mentioned in Chapter 1.

violent, with nine French missionaries and as many as 8,000 Korean converts dying for their faith.[29]

Several encounters with foreigners in the mid-nineteenth century did little to improve the general opinion of Koreans concerning the outside world. Particularly objectionable were the activities of an American ship, the *General Sherman*, which attempted in 1866 to force its way up the Taedong River to P'yŏngyang and was destroyed by inhabitants of the area, and the raid of Ernst Oppert, a Prussian adventurer who ransacked the tomb of the king's grandfather in 1868, ostensibly to force the Chosŏn Kingdom to open its doors to foreign trade. Chosŏn Korea's opinion of Westerners was hardly enhanced by the punitive missions sent by France in 1866 in response to the anti-Catholic purge and by the United States in 1871 to avenge the *General Sherman* incident. After brief skirmishes on Korea's western coast in which Korean soldiers fought valiantly, albeit with high casualties, the French and American forces withdrew. These events, more than any other, reinforced both Korea's determination to resist outside encroachment and its perception that such a course was feasible.[30]

Leading the plunge into even greater isolation was Yi Ha-ŭng, better known as the Grand Prince (Taewŏn'gun). In 1864, due to the frantic jockeying for behind-the-scenes power that followed the death of the heirless King Ch'ŏlchong (r. 1849–64), an eleven-year-old royal relative, Yi Myŏngbok, was chosen to inherit the throne (he would be known to posterity as King Kojong). Kojong's father, Yi Ha-ŭng, was elevated to the prestigious but rarely used rank of Grand Prince (Taewŏn'gun). Using this position, the Taewŏn'gun became *de facto* the ruler of Korea for the next decade. The Taewŏn'gun proved to be an ambitious and vigorous reformer in the domestic sphere, seeking to enhance central and, more significantly, royal prestige and resources at the expense of local *yangban* elites.[31]

When it came to foreign relations, he proved to be a staunch isolationist. Under his rule, the purchase or consumption of Western goods was prohibited.[32] In a communication to the American expedition of 1871, he

---

29. Yongkoo Kim, *The Five Years' Crisis*, 16–20; Wi Jo Kang, *Christ and Caesar in Modern Korea*, 1–8.

30. Yongkoo Kim, *The Five Years' Crisis*, 13–122.

31. Ching Young Choe, *The Rule of the Taewŏn'gun*; Palais, *Politics and Policy in Traditional Korea*.

32. *KS*, vol. 3, Nov. 24, 1866 (KJ 3.10.18).

expressed exasperation at the Americans' request to modify relations, a move that he argued would contravene 500 years of cordial relations with China and of eschewing relations with others.[33] After the Western punitive expeditions of 1866 and 1871, he ordered stone markers erected throughout the country with an inscription that captured the depth of his antiforeign sentiment: "Western barbarians invade our land. If we do not fight, we must appease them. To urge appeasement is to betray the nation."[34]

The threat to Korea's seclusion came not only from the West but also from Japan. Following the 1868 Meiji Restoration, Japanese officials and envoys became increasingly insistent in their demands for changes in Japanese-Korean relations, traditionally limited to trade by intermediaries from the Tsushima domain at the Korean port of Pusan. Local magistrates in the Pusan area and their superiors in Seoul rebuffed every Japanese request. They pointed to changes in Japanese nomenclature, protocol, and even attire as evidence of the unsavory nature of these new Japanese. Korea's consistent rejection of Japanese diplomatic overtures led to growing calls in Japan for military action both to enhance Japanese honor and to guarantee Japanese security in the face of the potential occupation of Korea by an outside power. Like Qing officials of the day, Japanese officials also described Korea as the "lips" that protected the Japanese teeth.[35]

The arrival of Western and Japanese "barbarians" had the interesting effect of softening anti-Manchu attitudes among some of Korea's Neo-Confucian elite. This is not to say that all Koreans now embraced the Manchus with open arms. Some Korean officials explained the Qing Empire's willingness to enter into relations with the West by blaming Prince Gong (a Manchu, the chief negotiator of the treaties ending the Anglo-French invasion of 1860, and a regent during the minority of the Tongzhi emperor [r. 1862–74]) and declaring that he had accepted bribes and that he lacked a "human heart."[36] Others implicitly highlighted the contrast between Korea, which had continued to follow the "way of the sages," and the Qing Empire, which was engaging in closer relations with the Western

---

33. *KS*, vol. 8, June 4, 1871 (KJ 8.4.17).

34. Eckert et al., *Korea Old and New*, 197.

35. Duus, *The Abacus and the Sword*, 35. For accounts of mid- to late nineteenth-century Japanese-Korean relations, see Conroy, *The Japanese Seizure of Korea*; Deuchler, *Confucian Gentlemen and Barbarian Envoys*; and Kim Key-hiuk, *The Last Phase of the East Asian World Order*.

36. Woong Joe Kang, *The Korean Struggle for International Identity*, 32.

barbarians.[37] Control over the expression of Korea's loyalty to an idealized Ming China was one of the axes on which domestic political struggles turned. One of the proximate causes of the heralded dispute between the Taewŏn'gun and local literati throughout the 1860s was the location of the Mandongmyo, a shrine dedicated to the Ming Wanli emperor (r. 1573–1620). The clash between the Taewŏn'gun and Korea's Neo-Confucian literati eventually forced the Taewŏn'gun from power.[38] However, it is clear that the growing Western and Japanese threat caused many Koreans to rethink their antipathy toward the Qing. In the continuum between "civilized" (i.e., Confucian) and "beasts" (the West), the Qing Empire was much closer to the former than the latter. The remarks of the Neo-Confucian scholar Yi Hang-no are typical: "The northern tribes [Manchus] were at least barbarians, and we could speak to them; but the Westerners are [subhuman] beasts, and we cannot speak to them."[39] Despite differences regarding domestic policy, Korea's Neo-Confucian elite were fairly unified concerning the nature of the Western and Japanese threat and the need for an unflinching response.

Some within the Qing Empire viewed the foreign attempts to open Korea with alarm. If the Qing Empire could not deny the foreigners the access they demanded in China, how much more vulnerable was Korea? Concerned that a foreign power—particularly Russia or Japan—might come to dominate Korea, some Qing officials began to consider modification of the established system of relations with Korea. In this, they had to be subtle because the Board of Rites generally resisted any attempt to move away from the established principles of hierarchy and noninterference that had long animated relations between China and Korea.

The Rise of Li Hongzhang

Opinion within the Qing ruling circles on how to deal with Korea was diverse and divided. Among the many voices advocating particular attitudes and actions toward the Chosŏn Kingdom, Louis Sigel emphasizes three

---

37. Hara, "Korea, China, and Western Barbarians," 426.

38. For more on the Mandongmyo and its role in the dispute between the Taewŏn'gun and local literati, see Palais, *Politics and Policy in Traditional Korea*, 120–24, 190–91, 228–31.

39. Chai-sik Chung, *A Korean Confucian Encounter with the Modern World*, 41, 134–37 (brackets in original).

groups that were of particular significance.[40] Most noteworthy were advocates of what Sigel labels the "mainstream approach": reform-oriented modernizers seeking first and foremost to avoid open conflict in order to buy time for Qing self-strengthening (*ziqiang*) efforts to bear fruit. Chief among this group was Li Hongzhang (1823–1901). Li first rose to prominence by commanding local militia groups in the suppression of the Taiping Rebellion. An acolyte of the famous Zeng Guofan, Li rapidly rose in prominence, attaining a series of important posts in various parts of the empire. Following his appointment as the governor-general of Zhili province in 1870, Li played a prominent role in the Qing Empire's foreign policy. His influence was enhanced by the establishment of the position "commissioner for the northern ports" as a post concurrently held by the Zhili governor-general. His official position, his political acumen, and his reputation meant that "up to the time when he was dismissed from his dual post at [Tianjin] in 1895, he was virtually China's 'foreign minister.'"[41]

Li represented a new generation of officials who were willing to adopt Western technology and military know-how in an attempt to strengthen the Qing Empire. But such self-strengthening efforts needed time to succeed.[42] Therefore, Li placed a premium on avoiding conflict in general and avoiding incidents in Korea in particular. In doing so, Li perhaps displays a tendency toward what Iain Johnston has labeled the "Confucian-Mencian" paradigm by placing a premium on "diplomatic maneuvering, bribes, formal and informal alliances, *he-qin* [alliance through marriage] type policies, trade, tributary relations, appeasement, and other policies within what could be broadly labeled accommodationist grand strategies."[43]

---

40. Sigel, "The Role of Korea in Late Qing Foreign Policy."

41. Meng, *The Tsungli Yamen*, 59. For more on Li Hongzhang, see Chu and Liu, *Li Hung-chang and China's Early Modernization*. See also Hummel, *Eminent Chinese of the Ch'ing Period*, 1: 464–71.

42. It is interesting to note that, for Li, "self-strengthening" initially included a strong component of antiforeignism as well as resentment of those Chinese merchants who cooperated and did business with the foreigners (Kwang-Ching Liu, "The Confucian as Patriot and Pragmatist," 23–25). Li's self-strengthening efforts would later appear to be the embodiment of the "Chinese learning for essence, Western learning for utility" (*tiyong*) principle. Moreover, he would employ and work very closely with a number of the compradors he once resented.

43. Johnston, *Cultural Realism*, 117–18. Johnston in general finds that traditional Chinese strategic thinking actually displayed more of the aggressive *parabellum* (prepare for war) tendencies than that of the Confucian-Mencian paradigm. However, his work

Li spoke highly of Korea as the "offspring of sages, a land of propriety and righteousness" (*liyi zhi bang*).[44] But he also feared that the Chosŏn Kingdom's weakness invited foreign, particularly Japanese, adventurism. Losing Korea would be tantamount to losing the protective screen (*fanbi*) for the three eastern provinces and the Manchu ancestral lands.[45] Therefore, he sought to reduce Korean intransigence in the face of Western demands for treaties and trade by continuing, albeit in a more frequent and pointed manner, the Zongli yamen's strategy of offering behind-the-scenes informal advice to the Korean court. This advice was transmitted via Chinese ceremonial envoys to Korea and Korean tribute emissaries to China. Yi Yu-wŏn, who served for a time as a chief state councilor in the Chosŏn government and who met Li Hongzhang on a special mission to China, frequently corresponded with Li.

Harshly critical of the efforts of Li Hongzhang and like-minded officials were members of the *qingyi* (pure discussion) group. Precise description and delimitation of this Purist Party group is difficult, not least because one of its tenets was that factional groupings were to be avoided. It is apparent, however, that a sizable and influential group of officials and scholars shared strongly held opinions about the need to resist "barbarian" incursions at all costs. They often vocally criticized the Qing Empire's "appeasement" policies and called for an aggressive defense against Western and Japanese incursions into what they saw as China's traditional sphere of influence. Their views found sympathetic ears among the highest echelons of the Qing government. Prominent officials including the influential imperial tutor and grand councilor Li Hongzao and the imperial tutor and president of the Board of Revenue Weng Tonghe supported many of the hard-line positions of the purists. Although generally described as "conservative" and even "reactionary," members of this group were willing to advocate radical measures—such as the incorporation of Korea into the

---

focuses primarily on the pre-Qing period. One might make a meaningful distinction between Qing expansion into Central Asia (which seems more in keeping with *parabellum* strategies) and Qing defensive efforts along the maritime littoral, which perhaps adhered more generally to the oft-cited but seldom actually used Confucian-Mencian paradigm.

44. Li Hongzhang, brush talk with Mori Arinori in 1873, *Li Wenzhong gong quanji yishu han'gao*, quoted in Nan-Tsung Kim, "Neighbour as Mirror," 49.

45. LHZ to Zongli yamen, Jan. 22, 1876 (GX 1.12.26), *ZRHGX*, 276–77.

Qing Empire proper and the invasion of Japan—in what they perceived as the defense of orthodoxy and China's traditional prerogatives.[46]

Sigel also highlights a third group he labels the treaty-port community. Consisting of wealthy "compradors, merchants and entrepreneurs," the treaty-port elite emphasized "the adoption of Western institutions to promote 'wealth and power,' while asserting their own interests in the name of China." They urged a variety of measures, such as the abolition of extraterritoriality, exclusion of foreigners from domestic shipping, recovery of tariff autonomy, industrial development, and government sponsorship of private railroad, mining, banking, and textiles ventures.[47] The treaty-port elites' agenda demonstrated that some in the Qing Empire were beginning to take note and make use of "commercial warfare" (*shangzhan*).[48] Although trade was nothing new to China, the nineteenth century saw a veritable explosion of commercial growth.[49] Buoyed by unprecedented wealth and success, powerful compradors began to push for official support for commerce both at home and abroad.[50]

The treaty-port community exerted a significant influence on the Qing Empire's policies toward Korea. Intellectuals such as Zheng Guanying and compradors such as Tang Tingshu (Tong King-sing) were instrumental in

---

46. This brief description hardly does justice to the complexity of "conservative" opinion in China. Nor does it give an adequate sense of how ideological and political configurations changed over time. For a more developed introduction to the subject, see Bonnie B. C. Oh, "The Leadership Crisis in China on the Eve of the Sino-Japanese War of 1894–1895." See also idem, "The Background of Chinese Policy Formation in the Sino-Japanese War of 1894–1895"; and Hao, "A Study of the Ch'ing-Liu Tang."

47. Sigel, "The Role of Korea in Late Qing Foreign Policy," 81–82. For more on Chinese compradors, see Hao, *The Comprador in Nineteenth Century China*. It should be noted that many have been harshly critical of compradors because of the way they facilitated imperialist inroads into their home countries. See, e.g., Dominic Lieven's (*Empire*, 23) observation that "one element in this dependency were native 'comprador' elites, who shared their countries' wealth with Western imperialist capital, whose agents they were and after whose luxuries and lifestyles they lusted."

48. For a discussion of "commercial warfare," see Wang Erh-min, *Zhongguo jindai sixiang shilun*, 233–380. For a brief reference in English, see Hao and Wang, "Changing Chinese Views of Western Relations, 1840–1895," 190–94.

49. See Hao, *The Commercial Revolution in Nineteenth-Century China*.

50. The confidence of the treaty-port elite in their potential is demonstrated in Chen Lanbin's call for the creation of a Chinese merchant marine with the long-term goal of competing for the carrying trade not just in China but along European coasts and rivers (Desnoyers, "Toward 'One Enlightened and Progressive Civilization,'" 147).

convincing Li Hongzhang to consider commerce as well as security in dealing with Korea. Tang Tingshu took a particular interest in Korea and had
the close ear of Li Hongzhang. An influential member of Li Hongzhang's
secretariat (*mufu*), Tang claimed, "The viceroy leads, but I am the man that
pushes."[51]

Li's resources and ability to maneuver were hampered by a strategic decision made by the Qing Empire in 1875. This decision had emerged out of
a spirited debate over whether the Qing should focus first and foremost on
suppressing the Muslim revolt in Central Asia and retaking and consolidat-
ing its control of that region (the "frontier defense," *saifang*) or whether
maritime defense (*haifang*) should take priority.[52] Li Hongzhang was an advocate of the latter, arguing that the most pressing threat to the Qing Empire was Japan, a nation that "is right on our threshold, capable of spying
out our weakness or readiness. She is China's most important permanent
problem."[53] However, the pleas of General Zuo Zongtang and others carried the day. Among other inducements, Zuo utilized a remarkably clear-
eyed assessment of the prevailing Western imperial strategies of the day to
justify his case: "Western nations, he asserted, driven primarily by the desire for trade profits, fought for harbors and ports, not for territory. The
danger from that quarter, therefore, was not immediate. Russia, on the
other hand, had territorial as well as commercial designs."[54] Given an imperial blessing and access to funds gathered from many Chinese provinces
as well as from foreign loans, Zuo embarked on an ambitious and aggressive military campaign that not only put down the Muslim rebellions but
also resulted in the direct incorporation of the region now known as Xinjiang as a province of the Qing Empire. For Li, however, the strategic deci-

---

51. Sigel, "The Role of Korea in Late Qing Foreign Policy," 84.

52. See Hsu, "The Great Policy Debate in China, 1874." For a detailed description of
the Muslim rebellion and its suppression, see Hodong Kim, *Holy War in China*. For
background on earlier Qing policies toward Central Asia, see Millward, *Beyond the Pass*.

53. Hsu, "The Great Policy Debate in China," 215. Writing elsewhere, Li concluded:
"It therefore seemed evident that 'Japan's greed for Korea has been firmly established
over many years'" (Li Hongzhang, *Li Wenzhong gong quanji yishu han'gao*, quoted in Nan-
Tsung Kim, "Neighbour as Mirror," 48).

54. Hsu, "The Great Policy Debate in China," 220. Of course, Zuo could not have
anticipated that most of the Western imperialist powers would soon eschew commerce-
seeking informal empire in favor of the great scramble for territory that characterized
the age of high imperialism beginning in the late nineteenth century.

sion to focus on Central Asia meant that he had fewer resources to devote to naval modernization and other self-strengthening efforts. As a result, Li placed an even higher premium on avoiding conflict with all outside powers.

The 1876 "Opening" of Korea

Busy building arsenals and developing a modern navy, Li Hongzhang sought to use behind-the-scenes persuasion and guidance to urge Chosŏn Korea to modify its unflinching resistance to more relations with the outside world. Several developments in Korea gradually rendered the powers-that-be in the Chosŏn Kingdom more amenable to Qing advice. First was the ouster of the Taewŏn'gun. Although most of Korea's Neo-Confucian elite heartily supported the Taewŏn'gun's foreign policies, many became increasingly dissatisfied with the regent's attempts at domestic reform. Costly palace construction projects (an attempt to shore up royal prestige and legitimacy) when government coffers were nearly empty, as well as the Taewŏn'gun's efforts to relocate or eliminate prominent shrines such as the Mandongmyo and Taebodan (Altar of Great Retribution) caused growing criticism of the Taewŏn'gun. In the end, however, it was the regent's decision to increase taxes on the Chosŏn Kingdom's *yangban* elite that cost him his base of support. Kojong, now in his early twenties, proved eager to step in and take direct control of the kingdom that had been ruled in his name for the past nine years. The young king initially demonstrated a determination to rule according to his Confucian training, but he also displayed a willingness to consider modifying Korea's relations with the outside world.[55]

A second development was the Qing Empire's granting of investiture to Kojong's infant son. The Taewŏn'gun had selected Queen Min as Kojong's primary consort largely because she hailed from an obscure family that he hoped would not play a prominent role in power struggles at the capital. Both the queen and her clan, however, proved able and aggressive at court, earning them the enmity of the Taewŏn'gun. Rumor had it that the Taewŏn'gun had a hand in the death of Queen Min's first son. A year after the birth of another son, the Chosŏn court, at the insistence of Queen Min, sought investiture from the Qing Empire, dispatching Yi Yu-wŏn to Beijing to accomplish this task in 1875. Yi's success in obtaining this rather irregular request solidified Queen Min's position in Chosŏn court politics and earned

---

55. Palais, *Politics and Policy in Traditional Korea*, 252–71.

the Qing Empire long-lasting gratitude from the queen and her powerful relatives.[56] Taken together, these developments—the ouster of the Tae-wŏn'gun, the ascendance of Kojong, and the pro-Qing sentiment of the Min clan—made it more likely that the Korean court would prove willing at least to entertain Qing advice on matters of the day.

Such advice came in prodigious amounts in 1875 and early 1876 when the Chosŏn Kingdom faced another powerful foreigner demanding new relations. The very type of conflict that Li Hongzhang had hoped to avoid in Korea took place in late 1875 when a Japanese survey vessel, the *Un'yō*, ventured too close to the coast of Korea's Kanghwa Island, the site of the French punitive expedition of 1866 and the American punitive expedition of 1871, and was fired on by Korean shore batteries. The Japanese responded by sending a flotilla to Korea in early 1876 with demands for a trade treaty. Korean refusal, the Japanese threatened, would be a cause for war.

Despairing at the prospect of being called on to fulfill the suzerain's duty by helping Korea repel a Japanese invasion (as Ming armies had done four centuries previously), Li Hongzhang frantically urged the Zongli yamen to write to Korea urging moderation and negotiation with Japan rather than conflict.[57] Li also echoed the same sentiments in a letter he personally sent to Yi Yu-wŏn. This encouragement, offered in the form of informal advice, was influential in convincing Kojong and his court to agree to negotiate with the Japanese. Also influential was the fact that the Qing had signed a new treaty with Japan just a few years earlier that signaled Qing willingness to entertain new forms of relations even with its East Asian neighbors and demonstrated that the Qing apparently had no problem with Japanese clothing and demeanor. Ultimately, the Chosŏn court signaled its willingness to talk rather than fight. The resulting Treaty of Kanghwa, concluded on February 22, 1876, is generally regarded as the first step in the opening of Korea.[58]

Japanese Monopolistic Imperialism

By attaching the prefix "gunboat" to its diplomacy, Meiji Japan was successful in causing Chosŏn Korea to sign and ratify its first Western-style treaty with an outside power. Historians have made much of the first arti-

---

56. Key-hiuk Kim, *The Last Phase of the East Asian World Order*, 249–52.

57. Li Hongzhang to Zongli yamen, Jan. 22, 1876 (GX 1.12.26), *ZRHGX*, 276–78.

58. Key-hiuk Kim, *The Last Phase of the East Asian World Order*, 248–55.

cle of the 1876 Treaty of Kanghwa, which states that Korea "being an independent State enjoys the same Sovereign rights as does Japan."[59] However, the Japanese motives for seeking a treaty were not limited to shaking Korea loose from its Sinocentric orbit by claiming that Chosŏn Korea was now a full-fledged member of the "family" of Western-style sovereign and independent nations; they also wanted trade, and more of it. Therefore, other articles of the treaty mandated the opening of two additional ports to trade, established Japan's right to consular jurisdiction in said ports, and promised to allow Japanese ships to survey the Korean coast without interference.

All these provisions have clear antecedents in the treaties signed between Japan and the United States two decades earlier. Indeed, the similarities were not lost on the Japanese themselves. An editorial in the *Chōya shinbun* newspaper compared Japanese negotiators Kuroda Kiyotaka and Inoue Kaoru with the Americans Matthew Perry and Adams.[60] There were, however, significant differences. Absent in the Treaty of Kanghwa is any mention of tariffs or other duties on foreign trade. In addition, there was no most-favored-nation provision. It became increasingly clear over the next several years that the treaty-port system that Japan introduced to Korea was rather different from its counterparts in China or Japan. In contrast to the emphasis on equal access in China and Japan, the system in Korea was designed to maximize Japanese access and privileges while keeping potential competitors away.

Whatever the significance of the 1876 Treaty of Kanghwa to later historians, at the time many Koreans did not expect to see a dramatic transformation of relations between the two nations. For the Koreans, signing the treaty was an expedient way to avoid a Japanese invasion. The Chosŏn Kingdom had enjoyed diplomatic and commercial relations, albeit rigorously restricted ones, with Japan for more than two centuries. It was not at all clear that the 1876 treaty signaled anything more than an effort to get relations back on an even keel after several years of rebuffs, recriminations, and generally chilly relations. Only two days after the treaty was signed, King Kojong assured Korean government officials that "the

---

59. For the full text of the treaty, see China, Imperial Maritime Customs, *Treaties, Regulations, Etc. Between Corea and Other Powers*, 1–17.

60. Duus, *Abacus and the Sword*, 46–47. Adams is probably Henry Adams, the deputy commander of the fleet led by Perry.

treaty was no more than a step toward restoring traditional relations with Japan."[61]

The same assumption held true concerning trade issues. Many Korean officials saw little use in increasing the level of trade with Japan above and beyond that of the long-established Japan House system in Pusan. Kim Ki-su, the Korean official sent to Japan in May 1876 as a "friendship envoy," spoke to Inoue Kaoru of Korea's intention to "always adhere to the ways of the Sage" and returned to Korea full of warnings about the abundance of "clever contrivances and trickeries" in commerce-happy Japan.[62] Subsequent trips to Japan by Korean officials generated some interest in trade among a small group of "progressive" officials, but even as late as the 1881 Gentlemen's Trip (*sinsa yuramdan*) to Japan, the official report of the journey was decidedly anti-commerce and pessimistic about the general state of affairs in rapidly commercializing Japan: "Not only is customs revenue low, the national debt grows daily. Not only are commercial conditions less than prosperous, but prices rise daily." It also warned against the dangers of growing materialism: "In the areas where trade is allowed by treaty, because the prices of goods are high, people's hearts are confused; they consider business matters to be true matters and take trivial profits to be essential."[63] At home, Korean officials warned of the deleterious effects of increased trade with Japan. Noting the increase in Korean exports to Japan, one memorialist complained: "The day is not far away when our people will go hungry because they have nothing left to eat, and they will be cold because they have nothing left with which to clothe themselves."[64]

---

61. Key-hiuk Kim, *The Last Phase of the East Asian World Order*, 258. See also Kojong's retrospective explanation of his decisions in 1876 in *Sŭngjŏngwŏn ilgi*, Sept, 16, 1882 (KJ 19.8.5) as cited in Ch'oe Tŏk-su, "The Dawning of a New World," 113–14.

62. Kim Chŏng-wŏn, "Cho-Chung sangmin suyuk muyŏk changjŏng e daehayo," 120–22; Key-hiuk Kim, *The Last Phase of the East Asian World Order*, 258–59.

63. Kim Chŏng-wŏn, "Cho-Chung sangmin suyuk muyŏk changjŏng e daehayo," 130. One Korean official, Ŏ Yun-jung, was much more sanguine about Japan and the benefits of trade there, but he was in the minority (ibid., 130–31).

64. Deuchler, *Confucian Gentlemen and Barbarian Envoys*, 68. As late as 1881 King Kojong wrote to the Qing Board of Rites: "Our people are poor. Our resources are meager. We do not produce gold or silver, pearls or jade. Nor have we an abundant supply of rice, grain, cloth, and silk. The products of our country hardly meet our own needs. If they be allowed to be exported overseas, it would lead to the eventual depletion of our domain and make the preservation of our feeble country even more difficult" (*Chouban yiwu*, 81: 11a–b, quoted in T. C. Lin, "Li Hung-Chang: His Korea Policies,"

Given this antipathy toward trade and the antiforeign sentiment still prevalent in much of Korea, it is not surprising to find that Korean officials utilized every available stratagem to resist and delay implementation of the treaty provisions. Frustrated Japanese diplomats and negotiators quickly found that their Korean counterparts objected to virtually every proposal they made. The promised twenty-month deadline for opening the two new ports passed with no progress whatsoever. All in all, it was not until 1880 that the eastern port of Wŏnsan (not the first choice of the Japanese) was officially opened. Chemulp'o, also known as Inch'ŏn, was not opened until 1883.[65] Japanese consular officials were not stationed in these new ports until even later.[66]

Japanese diplomats and merchants also discovered that establishing a presence in Korean treaty ports did not guarantee smooth and undisturbed relations with Chosŏn officials and the local Korean populace. In Pusan, local officials worked to see that dealings between Koreans and Japanese in Pusan were sharply restricted. In 1877, three Korean women discovered to have illicitly entered the Japanese settlement were decapitated, and several local officials including the prefect of Tongnae, Hong U-chang, were dismissed from their posts for lax enforcement of the rules demanding strict separation between Koreans and Japanese.[67] The Korean opinion of the virtues of the Japanese presence in Pusan was hardly enhanced by the 1879 riots of Japanese sailors, who, with the full knowledge and participation of the Japanese trade superintendent, stormed the Tongnae prefecture and wounded several Korean officials.[68]

In September 1878, the Korean government authorized an ad valorem tax of 15–20 percent on Korean merchants who traded or did business

---

204). Lin (204–5) concludes, "in the opinion of the Korean Government, there was no economic basis for a Korean-foreign trade."

65. The names Chemulp'o and Inch'ŏn, along with the Chinese (Jench'uan, Renchuan) readings and the Japanese (Jinsen) rendering of the latter, are often used interchangeably. For the sake of consistency, I will use "Inch'ŏn" unless the original source uses an alternative rendering.

66. This determined Korean resistance has led one Korean scholar to conclude that post-1876 Korea was not really "open." Only with the Korean-American, Korean-British, and Sino-Korean treaties of 1882 did Korea in fact open to international commerce (Kim Chŏng-wŏn, "Cho-Chung sangmin suyuk muyŏk changjŏng e daehayo," 123).

67. Deuchler, *Confucian Gentlemen and Barbarian Envoys*, 72–73.

68. Ibid., 77, 250*n*44.

with the Japanese in Pusan. Korean officials reasoned that such taxes were in keeping with the traditional levies imposed on the pre-1876 Tsushima trade. Moreover, they argued that since the tax was not directly charged to Japanese merchants but imposed on Korean merchants, there could be no objection based on treaty provisions. Nevertheless, trade slowed to a standstill since most Korean merchants could no longer afford to trade with the Japanese. Especially hard-hit were the small-scale Tsushima merchants who were already suffering from intense competition with merchants from other parts of Japan. One hundred and thirty-five of them marched on Tongnae in protest, but their pleas were ignored. Only the swift dispatch of the warship *Hiei* to Pusan harbor and the conducting of gunnery exercises and military maneuvers by Japanese marines convinced the Korean government to rescind the tax. This attempt to curtail Japanese commerce in Korea was ultimately counterproductive to Chosŏn Korea's desire to limit contact with Japan because Japanese diplomats were able to use the issue of compensation for the Japanese merchants affected by the tax as an excuse for traveling to Seoul to negotiate opening other ports in Korea.[69]

In Wŏnsan, the Japanese arrival met with resistance from the local Korean populace. Memorials of protest were sent to Seoul by literati from the neighboring towns of Togwŏn, Anbyŏn, and Munch'ŏn. The appearance of a wild tiger prowling the road in front of the newly constructed Japanese consulate was regarded as an extremely inauspicious sign by the local populace who frequently hurled insults and stones at Japanese nationals on the streets of the settlement. Small roving bands of Koreans also attacked any Japanese unwise enough to be out at night. Japanese officials responded by dispatching consulate guards to patrol the settlement day and night, by organizing Japanese nationals to travel in groups of four or more, and by discouraging the Japanese purchase of large amounts of rice or

---

69. The Japanese demanded compensation or, in lieu of cash, a number of privileges that would "give the Japanese the right to engage in trade between Japan and Korea and in retail and wholesale business within Korea as well. Moreover, they would guarantee the Japanese freedom of travel to virtually any part of Korea"; see Key-hiuk Kim, *The Last Phase of the East Asian World Order*, 268–71. For more on this incident, see Kim Sun-dŏk, "1876–1905 nyŏn kwanse chŏngch'aek kwa kwanse ŭi unyong," 5; Conroy, *The Japanese Seizure of Korea*, 95–96; and Deuchler, *Confucian Gentlemen and Barbarian Envoys*, 76. Korean officials argued that Japanese commerce in Pusan harmed the border trade at Ŭiju and also hoped that the tax would discourage smuggling.

other grains from the local populace.[70] Despite local resistance, the Japanese maintained their foothold in Wŏnsan, due in large part to an appreciation of the port's strategic significance and a desire to deny the Russians access to an ice-free port.

After finally securing a presence in Wŏnsan, the Japanese redoubled their efforts to open a port on Korea's west coast. After extensive surveys, Japanese negotiators decided on Inch'ŏn. Initially discouraged by the shallow water that made anchorage and docking of vessels of any significant size difficult, they ultimately chose Inch'ŏn because of its proximity to the capital and to the lack of a suitable alternative. The Koreans for their part had several compelling reasons to resist opening the port. As the gateway to the capital, Inch'ŏn had immense strategic and symbolic significance. Korean government officials were extremely anxious about the possibility of a widespread public protest against the opening of the port. In addition, there were concerns that allowing trade in Inch'ŏn would harm commercial interests in Seoul and would drain away precious foodstuffs from the capital region. And there was the practical matter that the nearly empty coffers of the Chosŏn government could not provide for the necessary improvements in the physical plant of the port. Korean negotiators used these reasons to extend negotiations over the port for twenty-one months. The redoubtable Hanabusa Yoshimoto, the Japanese minister to Korea, methodically worked his way through the Korean objections and finally, on January 28, 1881, reached an agreement with the Koreans to open the port. However, the Korean negotiators demanded that a minimum of two years elapse before the port actually opened, called for a prohibition of grain exports from the port, and requested that the Japanese minister reside in Inch'ŏn rather than in Seoul. Hanabusa granted the Koreans twenty months but refused to consider the other conditions. Inch'ŏn was not officially opened until January 1, 1883.[71]

---

70. The composition of the Japanese population in Wŏnsan in the early years of the settlement attests to the lack of commercial opportunities. In October 1880, there were some 210 male and 25 female Japanese in Wŏnsan. Seventy-five were attached to the consulate in some way or another, and another 100 or so were workers. Very few were merchants. Even in 1885, this number had not changed (Son Chung-mok, *Han'guk kaehanggi tosi pyŏnhwa kwajŏng yŏn'gu*, 120, 123).

71. Hanabusa skillfully dangled the possibility of his residing in Inch'ŏn rather than Seoul as an enticement for the Koreans to consider opening the port. But when push came to shove, it became clear that he had no intention of residing anywhere other than

The Growth of Japanese Commerce

The determined work of Japanese diplomats paid dividends for Japanese merchants. Enjoying the benefits of diplomatic representation, extraterritoriality, tariff-free trade, and a lack of competition, merchants from many parts of Japan came to Korean treaty ports to try their luck. Taking advantage of Korea's relative isolation and lack of information about regional or global prices, some Japanese merchants were known to have charged markups of up to 1,000 percent on sought-after imports.[72] Reliable and detailed information about the exact composition of the Korea-Japan trade during this period is lacking,[73] but anecdotal evidence indicates that the vast majority of Japanese imports during the period 1876–82 were of Western rather than Japanese manufacture. These were usually exchanged for Korean rice, soybeans, cowhides, and marine products.[74]

Although the advantages enjoyed by Japanese merchants during this period are clear, it is worth noting that Chosŏn Korea continued to trade with the outside world, most especially with China, through other avenues. The most significant of these were Korean tribute missions to China and periodic trade fairs on Korea's northern border. Exact figures for the amount of trade conducted by tribute envoys during the period 1876–83 are not available. However, one estimate of the level of trade (both legal and illegal) generated by tribute missions puts the figure at more than

---

the capital. Many details of the behind-the-scenes debates on the Korean side remain unclear. This is due in part to the fact that such discussions must have been held off the record and in secrecy so as to avoid criticism from conservative elements both inside and outside the government. See Deuchler, *Confucian Gentlemen and Barbarian Envoys*, 62–64. For a general narrative of the negotiation process, see Son Chŏng-mok, *Han'guk kaehanggi tosi pyŏnhwa kwajong yŏn'gu*, 125–126; and Conroy, *The Japanese Seizure of Korea*, 97.

72. Duus, *Abacus and the Sword*, 254.

73. Writing of a collection of trade statistics compiled for British use, Harry Parkes noted that "there being as yet no Customs Tariff in Corea, the officials of that country have no interest in exercising any supervision over the values either of imports or exports . . . much accuracy cannot be expect in results obtained in this way" (quoted in Pak Su-i, "Kaehanggi Han'guk muyŏk chabon e kwanhan yŏn'gu," 151). The most thorough and detailed examination of the various sources for trade data in this period is Kang Tŏk-sang, "Rishi Chōsen kaikō chokugo ni okeru bōeki no tenkai," 1–18. Other estimates can be found in Pak Su-i, "Kaehanggi Han'guk muyŏk chabon e kwanhan yŏn'gu," 152–58; and Conroy, *The Japanese Seizure of Korea*, 456–59.

74. Han'guk muyŏk hyŏphoe, *Han'guk muyŏksa*, 111.

500,000 taels of silver each year.[75] The tribute trade may have been influenced by the increased Japanese activity in Pusan and, later, Wŏnsan, but it is highly unlikely Japanese merchants in Pusan would have been able to meet all the demand for the Chinese medicines, silks, books, and other luxuries that came to Korea via tribute missions.

Equally significant was the Sino-Korean border trade. A Japanese report on Korean commerce estimated that in the late 1870s the value of this trade (both imports and exports) was as high as four million yen per year. The chief imports were Chinese silks and Western cotton textiles. Competition from Japanese merchants in Pusan, especially in the trade in Western textiles, resulted in a sharp decline in trade along the northern border. The same Japanese report estimated the level of trade in 1883 to be 1.2 million yen, well less than half the total of four or five years earlier; it noted that the cheaper prices of foreign goods in Pusan were winning the competition with their higher-priced counterparts on the northern border.[76] More exact and detailed records of the border trade are, unfortunately, unavailable.[77]

It is clear, however, that as the Japanese presence in Korea became more entrenched, Japanese merchants approaching Korea from the sea were slowly but surely crowding out the business done overland either on the border or via tribute missions. Thus, whereas the overall level of trade remained essentially the same, the primary orientation of the trade shifted from overland to maritime. The shift to maritime trade was further enhanced by the opening of Wŏnsan in 1880 and Inch'ŏn in 1883.

Qing Efforts to Counter the Growing Japanese Threat

The growing Japanese presence in Korea was resisted and resented by many Koreans. It was also watched with increasing alarm by Li Hongzhang and other Qing officials. The Japanese seizure of the Liuqiu (Ryūkyū)

---

75. Hae-jong Chun, "Sino-Korean Tributary Relations in the Ch'ing Period," 108.

76. *TSIS,* 4.256; Peter Duus (*Abacus and the Sword,* 256) notes that "a length of machine-made shirting that cost 4.8 yen in the north could be had for only 3.8 yen in Pusan or Wŏnsan. And the Japanese were more eager than the Chinese to buy Korean products like rice and leather, and they were willing to pay higher prices for them."

77. The only exception is a detailed report of trade at Chunggang (Zhongjiang), one of the three main sites of the legal border trade, in 1881 and 1882. Imports into Korea via Chunggang amounted to 395,066 yen in 1881 and 290,941 yen in 1882; see Han'guk muyŏk hyŏphoe, *Han'guk muyŏksa,* 113.

Islands in 1879 demonstrated Meiji Japan's willingness and ability to contest not only Qing claims of suzerainty (Liuqiu had been a tributary of China for centuries but had also, from time to time, paid tribute to Japan) but actually annex territory in the region. At the urging of many Qing officials, Li Hongzhang began to further modify the Qing Empire's longstanding commitment to noninterference in Korea. Li adopted a two-pronged strategy for shoring up the Chosŏn Kingdom's security and its position as the Qing Empire's pre-eminent vassal. First, he sought to encourage the Chosŏn Kingdom to enter into treaty relations with other foreign powers. Officials such as Ding Richang, a former governor of Fujian, called for the Qing court to order Korea to enter into relations with other powers as a means of counterbalancing Japanese and Russian designs on the peninsula. The court declined to issue the order, but Li Hongzhang was commanded to persuade and guide Korea in the direction of treaties with the West.[78]

As he had in 1876, Li resorted to informal advice and letters to Korean officials such as Yi Yu-wŏn to implement this policy. In addition, Chinese officials in Japan, most notably He Ruchang and Huang Zunxian, repeated the same advice to the Korean official Kim Hong-jip when he visited Tokyo in the summer of 1880. Kim brought back to Korea with him an essay written by Huang entitled *A Strategy for Korea* (K. *Chosŏn ch'aengnyak*; C. *Chaoxian celue*) and presented it to Kojong, who received it with enthusiasm. The essay's main recommendation was for Korea to have "intimate relations with China, association with Japan, and alliance with America" (*qin Zhongguo, jie Riben, lian Meiguo*).[79] Diplomatic relations with European nations would naturally follow. The result would be a situation in which no single outside power could become dominant in Korea.[80] In short, to offset the Japanese unilateral but informal colonialism, Li Hongzhang sought to introduce the same style of multilateral imperialism to Korea already present in China and Japan.

The second prong of Li's strategy was to promote self-strengthening efforts within Korea itself. Thus the Qing heartily endorsed Korea's first efforts to establish a new pseudo–foreign ministry, the Office of Extraordinary Affairs (T'ongni kimu amun), an institution that bore some resem-

---

78. Chien, *The Opening of Korea*, 63.
79. Huang Zunxian, *Chaoxian celue*, in Cho Il-mun, *Chosŏn ch'aengnyak*, 109.
80. Deuchler, *Confucian Gentlemen and Barbarian Envoys*, 88.

blance to the Qing Zongli yamen.[81] Li also encouraged the Chosŏn Kingdom's attempt to improve its military readiness, going so far as to invite a group of Korean students to travel to Tianjin to study armaments and their manufacture at the Tianjin Arsenal.

These attempts at reform were roundly criticized by many of Korea's Neo-Confucian elite. Memorialists also targeted Yi Yu-wŏn's correspondence with Li Hongzhang and Kim Hong-jip's presenting of Huang Zunxian's *A Strategy for Korea* to the throne. In every case, the Neo-Confucian literati saw significant threats to the Korean state and society and to Korea's position as the last bastion of orthodox Confucianism. This criticism was met at first with royal attempts at persuasion. However, as the number and intensity of the memorials mounted, the Korean government took more drastic measures, banishing several officials and beheading Hong Chae-hak, one of the most prominent and vocal critics of the government.[82] This growing disaffection with the government of Kojong caused many local literati to reconsider their rupture with his father, the Taewŏn'gun. An ill-planned attempt to bring the Taewŏn'gun back to power in 1881 was easily quashed. But it was far from apparent when or even if the Chosŏn Kingdom would agree to open itself to diplomatic and commercial relations with other non-Asian powers.

---

81. For the establishment of the T'ongni kimu amun, see Yi Kwang-nin, "T'ongni kimu amun ŭi chojik kwa kinŭng," 503–7. See also Kyung Moon Hwang, *Beyond Birth,* 52–58.

82. Cumings, *Korea's Place in the Sun,* 104–5.

THREE

Treaties and Troops

Bringing Multilateral Imperialism

to Korea

Eighteen eighty-two was a pivotal year in the history of relations between China and Korea. Qing influence on Chosŏn foreign policy, exerted through informal persuasion and advice, had been slowly growing in the preceding years. It was Japan, however, that appeared to be rapidly gaining the upper hand in Korea. Japanese diplomats and representatives alone were stationed in Seoul and the grudgingly opened treaty ports. Japanese merchants alone did business legally on the peninsula, and their commerce was thriving and threatening the viability of both the traditional tribute and the Sino-Korean border trades. A Japanese military officer was in charge of training a new elite unit of the Chosŏn army. And after the Japanese seizure of the Liuqiu (Ryūkyū) Islands, many in the Qing Empire worried that Korea might well be next.

Concerned about the growing Japanese threat, as well as the possibility of Russian incursions into Korea, Li Hongzhang moved to act on proposals that had been percolating throughout the Qing Empire which called for Korea to enter into treaty relations with a number of powers so as to minimize the likelihood that any single power would emerge dominant. Li took the unprecedented step of directly mediating Korea's first treaties with Western powers. His policy of using one barbarian to counter another (*yi yi zhi yi*) experienced a serious challenge in the chaos that followed the mutiny of Korean soldiers in the summer of 1882. Faced with an unanticipated and entirely unwelcome situation, the Qing Empire acted swiftly and decisively by dispatching troops to Korea, the first time in well over two centuries that a Qing army had set foot on Korean soil. Any doubt that the Qing had largely abandoned its long-standing policy of distance and noninterference in Korean affairs was swept away when its troops remained in Seoul after the mutiny was quelled. The subsequent promulgation of Sino-Korean commercial regulations, the first of their kind between China and Korea, served to accentuate the dramatic transformation in relations. These events marked a clear shift in imperial strategies and ambitions. Different groups within the empire itself had different visions of the scale and scope of this new Qing imperialism, and their goals and methods sometimes worked at cross-purposes. One of the most significant results of Qing activities in Korea was the replacement of the Japanese-imposed system of monopolistic privileges by a multilateral imperialism expressed in a treaty-port system based on equal access for all foreign powers.

Qing Mediation of Korea's Treaties with Western Powers

As noted in the previous chapter, many within the Chosŏn Kingdom resented and resisted the growing Japanese presence in Korea. They also criticized those who advocated further opening of Korea to relations with other powers and peoples. This domestic opposition made it extremely difficult for anyone, even King Kojong, to explicitly advocate expanding Korea's relations with the outside world. The United States' attempts to replicate in Korea its success in opening Tokugawa Japan were repeatedly stymied by Chosŏn officials. This Korean refusal frustrated American diplomats such as Frederick Low, who fumed that "the sea is the great highway of the nations, which no country is at liberty to obstruct with impunity."[1] Chosŏn Korea's lack of interest in facilitating international commerce also rankled American Commodore Robert Shufeldt, who made several attempts to engage Korea in negotiation. Chosŏn officials rejected these attempts on the grounds that Shufeldt was accompanied by Japanese diplomats and his letters were improperly addressed. In both cases, these served as excuses for avoiding negotiations that many in Chosŏn Korea had little desire to pursue in the first place.[2] Frustrated, Shufeldt traveled to

---

1. Frederick Drake, *Empire of the Seas*, 234.
2. That Shufeldt had grand designs for American involvement in the Far East is undeniable. He boldly declared that "the pacific is the ocean bride of America—China

Tianjin and asked Li Hongzhang for assistance in convincing Korea to negotiate a treaty.

Li Hongzhang's attempts at informal persuasion were similarly rejected. In a letter to Li, Yi Yu-wŏn wrote that "trade with Japan is already a concession under duress; trade with the West would be unthinkable."[3] Li also found elements within his own government opposed to any move toward expanding Korea's relations with foreign powers. As late as 1882, Chester Holcombe, an American diplomat in Beijing, complained that the Qing Board of Rites was proving extremely reluctant to consider modification of Korea's traditional relations with China or other powers.[4]

There were, however, officials in the Chosŏn government willing to at least entertain the notion of modifying Korea's relations with powers other than Japan. King Kojong counted himself among those who saw treaties and expanded relations as possibly beneficial for Korea. Motivated in part by Huang Zunxian's controversial essay, the Chosŏn court wrote to Li Hongzhang asking for copies of the Qing Empire's treaties with foreign powers as well as copies of commercial and customs regulations.[5] Li responded with alacrity and went one step further by giving the Chosŏn official Yi Yong-suk the draft of a proposed treaty between the United States and Korea written by Ma Jianzhong, an influential member of Li Hongzhang's secretariat.[6] A member of a group of students sent to study in Europe in 1877, Ma Jianzhong focused on politics, diplomacy, and interna-

---

and Japan and Corea—with their innumerable islands, hanging like necklaces about them, are the bridesmaids, California is the nuptial couch, the bridal chamber, where all the wealth of the Orient will be brought to celebrate the wedding. Let us as Americans—see to it that the 'bridegroom cometh'" (Cumings, *Korea's Place in the Sun*, 86). The Chosŏn minister of rites, Yun Cha-sŭng, admitted to the Japanese foreign minister that whatever the excuses Korean officials gave, the underlying reason for their rejection of Shufeldt's overtures was "mainly because his [Yun's] government did not intend to establish relations with any country other than Japan." Shufeldt suspected that the Japanese assistance he had received in approaching Korea was not given in good faith because "they wanted to monopolize the Korean trade" (Key-hiuk Kim, *The Last Phase of the East Asian World Order*, 303).

3. T. C. Lin, "Li Hung-chang: His Korea Policies," 220.

4. See Holcombe to Frelinghuysen, Feb. 4, 1882, no. 60, Confidential, *China Legations Despatches*, vol. 58, quoted in Chien, *The Opening of Korea*, 254n120.

5. Chien, *The Opening of Korea*, 70.

6. Key-hiuk Kim, *The Last Phase of the East Asian World Order*, 308.

tional law. After completing his studies in Paris, in 1879 he became the first Chinese student to earn a Western law diploma.[7]

Kojong's receptivity to the idea of treaties with Western powers as well as his approval of institutional reforms such as the creation of the Tongni kimu amun and the opening of Inch'ŏn led to widespread criticism and protest from Neo-Confucian stalwarts such as Yi Hang-no and Ch'oe Ik-hyŏn.[8] The strength of the domestic opposition gave Kojong pause, and he failed to respond positively to Li Hongzhang's requests for the dispatch of a Korean official to Tianjin to meet with Shufeldt.[9] As a result, Shufeldt became increasingly impatient, and Li increasingly anxious. Finally, Kim Yun-sik, the royally appointed adviser (*yŏngsŏnsa*) to a Korean student group, was dispatched to Tianjin in January 1882. Kim, however, was not an officially appointed plenipotentiary. Rather, he relayed Kojong's request that the Qing emperor command Korea to negotiate a treaty as a means of circumventing the intense domestic opposition to dealing with Westerners. Li refused to do so, not least because an imperial order would leave Cho-sŏn Korea little leverage in subsequent negotiations.[10] As the weeks wore on, Shufeldt threatened to leave Tianjin and go directly to Korea. This prompted Li to agree to enter into negotiations with Shufeldt on Korea's behalf. Overseeing the Korean student group in their studies at the Tianjin Arsenal, Kim Yun-sik remained in Tianjin but did not play a significant role in the subsequent negotiations.

The ensuing 1882 Treaty of Amity and Commerce has been regarded as a milestone in Chosŏn Korea's evolving relationship with foreign nations.[11]

---

7. For accounts of Ma's activities in Korea, see Ma Jianzhong, *Shikezhai jiyan*; idem, *Dongxing sanlu*; Bailey, *Strengthen the Country and Enrich the People*; and Yen-Lu Tang, "The Crumbling of Tradition."

8. Deuchler, *Confucian Gentlemen and Barbarian Envoys*, 104–5; Key-hiuk Kim, *The Last Phase of the East Asian World Order*, 309.

9. Key-hiuk Kim, *The Last Phase of the East Asian World Order*, 309.

10. Ibid., 311. The Qing minister in Japan, He Ruchang, had admonished the Qing Empire to order Chosŏn Korea to enter into treaty relations with Western powers; he feared that allowing Korea to negotiate treaties on its own would threaten the Qing Em-pire's suzerainty (He Ruchang to Zongli yamen, Nov. 18, 1880 [GX 6.10.16], *ZRHGX*, 440–41). But Li Hongzhang expressed confidence that entering into treaty relations with the West would not necessarily threaten Qing claims to suzerainty (T. F. Tsiang, "Sino-Japanese Diplomatic Relations, 1870–1894," 65).

11. *KS*, May 22, 1882 (KJ 19.4.6). For an English-language version, see Henry Chung, *Korean Treaties*, 197–204.

Li Hongzhang negotiated with Shufeldt for the express purpose of stabiliz-
ing Korea by the strategy of "attack one poison with another poison" (*yi du
gong du*).[12] But he also had additional motives and concerns that influenced
the Qing position in the treaty talks. Conservative officials in the Board of
Rites and Purist Party members alike were united in their determination to
maintain the longtime Qing claim of suzerainty vis-à-vis Korea. Li, too, saw
no reason to deny the Qing Empire's special relationship with its Korean
vassal. Li and his assistant Ma Jianzhong sought to declare this relationship
in the text of the treaty itself. In this, they found Shufeldt an implacable opponent. Shufeldt's refusal to acknowledge Qing claims to suzerainty in the
treaty and his firm support for the United States' "more enlightened policy"
toward Korea were reasons for some self-congratulation on his part.[13] Many,
however, including Shufeldt's biographer, have noted the incongruity of the
commodore's claim to be upholding Korean sovereignty and independence,
while "discussing the treaty with the viceroy of Chihli [Zhili] (and upbraid-
ing him for delaying action), writing it in Tientsin [Tianjin] in the Chinese
language, and arranging it through the agency of China's diplomats for a
Korean official he had never formally met and had seldom seen!"[14] Moreover, although they were unsuccessful in including a suzerainty clause
within the treaty itself, Li and Ma were able to convince the Chosŏn court
to attach a letter to the text of the treaty that acknowledged the special
Qing-Chosŏn relationship.[15] Thus, the 1882 treaty did not clarify Chosŏn

---

12. See the text of Li Hongzhang's letter to Yi Yu-wŏn in *KS*, Aug. 26, 1879 (KJ
16.7.9).

13. Frederick Drake, *Empire of the Seas*, 252, 255–56. Kim Wŏn-mo (*Han-Mi sugyosa*,
369) concludes that the 1882 Korean-American treaty amounted to Shufeldt's repudiation of Li Hongzhang's "suzerainty policy" (*sokbang chŏngch'aek*) and that it signaled Korea's casting-off of its traditional dependency on the Qing and entry into the family of
nations.

14. Frederick Drake, *Empire of the Seas*, 292. The text of the treaty uses dates from
both the Chosŏn and the Qing calendars (*KS*, May 22, 1882 [KJ 19.4.6]).

15. The text of the letter reads as follows:

The Chosen country (Korea) is a dependency of China, but the management of her
governmental affairs, home and foreign, has always been vested in the sovereign.

Now, as the Government of the United States and Korea are about to enter into
treaty relations, the intercourse between the two nations shall be carried on in every
respect on terms of equality and courtesy, and the King of Korea clearly asserts that
all the articles of the treaty shall be acknowledged and carried into effect concerning
the laws of independent States.

Korea's international position vis-à-vis the Qing Empire or other powers. Rather, it seemed that Korea was willing at the same time to function both as a Qing vassal and as an independent member of the "family of nations."

Much of the attention paid to the 1882 treaty negotiation has focused on the suzerainty issue. But maintaining Qing claims to suzerainty was not all that interested Li Hongzhang and Ma Jianzhong. They also sought to use the negotiations to protect their vassal as much as was feasible from the depredations and indignities that the Qing Empire itself had suffered from treaties imposed by force. Li Hongzhang consistently sought to draft a treaty that would, under the grossly unequal conditions of the day, maximize the benefits to Korea.[16] Li was initially reluctant to participate in the treaty negotiations because he feared that Chinese participation would encourage the Westerners to use the previously negotiated Sino-Western treaties (all of which had been negotiated under duress and included provisions contrary to international law [*wanguo tongli*]) as precedents, an outcome that would be harmful to Korea.[17] Once he became convinced that Qing mediation was necessary, however, Li sought to use the process to serve Qing as well as Korean interests and argued for a variety of provisions rather different from those found in earlier Sino-Western treaties. Extraterritoriality, while allowed, was to continue only until Korea reformed its penal code. The opium trade was to be strictly prohibited. Korea was to enjoy the right to establish tariffs and to tax foreign imports both in the treaty ports and in inland areas. Tariff rates were set at 10 percent for necessities and as high as 30 percent for luxuries. Korean officials were also to have the right to arrest Korean lawbreakers who worked for foreigners, even if they were in the houses of foreign merchants. The practice of appointing merchant

---

In the matter of Korea being a dependency of China (in) any question that may arise between them in consequence of such dependency the United States shall in no way interfere.

The King has accordingly deputed commissioners for the purpose of negotiating the treaty, and now, as in duty bound, addresses this communication for the information of the President of the United States. (Yur-bok Lee, "Establishment of a Korean Legation," 11–12)

For a slightly different translation of the letter, see Denny, *China and Korea*, 18–19.

16. Deuchler, *Confucian Gentlemen and Barbarian Envoys*, 115. Once he received the request for mediation from the Korean government, Li dispatched Ma Jianzhong and Zeng Zaoru to write a draft treaty "with all precautions for preserving Korean interests against foreign encroachment" (T. C. Lin, "Li Hung-Chang: His Korea Policies," 222–23).

17. Li Hongzhang to Zongli yamen, Dec. 23, 1880 (GX 6.11.22), *ZRHGX*, 449.

consuls was to be prohibited, as were Christian missionary work and the importation of religious books.

The influence of Ma Jianzhong on the provisions of both the Korean-American and the Korean-British treaty that was negotiated shortly thereafter is clear. Although Ma was unable to secure the inclusion of a provision declaring the Qing Empire's suzerainty over Korea, he was instrumental in pushing for a provision prohibiting the importation of opium. Ma had spent much of 1881 in India surveying the opium industry and searching for ways to reduce British India's exports of the drug to China, and his concern with the issue is obvious. Ma's work in India laid the foundation for the 1885 Chefoo Convention, which allowed the Chinese to impose significantly higher duties on opium imports.[18]

Li Hongzhang's efforts bore fruit. The treaty signed in May 1882 included a prohibition of merchant consuls (Article II); an agreement to abandon extraterritoriality "whenever the King of Chosen shall have so far modified and reformed the statutes and judicial procedure of his Kingdom that . . . they conform to the laws and course of justice in the United States" (Article IV); tariff autonomy for Korea, with tariffs set at 10 percent for necessities and 30 percent for luxuries (Article V); a prohibition on the American transport of goods into the interior (Article VI); a ban on the opium trade (Article VII); and recognition of Korea's right to arrest its own nationals on the premises of foreign residences or warehouses (Article X).[19]

In short, aside from the suzerainty clause and provisions banning missionary work and allowing Korea to exact duties on goods inland as well as in the treaty ports, the Qing negotiators got everything they wanted. The result was a somewhat kinder, gentler, albeit still unequal treaty. Compared to other treaties made between Western powers and China or Japan, or to the Korean-Japanese treaty of 1876, the decisions to give Korea tariff autonomy (and to allow Korea to charge what were then the highest duties

---

18. See Yen-Lu Tang, "The Crumbling of Tradition," 41, 63. Li Hongzhang anticipated British resistance to the prohibition on opium imports and said as much to Sir Harry Parkes in 1883. According to V. G. Kiernan (*British Diplomacy in China*, 106, 107), "Sir Harry denied it, and, a little irritated, said that Corea was likely to suffer more from importations of Chinese than of Indian opium (A hint at the poppies supposed to flourish on Li's Anhui estates?)." Whatever the case, "opium agitation at home was too strong to admit of opium being forced on a new country."

19. Henry Chung, *Korean Treaties*, 197–204; *KS*, May 22, 1882 (KJ 19.4.6).

in East Asia), to concede the possibility of an end to extraterritoriality, and to prohibit the opium trade were all of considerable benefit to Korea.[20]

After the negotiations in Tianjin were complete, Shufeldt, accompanied by Ma Jianzhong and Admiral Ding Ruchang, traveled to Korea where the treaty was signed in Inch'ŏn on May 22, 1882. Only when it came time to actually sign the treaty did Ma and Ding exit the tent where the ceremony was taking place. They returned after the signing and took part in subsequent festivities, including a banquet at which Shufeldt "gave the credit of the treaty to Li and Ma."[21]

Treaties with Great Britain and Germany were negotiated immediately thereafter.[22] Like its Korean-American counterpart, the Korean-British Treaty of June 6, 1882 (also known as the "Willes Treaty") was negotiated through the good offices of Chinese officials Ma Jianzhong and Ding Ruchang. The provisions of the Korean-British treaty (as well as the Korean-German treaty) were virtually indistinguishable from those of the Korean-American one.[23] The British diplomat Harry Parkes was highly

---

20. Woong Joe Kang (*The Korean Struggle for International Identity*, 140–41) claims that "contrary to some exaggerated claims, China's participation did not produce a treaty with liberal provisions. Compared with treaties she made with other Far Eastern powers, the United States gave what she had given to others and only what she wanted to give." However, it is clear that the American John Russell Young's assessment was more accurate: "It is a generous treaty when compared with conventions that have heretofore been signed between Western powers and Asiatic nations, superior I think, to any convention signed by Western powers, with China or Japan" (ibid., 147). This was especially true in terms of tariff rates; see Mun-hyung Choi, "Korean-British Amity and Its Historical Significance."

21. Fredrick Drake, *Empire of the Seas*, 298. For descriptions of the treaty negotiation and signing, see ibid., 297–98; Key-hiuk Kim, *The Last Phase of the East Asian World Order*, 303–13; and Woong Joe Kang, *The Korean Struggle for International Identity*, 138–39.

22. Great Britain did not wish to take the lead in opening Korea for fear that this would spur additional Russian activity in the region. However, once the Americans broke the ice, the British were ready and willing to pursue treaty relations with Korea; see Mun-hyung Choi, "Korean-British Amity and Its Historical Significance."

23. Both sides attempted to modify the treaty somewhat. Ma Jianzhong pushed for the inclusion of a provision declaring Korea to be a vassal of China. Vice Admiral George Willes, the British plenipotentiary, refused. Willes also sought to include some modifications, but these were rejected by Ma. The British desire to modify the treaty provisions was also discouraged by a practical matter: the Englishman who was to serve as the interpreter, a "Mr. Spence," failed to show up. Willes and the other British negotiators "did not trust themselves to alter the American phrasing for fear of losing the meaning" (Kiernan, *British Diplomacy in China*, 83). As was the case with the Korean-

critical of many of the provisions of the Willes Treaty, particularly its relatively generous tariffs, its failure to allow British gunboats access to Korean
treaty ports, and its prohibition of opium.[24]

Whether Li could have continued to uphold the paradox of simultane-
ous Korean dependency and autonomy while guaranteeing Korean security
by "using one barbarian against another" will never be known. Soon after
the signing of the Korean-American treaty of 1882, military unrest and the
return to power of the Taewŏn'gun in Korea would force additional modifications in Sino-Korean relations and further increase the tension between
traditional relations and the new policies and practices of the Qing Empire
in Korea.

The *1882* Imo *Soldiers' Mutiny*

Growing disaffection with Kojong's policy of accommodation with Japan
and the West healed, at least in part, the rift between the Taewŏn'gun and
many Neo-Confucian literati in Korea. Although out of power for nearly
ten years, the Taewŏn'gun was still an important figure. Resentful of his
loss of power and anguished at the direction in which his son was guiding
Korea, the Taewŏn'gun was implicated in many of the intrigues and assas-
sinations that plagued the Korean court during the late 1870s and early
1880s. His followers, led by his illegitimate son, attempted to seize power in
a coup in 1881.[25]

Arrayed against these forces was the increasingly powerful family of
Kojong's wife, Queen Min. Many members of the queen's family had used
newly established institutions such as the T'ongni kimu amun to propel
themselves into powerful positions in government. Among those not fortunate enough to belong to the Min clan, there was a growing fear of being

---

American Treaty, a letter declaring Chosŏn Korea's acceptance of Qing suzerainty was
sent to Queen Victoria. Reading this letter, Sir Harry Parkes wondered, "How are we to
recognise this quasi-dependent condition and at the same time to treat Korea as an
equal, the King being on the same footing as the Queen [of Great Britain] appears to
me to be a puzzling problem" (Sir Harry Parkes to Lord Tenterden, *Great Britain: Foreign
Office Confidential Papers*, no. 59 [21 June 1882], cited in Lisa Chung, "Somnolent in Korea," 5).

24. According to Ch'oe Mun-hyŏng (*Han'guk ŭl tullŏssan chegukchuŭi yŏlgang ŭi kakch'uk*, 46), these elements of the Willes Treaty made it an agreement that played into the
Qing Empire's hands.

25. Deuchler, *Confucian Gentlemen and Barbarian Envoys*, 106.

shut out. Coupled with the ongoing power struggle between the Tae-wŏn'gun and the king and his wife was a growing sense of unrest among the general populace. This was prompted in part by tales of the extravagance of the Queen Min–dominated court. The queen was known to invite shamans, fortunetellers, dancers, and other unsavory characters into the palace compound and reward them lavishly for their services. Since state revenues were declining, this extravagance had an even greater impact. The queen was not alone; other members of the Min family and their followers were also notorious for amassing huge fortunes by accepting bribes.[26] Interwoven into these domestic phenomena was the collision with the wider world. Many observers, both commoner and elite, felt that one cause of the widespread corruption and the perceived general lapse in morals was the growing influence of the outside world.

Criticism of the T'ongni kimu amun grew not only because the office served as a vehicle for promotion for members of the Min clan but also because it was of foreign origin and thus marked a break with tradition. There was similar resentment of the Special Skills Force (Pyŏlgigun), an elite military unit that was trained by Horimoto Reizō, a Japanese army instructor. Members of the old-style military units resented the special treatment and better pay received by the Special Skills Force; they also feared that the advent of such new-style military units signaled the beginning of the end of their livelihood.[27]

It is hardly surprising, then, that in July 1882, when soldiers from the old-style units found that the thirteen-months-overdue rice stipend they were given was adulterated with sand and chaff, some of them snapped. As vividly recounted by the historian Yi Sŏn-gŭn, looking at the bags of almost useless rice and hearing the din of shamanistic rites and drunken laughter from within the palace compound, the soldiers could not but protest. Their protests were met with stony silence and then arrest and even

---

26. One official, Left–State Councilor Yi Chae-ung, was said to have accepted more bribes and gifts than he could consume, causing his neighbors to complain that his home reeked of rotting pheasant and seafood. Popular rumor had it that horses owned by members of the Min clan turned up their noses at honey cakes; members of the Min were said to toss delicacies such as rice mixed with dates and chestnuts to their donkeys. See Yi Sŏn-gŭn, *Han'guksa*, 464–66.

27. Deuchler, *Confucian Gentlemen and Barbarian Envoys*, 103. For the suggestion, made by Japanese diplomat Hanabusa Yoshimoto, that Horimoto be hired to train Korean troops, see *KS*, May 20, 1881 (KJ 18.4.23).

execution for some. The comrades of the arrested and executed soldiers proceeded to enlist the assistance of the Taewŏn'gun.[28] Although publicly disassociating himself from the soldiers, he secretly plotted with their leaders. It became widely known that the Taewŏn'gun sympathized with the soldiers and blamed the uprising on "the corruption of the queen's party and the export of rice by Japanese merchants."[29] It also became clear that he hoped to utilize the righteous anger of the troops to exterminate the Min family and its followers, expel all Japanese from Korea, and recover the reins of power.

On July 23, 1882, soldiers, joined by a mob of commoners, stormed the Korean royal palace (the incident is known as the *imo* mutiny after the Korean name for the year in the sixty-year cycle). They also attacked the Japanese legation and burned it to the ground. The head of the legation, Hanabusa Yoshimoto, managed to escape with a small group of followers. The Japanese army instructor Horimoto was killed, as were a number of Korean high officials.[30] Queen Min was also rumored to have been killed in the melee but was later found to have slipped out of the palace in disguise. With the royal palace itself under attack and no succor in sight, King Kojong accepted the inevitable and declared the Taewŏn'gun *de facto* the ruler of Korea. The Taewŏn'gun promptly abolished the T'ongni kimu amun and reinstated the old military system.[31] He also purged the government of many of the Min family and their supporters and pardoned several Confucian officials involved in earlier antireform protests.

Had Korea still been in its state of nearly complete isolation from the outside world, the Taewŏn'gun's coup d'état may have succeeded. However, Hanabusa was swift to promise to return with Japanese troops and demands for reparations. Given that the iron-willed Taewŏn'gun was extremely unlikely to accede to further Japanese intervention, war between Chosŏn Korea and Meiji Japan, a war that Korea would certainly lose, seemed likely. The Qing policies of behind-the-scenes advice and mediation of Korean treaties with the United States and others were not sufficient to stave off Japan. More forceful action was required.

---

28. The soldiers first went to protest to Yi Kyŏng-ha, a venerable old general of the days of the Taewŏn'gun's isolationist policies. Yi, however, was not willing to do more than write a letter on behalf of the angry soldiers. See Yi Sŏn-gŭn, *Han'guksa*, 474.

29. Jerome Ch'en, *Yuan Shih-k'ai*, 5.

30. *KS*, July 23, 1882 (KJ 19.6.9).

31. *KS*, July 24, 1882 (KJ 19.6.10).

The Qing Responds: The Dispatch
of Troops to Korea

News of the uprising reached China via a cable from Li Shuchang, the Qing minister in Japan. Li Hongzhang had temporarily left office to mourn the death of his mother. Zhang Shusheng, acting commissioner for the northern ports, was forced to make the initial decision concerning the Qing response.[32] Zhang solicited the advice of Kim Yun-sik and Ŏ Yun-jung, Korean officials who were in Tianjin. Both Kim and Ŏ called for Qing warships and troops to be sent to Korea.[33] Zhang requested permission from the Zongli yamen to dispatch Qing warships to Korea to investigate the matter as well as to prepare to send troops if needed. Permission was granted on August 6, 1882.[34]

On the following day, Admiral Ding Ruchang and Ma Jianzhong, joined by Ŏ Yun-jung, left for Korea with three European-built Qing warships. Arriving in Korea on August 10, they found the capital in an uproar with the Taewŏn'gun propagating antiforeign slogans. In their report to Zhang, they advocated immediate action. Zhang, acting on the advice of, among others, Xue Fucheng, a member of Li Hongzhang's private secretariat, had already decided to take action even before he received the report. He requested that General Wu Changqing, commander of six Anhui army battalions stationed in Shandong, prepare his troops for departure to Korea. The throne approved of Zhang Shusheng's plans and even took the extreme step of ordering Li Hongzhang to cut short his mourning and return to Tianjin.[35]

General Wu's troops arrived in Korea on August 20. A Japanese contingent led by Hanabusa Yoshimoto had preceded them. Hanabusa had

---

32. Zhang Shusheng to Zongli yamen, Aug. 2, 1882 (GX 8.6.19), *ZRHGX*, 734.

33. Zhang Shusheng to Zongli yamen, Aug. 4, 1882 (GX 8.6.21), *ZRHGX*, 748–50.

34. Zongli yamen to Zhang Shusheng, Aug. 6, 1882 (GX 8.6.23), *ZRHGX*, 753.

35. Because many of General Wu's retinue had gone home to sit for the provincial examinations, the responsibility for mobilizing the troops fell largely on Wu's protégé Zhang Jian. With the assistance of Yuan Shikai and Xue Fucheng, Zhang had the troops ready to move by August 16. For a description of Chinese decision making and military preparations, see Key-hiuk Kim, *The Last Phase of the East Asian World Order*, 318–23; Deuchler, *Confucian Gentlemen and Barbarian Envoys*, 132–33; Chu, *Reformer in Modern China*, 12–14; Wang Bogong, *Quanlu suibi*, 11–12; and Lin Mingde, *Yuan Shikai yu Chaoxian*, 16–17.

stormed into Seoul and presented a seven-point ultimatum to the Chosŏn government. When the Koreans delayed their response, Hanabusa angrily left Seoul for Inch'ŏn. Thus, the Qing troops encountered no resistance from the Japanese (or the rebels) when they approached Seoul on August 25.

On the following day, Wu Changqing, Admiral Ding Ruchang, and Ma Jianzhong visited the Taewŏn'gun. Ma reported that they were impressed with his "refined taste."[36] Nevertheless, they had already concluded that the inflexible Taewŏn'gun must be removed. When the Taewŏn'gun paid a return visit to the Chinese camp the following day, he was forced into a sedan chair and marched under cover of a rainy night to the coast, where he was placed on a Qing ship bound for Tianjin. Once restored to power, the grateful Kojong requested Qing help in hunting down the leaders of the mutiny. Yuan Shikai led the effort to oust the rebels from their strongholds in the Korean towns of It'aewŏn and Wangsimni. Some 170 rebels were captured, but at the urging of General Wu's assistant Zhang Jian, most were released. The Korean king sent personal emissaries to Tianjin to thank the Qing Empire for its assistance. General Wu and Yuan Shikai were subsequently honored by the Korean court for their role in the suppression of the revolt.[37]

Given the obvious reluctance, up to this point, of the Qing Empire to directly intervene in Korean affairs, the speed and force with which the Chinese acted are nothing short of startling. Kim Key-hiuk succinctly summarizes: "The [Qing] government decided to intervene in Korean domestic politics within a week of receipt of the first report on the riot in Seoul. Precisely one month after he had been restored to power, the Taewŏn'gun was forcibly taken to China."[38] Far from simply advising and exhorting the Koreans through formal and informal channels, the Qing Empire had become directly involved in Korean domestic affairs and stationed more than 3,000 troops on Korean soil.[39]

---

36. Ma also noted in his journal: "This old man is very deep" (quoted in Jerome Ch'en, *Yuan Shih-k'ai*, 6).

37. Accounts of the uprising and its suppression can be found in Yi Sŏn-gŭn, *Han'guksa*, 462–518; Key-hiuk Kim, *The Last Phase of the East Asian World Order*, 316–25; Deuchler, *Confucian Gentlemen and Barbarian Envoys*, 130–34; Wang Bogong, *Quanlu suibi*, 11–12; and Zhang Ruogu, *Ma Xiangbo xiansheng nianbu*, 141–42.

38. Key-hiuk Kim, *The Last Phase of the East Asian World Order*, 325.

39. A North Korean account of the 1882 mutiny emphasizes how the soldiers' uprising invited not only intervention from "the feudal Chinese government" but also

Many scholars regard this Qing intervention as an irrevocable break with past practice.[40] The stationing of troops on Korean soil and the increasing Qing interference in Korean political affairs were far cries from the traditional policy of distance and nonintervention. Significantly, however, Qing policy makers and officials sought to explain and justify their actions in terms that made sense in the older tribute system as well as in the more recent Western-style international order. As Admiral Ding Ruchang summarized, "When Japanese aggression threatened to extend so near home as Corea, then China felt it was necessary to make a firm and decisive stand. In this Corean imbroglio China has been obliged to interfere as a father does when his son has got into some ugly scrape."[41]

Intervention, even military intervention, was not completely antithetical to the traditional system of relations. Nor was it without precedent. Just six years earlier, when Japan was threatening war with Korea, Li Hongzhang wrote of his fear that Korea might call on China to fulfill its duty as Korea's suzerain, just as the Chosŏn court had done in the late sixteenth century when Hideyoshi invaded Korea. In 1882, the Chosŏn Kingdom did precisely that, and the Qing Empire, recognizing the need to "be kind to the weak," responded.[42] Moreover, one of the chief explanations for kidnapping the Taewŏn'gun was the regent's disregard for his son, the rightful king, who had been granted investiture by the Qing emperor. On the day of the Taewŏn'gun's abduction, Ma Jianzhong, Ding Ruchang, and Wu Changqing issued a proclamation declaring that "Korea is China's dependent state" and called upon the rebels to lay down their arms and hand over their leaders.[43]

None of this is to say that Qing officials were not motivated by geopolitical and security concerns; they clearly were concerned with the need to avoid giving Japan a pretext for expanding its military presence in Korea.

---

from Japan and the "American and British invaders," who sent two gunboats, the *Monocacy* and the *Encounter*, to Inch'ŏn (*Chosŏn chŏnsa 13 kŭndae 1*, 169).

40. For a discussion of various schemes of periodization of this period and the significance of 1882, see Ku Sŏn-hŭi, *Han'guk kŭndae daeQing chŏngch'aeksa yŏn'gu*, 12–15.

41. Hall to Parkes, Dec. 11, 1882, *British Documents*, 2: 116.

42. LHZ to Zongli yamen, Jan. 22, 1876 (GX 1.12.26), *ZRHGX*, 276–77; for "be kind to the weak," see *WJSL*, 86: 10–12.

43. For the Chinese proclamation in Seoul, see Yur-bok Lee, *West Goes East*, 36. For an argument that the Qing dispatch of troops to Korea was an attempt to strengthen Qing suzerainty, see Han Yŏng-u, *Tasi ch'annŭn uri yŏksa*, 426.

However, they consistently sought to describe their actions in terms that made sense within the traditional system. Efforts to do this would become increasingly strained in the years ahead, but the ideological and ethical imperatives of the tribute system would continue to influence Qing policy in Korea, sometimes at the expense of the Qing Empire's attempts to implement a more vigorous imperialism in its old tributary state.

The parallels between the Qing dispatch of troops to Korea and similar actions taken by other imperialist powers were not lost on one British observer of the events. His description of Qing naval commanders and officers who transported the troops to Korea and maintained a powerful presence in Inch'ŏn captures the combination of confidence, condescension, and compassion that characterized many an imperialist's motivations and self-perceptions:

Most of them were Southern Chinese, and they all spoke English well. In talking with them about Corean affairs I was struck with the warmth of sympathetic interest they displayed. While deploring the backwardness and ignorance of the Coreans as loftily as the most conceited Europeans could have done, they, nevertheless, maintained that the people were pure Chinese. They posed themselves as deliverers and protectors of the country from Japanese aggression.[44]

The Qing decision to send troops to Korea is also a sign of the power of conservative Purist Party–style thinking in Korea. In an 1882 letter, the scholar Yao Wendong noted that "recently the *qingyi* [Purist Party adherents] in the capital and the public opinion throughout the empire have paid great attention to this affair and mostly advocate deploying troops."[45] One wonders what the Qing reaction to the 1882 soldiers' mutiny might have been, had the ever-cautious Li Hongzhang been at his post. Fearing that even the best of his self-strengthening efforts had not created a force that could best the Japanese, Li likely would have sought to avoid a direct confrontation.[46] However, in Li's initial absence, a chorus of calls for intervention carried the day. Given the ambition of some of the plans of the hard-liners—calls for the invasion of Japan were not uncommon—sending

---

44. Hall to Parkes, Dec. 11, 1882, *British Documents*, 2: 114.

45. Quoted in Nan-Tsung Kim, "Neighbour as Mirror," 52*n*8.

46. Jerome Ch'en (*Yuan Shih-k'ai*, 6) notes that "the dispatch of troops did not mean that Li was resolved to use force to obtain a Korean settlement. . . . He knew that his [Huai] Army, China's best fighting force, was not strong enough to defeat the Japanese."

troops to Korea to quell a domestic rebellion was easily within the scope of acceptable actions.[47] Powerful forces within the Qing Empire were willing to risk a clash with the Japanese to safeguard Korea's security and enhance the Empire's prestige.

For Kojong and the Min clan, Qing intervention was eagerly sought and gratefully received. The earlier Qing approval of Queen Min's son, known to posterity as Sunjong, as the heir apparent had enhanced the legitimacy of both king and queen, but Qing military intervention secured their very survival. A Korean mission of gratitude was swiftly sent to China in the aftermath of the rebellion. The Korean message of thanks was couched in terms that no one could mistake for anything but a reaffirmation of the suzerain-vassal relationship, beginning with King Kojong's observation: "In humble meditation your servant reflects on the worthless manner in which he has discharged the duties of the post to which he was appointed by Your Imperial Majesty."[48] Kojong would request Qing advice and assistance in many arenas in the coming years. And even when Qing policies under the Residency of Yuan Shikai took the luster off the Qing-Chosŏn relationship, Kojong often appeared to maintain a personal affection for China.

For some Koreans, especially a small group of younger officials who had connections with Japan, the signs of increased Qing influence in Korea were a source of dismay. Motivated in part by frustrated personal ambition and in part by the fear that Chinese influence would move Korea away from a Meiji-style reformation, these "progressives" chafed under the Qing military occupation and sought means to enhance their own power and influence at the expense of the Chinese and their allies, the Min clan.[49]

Once Li was back in Tianjin, he encouraged negotiation between Korea and Japan with Qing mediation. Ma Jianzhong played a key role in bringing the Koreans and Japanese to the negotiating table and gave detailed advice to the Korean envoys, Yi Yu-wŏn and Kim Hong-jip. The resulting Treaty of Chemulp'o and the Additional Convention called for Korea to pay a 500,000-yen indemnity to Japan, allowed for the stationing of Japanese soldiers in Korea to guard the Japanese legation, demanded the public

---

47. For bellicose Purist Party rhetoric on Japan, see, e.g., Bonnie B. C. Oh, "The Leadership Crisis in China on the Eve of the Sino-Japanese War of 1894–1895," 75–76.

48. Kiernan, *British Diplomacy in China*, 101. For the original of Kojong's declaration of thanks, see Li Hongzhang to Zongli yamen, Sept. 15, 1882 (GX 8.8.4), *ZRHGX*, 895–97.

49. Cook, *Korea's 1884 Incident*.

disclosure of all Korean treaties with Japan and other nations, and mandated the destruction of antiforeign stone tablets that had been erected by the Taewŏn'gun.[50] Li Hongzhang objected to the severity of some of the Japanese demands but thought it "inconvenient for China to overturn the agreement."[51]

Sino-Korean Trade Regulations

The need to intervene far more forcefully to quell the 1882 *imo* mutiny and forestall Japanese aggression in Korea did not distract from Li Hongzhang's continued efforts to use diplomacy and international law to promote Qing interests in Korea. After mediating Korea's first treaties with the United States, Britain, and Germany, Li Hongzhang turned his attention to commercial issues and the calls for a Sino-Korean commercial treaty. This was a step unprecedented in the relations between Korea and China. Although agreements concerning trade had been negotiated in the past, they invariably dealt with strictly controlling and limiting the amount of trade (and relations in general) between China and Korea. The Korean interest in increasing the level of trade with China was motivated in part by a desire to reduce Japanese influence on the peninsula. To this end, the Korean official Yi Yong-suk was sent to China in 1881 to discuss with Li Hongzhang the possibility of allowing Chinese merchants to trade in Korea. Li, aware of the calls of the Qing official Wu Dacheng and others for a more aggressive Chinese policy in Korea, agreed.[52]

Therefore, in 1882 Qing negotiators approached Korea with the express purpose of creating an agreement that would facilitate trade between China and Korea and, at the same time, reinforce Qing claims to suzerainty. Most examinations of the ensuing Regulations for Maritime and Overland Trade

---

50. *KS,* Aug. 30, 1882 (KJ 19.7.17). Although several authors, including Key-hiuk Kim and Martina Deuchler, use the name Treaty of Chemulp'o (named after the place where the treaty was negotiated), the official name is simply the Korean-Japanese Settlement Treaty (Cho-Il kanghwa choyak; C. Chao-Ri jianghe tiaoyue).

51. T. C. Lin, "Li Hung-Chang: His Korea Policies," 228.

52. In the name of stopping the Russians and Japanese in Korea, Wu called for coastal surveys by the China Merchants Steamship Company (in preparation for a more vigorous Chinese "gunboat diplomacy") and for Chinese commercial challenges to the Japanese monopoly; see Kim Chŏng-wŏn, "Cho-Chung sangmin suyuk muyŏk changjŏng e taehayŏ," 127–29.

Between Chinese and Korean Subjects conclude that suzerainty mattered most to the Qing negotiators. One argues that the Regulations "shed more light on politics than on economics." Another sees the Sino-Korean agreement as merely "a political tool for tightening Chinese control over Korea."[53] Ritual suzerainty did matter. Ma Jianzhong and Tianjin Customs Daotai Zhou Fu declared as much in the preamble to the Regulations: they "are understood to apply to the relations between China and Korea only, the former country granting to the latter certain advantages as a tributary Kingdom, and treaty nations are not to participate therein."[54]

Ritual suzerainty was not *all* that mattered, however. The preamble of the Regulations also states: "As now foreign countries entertain trade with Korea by water, it becomes necessary to remove at once the prohibition of sea trade . . . and let the merchants of both countries participate in all the advantages of commercial relations." Provisions guaranteeing such relations included those that gave Chinese merchants the right to live and work in Seoul; the right (with passports issued by the Korean government) to travel to the interior of Korea; and a very favorable tariff rate: 5 percent for most goods.[55] In addition, there were several provisions that established privileges similar to those enjoyed by the Japanese, Americans, and British. These included extraterritoriality and the right to establish "commissioners of trade" in Korean treaty ports.[56] The treaty also called for the China Merchants Steamship Company to provide regular service between China and Korea.[57]

---

53. Lin Mingde, "Li Hung-chang's Suzerain Policy Toward Korea, 1882–1894," 183; Dalchoong Kim, "Chinese Imperialism in Korea," 107; see also Deuchler, *Confucian Gentlemen and Barbarian Envoys*, 141; and Chien, *The Opening of Korea*, 197.

54. For the full text of the treaty, see China, Imperial Maritime Customs, *Treaties, Regulations, Etc., Between China and Other States*, 2: 847–53.

55. See ibid. Additional provisions allowed Korean merchants to bring ginseng into China (all others were prohibited from participating in the lucrative ginseng trade); Chinese merchants to participate in the inter-port trade in Korea; and Chinese to bring opium into Korea for personal use (the sale of opium was strictly forbidden). See "Memorandum comparing the regulations for trade between the Chinese and Coreans with the provisions of the British treaty with Corea," *British Documents*, 101–4.

56. The Qing deliberately avoided using the term "consul" to emphasize the uniqueness of the Sino-Korean relationship.

57. British observers were quick to note that this provision benefited not only Chinese commerce in general but also Li Hongzhang himself, who was thought to be "one of the principal shareholders" of the company ("Memorandum comparing the

The Sino-Korean trade regulations constitute the first time that the Qing Empire proactively sought to promote Chinese commercial interests beyond its borders through the use of treaties and international law. The influence of Tang Tingshu, the "man that pushes" Li Hongzhang, as well as other treaty-port elite advocates of "commercial warfare" on the provisions of the regulations is clear. In addition, the regulations highlight the willingness of the Qing Empire to assert the same types of unequal privileges in Korea that caused resentment when they were imposed on the Qing Empire itself. In the words of V. G. Kiernan, "We have come to one of the earliest concrete instances of the competition of an awakened China."[58] Whether China was ever asleep is an open question, but it is clear that Qing officials were more than willing to utilize the same mechanisms as the presumably more conscious Western powers.[59]

The Qing Empire would follow up on its success in promulgating the Regulations for Maritime and Overland Trade with a series of agreements, regulations, and rules designed to govern the long-standing border trade between Korea and China. These reflected the same combination of aims that motivated the 1882 Sino-Korean commercial agreement. The March 1883 Twenty-Four Rules for the Traffic on the Frontier between Liaodong [Fengtian] and Korea called for the establishment of customs houses to monitor and regulate the border trade. It also strictly stipulated that although Korea, as a Chinese dependency, could be seen as part of the "inner realm" (*neifu*), merchants from Fengtian (Liaodong) were not allowed to trespass on Korean territory. Like the 1882 Regulations for Maritime and Overland Trade, the Twenty-Four Rules repeatedly claimed that they applied only to China and Korea (and only to the people who lived, worked, or traveled near the border at that), not to other nations or to open ports in China and Korea.[60] The June 19, 1884, Rules for the Traffic on the Fron-

---

regulations for trade between Chinese and Coreans with the provisions of the British treaty with Corea," *British Documents*, 2: 101).

58. Kiernan, *British Diplomacy in China*, 103.

59. Writing of international law, Richard Horowitz ("International Law and State Transformation," 455) observes, "despite the patronizing tone of the international lawyers, it provided leaders of non-Western states, even those not fully 'civilized' in the international sense, with a set of tools for playing the games of international politics for their own benefit even though they remained in positions of profound military weakness."

60. China, Imperial Maritime Customs, *Treaties, Regulations, Etc., Between China and Foreign States*, 2: 854–63.

tier Between Jilin and Korea set similar regulations and limits on the border trade further east. As was the case in the 1883 Twenty-Four Rules, the 1884 Rules also claimed to apply only to China and Korea. And like their predecessor, the 1884 Rules included a provision instructing the Koreans to refer to the Qing Empire as the "Heavenly Court" (*tianchao*) or the "Superior Country" (*shangguo*) rather than using the character *zhong* (K. *chung*). Chinese should reciprocate by referring to Korea as either the "Chosŏn Country" (*Chaoxianguo*; K. Chosŏn'guk) or "your respected country" (*guiguo*; K. *kwiguk*).[61]

Treaty Renegotiation and Tariff Standardization

The promulgation of the Regulations for Maritime and Overland Trade also played an important role in Chosŏn Korea's efforts to impose tariffs on trade. One of the most glaring omissions in the 1876 Treaty of Kanghwa and its supplement of the same year was the lack of any provisions for tariff duties. Japanese negotiators had come to the bargaining table in 1876 prepared to accept a 5 percent *ad valorem* duty on Korean imports from Japan. However, the Korean negotiator Cho In-hŭi agreed to the proposal of his Japanese counterpart that "both countries exempt import and export duties for several years in order to promote trade between them."[62] That Korea would so willingly surrender sovereignty over such an important issue is usually blamed on Korean unfamiliarity with modern international law and trade. However, it is also likely that the decision was due in part to a general disdain for commercial affairs and in part to the Korean expectation that the 1876 treaty would lead more to continuity than to change. They expected that trade would continue to be regulated through traditional mechanisms such as the Japan House. Korean officials in Pusan had collected harbor dues from Japanese vessels long before 1876 and continued to do so after the Treaty of Kanghwa.[63]

---

61. *KS*, June 19, 1884 (KJ 21.5.6).

62. Key-hiuk Kim, *The Last Phase of the East Asian World Order*, 262.

63. For an examination of the traditional regulatory infrastructure in Pusan and how it changed after 1876, see Pusan chikhalshisa p'yŏnch'an wiwŏnhoe, *Pusanshisa*, 791–96. For Kojong's declaration that the 1876 Treaty of Kanghwa was merely a restoration of traditional "neighborly relations" (*kyorin*) between Korea and Japan, see *Sŭngjŏngwŏn ilgi*, Sept. 16, 1882 (KJ 19.8.5) as cited in Choe Tŏk-su, "The Dawning of a New World," 113–14.

When persistent Japanese efforts to obtain privileges stipulated in the 1876 Treaty began to convince many in the Korean government that continuing to insist that trade and interactions be conducted according to older rules and norms was untenable, some began to press for the introduction of a tariff. The Korean official Kim Hong-jip was sent to Japan in 1880 to discuss the issue of tariffs with the Japanese government. Although instructed to ask for the same 5 percent duty that Japan would have accepted in 1876, Kim was informed by the Qing Minister He Ruchang that Japan was in the process of negotiating with Western powers for a higher tariff. Therefore, when Kim met with the Japanese, he pressed for the same rate that the Japanese hoped to apply to Western exports to Japan. Using the rather flimsy excuse that the relatively shorter distance between Japan and Korea necessitated a lower tariff, the Japanese put off Kim's requests and the issue was not settled.[64]

When news of the 1882 Regulations for Maritime and Overland Trade became known, the reaction of other powers interested in Korea was predictable. The Japanese foreign minister noted that "China intended to assume great powers of control over Corea, and to secure exclusive commercial privileges in that country," an assessment not short on irony given that Meiji Japan had vigorously and successfully pursued such exclusive privileges over the course of the previous six years. Such actions were, he believed, "chiefly directed against Japan," but other nations were affected as well.[65] The British were also incensed at the special privileges accorded to China. Harry S. Parkes, Britain's minister in Tokyo, harangued visiting Korean delegates over the issue:

It would be vain, I thought, for Corea to suppose that the Western Powers would accept inferior terms to those which Corea had granted to China and Japan, as it was obvious that their people could conduct no trade in Corea unless they were placed, in regard to commercial advantages, on an equal footing with the subjects of those two nations.[66]

Parkes and other British officials were able to use the disorder surrounding the 1882 *imo* mutiny and the differences between the British and Chinese treaties to postpone ratification of the Korean-British treaty and to insist on new negotiations.

---

64. Key-hiuk Kim, *The Last Phase of the East Asian World Order*, 290–92.
65. H. Parkes to Earl Granville, Dec. 21, 1882, *British Documents*, 2: 104.
66. H. Parkes to Earl Granville, Jan. 12, 1883, *British Documents*, 2: 112.

Meanwhile, it was not until after the arrival of American Minister Lucius Q. Foote in Korea and the subsequent ratification of the Korean-American Treaty in May 1883 that the Japanese, bowing to the inevitable, agreed to allow the Chosŏn Kingdom to tax Japanese-Korean trade. The resulting Regulations Under Which Japanese Trade Is to Be Conducted in Korea were completed on July 25, 1883.[67] The tariffs included in the agreement were considerably lower than those found in Korea's treaties with the United States and (not yet ratified) Britain and Germany, but not as low as those stipulated in the Sino-Korean trade regulations. The Regulations also granted Japan most-favored-nation status.[68] Administrative delay meant that the rates stipulated in the Korean-American treaty were used until November 1883. Thereafter, the rates in the Korean-Japanese Regulations were in effect for nearly a year, until late 1884.[69]

After months of negotiating, the British were successful in obtaining a new treaty near the end of 1883. This new "Parkes Treaty" contained much lower tariff rates, especially for textiles; stipulated that British merchants would be able to purchase land and build factories in Korean ports; and allowed British warships to call in Korean ports. The new Korean-British Treaty became the model for subsequent treaties. The Germans signed a similar treaty the same day; Russia, Italy, and France followed in the next few years. The Americans obtained the benefits of the treaty, especially the low tariff rates, by claiming most-favored-nation status.

The alacrity with which Great Britain, the United States, and other foreign powers used the Sino-Korean trade regulations to assert the same level of tariffs and access to Korea for their own citizens is a sure sign of the coming of multilateral imperialism to Korea. In this respect, Li Hongzhang can be thought to have been successful in his efforts to secure the involvement and interest of a number of foreign powers in Korea so that no single power could emerge predominant. However, although multilateral imperialism would serve to destroy Japanese claims to exclusive privilege in Korea, it would also hamper the Qing Empire's own efforts to maintain claims to the fruits of a unique Sino-Korean relationship. Thus whereas Chinese merchants and their treaty-port elite sponsors may have been pleased with their privileges and access to Korean markets, they were

---

67. For the full text of the Regulations, see *Treaties, Regulations, etc.*, 82–119.
68. Mun-hyung Choi, " Korean-British Amity and Its Historical Significance," 16.
68. Han'guk kwanse yŏn'guso, *Han'guk kwansesa*, 72–74.

also likely to have been dismayed at the swiftness with which their exclusive privileges became the common property of any and all treaty powers in Korea.

The rush to use the 1882 Regulations for Maritime and Overland Trade to secure treaty revision and tariff standardization also highlights another tension brought about by the Qing Empire's introduction of multilateral imperialism to Korea: the very agreement that Britain and the United States used to claim equal commercial privileges in Korea also contained clear, unequivocal declarations that Chosŏn Korea remained a Qing vassal. Western diplomats tended to dismiss these claims as Oriental "romance and hyperbole," but nevertheless the fact remained that the Qing Empire and Chosŏn Korea had signed and ratified a modern treaty that clearly stated that Korea was a Chinese vassal. Moreover, by using the Sino-Korean Regulations for Maritime and Overland Trade to assert equal privileges in Korea, the Western powers and Japan were tacitly if not overtly demonstrating their acceptance of the regulations as international law, thus undermining the provisions in earlier treaties that declared Korea's independence. This tension between Qing suzerainty and Western-style independence would continue for at least the next twelve years.

FOUR

Soldiers, Diplomats, and Merchants

Establishing a Qing Presence

in Korea

Utilizing the mechanisms of international law and military intervention, the Qing Empire dramatically transformed its relationship with Chosŏn Korea in 1882. Both developments would play a prominent role in shaping the relationship in the years to come. The Qing military presence in Korea shaped the course of Korean military and political reform and would profoundly influence domestic political conflicts, particularly in the case of the *kapsin* coup attempt of 1884. Less visible but no less important was the expansion of the Qing diplomatic presence in Korea. For the first time in the history of the Qing Empire, it stationed permanent representatives on Korean soil. These officials not only influenced Korean domestic and foreign policy but also opened the gates for an influx of Chinese merchants, one of the first cases of the direct, overt official promotion of Chinese commerce beyond the confines of the Qing Empire itself.

Until the *imo* crisis of 1882, every action the Qing Empire had taken regarding Korea could be fit, however uneasily, within the framework of the traditional system of relations. Once the immediate crisis was defused and the rightful ruler was securely back on the throne, the question of the Empire's future course of action arose. Li Hongzhang regarded the stationing of troops in Korea as a temporary measure and sought to have them removed as soon as possible. He feared that a continued Qing military presence in Korea might lead foreign powers to conclude that the Qing Empire was responsible for Korea's security. Not wishing to take this course,

Li hoped to return, if at all possible, to the policy of behind-the-scenes advice and guidance.[1]

Other voices, many of the very voices that had urged the dispatch of troops in the first place, called for a much greater degree of intervention. These included Zhang Jian, a member of Wu Changqing's retinue, and the Purist Party scholar Zhang Peilun. Both submitted memorials calling for a dramatic increase in the scope and scale of Qing intervention in Korea. If not directly incorporate Korea into the Qing Empire (the desire of Zhang Jian), the Qing should at least post a high commissioner (*jianguo*) in Korea to oversee the Korean government and permanently station Qing military forces in Korean seaports. In addition, the Qing should promote the modernization of Korea's army and facilitate a greater degree of cooperation if not integration between the Qing and Korean armed forces.[2] A commentator in the newspaper *Shenbao* echoed that the Qing Empire should "abolish the Chosŏn Dynasty" if necessary.[3] Ironically, the groups in China usually labeled conservative were the advocates of radical changes that went far beyond the confines of the traditional system they claimed they were trying to defend.

Li Hongzhang, on the other hand, wanted to return as much as possible to past practice. He proved reluctant to adopt most of the radical measures advocated by the Purist Party. However, he heeded the calls, albeit unwillingly, for the continued presence of Qing troops in Korea and the facilitation of Korean military reform and modernization.

The Qing Military Presence in Korea

The 3,000 soldiers who came to Korea in August 1882 to put down the *imo* soldiers' mutiny established camps in and about Seoul. Li Hongzhang requested imperial permission to withdraw half the troops as early as spring 1883. This proposal was strongly resisted by Wu Changqing and King Ko-

---

1. Lin Mingde, "Li Hung-Chang's Suzerain Policy Toward Korea," 182; Deuchler, *Confucian Gentlemen and Barbarian Envoys*, 138–40.

2. Lin Mingde, *Yuan Shikai yu Chaoxian*, 30, 37–38; Deuchler, *Confucian Gentlemen and Barbarian Envoys*, 138–39; Bastid, *Educational Reform in Early 20th-Century China*, 21. The Purist Party even called for the invasion of Japan. Lin Mingde ("Li Hung-Chang's Suzerain Policy Toward Korea," 182) writes that "suddenly 'the idea of conquering Japan' was enthusiastically upheld."

3. Nan-Tsung Kim, "Neighbour as Mirror," 56n31.

jong, who sent a personal plea to Li urging him to keep Qing troops in Korea. However, Li eventually prevailed and General Wu and 1,500 men were transferred to Fengtian in May 1884. The remaining 1,500 soldiers were commanded by General Wu Zhaoyu (assisted by Yuan Shikai), and were stationed in Korea until all Chinese and Japanese troops were withdrawn in 1885.[4]

The presence of Qing troops in Korea gave their commanders significant influence at the Korean court. Wu Changqing and members of his staff, particularly Yuan Shikai and Huang Shilin, often paid visits to the royal court. Kojong returned the courtesy by leaving the royal compound and visiting General Wu at his headquarters. Wu did not hesitate to make suggestions and offer advice on a variety of topics including the need to establish a Korean foreign office (*t'ongni kyosŏp t'ongsangsamu amun*) and the desirability of minting a new currency.[5]

In addition to the obvious role of counterbalancing the Japanese, Qing troops served to reinforce the Qing Empire's ceremonial suzerainty over Korea. The Qing commanders made the most of King Kojong's visits to the Qing headquarters, drill grounds, and other locations. Given that Kojong rarely left the palace compound, the simple fact of his visits bolstered Qing claims to a special relationship with Korea. The presence of Chinese troops also provided a visual reminder of Qing influence and power. One Western observer was impressed by the sight of "the street guarded for a mile with Chinese soldiers, their red banners planted every ten feet" along the path that Kojong took on a visit to the Qing commander Wu Zhaoyu.

------

4. The headquarters of General Wu was established just outside the eastern gate of the royal palace. Six hundred men were stationed at this location. Four other regiments were scattered outside the gates of Seoul, one as far south as Suwŏn; see Yi Sŏn-gŭn, *Han'guksa*, 536. Martina Deuchler (*Confucian Gentlemen and Barbarian Envoys*, 140) speculates that Li's motivations included his "concern about the worsening situation in Annam" and his "desire to lower China's military profile in the peninsula as soon as possible." She also notes that Li's proposal demonstrates "that Li was not aware of how decisive a role the Chinese military had come to play in Korean politics." T. C. Lin ("Li Hung-Chang: His Korea policies," 229) notes that Li "considered the maintenance of Chinese troops in Korea as a great burden on the Chinese Government." See also Lin Mingde, *Yuan Shikai yu Chaoxian*, 40.

5. Yi Sŏn-gŭn, *Han'guksa*, 536; Deuchler, *Confucian Gentlemen and Barbarian Envoys*, 157. Kojong formally received Wu Changqing at least fourteen times during Wu's year-and-one-half stay in Korea; see *KS*, July 26, 1882–Feb. 20, 1884 (KJ 19.7.13–KJ 21.1.24).

Qing troops also participated in various ceremonies, such as the royal procession to a new palace.[6]

Although one British observer had nothing but praise for the deportment and behavior of the Chinese soldiers and their leaders, declaring them "to be on the best of terms with the populace," others noted that relations between occupiers and occupied were not always peaceful. When the troops first arrived in Korea, only several executions ordered by Yuan Shikai stopped the soldiers from plundering the local inhabitants.[7] The American doctor-missionary Horace Allen often complained of the behavior of the "rough" Chinese soldiers but was willing to treat the wounds they received from clashes with Japanese soldiers or Koreans.[8] The behavior of his troops was such that General Wu wrote a letter to Lucius Foote, the first American minister in Korea, apologizing for "the rude actions of our Chinese soldiers" and promising swift punishment of any Chinese offenders.[9]

One curious incident involving Chinese soldiers and their Korean hosts took place in early 1884. On January 30, the newly established Korean newspaper, the *Hansŏng sunbo*, reported that a Chinese soldier had wounded the owner of a Seoul pharmacy and had shot and killed the pharmacist's son.[10] A thorough investigation conducted by both Chosŏn and Qing authorities failed to locate the culprit. After the publication of the story, Chen Shutang, the newly appointed Qing commissioner of trade in Korea, wrote a stern letter to the Chosŏn Foreign Office. In it he criticized the *Hansŏng sunbo*, a semi-official publication, for broadcasting half-truths before the full facts were known and insisted that the paper and the Korean government be prepared to make a full apology once the case was fully resolved.[11]

---

6. Kim Wŏn-mo, ed., *Allen ŭi ilgi*, 436–37, 453.

7. Hall to Parkes, in *British Documents*, 2: 120; Jerome Ch'en, *Yuan Shikai*, 6. The plundering on the part of Qing troops may have been a result of the general lack of a commissariat in Qing armed forces, a fact that usually meant that "troops in the field had to find their own provisions" (Paine, *The Sino-Japanese War*, 142).

8. Kim Wŏn-mo, ed., *Allen ŭi ilgi*, 444, 454, 457, 464. In March 1885, Allen sent a bill to the Qing commissioner of trade, Chen Shutang, for $215, which was for 43 calls to wounded Chinese soldiers at $5 a call. Chen also sent "two jars of preserves" to the Allen family as thanks for Horace Allen's tending to wounded Chinese (ibid., 433, 455).

9. Kuksa p'yŏnch'an wiwŏnhoe, *The Collected Letters of Yun Tchi Ho*, 226–27.

10. *Hansŏng sunbo*, no. 10, Jan. 30, 1884.

11. Chen Shutang to Chosŏn Bureau of Information (Chosŏn pangmun sunboguk), Apr. 13, 1884 (KJ 21.3.18), *Ch'ŏngan*, 1: 64. See also Chen Shutang to Kim Pyŏng-si,

Months later, the culprit still at large, the paper published a proclamation of Chen Shutang which made the rather tenuous claim that the culprit was actually a Korean vagabond who happened to be wearing Chinese-style clothing.[12] In a private letter to Chen, the Korean Foreign Office wondered how a Korean vagabond could mimic a Chinese accent so fluently and how he had managed to obtain a Western-style gun.[13] Still, Qing pressure was sufficient for the paper to publish Chen's explanation of the affair and may have resulted in the ouster of the paper's Japanese publisher, Inoue Kakugorō.[14]

Qing-Chosŏn Military Cooperation

In addition to maintaining a military presence on Korean soil, the Qing Empire also facilitated efforts to improve Chosŏn Korea's own armed forces. Li Hongzhang, ever eager to reduce the number of Qing troops in Korea, was willing to accommodate calls for assistance to Korean efforts to modernize its military because he hoped that Korea would eventually prove able to defend itself, thus obviating the need for Qing troops on the peninsula. As part of this plan to assist Korea's self-strengthening, the Qing Empire allowed Korean students to travel to China and study the best in armaments manufacturing that the Qing Empire had to offer. In addition, Qing officers trained Korean troops in Korea itself.

Chosŏn Korea had requested Qing assistance in improving Korea's army well before Qing troops first arrived in Korea. An official request to allow Korean students to travel to China to study came from King Kojong in August 1880. Bureaucratic wrangling and logistical problems delayed the actual dispatch of Korean students until 1882, when the scholar-official Kim Yun-sik led a group of 87 students to study at the Tianjin Arsenal.[15]

Apr. 13, 1884 (KJ 21.3.18), *Ch'ŏngan*, 1: 64–65; and Kim Pyŏng-si to Chen Shutang, Apr. 19, 1884 (KJ 21.3.24), *Ch'ŏngan*, 1: 71–72.

12. *Hansŏng sunbo*, no. 18, Apr. 16, 1884.

13. Kim Pyŏng-si to Chen Shutang, Apr. 19, 1884 (KJ 21.3.24), *Ch'ŏngan*, 1: 71–72.

14. Conroy, *The Japanese Seizure of Korea*, 140–41.

15. The Tianjin Arsenal began to produce Remington-type rifles and ammunition in 1876, and by the late 1870s, its production of munitions such as powder, cartridges, and artillery ammunition was greater than that of even the famed Jiangnan Arsenal. Korean students as well as officials stationed at the Korean legation in Tianjin often consulted with Fan Junde and Wang Dejun, the managers of the two "bureaus" of the Tianjin Arsenal, with questions concerning production and the establishment of a munitions

These students were allowed to travel to Tianjin by sea, one of the first pieces of evidence of a willingness to reconsider the centuries-old ban on maritime transportation between the Qing Empire and Korea. A smaller delegation of Korean students was sent to Tianjin in 1883, and another mission to Shanghai seems to have been considered if not sent in early 1884.[16]

The Qing Empire was also instrumental in the establishment of the Machine Hall (Kigiguk), Chosŏn Korea's first domestic armaments factory.[17] Prominent Korean officials supervised the project with the assistance of Yuan Rongcan and three other Chinese advisers invited to Korea for the express purpose of assisting operations in the Hall.[18] In addition, the Chosŏn government borrowed money from a variety of Chinese sources to

---

factory in Korea. See Thomas L. Kennedy, "Li Hung-chang and the Kiangnan Arsenal, 1860–1895"; and Kim Chŏng-gi, "1876–1894 nyŏn Ch'ŏng ŭi Chosŏn chŏngch'aek yŏn'gu," 36. Training in Tianjin focused on the production of small arms and ammunition. However, the students' stay in Tianjin was cut short, since most returned home once they received news of the 1882 mutiny. This short-lived training must have been somewhat effective because several of the students would later play prominent roles in the Machine Hall (Kigiguk; established in 1883), the Telegraph Bureau (Chŏnboguk; established in 1885), and the T'ongni kimu amun and its successors. See Kim Chŏng-gi, "1876–1894 nyŏn Ch'ŏng ŭi Chosŏn chŏngch'aek yŏn'gu," 37.

16. In December 1883, the Korean president of the Foreign Office, Min Yŏng-mok, wrote requesting passports for Yi Kyu-wŏn, Kim Wan-sik, and Kim Hak-sŏng to travel to Shanghai to study armaments (Min Yŏng-mok to Chen Shutang, Jan. 1, 1884 [KJ 20.12.4], *Ch'ŏngan*, 1: 16). The Qing commissioner of trade, Chen Shutang, replied that he would forward the request to the relevant authorities in Shanghai (Chen Shutang to Min Yŏng-mok, Jan. 2, 1884 [KJ 20.12.5], *Ch'ŏngan*, 1: 16). There is, however, no further correspondence concerning this mission.

17. Manufacture of cartridges and other munitions as well as the repair of weapons was conducted in the Machine Hall largely with hand tools; see Deuchler, *Confucian Gentlemen and Barbarian Envoys*, 156, 268*n*7; Cho Ki-Jun, "The Impact of the Opening of Korea on Its Commerce and Industry," 39; Kuksa p'yŏnch'an wiwŏnhoe, *Kojong sidaesa*, 2: 447; and Kim Chŏng-gi, "1876–1894 nyŏn Ch'ŏng ŭi Chosŏn chŏngch'aek yŏn'gu," 36–38.

18. Korean officials associated with the Machine Hall constitute a veritable who's who of prominent scholar-officials of the 1880s, such as Min Yong-ik, Kim Yun-sik, Yun T'ae-jun, Pak Chŏng-yang, Yi Cho-yŏn, Pyŏn Wŏn-gyu, Han Kyu-jik, Paek Nak-non, An Chŏng-ok, Kim Myŏng-gyun, and Ku Tŏk-hui (Kuksa p'yŏnch'an wiwŏnhoe, *Kojong sidaesa*, 2: 449).

purchase weapons, munitions, military equipment, and military-related literature.[19]

Military Training Under Qing Supervision

After the violent expression of anti-Japanese sentiment among the Korean populace during the 1882 riots, few Chosŏn officials thought it prudent to request the services of another Japanese drill instructor. However, the need for military training along more modern lines was still evident. Therefore, the Korean court turned to the Qing Empire for assistance. The fact that a ready supply of Qing military officers was stationed in Korea made the utilization of them for training purposes all the easier.

Kojong renewed his requests for Qing assistance in military training when he sent a delegation to Tianjin to express thanks for the Qing aid in suppressing the soldiers' mutiny. Acknowledging the need for Korean self-strengthening, the Qing agreed to provide assistance. Immediately following the suppression of the 1882 mutiny, Yuan Shikai met with Korean officials and hammered out a plan to equip and train two units of 500 men

---

19. In 1882, Kim Yun-sik arranged for a 3,000-*liang* loan from the Qing Empire for the purpose of facilitating the purchase of a wide range of military equipment. Kim returned from Tianjin with 62 different items including gun caps, corrosive acids, chemical testing equipment, gun repair equipment, a crane, electrical equipment, and materials to make gun caps, gunpowder, and bullets. He also brought back books on 53 subjects ranging from chemistry and mathematics to military tactics. A year later, Kim Myŏng-gyun, a member of the Korean legation in Tianjin, spent upward of 10,000 *liang* on equipment and tools ordered from Shanghai. Korean purchases continued with the 1884 arrival in Tianjin of Pyŏn Wŏn-gyu. Not only did Pyŏn repay outstanding debts accrued by earlier buying trips, but he arranged for further purchases of equipment and munitions, including gun caps and training rifles, and 2,000 pounds of bullets and powder. See Li Hongzhang to Zongli yamen, Mar. 19, 1884 (GX 10.2.22), *ZRHGX*, 1348; Kim Chŏng-gi, "1876–1894 nyŏn Ch'ŏng ŭi Chosŏn chŏngch'aek yŏn'gu," 37; and Min Yŏng-mok to Chen Shutang, Feb. 2, 1884 (KJ 21.1.25), *Ch'ŏngan*, 1: 32. The Koreans received financial assistance and advice from Chinese officials in Tianjin. Director Wang Dejun of the Tianjin Arsenal arranged for a Korean purchase of sulfuric acid and paid the freight insurance for shipments back to Korea. Korean officials and students also regularly borrowed money from local Qing officials, even for expenses not directly related to arms purchases. For a detailed list of Qing loans to Korean officials, see Chen Shutang to Min Yŏng-mok, Feb. 18, 1884 (KJ 21.1.22), *Ch'ŏngan*, 1: 29–30. See also *KS*, June 15, 1883 (KJ 20.5.11).

each.[20] These Korean troops were supplied with arms donated by the Qing, including 10 twenty-pound cannons, 1,000 Peabody-Martini rifles, and generous amounts of munitions and supplies.[21]

Training was conducted along the pattern established in the Chinese Huai Army. Korean officials were attached to each unit, but actual drill instruction was managed by the Chinese officers.[22] By November 1882, they felt sufficiently confident of their work to put on a display for King Kojong. The king was impressed with the precision of the marching and the competence with which the soldiers handled their weapons. He reserved special praise for Yuan Shikai, declaring that the young Chinese officer clearly "knows how to train." Kojong even requested that Yuan be made marshal of the new army rather than merely the commander of one 500-man unit. This proposal, however, was rejected by Wu Changqing.[23]

Kojong later requested that the Qing officers expand their training operations to include 500 soldiers stationed on the strategically important island of Kanghwa. The Kanghwa contingent was reorganized under Qing direction in January 1883. Korean officers were sent to Seoul for training, and the organization of the new unit on Kanghwa mirrored that of the Chinese-trained units in Seoul. However, rather than the Chinese Huai Army methods, the Kanghwa unit was trained using newer British and German methods.[24]

———

20. In the planning sessions, Yuan emphasized the importance of a strong Korean force as a defense against Japanese encroachment and called for fiscal austerity to help pay for the proposed reforms; see Lin Mingde, *Yuan Shikai yu Chaoxian*, 29–31.

21. Li Hongzhang to Zongli yamen, Oct. 8, 1882 (GX 8.8.27), *ZRHGX*, 976; Li Hongzhang to Zongli yamen, Nov. 12, 1882 (GX 8.10.2), *ZRHGX*, 1016–17; Li Hongzhang to Zongli yamen, Jan. 18, 1883 (GX 8.12.10), *ZRHGX*, 1090.

22. Yuan Shikai directly commanded one unit but left the actual training to Wang Degong, a Chinese officer who had experience in Germany. This unit was stationed and trained just outside the Qing army headquarters near the main gate to Kyŏngbok Palace. The other unit was commanded by Zhu Xianmin and trained by He Zengzhu and was stationed in Seoul near the Tongbyŏl Palace; see Wang Bogong, *Quanlu suibi*, 9–10.

23. Lin Mingde, *Yuan Shikai yu Chaoxian*, 32; Jerome Ch'en, *Yuan Shih-k'ai*, 9. For a description of the rather harsh training methods utilized by Wang Degong, see Wang Bogong, *Quanlu suibi*, 9–10. Although Wu Changqing was a friend of Yuan Shikai's adopted father, there apparently was some tension between Yuan and Wu in Korea (Wang Bogong, *Quanlu suibi*, 8–9).

24. While surveying the troops on Kanghwa Island, Yuan Shikai met Tang Tingshu, who, along with some British mining experts, was on the island surveying mining prospects. Yuan and Tang agreed that if any mining operations on the island proved profit-

Relations between the newly organized units and the old-style troops were less than cordial. Zhou Jialu, a member of Wu Changqing's retinue, noted that the old-style troops deeply resented the higher pay received by the Chinese-trained units. Zhou feared that this resentment might turn into outright conflict.[25] In addition, the new units became a battleground for the ongoing conflict between the Min clan and other Korean elites. The Korean officers attached to the Chinese-trained units initially included a number who had received some military instruction in Japan. However, once Min Yŏng-ik became the Korean commander of the Right Barracks, he managed to oust Sŏ Chae-p'il and the other Japanese-trained instructors and replace them with additional Chinese instructors.[26]

Qing Advisers in Korea

During the period 1882–85, in addition to military advice and training, the Qing Empire also dispatched advisers to assist the Korean government. The practice of utilizing foreign advisers in important positions was hardly a new one for the Qing Empire. Sometimes willingly, sometimes not, the Qing Empire had employed foreign officials and advisers in a number of key institutions, particularly those that dealt with foreign commerce and relations. When the Chosŏn court asked for assistance and advice, the decision to dispatch advisers was, therefore, a rather natural response.

The most prominent of the advisers during this period was Paul Georg Moellendorff, a Prussian employee of the Chinese Imperial Maritime Customs Service. Moellendorff was instrumental in the establishment of a maritime customs service in Korea. Two Chinese students, who had recently returned from study in America, Tang Shaoyi and Wu Zhongxian, were also sent to Korea to assist Moellendorff; they were later joined by at least four more returned students from the United States. Moellendorff was also active in a number of other arenas, including negotiation of tariff regulations with Japan, the establishment of a new mint, the operation of the Machine Hall, the introduction of Western agricultural techniques to Korea, and the establishment of a foreign-language school. In addition to functioning as the inspector general of the new customs service,

---

able, part of the money would be used to assist in the training of the cash-poor Korean troops there; see Lin Mingde, *Yuan Shikai yu Chaoxian*, 32–33.

25. Ibid., 33.

26. Deuchler, *Confucian Gentlemen and Barbarian Envoys*, 203–4, 281n14;

Moellendorff served as a vice minister (*ch'amp'an*) in the newly created Foreign Office.[27]

To complement Moellendorff's role in foreign affairs, Ma Jianchang, a brother of Ma Jianzhong, was sent to advise the Chosŏn Kingdom in managing its relations with foreign powers. A Jesuit priest and diplomat (he had served in Tokyo before coming to Korea), Ma had high hopes for the assistance he could render to Korea. Noting that outside powers had in the past taken advantage of Korea's ignorance of international law and had acted "haughtily," he confidently declared that his advice would help Korea avoid problems in the future. His bold expectations reflect a confidence in the Qing Empire's knowledge and ability to meet the West on its own terms: "Whatever ability they [foreign diplomats] have, I have; whatever knowledge they have, I have; when, in the future, they act haughtily, we can restrain them with law. Before long, they will behave properly." He established a good rapport with Kojong and was appointed to a high-level domestic position in the powerful State Council (Ŭijŏngbu) in March 1883.[28]

These high-level advisers served to augment the Qing Empire's power and influence in Korea. Their advice was not, however, always well received by their Korean hosts. Ma Jianchang complained of what he described as the duplicity and timidity of the Korean officials he worked with. When they received the detailed plans for reform Ma presented to them, they failed to act on them, citing the need for additional deliberations, causing Ma to fume that "a hundred plans are useless if they are not carried out." After only three frustrating months, Ma traveled to Tianjin, reported to Li Hongzhang, and requested not to be sent back to Korea. Li agreed to recall Ma and explained his decision by declaring that it was not suitable for officials of a suzerain to accept appointments in the government of a vassal state.[29]

This explanation of events illustrates one of the more difficult challenges that confronted Li Hongzhang: how to maximize Qing interests through informal rule while avoiding ever greater responsibilities that inexorably lead toward formal colonization. When he dispatched Ma Jianchang, as well as other Chinese advisers including Wang Bogong, Tang

---

27. For more on Moellendorff, see Yur-bok Lee, *West Goes East*; and Leifer, "Paul-Georg von Mollendorff and the Opening of Korea."

28. Zhang Ruogu, *Ma Xiangbo xiansheng nianbu*, 139–40.

29. For Li's recall of Ma Jianchang, see *ZRHGX*, 1140–42; and Zhang Ruogu, *Ma Xiangbo xiansheng nianbu*, 146–47; see also Wang Bogong, *Quanlu suibi*, 12–13.

Shaoyi, and Wu Zhongxian, to Korea to advise the Korean government (all of them traveled to Korea on the same boat as Moellendorff), he explicitly instructed them to emphasize that they were stationed in Korea at the express request of the Korean king. This was because Li feared that the unsolicited dispatch of Chinese officials to Korea not only contravened the traditional policy of noninterference but also might invite a Japanese response.[30] However, the thought of a Qing official serving the Korean government in any official capacity disturbed those who regarded as anathema any threat to the Qing Empire's superior position in the hierarchical Sino-Korean relations. Recalling Ma Jianchang may have pleased some of the Purist Party offended at the thought of a Chinese official serving in the Korean government, but it did little to enhance the Qing's practical influence in the peninsula.

The case of Moellendorff presented a different type of problem. Li Hongzhang had personally selected Moellendorff but was uneasy about the close ties between the Prussian and Robert Hart, the inspector general of the Chinese Imperial Maritime Customs. His fears of undue collusion between Hart and Moellendorff were not realized, but Moellendorff proved much more treacherous to Qing interests. In 1885, Li learned that Moellendorff was playing an instrumental role in the Korean effort to seek a secret alliance with Russia. Outraged at this flagrant violation of his instructions, Li recalled Moellendorff in December 1885.

The advisers dispatched to Korea represented, in many ways, the cream of the crop of those responsible for the Qing Empire's own efforts at reform and self-strengthening. Li Hongzhang, one of the chief architects of self-strengthening in the Qing Empire, used some of the best talent available to project Qing influence in Korea and assist Korean reform.[31] He utilized Ma Jianzhong, the first Chinese to study politics and law and obtain a degree in France, to mediate Korea's negotiations with the United States and other Western powers. He dispatched military officers such as Wang Degong who had first-hand experience with European military practices. He sent Moellendorff, a member of the Chinese Imperial Maritime Customs Service, one of the most efficient bureaucratic institutions in the Qing Empire, to establish a similar institution in Korea. Moellendorff was

---

30. Wang Bogong, *Quanlu suibi*, 12–13.

31. For various assessments of Li Hongzhang's self-strengthening measures, see Chu and Liu, *Li Hung-chang and China's Early Modernization*.

assisted by some of the first Chinese students to study in the United States. Gunboats of Li's Northern (Beiyang) Fleet often visited Korean ports. The products of the arsenals in Tianjin and Shanghai, the most modern in the Qing Empire, were given to Korea to assist military strengthening and reform. In short, the Qing Empire's policies in Korea were intimately bound up with its own self-strengthening efforts.

Commercial Warfare and Chinese Commerce in Korea

In late 1883, Gong Liande, a young Shandong merchant, arrived in Seoul. With only a small amount of capital, 60 taels (*liang*) of silver, he set up a tiny shop in one of the city's market districts to sell thread, matches, pipes, hand towels, and other sundries. Gong's expectations for this venture may have been evident in the name he chose for his business, Gongshenghe, which has connotations of great prosperity and success. His expectations were met and exceeded more swiftly than he could have imagined. Less than two months after he established his business, Gong was able to purchase a large piece of property in Seoul for the sum of 1,270 taels.[32] Gong was part of a growing influx of Chinese who came to Korea to live and do business. Chinese from Guangdong, Zhejiang, Jiangsu, Jiangxi, Hubei, Hunan, Zhili, Anhui, Henan, and Shandong, as well as the cities of Shanghai and Tianjin, were to be found in Korea after 1882.

In some respects, Gong's success in Korea can be seen as not unlike the commercial success of Overseas Chinese (*huaqiao*) in many other parts of Asia. There are some key differences, however, between the Chinese who came to Korea in the 1880s and their counterparts in Southeast Asia and elsewhere. Unlike many Chinese in other parts of Asia in previous periods, Chinese sojourners and migrants traveled to Korea with the express permission, even encouragement, of the Chinese government, in this case, the Qing Empire. Before the late nineteenth century, Chinese who left China proper were officially regarded as "deserters," "criminals," and "potential traitors" (appellations that go back at least to the Ming period) tainted by their commercial dealings and their contact with the West.[33] By contrast,

---

32. For a brief description of Gong and his success, see Qin Yuguang, *Lü Han liushinian jianwenlu*, 23. For Gong's property purchase, see Chen Shutang to Kim Yunsik, Mar. 8, 1885 (KJ 22.1.22), *Ch'ŏngan*, 1: 232–33.

33. Yen, *Coolies and Mandarins*, 18–22.

those Chinese who traveled to Korea benefited from the Qing Empire's growing appreciation of the need to protect the lives and interests of Chinese abroad. Moreover, official support for migration in Korea came more swiftly and forcefully than in many if not most other areas.[34] Chinese in Korea enjoyed consular representation almost as soon as they first arrived in Korea in the early 1880s. This contrasts with the Philippines, where repeated requests for consular protection from Chinese residents were granted only in 1898.[35]

In short, the Chinese commercial community came to Korea at the explicit invitation of the Qing Empire. Heeding the calls of the treaty-port elite in Korea, Li Hongzhang went to great lengths to facilitate the creating of a diplomatic, legal, and physical infrastructure in Korea to protect and support the efforts of Chinese merchants there. Korea was a case of the Qing Empire's taking "commercial warfare" (*shangzhan*) beyond the confines of the Empire itself.

Chen Shutang and the Establishment of an Official Qing Presence in Korea

The task of taking advantage of the opportunities afforded by the 1882 Regulations for Maritime and Overland Trade Between Chinese and Korean Subjects fell to Chen Shutang. Chen was on the China Merchants steamer *Xingxin* when it dropped anchor off Inch'ŏn in 1882. The exact nature of his activities in Korea on his December 1882 trip to Korea is not clearly known.[36] However, Chen did have a personal audience with King

---

34. Even before the completion of the 1882 Regulations for Maritime and Overland Trade, Chinese newspapers such as *Shenbao* were discussing trade prospects in Korea. According to Nan-tsung Kim ("Neighbour as Mirror," 56*n*29; citing *Shenbao*, 31.3.1882, p. 2; 23:6.1882, p. 1; 8.7.1882, p. 1; 22.7.1882, p. 1; 27.7.1882, p. 1), "Hopes for a swift Chinese success on the Korean market were raised by analyses of Japanese difficulties in the Korea trade. It was noted with satisfaction that the Japanese balance of trade was negative, and that the combination of Korean anti-Japanese sentiment . . . and Japanese overbearing [behavior] made for an excellent starting position for Chinese merchants."

35. This in spite of the fact that the Chinese in the Philippines were far more numerous (at least in the 1880s) and had suffered far more at the hands of both the local authorities and the general populace than had the Chinese in Korea; see Wilson, "Ambition and Identity."

36. For Korean acknowledgment of the arrival of Tang Tingshu, Chen Shutang, Moellendorff, and others, see *KS*, Dec. 14, 1882 (KJ 19.11.5).

Kojong on January 11, 1883, and returned from his trip to Korea having become, in Li Hongzhang's words, "quite familiar with the conditions and the people there."[37]

Li Hongzhang called for the stationing of a commissioner of trade in Korea in mid-1883. His first choice for the position was He Ruchang, the Qing minister in Tokyo, but his services in Japan were considered indispensable.[38] Li then turned to Chen Shutang, an expectant circuit intendant (*heru daotai*) who had served as a consul in San Francisco. The Guangdong native had lived in the United States for ten years and was regarded as "sincere, honest, upright, intelligent, well trained," and "well versed in commercial matters." Li noted that commerce in San Francisco had flourished under Chen's direction and that the local Chinese merchants seemed to have approved of his services.[39] Li proposed that Chen be sent to Korea to "manage trade." As such, his duties would include writing annual reports on the numbers of Chinese in Korea and the amount of trade conducted by them, constructing official buildings in Seoul and the treaty ports, and conferring and consulting with Korean officials. An imperial edict approved Li's choice on August 22, 1883; Chen arrived in Seoul on October 16 and took up his official duties on October 20.[40]

Although Chen's official title implies that he was to focus on the commercial aspects of the new Qing-Chosŏn relationship, he also sought to act as a Qing diplomatic representative. Soon after his arrival in Seoul, he attempted to enhance the position and prestige of the Qing Empire in Korea by issuing a proclamation that declared "Korea is a dependency of China" and noted that because Korea was opening commercial relations with various nations, the Qing Empire had "issued trade regulations benefiting

---

37. Board of Personnel to Zongli yamen, Aug. 23, 1883 (GX 9.7.21), *ZRHGX*, 1183; Li Hongzhang to Zongli yamen, Aug. 23, 1883 (GX 9.7.21), *ZRHGX*, 1184; Li Hongzhang to Zongli yamen, Sept. 3, 1883 (GX 9.8.3), *ZRHGX*, 1185.

38. Tan Yongsheng, "Chosŏn malgi ŭi Ch'ŏngguk sangin," 24.

39. Board of Personnel to Zongli yamen, Aug. 23, 1883 (GX 9.7.21), *ZRHGX*, 1183; Tan Yongsheng, "Chosŏn malgi ŭi Ch'ŏngguk sangin," 25.

40. Zongli yamen memorial, Aug. 22, 1883 (GX 9.7.20), *ZRHGX*, 1181–83; Kuksa p'yŏnch'an wiwŏnhoe, *Kojong sidaesa*, 2: 504; Chen Guding, *Zhong-Ri-Han bainian dashiji*, 40; Sin Pok-kyŏng and Kim Un-gyŏng, *Moellendorop'u munsŏ*, 50–51. For the Qing Empire's notification to Chosŏn Korea of Chen's impending arrival and requests for logistical assistance, see Chen Shutang to Cho Yŏng-ha, Sept. 5, 1883 (KJ 20.8.5), *Ch'ŏngan*, 1: 2–3.

Korea" and had sent Chen to manage Chinese commerce on the peninsula. He had this proclamation posted on at least one of the main gates of Seoul.[41]

The issue of Chen's precise status arose when Chen, officially designated as a "high commissioner of trade" (*zongban Chaoxian gekou shangwu*), attempted to participate in diplomatic as well as commercial affairs in Korea. Confused and disturbed by Chen's efforts to be treated on an equal basis with Western ministers, Britain's minister in Beijing (recently transferred from his post in Tokyo), Harry Parkes, requested clarification from the Qing government. The reluctant answer was that, even after an 1884 upgrade in status to "chief commissioner of diplomatic and commercial affairs for the several Korean ports" (*zongban Chaoxian gekou jiaoshe tongshang shiwu*), Chen's rank (and salary) was that of a consul-general.[42] Chen's unsuccessful efforts to assert his influence combined with an inherent proclivity for equivocation—the Korean reformer Kim Ok-kyun referred to Chen as a "boneless slug"—led many contemporary observers as well as subsequent historians to regard Chen's tenure in Korea as ineffective and of little significance, especially in comparison to the aggressive actions and far-reaching influence of his successor, Yuan Shikai.[43]

Chen was successful, however, in establishing and promoting an official Qing diplomatic and commercial presence in Korea. This presence was facilitated by the construction of official Qing buildings, by the stationing of Qing commercial officials in Korea's treaty ports, and by the negotiation and establishment of Chinese settlements in several treaty ports (the first time that the Qing obtained the same treaty-port privileges that other nations had enjoyed in China for decades). Throughout his tenure in Korea, Chen took full advantage of the privileges and opportunities afforded the Qing Empire by its unequal commercial treaty with Korea and by the introduction of multilateral imperialism to Korea. The Qing presence and privileges in Korea were resisted by the Japanese and resented by some Koreans. But much like his earlier Japanese counterpart Hanabusa Yoshimoto's

---

41. Dennett, *Americans in Eastern Asia*, 475–76.

42. Deuchler, *Confucian Gentlemen and Barbarian Envoys*, 143–44. For details on Chen's salary, see Zongli yamen memorial, Aug. 22, 1883 (GX 9.7.20), *ZRHGX*, 1181–83.

43. For the "boneless slug" designation, see Jerome Ch'en, *Yuan Shih-k'ai*, 10. Martina Deuchler (*Confucian Gentlemen and Barbarian Envoys*, 144) concludes that Chen Shutang was a "minor official," whose "exercise in 'tributary diplomacy' . . . was largely ineffective."

attempts to secure on the ground the privileges supposedly guaranteed by treaty, Chen persevered in establishing and upholding a Qing presence in the Korean capital and treaty ports.

When Chen Shutang returned to Korea in 1883 as the first Qing commissioner of trade, he traveled from Shanghai to Inch'ŏn (via Yantai) on a China Merchants Steamship Company ship, the *Yongqing*. His initial funds for operating in Korea, 100,000 taels, were obtained from the Shanghai Customs Bureau. Clearly, influential members of the Chinese treaty-port community were interested and supportive of an expanded Qing official presence in Korea. Members of Chen's retinue, some of whom arrived in Korea shortly before Chen himself, would play important roles in the expansion of the Qing presence in Korea.[44]

Soon after he assumed his post in Korea, Chen made preparations for the unprecedented step of acquiring land and constructing a permanent Chinese official building in the Korean capital. In early January 1884, he acquired a wide plot of land in Nak-tong, near the main south gate (Namdaemun) of Seoul. Over six months of construction resulted in an impressive complex; the main gate and central building were constructed in "the fashion of official Chinese buildings," and the remaining buildings in "Korean style." Additional land was acquired to connect the complex with the main road leading to Namdaemun. This complex would serve as the center of the official Qing presence in Korea and was substantially expanded during Yuan Shikai's tenure in Korea.[45]

---

44. Tan Yongsheng, "Chosŏn malgi ŭi Ch'ŏngguk sangin," 25; Li Hongzhang to Zongli yamen, Oct. 22, 1883 (GX 9.9.22), *ZRHGX*, 1206–7. Li's dispatch gave the names and duties of Chen's retinue—attendants: Chen Weikun, Li Nairong; English interpreter: Chen Baoqiu; secretaries: Chen Xueyuan, Zheng Dianjia; and messengers: Wang Jiuling, Chen Shen, Fang Kerong, Zhang Si, Liang Junxiu, and Du De. A Korean interpreter was attached to Chen's group after his arrival in Seoul. At least three of these, Li Nairong, Chen Weikun, and Chen Baoqiu, were to hold important positions at Chinese consulates in the treaty ports.

45. The exact location of the site is Seoul, Nam-bu, Hoehyŏn-bang, Nak-tong. For Chen's description of the purchase of land and subsequent construction, see Li Hongzhang to Zongli yamen, Jan. 2, 1884 (GX 9.12.5), *ZRHGX*, 1314–15; and Tan Yongsheng, "Chosŏn malgi ŭi Ch'ŏngguk sangin," 33–34. For the contracts covering the sale of the land from a Mr. Pak as well as the subsequent purchases from a Yu Song-ho and Ch'oe Tae-yong, see Chen Shutang to Min Yŏng-mok, Nov. 15, 1883 (KJ 20.10.16), *Ch'ŏngan*, 1: 7–8. Min Yŏng-mok to Chen Shutang, Nov. 18, 1883 (KJ 20.10.19), *Ch'ŏngan*, 1: 8; and Chen Shutang to Min Yŏng-mok, Feb. 21, 1884 (KJ 21.1.25), *Ch'ŏngan*, 1: 33.

Japanese Resistance: The "Dexinghao Incident"

In addition to establishing an official Qing presence in Korea, Chen Shutang also had to contend with Japanese opposition. Despite the fact that the Qing was merely asserting treaty-guaranteed privileges, Japanese officials and merchants on the ground in Korea were reluctant to relinquish their exclusive privileges in the Chosŏn Kingdom. The tradition of monopolistic, exclusive Japanese privilege and prerogative would not vanish overnight. Nowhere was this more evident than in the Japanese stronghold of Pusan.

Soon after Chen arrived in Korea, he learned that in late October 1883, a Kobe-based Chinese firm by the name of Gongxinghao, managed by one Huang Yaodong, had sent two Guangdong merchants to Pusan to open up shop there. These two brothers, Zheng Yizhi and Zheng Weisheng, brought a large stock of food and various Western goods with them and, with the assistance of Chesney Duncan, an Englishman who had come to Pusan to work for the Korean Customs Service, managed to secure the use of a building in the Japanese settlement. The Zheng brothers were soon ready to open for business under the name Dexinghao. Once their plans for opening were made known, however, they quickly encountered opposition from the local Japanese merchant community. On opening day, local Japanese merchants hovered around the entrance to the building uttering curses and threats. When the Chinese merchants ignored these not so subtle demands to refrain from doing business, a large crowd gathered by the door, blocking the entrance, and threatened to burn the goods inside the building if the business was not shut down. In the face of determined resistance from the shopkeepers, the crowd eventually dispersed, but they promised to return if Dexinghao ever opened its doors.

Fearing for their goods if not their lives, and in the absence of any Qing official in the port, the Zheng brothers appealed to the Japanese consul, Maeda Kenkichi, for protection. Maeda agreed to meet with the Chinese but declared himself unwilling to restrain the Japanese merchants, claiming that the port of Pusan, not to mention the Japanese settlement, was open only to Japanese. Dexinghao had no choice but to postpone its opening day, a decision that cost the merchants dearly.[46]

----

46. For a brief summary of the incident, see Qin Yuguang, "Hwagyo"; see also Son Chŏng-mok, *Han'guk kaehanggi tosi pyŏnhwa kwajŏng yŏn'gu*, 108. The Zheng brothers justified their appeal to Maeda by explaining that China lacked consular representation

News of the incident soon reached Seoul as well as Japan. In Japan, the Qing minister Li Shuchang reported the incident back to China, noting that he had already requested that the Japanese Foreign Ministry restrain its overzealous consul in Pusan. Li also noted that this incident was sparked at least in part by Japanese anxiety over the prospect of Chinese competition in Korea and in part by Japanese resentment at not being able to obtain all of the commercial privileges it desired in China. He suggested that Chinese settlements be established in Pusan and other open ports in Korea so as to avoid future conflicts.[47] In Seoul, Chen Shutang reached essentially the same conclusion. In November, accompanied by Moellendorff, he traveled to Pusan to investigate the situation personally. He found the Japanese, claiming traditional monopoly rights in Pusan, still resisting the opening of the Chinese shop. Chen, aided by Moellendorff and other newly appointed customs officials in Pusan, attempted to convince the Japanese consul that recent treaties superseded traditional Japanese prerogatives. He also demanded that the Japanese consul select another site for Dexinghao to use and called for reparations from the Japanese government.[48]

Official Qing communications on this issue reveal striking similarities between Qing rhetoric and that used by foreign powers in China itself. For example, Li Shuchang wrote: "Pusan is an open port. All those who have a treaty with Korea can come there to trade. How is it, then, that Chinese merchants are not allowed to do business there? This makes no sense!"[49] This is consistent with Chen Shutang's declaration that "the world has now become one family, and the various nations thereof trade with one another, exchanging each other's resources for their respective needs."[50]

While in Pusan, Chen and Moellendorff also explored potential sites for a Chinese settlement and drew up a draft for a proposed site.[51] Chen later

---

in Pusan, and they had no other alternative. For an enumeration of Dexinghao's losses, see Chen Shutang to Kim Pyŏng-si, Apr. 19, 1884 (KJ 21.3.24), *Ch'ŏngan*, 1: 73–74.

47. Li Shuchang to Zongli yamen, Dec. 29, 1883 (GX 9.12.1), *ZRHGX*, 1258–60.

48. Qin Yuguang, "Hwagyo"; Son Chŏng-mok, *Han'guk kaehanggi tosi pyŏnhwa kwajŏng yŏn'gu*, 108.

49. Li Shuchang to Zongli yamen, Dec. 29, 1883 (GX 9.12.1), *ZRHGX*, 1258–59.

50. Kiernan, *British Diplomacy in China*, 109. Noting Chen Shutang's declaration, Kiernan sardonically concluded: "China could sound very modern and sophisticated when lecturing her admiring little tributaries."

51. Chen Shutang to Min Yŏng-mok, Dec. 13, 1883 (KJ 20.11.14), *Ch'ŏngan*, 1: 13–14; Chen Shutang to Min Yŏng-mok, Jan. 15, 1884, (KJ 20.12.18), *Ch'ŏngan*, 1: 20–21; Son Chŏng-mok, *Han'guk kaehanggi tosi pyŏnhwa kwajŏng yŏn'gu*, 108.

reported to his superiors on the commercial potential of both Pusan and Wŏnsan, and of the need to send Qing officials there to protect and promote Chinese commerce. Chen noted that Chinese merchants in Japan had their eyes on the trade of goods between Hong Kong, Shanghai, and Korea, a trade that was currently dominated by Japanese merchants. He predicted that a flood of Chinese merchants would follow the posting of a Qing official in these ports.[52]

What remained was for the Qing Empire to station an official in Pusan to take care of the details of a Chinese settlement and act as Chinese merchants' first line of defense in the case of future problems. This was not accomplished until June 1884 when Chen Weikun was sent to Pusan. Consulting with the local port superintendent (*kamni*), Chen Weikun followed up on the proposals made by Chen Shutang and Moellendorff. A Chinese settlement was demarcated at Ch'ŏryang, near the Japanese settlement. A modicum of protection was thus secured for the small number of Chinese merchants who had braved Japanese opposition and had come to Pusan to trade.[53] The establishment of a Chinese settlement in Pusan was motivated

---

52. Li Shuchang to Zongli yamen, Dec. 29, 1883 (GX 9.12.1), *ZRHGX,* 1258–61. Li Shuchang attached translations of an English newspaper in Yokohama to his report on the incident. It was, apparently, important to Li that British public opinion agreed with him that the Qing Empire's treaty privileges should be aggressively pursued and protected; see Li Hongzhang to Zongli yamen, Mar. 29, 1884 (GX 10.3.3), *ZRHGX,* 1349. Chen also pointed to the need for a Japanese interpreter to facilitate better relations with the growing numbers of Japanese in Korean treaty ports. The Japanese consul in Pusan, claiming he lacked instructions from the home government, continued to oppose Chinese competition. Although he facilitated the move of Dexinghao to another location, he instructed the building's owner to raise the rent to prohibitive levels. Chinese requests for Korean intervention in the affair were singularly ineffective. The Korean Foreign Office initially chided the Chinese merchants for not consulting with the Korean port superintendent and other Korean authorities until after they got into trouble. It then duly forwarded Qing requests for mediation, resolution, and reparations to Japanese officials but apparently took no active role. Six months after the incident, Chen was still demanding reparations to no avail. See Chen Shutang to Min Yŏng-mok, Jan. 15, 1884 (KJ 20.12.18), *Ch'ŏngan,* 1: 22–23; Min Yŏng-mok to Chen Shutang, Jan. 16, 1884 (KJ 20.12.19), *Ch'ŏngan,* 1: 23; Min Yŏng-mok to Chen Shutang, Jan. 19, 1884 (KJ 20.12.22), *Ch'ŏngan,* 1: 23–24; Chen Shutang to Kim Hong-jip, Feb. 24, 1884 (KJ 21.1.28), *Ch'ŏngan,* 1: 34–35; Kim Hong-jip to Chen Shutang, Feb. 25, 1884 (KJ 21.1.29), *Ch'ŏngan,* 1: 35; Chen Shutang to Kim Pyŏng-si, Apr. 19, 1884 (KJ 21.3.24), *Ch'ŏngan,* 1: 73–74.

53. For the official announcement of Chen Weikun's appointment, see Chen Shutang to Kim Pyŏng-si, June 7, 1884 (KJ 21.5.14), *Ch'ŏngan,* 1: 101–2. There is some disagreement over the actual date of the creation of the Chinese settlement. Some scholars,

as much by symbolic concerns as by perceived opportunities for Chinese commerce there. Li Shuchang's calls for a Chinese settlement in Pusan were clearly cast in the larger context of Sino-Japanese relations and were seen as part of the process of both securing treaty-guaranteed privileges and demolishing Japan's claims to monopolistic privileges in Korea. Still, the establishment of a Chinese settlement in Pusan facilitated the greater participation of Chinese merchants, particularly those based in Japan in what was formerly a Japanese stronghold.[54]

Expanding the Chinese Presence in Inch'ŏn

The Dexinghao Incident and the Qing Empire's subsequent attempts to establish a Chinese settlement in Pusan did not distract Chen Shutang from focusing on a much more important prize: the port city of Inch'ŏn. Chen was originally sent to Korea to oversee Chinese commerce generally and also to act as the Qing commissioner of trade in both Seoul and Inch'ŏn. Chen soon reported back to his superiors that the distance between Seoul and Inch'ŏn (a journey of at least several hours on horseback) made it extremely difficult for him to oversee Chinese commerce in both places. The vast majority of Chinese merchants who came to Korea landed in Inch'ŏn. The Japanese had already established a consulate there, and the Americans were rumored to have plans to do the same in the near future. It was imperative for China to follow suit and to place an official in this in-

---

Tan Yongsheng ("Chosŏn malgi ŭi Ch'ŏngguk sangin," 36), for example, argue that the settlement was not officially established until 1887. Although there is some question concerning the actual ratification of the agreement, it is clear that signposts demarcating the settlement were erected on July 4, 1884. Chinese merchants moved in soon thereafter. Subsequent negotiations between Chinese and Korean officials seem to have dealt with particular aspects of the settlement agreement, such as the responsibilities for maintaining settlement facilities, rather than the existence of the settlement itself. For a detailed discussion of different opinions on the date of the settlement, see Son Chŏng-mok, *Han'guk kaehanggi tosi pyŏnhwa kwajŏng yŏn'gu*, 109. Upon the establishment of the settlement, there were only fourteen Chinese merchants in Korea. Four were connected to the intrepid Dexinghao business, three more bought and sold dried fish, and the occupations of the remaining seven are unknown; see ibid., 108.

54. Tan Yongsheng ("Chosŏn malgi ŭi Ch'ŏngguk sangin," 17) notes that in the second half of 1884, of the 87 Qing merchants who went to Pusan, 27 stopped briefly in Pusan and then went to Japan. An even greater proportion of the Chinese doing business in Wŏnsan were based in Japan: of the 47 Qing merchants who came to the port in mid- to late 1884, 26 were from Nagasaki.

creasingly important town. Chen suggested that his attendant, Vice Prefect Li Nairong, fill the post. Approval was soon granted, and Li took up office in Inch'ŏn on February 8, 1884.[55] Soon after his trip to Pusan, Chen Shutang traveled with Moellendorff to Inch'ŏn. While there, he surveyed the commercial potential of the port and drew up plans for the establishment of a Chinese settlement.[56] After a few months of negotiation between Li Nairong and Korean authorities, the Agreement for the Establishment of a Chinese Settlement was ratified on April 2, 1884.[57]

Although the Agreement declared that the initial preparation of the settlement was Korea's responsibility, it soon became clear that the Korean government lacked the funds and the wherewithal to proceed with any speed. Most of the settlement land was situated on fairly steep terrain. In order to expedite the preparation, 500 Qing soldiers were transferred from Seoul to Inch'ŏn and were put to work grading land and constructing roads.[58] Two prominent merchants, Tai Tinghan and Zhu Guanguang, were appointed as directors of the effort to level and prepare the settlement.[59] Still, it was over a year before the first land auction was held.

In the meantime, Chinese merchants had been entering Inch'ŏn in growing numbers. The first Chinese merchants in the port were a group that set up shop behind the Customs Office and provided food and water

---

55. Li Hongzhang to Zongli yamen, Jan. 2, 1884 (GX 9.12.5), *ZRHGX*, 1314–16; Chen Shutang to Min Yŏng-mok, Feb. 8, 1884, *Ch'ŏngan*, 1: 27.

56. Pak Kwang-song, "Inch'ŏnhang ŭi chogye e taehayŏ," 293.

57. For the full text of the agreement, see *KS*, Apr. 2, 1884 (KJ 21.3.7); Chen Shutang to Kim Hong-jip, Mar. 4, 1884 (KJ 21.2.7), *Ch'ŏngan*, 1: 35–38. For subsequent modifications of the agreement, see Kim Hong-jip to Chen Shutang, Mar. 17, 1884 (KJ 21.2.20), *Ch'ŏngan*, 1: 48–51. The agreement, which largely followed the pattern established by the Japanese settlement agreement, arranged for a Chinese settlement to be established in an uninhabited area northwest of the Customs Office and the Japanese settlement. Land in the settlement was graded according to its usefulness (the best land being on the waterfront) and would be auctioned and taxed accordingly. Once the Chinese settlement was filled, Chinese could then rent or construct buildings in the anticipated but not yet established general foreign settlement. A special municipal fund was established to meet the expenses of maintaining the settlement.

58. Son Chŏng-mok, *Han'guk kaehanggi tosi pyŏnhwa kwajŏng yŏn'gu*, 148n58.

59. Chen Shutang to Kim Pyŏng-si, May 3, 1884 (KJ 21.4.8), *Ch'ŏngan*, 1: 78. Tai Tinghan and Zhu Guanguang, both merchants with low-level purchased official titles, were not only to oversee development of the settlement but also to be consulted in other public and commercial matters such as the establishment of a hospital and the management of common properties.

for foreign ships in the harbor. Their numbers were soon augmented by
merchants who hoped to sell British textiles, Chinese silks, and other
goods. Not waiting for the official auction of land, some set to work securing permission to erect a kiln for the production of bricks as well as permission to travel to Kanghwa Island and other areas in the interior to
gather fuel for brick production.[60] The number of eager Chinese merchants in the port is indicated by the fact that when the first land auction
was held in August 1885, all of the top- and middle-grade land was immediately purchased, and only a portion of the low-grade land remained for
subsequent auctions.[61] The Chinese presence in Inch'ŏn attracted considerable attention. The Korean newspaper, the *Hansŏng sunbo*, noted that
Inch'ŏn was filled with the signboards of Chinese merchants and that piles
of their goods were everywhere. However, since the Chinese found nothing of worth to trade for their goods, payment had to be made in specie, a
fact that dismayed many customers.[62]

The influx of Chinese merchants into Inch'ŏn was indicative of the
larger flood that washed across Korea after the arrival of Qing diplomatic
and consular representatives. Although only a handful of Chinese merchants braved the Japanese stronghold of Pusan, larger numbers flocked to
Wŏnsan and more still to Inch'ŏn and Seoul.[63] Many of the first arrivals

----

60. For more on the efforts of Chinese merchants Tang Chengjiu, Wang Yixian,
and Zhang Motai to find a site for a kiln and to secure permission from the Korean
government, see Chen Shutang to Kim Hong-jip, Mar. 7, 1884 (KJ 21.2.10), *Ch'ŏngan*, 1:
39; Chen Shutang to Kim Pyŏng-si, Apr. 24, 1884 (KJ 21.3.29), *Ch'ŏngan*, 1: 76; Kim Pyŏng-si to Chen Shutang, Apr. 26, 1884 (KJ 21.4.1), *Ch'ŏngan*, 1: 77; Chen Shutang to Kim
Pyŏng-
si, May 25, 1884 (KJ 21.5.1), *Ch'ŏngan*, 1: 95; Chen Shutang to Kim Yun-sik, Aug. 10, 1884
(KJ 21.6.20), *Ch'ŏngan*, 1: 150; Kim Yun-sik to Chen Shutang, Aug. 12, 1884 (KJ 21.6.22),
Ch'ŏngan, 1: 150–151.

61. Inch'ŏn chikhalsisa p'yŏnch'an wiwŏnhoe, *Inch'ŏnsisa*, 1: 226; Son Chŏng-mok,
Han'guk kaehanggi tosi pyŏnhwa kwajŏng yŏn'gu, 148; Pak Kwang-song, "Inch'ŏnhang ŭi chogye e taehayŏ," 294.

62. The paper optimistically concluded that, when one compares the situation to
how things were before and observes the changes that are taking place on a daily basis,
it is clear that all will be rich and prosperous in less than ten years (*Hansŏng sunbo*, Jan. 30,
1884).

63. By the spring of 1884, Chen Shutang was able to report that approximately a
thousand Chinese had spent time in Korea. They included merchants from Zhejiang,
Guangdong, Shandong, and elsewhere, laborers, and assistants at the Customs Service,

were already familiar with East Asian trading patterns and networks from their previous experience living and doing business in Japan or in prominent Chinese entrepôts such as Shanghai and Hong Kong. These merchants were quick to take advantage of their intimate knowledge of markets from Hong Kong to Kobe as well as the geographical proximity of the Chinese coast to most Korean treaty ports to mount a serious challenge to the Japanese monopoly in the trade in Western manufactured goods. Chinese merchants also sought to meet the needs of Chinese soldiers and officials in Korea. In addition, the traditional tribute and border trades continued; however, their significance vis-à-vis the rapidly growing maritime trade continued to decline.

Expanding a Chinese Presence in Hansŏng (Seoul)

At the same time that Chen Shutang was working to establish an official Chinese presence in Korea's treaty ports, he also sought to protect and promote Chinese commercial interests in Hansŏng (Seoul), the capital of the Chosŏn Kingdom. The Chinese presence in Hansŏng began at gunpoint when Qing troops entered the city to quell the *imo* mutiny in 1882. The Sino-Korean trade regulations established later that year granted Chinese merchants the right to set up shop in Yanghwajin and Hansŏng.[64] The Chinese monopoly on this privilege ended with the ratification of the Korean-British treaty negotiated by Harry Parkes in late 1883. After this time, citizens of all nations who had a treaty with Korea could reside and do business in the Korean capital.

Following Chen Shutang's official arrival in Seoul in October 1883, he worked to enhance the prospects for Chinese business through, among other activities, obtaining permission for Chinese junks to sail up the Han River, aiding Chinese merchants in their efforts to rent or purchase land and buildings, and mediating between Chinese merchants and the Korean government in a wide variety of disputes. Chen's efforts did not always meet with success but they clearly helped advance Chinese commerce in Seoul.

A problem confronted by all visitors traveling to Seoul via Inch'ŏn was the overland journey. A traveler on a good horse could make the trip in

---

foreign legations, and other institutions (Li Hongzhang to Zongli yamen, Mar. 8, 1884 [GX 10.2.11], *ZRHGX*, 1337–41).

64. China, Imperial Maritime Customs, *Treaties, Conventions, Etc., Between China and Foreign States*, 2: 850.

around four hours. For those laden with goods, however, the trip went much more slowly. The absence of reliable overland transport substantially increased costs for those merchants who desired to sell goods in Seoul. In early 1883, several Shandong merchants, traveling to Korea in traditional Chinese junks, bypassed this problem by sailing up the Han River and docking at Map'o, a town on the river a few miles outside Seoul. The river passage was not without its own challenges and perils, but water transport was considerably cheaper and more convenient than the overland passage.

A problem arose in early March 1884 when some of the same junks, chartered by the Shandong merchant Li Mingjin, were detained in Inch'ŏn by the Inch'ŏn Customs Commissioner A. B. Stripling.[65] The Chinese merchants complained to Chen Shutang, who inquired of the Korean Foreign Office as to the reason for the detention.[66] Chen learned that the Koreans would not allow foreign ships to use the Han River. This prompted a series of protests from Chen. The Koreans replied that the Regulations for Maritime and Overland Trade merely allowed Chinese merchants to conduct business in Seoul; they said nothing about how they might reach the capital. When Li Mingjin sailed up the Han River in 1883, he was informed that he would not be allowed to repeat the trip.[67]

This led to a protracted debate over the meaning of the term *tongshang kou'an* (K. *t'ongsang kuam*), often rendered in English as "open port." In addition, Chinese merchants complained about the lack of space in Inch'ŏn to warehouse their goods while they arranged overland transport with the unreliable and overpriced Korean porters. Korean ships were equally unreliable and expensive, with the additional drawback of being leaky.[68] Chen also relayed to the Chosŏn Foreign Office the complaints and arguments of Li Hongzhang, who noted that prohibiting Chinese ships from traveling to Yanghwajin and Map'o was tantamount to denying the treaty-guaranteed privilege of trading in Seoul.[69]

The repeated weight of Qing protests finally caused the Korean government to allow ships of under 200 tons to ply the Han River, but only

---

65. Chen Shutang to Min Yŏng-mok, Mar. 12, 1884 (KJ 21.2.15), *Ch'ŏngan*, 1: 42–43.
66. Chen Shutang to Min Yŏng-mok, Mar. 13, 1884 (KJ 21.2.16), *Ch'ŏngan*, 1: 43–44.
67. Kim Hong-jip to Chen Shutang, Mar. 14, 1884 (KJ 21.2.17), *Ch'ŏngan*, 1: 44–45.
68. Chen Shutang to Kim Hong-jip, Mar. 24, 1884 (KJ 21.2.27), *Ch'ŏngan*, 1: 58–59.
69. Chen Shutang to Kim Pyŏng-si, May 9, 1884 (KJ 21.4.14), *Ch'ŏngan*, 1: 80–81; Chen Shutang to Kim Pyŏng-si, May 20, 1884 (KJ 21.4.25), *Ch'ŏngan*, 1: 88–89; Li Hongzhang to Zongli yamen, June 17, 1884 (GX 10.5.24), *ZRHGX*, 1396.

after they had docked in Inch'ŏn and been inspected by the Customs Service there. The same ships were required to report at Inch'ŏn again upon their return from Seoul.[70] In all, the process took as long as ten days, a fact that caused no small amount of grumbling on the part of Chen and the Chinese merchant community.[71] Chen's repeated calls for the establishment of a customs office at Map'o, which would enable Seoul-bound Chinese ships to avoid Inch'ŏn altogether, were ignored for years. It was only in 1889 that a branch of the Customs Service was established at Map'o, and the general lack of business there combined with Japanese pressure resulted in the closing of this office five years later.[72]

Chen also assisted Chinese merchants in their attempts to travel and do business in the interior. Article IV of the Sino-Korean Regulations for Maritime and Overland Trade guaranteed Chinese merchants the right to travel within Korea to purchase Korean goods.[73] Those desiring to travel to the interior were to apply to the local Qing commissioner of trade, who would, in conjunction with local Korean authorities, issue a restricted passport. Qing commissioners of trade in the treaty ports were to handle most of the requests. In the early years of an official Chinese presence on Korean soil, however, many of the requests for passports were funneled through Chen Shutang. In 1884, Chen made at least nineteen requests to permit Chinese merchants to travel to the interior, in most cases to areas in northwest Korea. A similar number of applications was made in 1885. In virtually every case, Chen's requests were granted.[74]

---

70. Kim Pyŏng-si to Chen Shutang, May 9, 1884 (KJ 21.4.14), *Ch'ŏngan*, 1: 82.

71. Chen Shutang to Kim Pyŏng-si, May 10, 1884 (KJ 21.4.15), *Ch'ŏngan*, 1: 82–83; Chen Shutang to Kim Yun-sik, July 25, 1884 (KJ 21.6.4), *Ch'ŏngan*, 1: 142–43.

72. Ch'oe T'ae-ho, "Map'o haegwanbun'guk ŭi sŏlch'i wa hyŏkp'a." Rampant smuggling at Map'o by both Chinese and Japanese prompted Henry Merrill, the chief commissioner of the Korean Customs Service, to call for the establishment of a customs office there as early as 1886.

73. China, Imperial Maritime Customs, *Treaties, Conventions, Etc., Between China and Foreign States*, 2: 850–51.

74. Article IV of the Sino-Korean Regulations for Maritime and Overland Trade also prohibited the direct sale of foreign merchandise in the interior. Given the lack of monetization in much of Korea, however, it is difficult to see how foreign merchants would have been able to obtain Korean goods except by barter. Determining the exact number of passports requested and issued is somewhat difficult because a single piece of correspondence often included multiple requests. They were generally listed under the name of the first merchant to request a passport (e.g., Tai Tinghan et al. (C. *deng*; K. *tŭng*) request passports for travel to . . .). For examples of passport requests made by

At the same time that Chen Shutang and other Chinese officials were working to establish safe havens for Chinese merchants in the treaty ports, Chinese merchants were also entering Seoul in ever-greater numbers. Chen worked to further the interests of these merchants in many ways. He assisted in property purchases, attempted to mediate in cases of disputed debt payments and theft, and aggressively defended Chinese interests in conflicts with Korean citizens and the Korean government.

As the first significant group of non-Japanese foreigners in Hansŏng, Chinese merchants fanned out through the city in search of property and buildings for lodging, business, and social organizations and activities. Chen Shutang assisted individual merchants and companies in their efforts. He was also careful to report such efforts to the Korean Foreign Office in order to secure legal sanction for the purchases. These purchases ranged in size from tiny shops in one of the city's market districts to the spacious accommodations secured for a Chinese merchant guild hall (*huiguan*).[75]

Chen also relayed the complaints and claims of Chinese merchants to the Korean Foreign Office. These sometimes centered on the failure of Koreans to repay debts owed to Chinese merchants. In some cases in which the culprits were known and quickly apprehended, such as when the Koreans Kim Yun-p'yŏng and Kim Song-bŏm tried to skip town without paying for the cases of matches they had bought from the Chinese firm Fuyuhao, Chen's requests for action by the Korean government bore swift fruit. The Kims were ordered to make restitution (there is, however, evidence of only one partial payment made to Fuyuhao). But in many cases, the Chinese demands for repayment and damages were never met.[76]

Chen also conveyed the complaints of Chinese merchants in cases of outright theft. Generally unfamiliar with their Korean surroundings and often

----

Chen Shutang, see Chen Shutang to Min Yŏng-mok, Feb. 21, 1884 (KJ 21.1.25), *Ch'ŏngan*, I: 32; Min Yŏng-mok to Chen Shutang, Feb. 22, 1884 (KJ 21.1.26), *Ch'ŏngan*, I: 34; Chen Shutang to Min Yŏng-mok, Mar. 11, 1884 (KJ 21.2.14), *Ch'ŏngan*, I: 40; Chen Shutang to Kim Pyŏng-si, Apr. 14, 1884 (KJ 21.3.19), *Ch'ŏngan*, I: 69–70.

75. While Chinese purchases of land and buildings in Seoul undoubtedly continued after 1885, this detailed reporting of property transactions ended with the appointment of Yuan Shikai as the Qing Resident in Korea. Yuan, apparently, had other things to do with his time than report to the Korean Foreign Office on property acquisitions.

76. Tan Yongsheng, "Chosŏn malgi ŭi Ch'ŏngguk sangin," 67–69. For more on the Fuyuhao case, see Chen Shutang to Kim Pyŏng-si, May 8, 1884 (KJ 21.4.13), *Ch'ŏngan*, I: 79–80; Chen Shutang to Kim Pyŏng-si, May 16, 1884 (KJ 21.4.21), *Ch'ŏngan*, I: 85–86; Kim Pyŏng-si to Chen Shutang, May 17, 1884 (KJ 21.4.23), *Ch'ŏngan*, I: 87–88.

more conspicuous than their Korean counterparts, Chinese merchants and businesses were easy targets for Korean burglars and bandits. During Chen Shutang's tenure, he reported no fewer than seventeen cases of major theft, robbery, and loss of goods. These cases ranged from itinerant Chinese merchants who were held up by Korean bandits as they made their way into the interior to purchase Korean goods[77] to the hapless merchant whose horse went lame on the road from Inch'ŏn to Seoul and whose bolts of heavy cloth "disappeared" when he left his cargo in search of help.[78]

Burglary in Seoul was also common. Lost or stolen goods reported by Chen Shutang include cotton textiles, silk, cowhides, beer, kerosene, tin, matches, silver, and strings of copper cash. In most cases, such as the May 1884 nighttime burglary of the Shengshenghao firm, despite Chen's persistent calls for action, no culprit was ever captured—this in spite of the fact that Chen gave a detailed listing of the stolen goods: 23 pieces of Yiyuan brand Western-style cloth (wrapped in a bolt with the characters *jicheng* written on the outside) and five jugs of Yantai beer. Reports of thefts to the Korean government virtually disappeared when Yuan Shikai succeeded Chen Shutang. This is probably due as much to the realization that appeals to the Korean Foreign Office were singularly ineffective as to any real decline in robberies of Chinese goods.[79]

---

77. See, e.g., Chen Shutang to Kim Yun-sik, July 21, 1884 (KJ 21.5.29), *Ch'ŏngan*, 1: 138; Kim Yun-sik to Chen Shutang, July 23, 1884 (KJ 21.6.2), *Ch'ŏngan*, 1: 139; Kim Yun-sik to Chen Shutang, Aug. 7, 1884 (KJ 21.6.17), *Ch'ŏngan*, 1: 149–50.

78. See Chen Shutang to Kim Hong-jip, Oct. 17, 1884 (KJ 21.8.29), *Ch'ŏngan*, 1: 188.

79. For the specifics on the Shengshenghao case, see Chen Shutang to Kim Pyŏng-si, May 21, 1884 (KJ 21.4.26), *Ch'ŏngan*, 1: 90; Kim Pyŏng-si to Chen Shutang, May 22, 1884 (KJ 21.4.27), *Ch'ŏngan*, 1: 92; Kim Pyŏng-si to Chen Shutang, June 10, 1884 (KJ 21.5.17), *Ch'ŏngan*, 1: 104; Chen Shutang to Kim Pyŏng-si, July 9, 1884 (KJ 21.5.17), *Ch'ŏngan*, 1: 126–27; For Chen Shutang's reports to the Korean Foreign Office on other cases and the Korean replies, see Chen Shutang to Kim Hong-jip, Nov. 6, 1884 (KJ 21.9.19), *Ch'ŏngan*, 1: 199; Kim Hong-jip to Chen Shutang, Nov. 7, 1884 (KJ 21.9.20), *Ch'ŏngan*, 1: 199–200; Chen Shutang to Kim Yun-sik, Jan. 31, 1885 (KJ 21.12.16), *Ch'ŏngan*, 1: 220; Chen Shutang to Kim Yun-sik, Feb. 9, 1885 (KJ 21.12.25), *Ch'ŏngan*, 1: 223; Kim Yun-sik to Chen Shutang, Feb. 12, 1885 (KJ 21.12.28), *Ch'ŏngan*, 1: 224; Chen Shutang to Kim Yun-sik, Mar. 13, 1885 (KJ 22.1.27), *Ch'ŏngan*, 1: 236–37. It is not possible at this point to determine whether the failure of the Korean government to capture thieves who robbed Chinese of their goods was due to a lack of effort or simply to a more general inability to control and prosecute crime. By most accounts, few criminals of any kind were caught and apprehended by the Korean authorities, regardless of whether their victims were natives or foreigners. There is some evidence that goods stolen from

Chen Shutang was also active in representing the claims of Chinese merchants vis-à-vis the newly established Korean Customs Service. In April 1884, he forwarded the arguments of merchants who felt that their goods were being overvalued by the customs officials in Inch'ŏn.[80] In July of the same year, he complained that Inch'ŏn customs officials were blocking Chinese-chartered Korean ships from docking at Madu, the pier nearest the newly demarcated Chinese Settlement. He proposed the creation of a system of passes and banners that would allow Korean ships to avoid interference from customs officers.[81] In the same month Chen responded to the complaints of merchants in Pusan by pressing the Korean Foreign Office to standardize tariffs in all the treaty ports.[82] In July 1885, he relayed the claims of merchants in Wŏnsan who had imported grain into the famine-stricken region on the understanding that the much-needed grain would be imported duty-free. Chen reminded the Korean government of its proclamation of a six-month moratorium on duties levied on grain imports at Wŏnsan and called for and received refunds of the duties assessed.[83]

Chen also assisted in the construction of a merchants' guild hall in Seoul. In May 1884, the nascent Chinese merchants' association negotiated to purchase the land and buildings owned by the three sons of one Yi Kyŏng-hak for this purpose. Although all three brothers initially agreed to sell their share of the family compound, at the last minute, the eldest son, Yi Pŏm-jin, suffered a change of heart and refused to sell his portion.[84] The two younger brothers, Yi Pŏm-jo and Yi Pŏm-dae, observed the agreement and sold their shares, but this left the Chinese merchants with the some-

---

Chinese firms were shipped out of the capital and sold in the hinterland to evade detection; see Han U-gŭn, *Han'guk kaehanggi ŭi sangŏp yŏn'gu*, 113.

80. Kim Hong-jip to Chen Shutang, Apr. 1, 1884 (KJ 21.3.6), *Ch'ŏngan*, 1: 61; Chen Shutang to Kim Pyŏng-si, May 20, 1884 (KJ 21.4.25), *Ch'ŏngan*, 1: 88–89; Kim Pyŏng-si to Chen Shutang, May 28, 1884 (KJ 21.5.4), *Ch'ŏngan*, 1: 97.

81. Chen Shutang to Kim Yun-sik, July 25, 1884 (KJ 21.6.4), *Ch'ŏngan*, 1: 142–43.

82. Chen Shutang to Kim Pyŏng-si, July 15, 1884 (KJ 21.5*.23), *Ch'ŏngan*, 1: 129–30.

83. Kim Hong-jip to Chen Shutang, Nov. 11, 1884 (KJ 21.9.24), *Ch'ŏngan*, 1: 201; Chen Shutang to Kim Hong-jip, Nov. 12, 1884 (KJ 21.9.25), *Ch'ŏngan*, 1: 202; Chen Shutang to Kim Yun-sik, July 7, 1885 (KJ 22.5.25), *Ch'ŏngan*, 1: 264; Kim Yun-sik to Chen Shutang, July 8, 1885 (KJ 22.5.26), *Ch'ŏngan*, 1: 264–65.

84. Yi Pŏm-jin would later be a prominent member of the "pro-Russian faction" in the Chosŏn court. Still later, he would serve as the Korean minister in Washington, DC, and Moscow.

what untenable arrangement of owning the northern and southern sections of a compound while the central section remained under other ownership. To facilitate access to the portions that they owned, the Chinese merchants pushed for the inclusion of a clause in the contract that allowed them to use the main gate and paths that led from the gate to the northern and southern sections of the compound. Less than a month after this arrangement was reached, Yi Pŏm-jin had the main gate nailed shut and denied access to the paths that led to the sections now owned by the Chinese. Repeated protests by Tai Tinghan and other Chinese merchants were met with refusals and, according to the Chinese accounts, increasingly abusive behavior from Yi Pŏm-jin.

Tai Tinghan decided to take matters into his own hands. He gathered a group of some thirty merchants and proceeded to enter Yi Pŏm-jin's house. The Chinese merchants beat Yi and dragged him to the Qing legation for "adjudication." Chen Shutang was present at the legation but, rather than involving himself directly in the case, deputized Liu Jiacong, a Qing official who would later serve as Commissioner of Trade in Wŏnsan, and two Korean officials, Sin Hak-hyu of the Board of Punishments and Han Yong-gil of the Hansŏng city police, who happened to be there on other business, to look into Tai's grievances. After interrogating all the principals, these officials essentially found in favor of the Chinese and forced Yi Pŏm-jin to write and sign a "confession" and a promise to refrain from blocking access to the "public paths" in the future.

This incident caused a firestorm of controversy and criticism of Chen Shutang and the Chinese by the Korean Government. Kim Yun-sik secretly wrote to Tianjin Customs Daotai Zhou Fu complaining of the incident. British Consul William George Aston joined in the chorus of criticism. Although Chen quibbled with the particulars of the Korean accusations, he eventually demoted Tai Tinghan and apologized for the whole affair, but relations between Chen and the Korean government were strained for some time afterward.[85]

---

85. Kuksa p'yŏnch'an wiwŏnhoe, *Kojong sidaesa*, 2: 606–7; Tan Yongsheng, "Chosŏn malgi ŭi Ch'ŏngguk sangin," 70–71; Chen Shutang to Kim Pyŏng-si, June 21, 1884 (KJ 21.5.28), *Ch'ŏngan*, 1: 111–13; Kim Pyŏng-si to Chen Shutang, June 22, 1884 (KJ 21.5.29), *Ch'ŏngan*, 1: 113–14; Chen Shutang to Kim Pyŏng-si, June 23, 1884 (KJ 21.5*.1), *Ch'ŏngan*, 1: 114–16; Kim Pyŏng-si to Chen Shutang, June 24, 1884 (KJ 21.5*.2), *Ch'ŏngan*, 1: 116–17. Some Korean sources indicate that the Korean officials Sin and Han politely demurred from participating in the extrajudicial proceedings against Yi Pŏm-jin. However, the

1884: The Kapsin *Coup*

The bad blood caused by the Yi Pŏm-jin incident, the controversy over the *Hansŏng sunbo* report of the Chinese murder of a Korean shopkeeper's son (see above), and other incidents caused no small resentment in some circles in Korea. In addition, the Qing domination of the training of the Korean army came at the expense of Korean officers and officials in general and those who had studied in Japan in particular. Among the latter group were a small number of younger officials whose plans for reform have earned them the title the "Progressives." The unwillingness of the Qing Empire to allow the Progressives to participate meaningfully in military reform contributed to the more general frustration of these officials. Unable to obtain the high positions that might allow them to implement their reform agenda, the Progressives plotted to seize power in late 1884 (the *kapsin* year in the traditional sixty-year cycle).[86]

With the encouragement of the Japanese legation in Korea (though without the express approval of the Japanese government), the leaders of the plot, most notably Pak Yŏng-hyo and Kim Ok-kyun, hoped to take advantage of the opportunity offered by the Qing Empire's involvement in an undeclared war with France. While the Qing was thus distracted, the

---

Chinese produced Yi Pŏm-jin's "confession," which was signed and witnessed by the Korean officials. All of them were summarily dismissed from their posts, as was Yi Pŏm-jin. Several months later, Tai Tinghan was accused of beating another Korean, one Yi Sun-hŭi. Chen Shutang was successful in disparaging the testimony of two Korean witnesses to the incident and in implicating one Hong Chun-guk, a shadowy Seoul criminal. See Chen Shutang to Kim Yun-sik, Aug. 13, 1884 (KJ 21.6.23), *Ch'ŏngan,* 1: 152; Kim Yun-sik to Chen Shutang, Aug. 15, 1884 (KJ 21.6.25), *Ch'ŏngan,* 1: 153–54; Chen Shutang to Kim Yun-sik, Sept. 18, 1884 (KJ 21.7.29), *Ch'ŏngan,* 1: 171; Kim Yun-sik to Chen Shutang, Sept. 18, 1884 (KJ 21.7.29), *Ch'ŏngan,* 1: 172; Chen Shutang to Kim Hong-jip, Oct. 31, 1884 (KJ 21.9.13), *Ch'ŏngan,* 1: 194; Chen Shutang to Kim Hong-jip, Nov. 5, 1884 (KJ 21.9.18), *Ch'ŏngan,* 1: 197; Kim Hong-jip to Chen Shutang, Nov. 6, 1884 (KJ 21.9.19), *Ch'ŏngan,* 1: 198; Chen Shutang to Kim Hong-jip, Nov. 28, 1884 (KJ 21.10.11), *Ch'ŏngan,* 1: 203–4; Kim Hong-jip to Chen Shutang, Dec. 1, 1884 (KJ 21.10.15), *Ch'ŏngan,* 1: 208; Chen Shutang to Cho Pyŏng-ho, Jan. 17, 1885 (KJ 21.12.2), *Ch'ŏngan,* 1: 213–14; Cho Pyŏng-ho to Chen Shutang, Jan. 18, 1885 (KJ 21.12.3), *Ch'ŏngan,* 1: 215; Chen Shutang to Kim Yun-sik, Mar. 7, 1885 (KJ 22.1.21), *Ch'ŏngan,* 1: 230.

86. For an account of the 1884 *kapsin* coup and its background, see Cook, *Korea's 1884 Incident.* See also Yŏng-ho Ch'oe, "The *Kapsin* Coup of 1884: A Reassessment."

Progressives planned to oust many of the Min faction and move Korea on a path of sweeping reform under Japanese tutelage.

The coup plotters decided to strike during a banquet held on December 4, 1884, in honor of the inauguration of Korea's first post office (Hong Yŏng-sik, a prominent Progressive, was president of the Post Office). During the banquet, a fire was started nearby, and as several of the banquet participants rushed outside to observe the conflagration, they were attacked by Korean and Japanese recruits of the coup plotters. The coup leaders rushed to the palace, informed Kojong that the Chinese were running rampant through Seoul, and coerced him into requesting Japanese protection. Kojong and his court were soon surrounded by Japanese legation troops. As the Korean commanders of the Qing-trained battalions came to the palace to protect the king, they were executed on the spot.[87] The following day, a new government was organized, and several reforms including the severing of traditional ties with the Qing Empire were announced.[88]

On learning of the coup, the Qing military and civil officials Wu Zhao-yu and Chen Shutang were indecisive and were inclined to wait for instructions from the Qing government before taking action. Yuan Shikai, on the other hand, had anticipated the coup for some time; more than two weeks earlier, he had ordered his troops "to sleep in their tunics and boots."[89] He sprang into action, ordered Qing and Korean troops to surround the palace, and attempted to visit the king personally. After a day of tense stand-off, shots were fired (who fired the first shot is still a matter of debate), and the Qing and Qing-trained Korean troops stormed the palace. In contrast to the timidity of Wu Zhaoyu, who had to be carried trembling from the field of battle, Yuan Shikai moved forward fearlessly and aggressively. In the melee, the Korean queen and the heir apparent fled the palace and sought protection in the Chinese camp. King Kojong demanded to be accorded the same privilege but was held by the coup plotters for a few more desperate hours. When it became apparent that they were hopelessly outnumbered, the Japanese troops fought their way out of the palace and retreated to Inch'ŏn, much in the same way as Japanese legation troops had fled during the 1882 *imo* mutiny. They took Kim Ok-kyun and other

---

87. *KS*, Dec. 4, 1884 (KJ 21.10.17).
88. Kim Ok-kyun, "*Kapsin* Reform Edict."
89. Jerome Ch'en, *Yuan Shih-k'ai*, 11.

Progressives with them and eventually fled to Japan.[90] Kojong was escorted by Hong Yŏng-sik to the gate of another palace, where they were met by Qing soldiers and officers. Hong was executed on the spot, and Kojong remained under Chinese protection until December 10.

In Seoul, as news of the Japanese-aided coup attempt spread, Korean mobs, crying "Death to the Japanese," attacked the Japanese legation and any other Japanese building or citizen they could find.[91] Order was fully restored only after the arrival of additional troops from China and Japan. A potential conflict between the Qing Empire and Japan was avoided by a series of negotiations. The Treaty of Hansŏng, signed in January 1885, arranged for Korean reparations to be paid to Japanese victims of the anti-Japanese rampages, an official Korean apology, and an increase in the Japanese legation guard to 1,000 men.[92] A later treaty, the Convention of Tianjin, negotiated between Li Hongzhang and Itō Hirobumi, led to the mutual withdrawal of troops, encouraged improvements in Korea's army (trained by officers from a third country), and contained a promise that both Japan and the Qing Empire would notify the other in the event of dispatching troops to Korea.[93]

From the perspective of Qing policy makers, the resolution of the *kapsin* coup attempt must have seemed a significant victory. Like many other imperialists of the day, the Qing Empire had resorted to military force to protect its interests. Qing troops and their Korean protégés united

---

90. This retreating party was escorted by Korean and Chinese troops on its way to Inch'ŏn. See Foote to U.S. Secretary of State, Dec. 17, 1884, *KAR*, 1: 100. Yuan Shikai, along with the Chosŏn officials Ŏ Yun-jung and Kim Yun-sik, also worked to prevent the mutilation of the body of Pak Yŏng-hyo's father, who was executed in the aftermath of the *kapsin* coup attempt (Yŏng-ho Ch'oe, "The *Kapsin* Coup of 1884: A Reassessment," 115).

91. Horace Allen wrote in his diary that there was some evidence of official collusion in the anti-Japanese violence. He records a translation of an official notice (*taegunju ŭi konggomun*) sent by the Hansŏng (Seoul) city *chaep'ansŏ* (court) to the Peddlers (Pobusang) Guild. It read: "The Chinese Emperor silently aids us, and the Chinese General [Yuan Shikai] has summoned his soldiers and fought. . . . We now as volunteers must assist the Chinese, gritting our teeth in our desire to destroy the Japanese villains" (Kim Wŏn-mo, ed., *Allen ŭi ilgi*, 420).

92. *KS*, Jan. 9, 1885 (KJ 21.11.24). The treaty used the Meiji and Korean Chosŏn calendars but not the Qing calendar.

93. China, Imperial Maritime Customs, *Treaties, Conventions, Etc., Between China and Foreign States*, 2: 588–89, 706.

to quell a serious threat to the Korean monarch's autonomy and a threat to the stability of the region. Despite the fearful vacillation of some of the army's commanders, enough of the troops, particularly those led by Yuan Shikai, displayed sufficient aggressiveness and forcefulness to put to flight the Korean and Japanese participants in the coup. One of the most significant threats to the security of the Qing Empire, Japanese expansion into Northeast Asia, was checked for the next decade.

The successful suppression of the *kapsin* coup attempt represents one of the few victories of the Self-strengthening Movement in the military arena, either in China or abroad. In terms of the development of the Korean army itself, Qing training and assistance, whatever its shortcomings, was at least as substantive and effective as anything that was to follow for the next six decades, if not more so. However, the cases of Moellendorff and Ma Jianchang demonstrated that the use of advisers did not always achieve desired goals. The Qing Empire's attempt to project its influence through foreign advisers foundered on Korean resistance, differences of opinion in China, and the personalities and behavior of the advisers themselves.

In the cases of both military reform and Qing advisers in Korea, the desire of Qing statesmen such as Li Hongzhang to assist in Korean self-strengthening efforts was motivated in large part by the hope that a stronger Korea would improve the security of the Qing Empire. Many Korean officials agreed with the need for self-strengthening reforms, although their emphasis was naturally on guaranteeing the security of Korea itself. Neither Li Hongzhang nor the majority of Korean officials seriously entertained the idea of formally incorporating Korea into the Qing Empire. However, the aftermath of the *kapsin* coup attempt necessitated an adjustment in the mechanisms of the Qing informal empire in Korea.

FIVE

The Residency of Yuan Shikai

In October 1885, another Chinese ship arrived in Inch'ŏn bearing passengers whose fates would be intertwined with those of the Qing Empire and Chosŏn Korea. The Taewŏn'gun returned after three years of exile in China. Demonstrating his Confucian filial piety, Kojong had repeatedly requested his father's repatriation despite the Taewŏn'gun's proven willingness to remove his son from power in the past.[1] Chafing under house arrest south of Beijing in Baoding, the Taewŏn'gun convinced his captors that he had experienced a change of heart and would cooperate with the Qing Empire.[2] Li Hongzhang, the Qing official instrumental in securing the Taewŏn'gun's return, was not motivated solely by Confucian ethics; he also hoped that the return of the king's father would prove useful to Qing interests by providing a counterbalance to the growing power of Queen Min's family in the Chosŏn government. The Min clan, particularly its unofficial spokesman, Min Yŏng-ik, opposed the Taewŏn'gun's return, but Kojong did not heed their protests, and the old regent was escorted back to Seoul on October 5 by 40 Qing soldiers and was greeted enthusiastically by large crowds. The queen and her family made their displeasure known by ordering the execution of three officials implicated in the Taewŏn'gun-

---

1. For examples of Kojong's expressions of concern about his father and his hopes for his swift return, see *KS*, Dec. 14, 1882 (KJ 19.11.5), Dec. 15, 1882 (KJ 19.11.6), and Dec. 18, 1884 (KJ 21.11.2).

2. The Taewŏn'gun still had his doubts about Korea's opening to relations with foreigners. In a discussion with his Chinese captors in Baoding, he was asked why Korea should not have relations with the outside world. He replied that the Qing Empire had had increased relations with foreigners for decades but little good had come of it (Wang Bogong, *Quanlu suibi*, 15).

directed attempt to kill the queen during the 1882 *imo* mutiny.[3] Nevertheless, the Taewŏn'gun was back in Korea to stay. He would be a permanent
fixture in a series of plots and intrigues—both real and imagined—for the
next decade.[4]

On board the Chinese ship with the Taewŏn'gun was Henry F. Merrill,
the Qing-appointed successor to Moellendorff as overseer of the Korean
Customs Service. Frustrated with the independent-minded activities of
Moellendorff, especially his attempts to negotiate a secret Russo-Korean alliance, Li Hongzhang and other Qing policy makers carefully delimited
Merrill's duties. He was to focus solely on the Customs Service and refrain
from engaging in political activities. His arrival signaled the continued albeit
considerably diminished determination of the Qing Empire to use advisers
to the Chosŏn government to protect and promote its interests in Korea.

Yuan Shikai returned to Korea on the same ship. Having previously
served in Korea as an officer in the Qing army and as an instructor of Korean troops, Yuan returned to Korea as the chief representative of the
Qing. He would be instrumental in the implementation, and in some cases
instigation, of Qing imperialist policies in Korea for the next decade. He
would vigorously press the Qing Empire's claims to a special suzerain-
vassal relationship with Chosŏn Korea, notwithstanding Korea's putative
entrance into the "family of nations." Despite grumbling from some cor-
ners, these claims were recognized, tacitly if not overtly, by most of the
foreign powers in Korea. In addition, Yuan Shikai would facilitate the expansion of Qing imperialism in Korea in ways never before imagined. This
two-pronged attempt to maintain traditional prerogatives and pursue new
power and privileges (while at the same time strenuously denying responsibility for Korean affairs) would lead to an anomalous situation in which
Korea was simultaneously a Qing vassal and an autonomous nation, both
welcoming and resenting Qing intervention. Only the Sino-Japanese War
of 1894–95 would impose, with force of arms, some clarity on the irregular

---

3. Theodore Critchfield ("Queen Min's Murder," 46) notes that the queen "had further spectacles scheduled, but these were forestalled and the dismembered bodies of
the first victims were removed from exposure in the streets by the newly arrived Chinese resident."

4. For the repatriation of the Taewŏn'gun, see Lensen, *Balance of Intrigue*, 69; and
Deuchler, *Confucian Gentlemen and Barbarian Envoys*, 216. For an example of allegations of
the Taewŏn'gun's involvement in intrigue, see Hwang Hyŏn, *Maech'ŏn yarok*, 119. See
also Kwŏn Sŏk-pong, "Ch'ŏngjŏng e issŏsŏ ŭi Taewŏn'gun kwa kŭ ŭi hwan'guk."

status of Korea in the world and signal the beginning of the end of Qing traditional suzerainty, but not of the system of multilateral imperialism introduced to Korea by the Qing Empire.

The next three chapters explore various facets of Yuan Shikai's Residency in Korea. Among other things, Yuan expanded the Qing imperial presence in Korea, taking an active role in the construction and management of key institutions such as overland telegraph lines and the Korean Maritime Customs Service. Yuan also influenced the Qing policy on Korea's attempts to borrow money from abroad. The Resident played an important part in the Qing Empire's efforts to maintain its claims to suzerainty while avoiding the entanglements and responsibilities of greater involvement in Korea. Finally, Yuan was also active in the execution of "commercial warfare" in Korea.

"De Facto *the King of Korea*"

In the aftermath of the 1884 *kapsin* coup attempt, the Qing Empire introduced a new type of official to Chosŏn Korea. Purist Party adherents in China, angry at Li Hongzhang's bargaining away of Qing advantages in the negotiations that resolved the 1884 coup attempt, continued to call for more aggressive action in Korea. Surprisingly, adding their voices to these calls were important Japanese diplomats as well as the Taewŏn'gun.[5] Although the ever-cautious Li Hongzhang refused to heed the most aggressive of the proposals he received, he did agree to the dispatch of a Qing high commissioner to Korea. The person he selected for the post was Yuan Shikai. Li justified his choice as follows:

The reason for the appointment of a Commissioner for Trade is to station a high-ranking official whose duties are to report the political development of that country. . . . Yuan Shikai twice went to the King's aid, his meritorious deeds have earned him admiration among Korean officials and common people, and he has shown great promise and loyalty. Furthermore, he and the Korean Ministers Kim Yun-sik, Kim Hong-jip, and others are very close friends. . . . When Chen Shutang was there in charge of commercial affairs, other diplomatic representatives in Seoul

---

5. Before being repatriated to Korea, the Taewŏn'gun argued for the dispatch of a Qing imperial supervisor to Korea, "following the precedent of the Mongol superintendent at the Koryŏ court as a means of arresting the decline of the Yi dynasty, which he attributed to the perpetuation of misgovernment by the 'wayward and spendthrift' Queen Min" (Young Ick Lew, "Yuan Shih-k'ai's Residency," 69–70).

considered him lower in rank than a Consul-General. This made it rather difficult for him to behave according to etiquette on social occasions. It seems advisable that Your Majesty should appoint a Consul-General as other countries.[6]

As a result, Yuan arrived in Seoul on October 5, 1885, with the title "commissioner of trade of the third rank" (*zongli Chaoxian jiaoshe tongshang shiyi*). The title Yuan had printed on his English-language calling cards told a rather different story: "His Imperial Chinese Majesty's Resident, Seoul."[7]

Yuan was only 26 when he took up his official diplomatic duties in Korea. However, according to one observer, Yuan "projected an image of maturity and solemnity beyond his years. A short, heavyset man who wobbled when he walked, Yuan was physically unimpressive. It was his prematurely grey hair and penetrating eyes of almost demonic intensity and intelligence which commanded one's attention."[8] Another noted that Yuan "affects a rather coarse joviality but . . . is unquestionably an able man, and, although he speaks no English, even through an interpreter impresses one conversing with him of the alertness and quickness of his intellect."[9]

Born in 1859 to a central Henan farming family, Yuan Shikai was adopted by Yuan Duchen, himself the adopted son of a prominent general, Yuan Jiasan. Although given the benefits of a classical education and a private tutor, Yuan Shikai proved unable (or unwilling) to pass the civil service examination. After three failures, he decided to pursue a military career, joining the Qing brigade commanded by General Wu Changqing in 1880. There, he was befriended by Zhang Jian, who assisted his protégé in moving swiftly up the ranks in General Wu's brigade. Consequently, Yuan was able to play a pivotal role in the suppression of the 1882 *imo* mutiny and an even larger role in the training of Korean troops and the subsequent quashing of the 1884 *kapsin* coup attempt.[10]

---

6. Jerome Ch'en, *Yuan Shih-k'ai*, 33.

7. Ibid., 33–34.

8. MacKinnon, *Power and Politics in Late Imperial China*, 16–17.

9. Heard to Blaine, no. 12, DS, Seoul, June 3, 1890, USDD, Korea, 134/6, cited in Lensen, *Balance of Intrigue*, 369n4. The role of interpreters and secretaries in fostering this impression of "quickness and intellect" should not be underestimated. Wang Bogong (*Quanlu suibi*, 12–13), who served as one of Yuan Shikai's secretaries in Korea, records that he often corrected Yuan's laughable errors in order to spare him embarrassment.

10. For biographies of Yuan Shikai, see Jerome Ch'en, *Yuan Shih-k'ai*; and Hou Yijie, *Yuan Shikai quanzhuan*.

Although many observers were impressed with Yuan personally, they had concerns and questions concerning Yuan's official rank and role in Korea. Endeavoring to clarify Yuan's status and its implications occupied the energy of many a foreign diplomat for years to come. Equally ambiguous—in the eyes of both contemporary observers and subsequent scholars—was the influence Yuan wielded over Chosŏn Korea during this critical time. Many have attributed nearly omnipotent powers to the Qing official. One noted: "Yuan, Li Hung-chang's deputy, little if at all less able and astute than the great chief, was at the Capital, no longer as a Commissioner, but as *Resident*, a semi-gubernatorial office, and he was *de facto* the King of Korea. Nothing was done without consulting him, nor without his sanction."[11] Another concurred: "Notwithstanding his youth, Yuan was 'past master in diplomatic intrigue and bluff' and skillfully restored effective Chinese domination in Korea."[12] In his biography of Yuan, Jerome Ch'en concludes: "As a struggling young man in Korea, Yuan had served the throne well."[13]

Yet, there were many critics of Yuan's behavior in Korea. Owen Denny, an American adviser to the Korean king, described Yuan's behavior less favorably: "For petty schemes, criminality, injustice and brutality, [it] has seldom, if ever, been equaled in the annals of international intercourse."[14] Scholars have also emphasized Yuan's influence in Korea, calling the period of his Residency "the decade of Yuan Shih-k'ai"[15] and concluding that it was "a dark age for the Korean enlightenment movement."[16] Yuan was all of this and both more and less.

The Decline of Self-strengthening

As Yuan Shikai worked to enhance Qing ritual suzerainty and consolidate Qing informal imperial rule, Qing attempts to support Korean self-strengthening efforts, particularly in the military arena, diminished. The successful quelling of the 1884 *kapsin* coup attempt by Qing and Qing-trained Korean troops was a sign of the success of Li Hongzhang's efforts to transplant self-strengthening to Korea. In winning the battle, however,

---

11. J. H. Longford, quoted in Jerome Ch'en, *Yuan Shih-k'ai*, 34.
12. J. O. P. Bland, *Li Hung-chang*, 169; cited in Lensen, *Balance of Intrigue*, 69–70.
13. Jerome Ch'en, *Yuan Shih-k'ai*, 206.
14. Denny, *China and Korea*, 32.
15. Chandra, *Imperialism, Resistance, and Reform in Late Nineteenth-Century Korea*, 52.
16. Eckert et al., *Korea Old and New*, 213.

Li lost the war. For in the resolution of the various Qing and Japanese claims and demands following the coup, Li agreed in the Convention of Tianjin to a joint withdrawal of Qing and Japanese troops from Korea. Moreover, both the Qing Empire and Meiji Japan agreed to encourage Chosŏn Korea to seek military instructors from a third-party nation.[17] Li Hongzhang expressed some resistance to this measure, but ultimately he acquiesced to it.[18] King Kojong turned to the United States for assistance. The American response was lukewarm at best. After years of delay, in part because the official Korean request for instructors was apparently misplaced by the U.S. State Department for more than a year, an alcoholic ex-Confederate officer accompanied by two other "officers" whose claims to military experience far exceeded the reality arrived in Korea. They succeeded only in demonstrating their incompetence, and the Chosŏn court quickly embarked on the difficult process of extricating itself from its now-unwanted contracts with the Americans. The Qing Empire would never again play a prominent role in Chosŏn Korea's efforts to reform and strengthen its military. It may not be entirely coincidental that the Chosŏn army never again engaged in a successful campaign.[19]

Other avenues of Qing assistance to Korean self-strengthening and modernization programs did continue, albeit with little concrete results. The occasional Korean continued to travel to China to study and to purchase military and industrial machinery, for example, Ch'oe Sŏk-yong's trip to Yantai and Shanghai in 1888.[20] Another Korean, Tang Po-sin, took at least four others to Jiangxi to study porcelain-making techniques. Local

---

17. China, Imperial Maritime Customs, *Treaties, Conventions, Etc., Between China and Foreign States*, 2: 588–89, 706.

18. Li's proposal that twenty Qing instructors remain in Korea after the withdrawal of Qing and Japanese troops was rejected by Itō Hirobumi. A similar suggestion was again proffered later, but King Kojong's reluctance combined with international pressure to hinder Li's plan; see Chien, *The Opening of Korea*, 181, 185.

19. Bishop, "Shared Failure." Korean troops proved unable to suppress the Tonghak Rebellion of the early 1890s and unable to resist growing Japanese power in Korea.

20. Cho Pyŏng-jik to Yuan Shikai, Aug. 11, 1888 (KJ 25.7.4), *Ch'ŏngan*, 1: 475–76; Yuan Shikai to Cho Pyŏng-jik, Sept. 1, 1888 (KJ 25.7.25), *Ch'ŏngan*, 1: 480–81; Yuan Shikai to Cho Pyŏng-jik, Oct. 23, 1888 (KJ 25.9.19), *Ch'ŏngan*, 1: 488; Cho Pyŏng-jik to Yuan Shikai, Oct. 25, 1888 (KJ 25.9.21), *Ch'ŏngan*, 1: 489; Yuan Shikai to Cho Pyŏng-jik, Oct. 29, 1888 (KJ 25.9.25), *Ch'ŏngan*, 1: 490–91; Cho Pyŏng-jik to Yuan Shikai, Nov. 6, 1888 (KJ 25.10.3), *Ch'ŏngan*, 1: 492; Cho Pyŏng-jik to Yuan Shikai, Dec. 19, 1888 (KJ 25.11.17), *Ch'ŏngan*, 1: 505; Yuan Shikai to Cho Pyŏng-jik, Dec. 22, 1888 (KJ 25.11.19), *Ch'ŏngan*, 1: 506.

Chinese officials, incensed that outsiders were attempting to steal their secrets, arrested the Korean group, and it was discovered that they were traveling without proper documentation. A flurry of diplomatic correspondence revealed that both Korean and Qing officials in Korea had approved of the trip, but the official authorization did not reach Jiangxi until after Tang had been punished by local authorities and his party sent home.[21] Whether they learned anything of practical use is unknown.

Chinese advisers continued to assist in various Korean industrial and official commercial ventures particularly in the area of sericulture and textile weaving. But, as was often the case with foreign advisers from other nations, the payment of salaries was inconsistent at best and complaints concerning remuneration and lodging were seldom heeded.[22] Chinese-language instructors and interpreters expressed similar grievances and concerns.[23]

Another group of Qing-appointed advisers played a larger role in Chosŏn Korea. As noted above, Li Hongzhang appointed the American Henry Merrill to replace Moellendorff as head of the Korean Maritime Customs Service. Moellendorff's domestic advisory role was assumed by another American suggested by the Qing: the Oregon "judge" Owen Denny.[24] Both

---

21. Kim Hong-jip to Chen Shutang, Nov. 5, 1884 (KJ 21.9.18), *Ch'ŏngan*, 1: 197; Chen Shutang to Kim Hong-jip, Nov. 6, 1884 (KJ 21.9.19), *Ch'ŏngan*, 1: 198; Chen Shutang to Kim Pyŏng-ho, Jan. 15, 1885 (KJ 21.11.30), *Ch'ŏngan*, 1: 212–13; Chen Shutang to Kim Yun-sik, Feb. 13, 1885 (KJ 21.12.19), *Ch'ŏngan*, 1: 224–27.

22. For requests that the Chinese sericulture expert Zhang Baozhong be paid, see Yuan Shikai to Sŏ Sang-u, Aug. 23, 1886 (KJ 23.7.24), *Ch'ŏngan*, 1: 313; Yuan Shikai to Min Chong-muk, Oct. 23, 1889 (KJ 26.9.29), *Ch'ŏngan*, 1: 620–21; and Min Chong-muk to Yuan Shikai, Nov. 10, 1889 (KJ 26.10.18), *Ch'ŏngan*, 1: 629–30. For complaints concerning the lodging of Chinese textile advisers, see Chen Shutang to Kim Yun-sik, July 12, 1885 (KJ 22.6.1), *Ch'ŏngan*, 1: 265–66. At least one Chinese worker was connected to the Korean Textiles Bureau (Chikjogŭk) as late as 1891, when he requested to be allowed to return home; see Min Chong-muk to Tang Shaoyi, Nov. 23, 1891 (KJ 28.10.22), *Ch'ŏngan*, 2: 74–75; and Tang Shaoyi to Min Chong-muk, Dec. 3, 1891 (KJ 28.11.3), *Ch'ŏngan*, 2: 76.

23. Min Chong-muk to Cha Yisong, Sept. 30, 1892 (KJ 29.8.10), *Ch'ŏngan*, 2: 131; Cha Yisong to Min Chong-muk, Sept. 30, 1890 (KJ 29.8.10), *Ch'ŏngan*, 2: 131; Cha Yisong to Nam Chŏngch'ŏl, June 16, 1893 (KJ 30.5.3), *Ch'ŏngan*, 2: 203–4; Cho Pyŏng-sik to Xu Taishen, Mar. 24, 1904 (KM 8.3.24), *Ch'ŏngan*, 2: 679; Xu Taishen to Cho Pyŏng-sik, Mar. 29, 1904 (KM 8.3.29), *Ch'ŏngan*, 2: 681.

24. Denny had served as a judge in Wasco county, Oregon, in the 1860s and was elected police court judge in Portland, Oregon, in 1870. Subsequently Denny was

would play prominent roles in Korea's politics and government, although not always in the ways Li Hongzhang and particularly Yuan Shikai expected. Denny became a vocal and implacable opponent of Yuan and openly called for Yuan's dismissal in an incendiary tract, *China and Korea*.[25] Merrill kept a lower profile, but his efforts to develop and promote the operations of the Korean Customs Service often ran afoul of Yuan Shikai's claims of special Qing privilege in Korea.

All in all, Qing efforts to stimulate and promote self-strengthening reforms in Korea enjoyed little if any success after 1885. It is far from clear that any degree of modernizing reforms would have enabled Chosŏn Korea to extricate itself from its extremely difficult geopolitical circumstances. Whatever the case, the gradual demise of self-strengthening would influence the future course of Qing imperialism in Korea.

In the ensuing years, the Qing Empire sought to maintain the security of Korea and its privileged position there through a combination of tactics not altogether dissimilar from those used by other imperialists trying to maximize their interests while minimizing entanglement and responsibility. Qing troops were gone, but gunboats from Li Hongzhang's Northern (Beiyang) Fleet made frequent visits to Korean treaty ports.[26] More important, the Qing Empire took the lead in connecting Korea to global communications networks via overland telegraph lines. It also played a complex and somewhat ambiguous role in the operation of the Korean Maritime Customs Service. Finally, the Qing Empire wielded a strong influence over Chosŏn Korea's attempts to borrow money from abroad.

Sinews of Informal Empire: Construction and Control of Telegraph Lines

The fact that it took several days for officials in the Qing Empire to learn of the 1884 *kapsin* coup attempt highlighted the need for improved communications between China and Korea. From the mid-nineteenth century

---

known as "the Judge" by "friend and foe alike" (Swartout, *Mandarins, Gunboats, and Power Politics*, 1–2).

25. Denny, *China and Korea*. For more on Denny, see Swartout, *Mandarins, Gunboats, and Power Politics*.

26. However, Li Hongzhang often dispatched the oldest and most decrepit ships in his fleet for duty in Korean ports; see Kim Chŏng-gi, "1876–1894 nyŏn Ch'ŏng ŭi Chosŏn changch'aek yŏn'gu," 131*n*.

on, imperialist powers were quick to recognize and utilize the potential of the telegraph as a facilitator of heretofore unimaginably swift communications across the globe. Describing telegraph cables as "an essential part of the new imperialism," Daniel Headrick notes the multifaceted uses of this new technology: "In times of peace, they were the lifelines of the ever-increasing business communications that bound imperialist nations to their colonies around the world. In times of crisis, they were valuable tools of diplomacy. . . . And in times of war, the cables were security itself."[27]

Japan had secured Korean permission to construct an undersea cable from Nagasaki to Pusan in 1883, but the rest of the peninsula including the Korean capital remained relatively unconnected to the outside world. News traveled either by steamship or by overland courier from Seoul to Pusan, via cable from Pusan to Nagasaki, and from thence to other parts of the world via cables from Japan. Events made it increasingly clear that the Qing Empire needed to have closer communications with the Korean peninsula.

After the construction of the Japanese Nagasaki–Pusan line, Li Shuchang, the Qing ambassador to Japan, warned of the dangers of a Japanese monopoly on communications in Korea. After the December 1884 coup attempt, Wu Dacheng called for the construction of an overland telegraph line from Lüshun to Seoul in his "Plan for Managing Korean Affairs."[28] Astute Japanese telegraph officials saw the implications of a competing Chinese line, but their proposals for a Japanese-constructed line from Pusan to Seoul and Inch'ŏn were ignored by the now very cautious Japanese government.[29] Li Hongzhang, on the other hand, recognized the need for a telegraph line not only to counter Japanese influence but also to reduce the inefficiency and waste of the traditional post-horse system. King Kojong agreed and, after consulting with Qing officials, sent an official request for Qing assistance in the construction of a telegraph line in May 1885.[30]

----

27. Headrick, *Tools of Empire*, 163–64.

28. Lin Mingde, *Yuan Shikai yu Chaoxian*, 227.

29. Yi Sŏn-gŭn, *Han'guksa*, 888–89.

30. Yi Yang-ja, "Ch'ŏng ŭi tae Chosŏn kyŏngje," 134; Lin Mingde, *Yuan Shikai yu Chaoxian*, 228. Kojong expressed concerns about the potential disruption caused by the introduction of such a modern device into the countryside and wondered whether an undersea cable might not be preferable. Japanese telegraph officials had also noted the potential obstacle posed to an overland line by a suspicious peasantry. Li Hongzhang replied that overland lines were cheaper and easier to maintain; moreover, China had

Once the official Korean request was made, the Ŭiju Telegraph Agreement was swiftly drawn up and signed. The agreement provided that the Qing would oversee construction and supply a no-interest loan of 100,000 taels to finance the project. Korea was not to cede control of the telegraph lines to others for at least 25 years and was to seek Qing permission before expanding existing lines or establishing new ones.[31] Despite protests by the local populace over the confiscation of land and lumber for the project, construction proceeded at a rapid pace. The line between Inch'ŏn and Seoul was completed by September 1885, a branch office was opened in P'yŏngyang in October, and the line to the border town of Ŭiju was completed by the end of November, thus linking Korea with the outside world in a manner unprecedented in its long history.[32] After some delays, Korea's telegraphic network was expanded to include lines connecting Seoul to Pusan (1888) and Wŏnsan (1891).

The Qing efforts to construct and control Chosŏn Korea's overland telegraph lines were met by resistance and challenges from both Japan and Russia. Citing a provision in the Pusan–Nagasaki undersea cable agreement that gave Japan a 25-year monopoly on telegraph construction in Korea, Japanese officials demanded reparations and concessions in return for what they regarded as a breach of contract. Qing and Chosŏn officials deflected the initial claim by making a distinction between underwater cables and overland telegraph lines. Some Korean officials were more receptive to Japanese demands for the right to construct a line from Seoul to Pusan, but Yuan Shikai and the Qing Commissioner of Trade in Pusan Tan Gengyao labored to convince Korean officials, particularly Kim Yun-sik, that the Seoul–Pusan line was best kept out of the hands of a third party. Some feared that the construction of the line linking Seoul to Wŏnsan, and potentially to points farther north, was merely the precursor to an enhanced Russian presence in Korea. Counseled by Li Hongzhang to be vigilant

---

no experience laying undersea cables. It is likely that Li had an ulterior motive in promoting an overland line: when the Japanese protested the Sino-Korean telegraph agreement, arguing that the Pusan-Nagasaki undersea cable agreement gave Japan a monopoly on all future telegraph construction, they were informed by Kim Yun-sik that the Korean-Japanese agreement referred only to undersea cables; see Chien, *The Opening of Korea*, 193–94.

31. For text of the agreement, see *KS*, July 17, 1885 (KJ 22.6.6).

32. Kim Chŏng-gi, "1876–1894 nyŏn Ch'ŏng ŭi Chosŏn chŏngch'aek yŏn'gu," 139.

about this possibility, Yuan Shikai repeatedly invoked the provisions of the Ŭiju Telegraph Agreement to ensure Qing control of the Wŏnsan line.[33]

After the lines were constructed, Japanese officials were swift to protest what they regarded as unfair rates. They noted that rates for the Inch'ŏn–Seoul–Ŭiju line were considerably lower than for the Seoul–Pusan line and demanded equal if not special treatment. At stake was the revenue from virtually all communications between the Korean capital and the outside world beyond China and Japan. Since both China and Japan were connected to a growing worldwide communications network, foreigners and Koreans alike naturally chose the cheaper route for telegraphic transmissions. Also at stake were Japan's long-term plans for wresting control over the southern portion of Korea's telegraph lines. Hence, the Japanese demand that the Inch'ŏn–Seoul line be merged with the Seoul–Pusan line. Japanese officials sought to resolve the issue through direct negotiations with the Koreans. However, the Qing superintendent of the Korean Telegraph Office, Chen Tongshu, had already firmly declared: "The line from Seoul to Pusan is Korea's line; the line from Inch'ŏn to Ŭiju is China's line; there is no reason to entertain Japanese demands."[34] Therefore, the Korean-Japanese negotiations resulted only in an agreement to allow non-Chinese officials to use the telegraph for half price (Qing officials already used it for free) with funds from a monthly 5,000-tael stipend to make up the difference in revenues. Aside from this concession, the Qing Empire and Chosŏn Korea held firm in the face of Japanese demands.[35]

Equally troublesome in the eyes of Qing officials were the Korean demands for greater control over the telegraph lines. In order to assuage Korean anxieties about the Seoul–Pusan line, Yuan Shikai promised to allow the Chosŏn government to send apprentices and watchmen to each telegraph office along the line and agreed to pay some of the expenses of operating the line; however, control of the telegraph remained firmly in Chinese hands. This was somewhat paradoxical because Qing officials and telegraph administrators used Korea's putative control of the Seoul–Pusan line to keep the Japanese at bay even as they denied Korean requests for greater autonomy.[36]

---

33. Lin Mingde, *Yuan Shikai yu Chaoxian*, 233–34.
34. Ibid., 231–32.
35. Ibid., 232; Yi Yang-ja, "Ch'ŏng ŭi tae Chosŏn kyŏngje," 141.
36. Lin Mingde, *Yuan Shikai yu Chaoxian*, 229–30.

In late 1888, Korean officials requested permission from Yuan Shikai to take managerial control of the Inch'ŏn–Seoul–Ŭiju line. Yuan replied that such a move would contravene the Ŭiju Telegraph Agreement. Li Hongzhang, fearing the implications for Qing security, concurred with Yuan. Li and Yuan also opposed an 1890 attempt by Korea to borrow money from France to repay the telegraph loan from the Qing and recover control of the line.[37]

In the end, despite challenges, the Qing Empire maintained a firm grip on Korea's telegraph lines until its defeat in the Sino-Japanese War. Yuan Shikai exercised ultimate power over the line. Qing officials, notably Chen Tongshu and Chen Chongyi, managed the head office in Seoul, and Qing officials were stationed in all the branch offices. They used the line free of charge, whereas the officials of other nations paid a half-price rate for use. The Qing also managed to keep the general fares along the Ŭiju line cheaper than those along the line leading to Japan. This monopolistic control, combined with waste and extravagance at the branch offices, especially along the Ŭiju line, made it extremely difficult for the revenues to cover operating expenses. The Korean government was forced at times to subsidize the line to keep it in operation.[38]

Although the Qing gained little commercial advantage from its control of Korea's telegraph lines, the symbolic value of being the nation to construct and operate Korea's first modern communication lines with the outside world was significant. Michael Adas has eloquently described how Western imperialist powers used their perceived technological superiority both to explain and to justify their expansion.[39] To be able to wield modern communications technology for the benefit of the colony as well as the enhanced control and prestige of the metropole was, in part, what made a late nineteenth-century power an imperialist one. It is unlikely that this fact was lost on the Qing, the Japanese, or the Koreans.[40]

Qing control had strategic advantages. Nearly instant communications allowed the Qing to react quickly to events and developments on the

---

37. Ibid., 233; Yi Yang-ja, "Ch'ŏng ŭi tae Chosŏn kyŏngje," 142.

38. Yi Yang-ja, "Ch'ŏng ŭi tae Chosŏn kyŏngje," 141.

39. Adas, *Machines as the Measure of Men.*

40. A Japanese military report stressed that "all countries of the world consider autonomy in communications a basic tenet in national defense. All aspire to possess their own communications systems" (cited in Daqing Yang, *Technology of Empire: Telecommunications and Japanese Imperialism, 1930–1945,* 45).

peninsula. Moreover, the telegraph enabled Qing officials to rein in overly aggressive on-the-spot officials, such as Yuan Shikai, who had previously acted with relative freedom in Korea. It also enhanced the Qing ability to observe and influence the activities of its putative vassal.[41] In many ways, the telegraph served as an adequate replacement for the troops withdrawn in accordance with the 1885 Convention of Tianjin. Kim Chŏng-gi concludes that the telegraph line, combined with an enhanced naval presence, served to project Qing influence and protect Qing interests in Korea almost as ably as had the Qing troops once stationed there.[42]

The Qing monopoly was sometimes used for tactical advantage. Foreign officials complained that the telegraph line was suspiciously out of order during times of crisis, especially before the completion of the Seoul–Pusan line. The American missionary-diplomat Horace Allen noted that during what some suspected was a Qing-instigated coup attempt in 1886, "the Chinese here ordered the telegraph circuit interrupted and had things all their own way."[43] Foreign officials also complained of telegrams arriving in an unintelligibly garbled state and often blamed Chinese interference.[44] Japanese officials even attempted to circumvent Qing control by asking the American naval attaché George C. Foulk to send their coded messages to Japan. Once he realized the nature of the Japanese designs, however, he declined to assist them.[45]

Much of the Inch'ŏn–Seoul–Ŭiju line was destroyed during the Sino-Japanese War. When the lines were rebuilt, the Qing Empire was not in a position to interfere or assert any sort of control. Korean autonomy over the lines was to be short lived, however, as growing Japanese political influence translated into control over key institutions, including the telegraph.

---

41. An American diplomat noted that the construction of the telegraph was motivated in part by Chinese "suspicions": "the Chinese were not only 'suspicious of Russian designs upon Korea to an unusual degree,' but that they were 'suspicious, as well, of the Koreans themselves'" (Lensen, *Balance of Intrigue*, 70).

42. Kim Chŏng-gi, "1876–1894 nyŏn Ch'ŏng ŭi Chosŏn changch'aek yŏn'gu," 137.

43. Kim Wŏn-mo, ed., *Allen ŭi ilgi*, Sept. 5, 1886, 508–9. Owen Denny's wife, Gertrude, concurred: "For more than two weeks we have been bottled up here, unable to get a word over the telegraph lines." Mrs. Denny continued, "We were always told it was broken and yet we knew positively messages were going back and forth to Tientsin all the time" (quoted in Swartout, *Mandarins, Gunboats, and Power Politics*, 85).

44. Kim Wŏn-mo, ed., *Allen ŭi ilgi*, Oct. 1, 1887, 517.

45. Ibid., Dec. 20, 1885, 497.

The Korean Maritime Customs Service

The arrival of the American Henry F. Merrill to replace Moellendorff as the chief commissioner of the Korean Maritime Customs Service was a sign of the continuing Qing interest in and commitment to the Korean counterpart of the Chinese Imperial Maritime Customs Service. Some saw it as additional evidence of greater Qing intervention and assertion of exclusive privilege in Korea. But in the end, the Korean Maritime Customs Service was less the embodiment of Qing claims to suzerainty and more an expression of the multilateral imperialism introduced into Korea by the Qing Empire. The advent of a maritime customs service was another indication of the end of Japan's exclusive, monopolistic privileges in Korea. The days of Japanese merchants enjoying tariff-free trade in Korea were over.

The Korean Maritime Customs Service was established and initially overseen by Paul Georg Moellendorff.[46] Moellendorff's dispatch to Korea was a response to repeated Korean requests for assistance. His selection was the result of considerable debate between Li Hongzhang, Robert Hart (the commissioner of the Imperial Chinese Maritime Customs Service), and other Qing officials.[47] Moellendorff consulted frequently with Qing officials and relied on a 200,000-tael loan for construction and operating expenses. He staffed the offices with large numbers of Westerners and smaller numbers of Chinese.[48] The Customs Service quickly became an important source

---

46. For evaluations of Moellendorff, see Yur-Bok Lee, *West Goes East*; and Leifer, "Paul-Georg von Moellendorff and the Opening of Korea." For a less laudatory view, see Foulk to U.S. Secretary of State, Aug. 4, 1885, *KAR*, 1: 120–23.

47. Han'guk kwanse yŏn'guso, *Han'guk kwansesa*, 101. Hart's initial choices for the position included a Mr. Cartwright and a Mr. Carral, but both declined the post; see Hughes to Grosvenor, Dec. 13, 1882, *British Documents*, 2: 100. Hart's disapproval of Moellendorff was motivated in part by his fear that the German would work to hinder British interests in Korea. Moreover, he complained that Li's selection of Moellendorff was due to Li's desire to appoint "men who will obey orders rather than . . . men who will give advice." The American minister in China, John Russell Young, also opposed the selection of Moellendorff. Ma Jianzhong, on the other hand, enthusiastically supported Moellendorff, declaring him to be the "most confident man for the job"; see Yur-Bok Lee, *West Goes East*, 45–46; see also Woo, "The Historical Development of Korean Tariff and Customs Administration, 1875–1958," 33.

48. The actual number of advisers is not entirely clear. Yur-Bok Lee (*West Goes East*, 50) states that Moellendorff chose 28, of whom 23 were Europeans, four Chinese, and one Japanese. A list included in Han'guk kwanse yŏn'guso, *Han'guk kwansesa* (103) also

of revenue for the Chosŏn government. Revenue from the first three months of the year was generally sufficient to pay for all overhead and oper- ating costs, leaving three-quarters of the customs revenue available for use by the Korean government, which used the money for a variety of purposes.[49] Despite his successful establishment and management of the Korean Maritime Customs Service, Moellendorff was recalled to China in 1885 because of his role in a Korean attempt to secure a secret alliance with Russia.

Merrill received explicit instructions not to meddle in political or diplo- matic affairs in Korea. However, before leaving for Korea, Merrill was in- structed by Hart: "You are the suzerain's man and must keep the tributary rights as far as in your power."[50] The open secret of such instructions and the fact that, under Merrill's administration, the annual reports of the Ko- rean Customs Service were appended to the annual reports of the Chinese Imperial Maritime Customs Service were taken as indications of Qing con- trol over the institution. The American George C. Foulk noted that "the Customs of Korea would appear to have been incorporated in the Customs of China, the most direct evidence being that the Customs Trade Reports . . . appear as a section merely of the General Report of the Chinese Customs— in the same manner as though Korea were but a province of China."[51]

The reality was more complex. The Korean Maritime Customs Service stood at the crossroads of a number of discrete and sometimes competing strands of Qing imperial strategy. Purist Party supporters were likely to have applauded the symbolic significance of the inclusion of Korean Cus-

---

contains 28 names but this list includes the names of five Chinese. Louis Sigel ("The Role of Korea in Late Qing Foreign Policy," 86) contends that six Chinese students who had studied in America were selected by Moellendorff. Of the six listed by Sigel, two are not on the *Han'guk kwansesa* list. On the other hand, the *Han'guk kwansesa* list includes the name of one Chinese not mentioned by Sigel. In the end, it appears that at least seven Chinese, Wu Litang, Tang Shaoyi, Wu Zhongxian, Zhou Zhangling, Liang Ruhao, Cai Shaoji, and Lin Peiquan, worked in the Korean Customs Service in the early years of its existence.

49. Han'guk kwanse yŏn'guso, *Han'guk kwansesa*, 94–95; Moellendorff was also able to use customs revenue to pay the first installment of the indemnity owed to Japan fol- lowing the 1882 *imo* mutiny (Woo, "The Historical Development of Korean Tariff and Customs Administration, 1875–1958," 51).

50. Morse, *The International Relations of the Chinese Empire*, 3: 14.

51. Foulk to U.S. Secretary of State, Apr. 23, 1886, *KAR*, 1: 148.

toms Service reports in the much larger reports of the Chinese Customs Service. The fact that the salaries of most if not all the foreign employees of the Korean Customs Service were paid by its Chinese counterpart could be taken as yet another sign not only of Qing benevolence toward its Korean vassal but also of continued support for self-strengthening measures in the non-military arena. But Li Hongzhang proved far more concerned that the foreign commissioners he appointed did not unduly entangle Chosŏn Korea and the Qing Empire into dangerous arrangements such as the Korean-Russian agreement sought by Moellendorff. As long as Merrill and his successors focused on their administrative duties and stayed out of politics, Li seemed content. In addition, Li often saw Hart as a competitor and, therefore, proved reluctant to heed Hart's calls for a complete merger of the two customs services. Moreover, Li consistently avoided any official declaration of Qing responsibility for Korea that extended beyond the traditional prerogatives of the tribute system.

Tang Tingshu, a chief representative of the Chinese treaty-port community, provided the initial loan for the establishment of the Korean customs service, an indication that he saw the institution as consistent with his larger goals in Korea. On the other hand, Tang balked when he was unable to secure a Qing government guarantee for the loan and disagreed with Moellendorff over many of the specific terms of the loan. The end result was a loan of the more modest sum of 200,000 taels rather than the 500,000 Moellendorff had requested.[52] On the ground, it is evident that Chinese merchants often sought special or even illegal privileges and prerogatives based on the Qing Empire's status as Chosŏn Korea's suzerain. Although these efforts were frequently abetted by Qing officials in Korea, most notably Yuan Shikai, they found in Merrill a forceful opponent. Time and again, Merrill's emphasis proved to be more on administrative

---

52. Many sources mistakenly conclude that Korea actually received the initially proposed 500,000 taels from the China Merchants Steamship Company and the Kaiping Mines. For example, see Sigel, "The Role of Korea in Late Qing Foreign Policy," 88; Yi Yang-ja, "Ch'ŏng ŭi tae Chosŏn kyŏngje," 122–23; and Lin Mingde, *Yuan Shikai yu Chaoxian*, 206. For Tang Tingshu's desire to micro-manage Korea's use of the loan money and the ultimate compromise on a loan for 200,000 taels, see Deuchler, *Confucian Gentlemen and Barbarian Envoys*, 174–75; and Sin Pok-kyŏng and Kim Un-gyŏng, *Moellendorŭp'u munsŏ*, 60. That only 200,000 taels were actually loaned is clearly indicated in the record books of the China Merchants Steamship Company (Feuerwerker, *China's Early Industrialization*, 158–59).

efficiency than on enhancing Korea's political subordination to the Qing Empire or helping Chinese merchants.[53]

The Qing Empire in general and Yuan Shikai in particular did pay close attention to the role of customs revenue in Chosŏn Korea's finances. Yuan steadfastly opposed Korean attempts to use customs revenue as collateral or security for loans from abroad. He had no objection to using such revenue for loans from Chinese companies, as, for example, in the case of loans from the Chinese firm Tongshuntai in the early 1890s. But aside from exercising this negative veto, Yuan and other Qing officials appear to have played little role in the spending of customs revenues. Among other uses, these funds were used to pay the operating expenses of the Customs Service itself; the salaries and operations of the Korean port superintendents (*kamni*); the salaries and expenses of foreign advisers in Korea such as those connected with the mint, the Machine Hall, the Sericulture Bureau, and schools; and other modernization projects, including the sending of students abroad and the improvement of treaty-port facilities.[54] Years later, under the management of John McLeavy Brown, the Customs Service would oversee a diversity of projects ranging from bridge building and urban planning to newspaper publishing.[55]

The Korean Maritime Customs Service functioned well as a tool of the type of multilateral imperialism that held sway throughout much of East Asia at the time. Chosŏn Korea did not enjoy tariff autonomy. Most-favored-nation clauses in Korea's treaties with other nations ensured that all foreign merchants enjoyed the lowest tariff rates. But access was granted equally to all applicants, a stark contrast to the days of Japanese domination of a duty-free maritime trade in Korea. The operation of the Customs Service, particularly its foreign management, reflected the British-dominated ethos that prevailed both in the Imperial Maritime Chinese Customs Service and throughout the British Empire more generally. British diplomats and consuls alike, as well as customs service officials generally, heeded Palmerston's advice that "it is the business of the Government to open and to

---

53. For a detailed summary of scholarly evaluations of the relative independence of the Korean Customs Service, see Woo, "The Historical Development of Korean Tariff and Customs Administration, 1875–1958," 57–60, 58*n*25. Woo concludes that Merrill's emphasis was on independence from diplomatic and political affairs.

54. Han'guk kwanse yŏn'guso, *Han'guk kwansesa*, 94–95.

55. Nish, "John McLeavy Brown in Korea," 42.

secure the roads for the merchant," but in a fashion that facilitated equal access to all comers.[56]

Each of the various groups that influenced Qing imperial policy toward Korea could point to some aspect of the Korean Customs Service with satisfaction: the joint annual reports and the paying of Korean Customs Service officials' salaries pleased those who insisted on the primacy of suzerainty. And although Tang Tingshu never received full compensation for his loan to Korea, some of his countrymen enjoyed the security of knowing that customs revenue would be used for repaying their loans. Li Hongzhang was able to continue walking the tightrope between influencing and controlling events and developments in Korea while eschewing direct control of or responsibility for the Qing Empire's Korean vassal.

Qing Intervention in Chosŏn Financial Affairs: Foreign Loans

Imperialist meddling in the financial affairs of the periphery is a well-known phenomenon. For example, the inability of Egypt to pay the huge debts owed to European financial groups resulted in increased British interference in Egypt's domestic affairs and paved the way for occupation in 1882.[57] Westerners and Japanese used loans and indemnities to increase influence or gain concessions in China throughout much of the nineteenth and early twentieth centuries. Loans were also often regarded as a means to

---

56. Lynn, "British Policy, Trade, and Informal Empire in the Mid-Nineteenth Century," 105. Lynn notes further that "the free trade treaties the Foreign Office pushed for were restricted to 'equal favor and open competition' for all powers. . . . The 'Open Door' was open to everyone. There was no policy here of obtaining exclusive privileges for Britain." This was due in part to a philosophical commitment to free trade but also because, for much of the nineteenth century, "The government did not need to go beyond the 'Open Door' to obtain exclusive privileges in this period; the British economy's success made it possible to entertain ambitions of dominating large areas of the globe almost by default. Given the favorable international situation and that Britain's industrial and financial lead was so great, opening an area to outside influences by treaty was often sufficient to ensure that British trade and finance, rather than any rival's, would be paramount in the region" (ibid., 105–6).

57. For an introduction to the literature on the British Empire in Egypt, see Sluglett, "Formal and Informal Empire in the Middle East." See also Welch, *No Country for a Gentleman*.

secure greater access to markets and to facilitate exports.[58] In the words of an American Commerce Department official, "It is sometimes said that foreign trade follows the flag, but it is more truly said that foreign trade follows the loan."[59]

Although it may have been aware of the risks associated with borrowing from abroad, the cash-strapped Chosŏn government often found itself seeking foreign loans in order to weather short-term revenue shortfalls, maintain current levels of spending, and engage in desired reforms. Widespread corruption, the gradual disappearance of many local *yangban* elites from the tax rolls, and royal extravagance limited the amount of revenue the central government obtained and retained. In 1884, state revenues were barely higher than they had been twenty years before and were actually lower than at the height of the Taewŏn'gun's fiscal reforms.[60] As a result, many Chosŏn officials concluded that borrowing from abroad was an unavoidable necessity. Indeed, it can be argued that seeking foreign loans was a very important component in several of Chosŏn Korea's diplomatic overtures to its neighbors, including trips by Koreans to Japan in the early 1880s and to the United States years later.[61]

Many Korean historians, particularly those highly critical of Qing intervention in late nineteenth-century Korea, see the Qing Empire in general, and Yuan Shikai in particular, as an implacable and mostly insurmountable obstacle to Korea's attempts to borrow from abroad. Yur-Bok Lee expresses this view when he states, "Whenever the Korean government and the king sought loans from other countries than from China, Yuan successfully blocked the effort."[62] The Qing Empire's attitudes toward and ac-

---

58. Horowitz, "International Law and State Transformation," 472–73.

59. Pratt, "The Attitude of Business Towards Foreign Trade," 296. Pratt continues: "There is no doubt that unless the United States can make loans and investments in foreign countries, our manufacturers and merchants will not be able to develop their export trade to any considerable degree" (ibid.).

60. The amount of land subject to the land tax, Korea's chief source of revenue, in 1863 was 776,709 *kyŏl*; in 1874, the figure was 805,303 *kyŏl*; the figure had dropped to 799,123 *kyŏl* in 1884 (Yi Sŏn-gŭn, *Han'guksa*, 466).

61. For the efforts of Korean officials such as Kim Ok-kyun to obtain loans from Japanese and other sources in the early 1880s, see Cook, *Korea's 1884 Incident*. For the influence of seeking a loan on the decision to establish a legation in Washington, DC, see Harrington, *God, Mammon, and the Japanese*, 226–27.

62. Yur-Bok Lee, *West Goes East*, 177. Similar expressions can be found in Young Ick Lew, "Yuan Shih-k'ai's Residency," 93–97; Bonnie B. C. Oh, "The Background of

tions regarding foreign loans to Korea were actually much more complex. Both Yuan Shikai and Li Hongzhang recognized the potential for loans as a mechanism for increasing Qing influence and power in Korea, and they encouraged Korean borrowing from Chinese sources whenever possible. They also recognized that the same tool might be used by other competing powers.[63] As such, they often sought to control if not prohibit Korea's attempts to borrow from other non-Chinese sources abroad, particularly if such a loan would seemingly grant monopolistic privileges to a single outside power. On the other hand, Yuan and Li demonstrated less concern over a flurry of smaller-scale borrowing from non-Chinese sources. But since Korea proved unsuccessful in obtaining massive foreign loans, it was, in the words of Young Ick Lew, prevented from becoming an "Egypt of Asia."[64]

As was the case in other areas of its Korea policy, the Qing Empire's attitude toward foreign borrowing was hardly monolithic. Many, such as Grand Councilor and President of the Board of Revenue Weng Tonghe, adopted a rather conservative position on government finances. Fang Chaoying describes Weng as "a financier of the old school, [who] tried to balance the expenditures of the government with the small revenue from agriculture. He opposed the provincial officials who were experimenting with commercial and industrial capitalism with funds borrowed from foreign banks."[65] Yuan Shikai appears to have been influenced by this sentiment; he strongly supported what Lew Young-ick describes as "the Confucian economic ideal of a balanced budget." After his appointment as the Qing Empire's Resident, Yuan frequently reminded King Kojong that Korea's poverty and inability to collect revenue necessitated a very cautious economic strategy in which reform of administration and exploitation of natural resources should take precedence over borrowing money from

---

Chinese Policy Formation in the Sino-Japanese War," 152; and Dalchoong Kim, "Korea's Request for Reform and Diplomacy in the 1880s," 485.

63. Akira Iriye ("Imperialism in East Asia," 142–43) notes that some Japanese officials adopted the explicit strategy of using loans to increase power in China in an era of Great Power competition there: "As Kurino Shinichiro, minister to France, wrote in 1897, Japan should extend loans to China, obtain railway concessions, and invest in China's industrial development. Strictly speaking, Japan could not afford to export capital, but for this very reason it was imperative to establish close connections with parts of China. Otherwise the whole of China would be subdivided into Western spheres of influence, and there would be little chance for Japan to join the game."

64. Young Ick Lew, "Yuan Shih-k'ai's Residency," 96–97.

65. Fang Chaoying, "Weng T'ung-ho" [Weng Tonghe], 860.

abroad.[66] Yuan's anxiety concerning Korean insolvency was only increased by the fact that the Chosŏn government seemed to be continually borrowing money to pay off earlier loans, yet seemed unable to make significant progress toward that goal.[67] This cautious outlook was echoed by one Japanese observer of Korea who recommended that "expenditures must meet revenues . . . so that debt is not incurred."[68]

Not all Qing officials were philosophically opposed to the idea of borrowing from abroad. Ma Jianzhong, for example, expressed guarded approval of loans. Writing of the possibility of China borrowing from abroad to finance railroad construction, Ma noted that "if instead we worry about what could go wrong and reject the idea of a loan altogether, would this not be the same as worrying about sexual indulgence and therefore banning marriage, or worrying about a shortage of wild animals and therefore proscribing the hunt? Surely, we dare not imagine this!"[69] Ma was, however, very concerned about the purpose and proper implementation of foreign loans. Offering advice to Kim Hong-jip in 1882, he noted that loans should "bring benefits to the common people" and "enhance commerce." Moreover, special attention should be devoted to the loan negotiations in order to avoid unnecessary problems.[70]

In contrast to Qing officials who supported the idea of loans only under circumscribed conditions, some elements called for the aggressive promotion of loans to Korea. Hailing largely from China's treaty-port community, these businessmen and officials saw the extension of loans to Korea as part of the larger project of supporting Korean self-strengthening reforms, enhancing Qing influence in the peninsula, and promoting Chinese commercial activities there. The intellectual and reformer Zheng Guanying wrote

---

66. Young Ick Lew, "Yuan Shih-k'ai's Residency," 93. For Yuan's admonitions to Kojong, see "Yuan Shikai zhujie Chaoxian qijian handu xuanji"; a portion of one of these letters is translated into English in Young Ick Lew, "Yuan Shih-k'ai's Residency," 93.

67. For example, in 1893 Korea still owed the German firm Myer and Company at least 100,000 taels of interest on a steamship purchased years earlier; see *JSSL*, 12:.7. See also Lin Mingde, *Yuan Shikai yu Chaoxian*, 208.

68. Schmid, *Korea Between Empires*, 116.

69. Bailey, *Strengthen the Country and Enrich the People*, 85–86.

70. Zhang Shusheng to Zongli yamen, June 10, 1882 (GX 8.4.25) *ZRHGX*, 659; writing elsewhere, Ma noted that "contracting a loan is a torturous and difficult business." He warned that foreigners often sought concessions in return for loans and that careless granting of concessions could lead to undue foreign influence and control (Bailey, *Strengthen the Country and Enrich the People*, 81).

that in the case of Korea, "China should be first in providing finance for reform through loans repayable on an annual basis and should take the lead in training officials and officers." The treaty-port community was well aware of the potential for informal empire in Korea and saw the provision of loans as an important part of this strategy.[71] There is no doubt that this group also saw the potential for considerable personal profit in Korea as well.[72]

All three of these positions regarding foreign loans were expressed at various times in Qing policy toward Korea's attempts to borrow from abroad. The Qing Empire opposed loans in certain situations, tolerated them in others, and actively promoted them in still others. A detailed examination of Korea's foreign debts and obligations is extremely difficult. This is due in part to the lack of official Chosŏn government records on the subject and in part to the fact that there was no single government institution entrusted with financial affairs. Thus, whereas King Kojong personally authorized the solicitation of some loans, in other cases Korean officials or even foreign advisers to the Korean government sought and sometimes obtained loans without the knowledge or approval of the court. An additional problem is the matter of definition. Some cases clearly fall within the definition of a "foreign loan," however conceived. However, other cases are not as clear-cut.[73] The problems of definition and lack of adequate documentation create a situation in which estimates of Korean indebtedness vary widely.[74]

---

71. Sigel, "The Role of Korea in Late Qing Foreign Policy," 81–83.

72. Sigel, "Business-Government Cooperation in Late Qing Korean Policy," 162–63.

73. For example, while in Japan, Kim Ok-kyun received an advance payment of 2,750 yen from Takasu Kenzō, a Japanese businessman, for timber on the Korean island of Ullŭng. Kim subsequently granted permission to harvest timber on Ullŭng-do to the American Walter Townsend, and Takasu never received his promised wood. Kim negotiated the contract with Takasu in an official capacity. Should the 2,750 yen for which the hapless Japanese merchant attempted to sue in a Kobe court, be considered a "loan"? If not, should it be considered a "debt," or an "obligation" or something else entirely? Numerous examples of this type of small-scale debt appear in the extant records. For Kim Ok-kyun's contract with Takasu, see Cook, *Korea's 1884 Incident*, 87.

74. Yur-Bok Lee ("Politics over Economics," 83) writes that Kojong wanted loans so badly that "his closest advisers began to entreat foreign loans on their own without going through regular government channels." For estimates of Korea's level of debt and the difficulty of making such estimates, see Lin Mingde, *Yuan Shikai yu Chaoxian*, 209; Tsiang, "Sino-Japanese Diplomatic Relations, 1870–1894," 103; and Bonnie B. C. Oh, "The Background of Chinese Policy Formation in the Sino-Japanese War," 153. At the

Encouragement and Facilitation
of Foreign Borrowing

Whatever the case, it is clear that the Qing Empire loaned considerable sums of money to the Korean government (see Table 1). During 1882–85, the period of the greatest level of Qing support for Korean self-strengthening measures, Li Hongzhang orchestrated loans from the China Merchants Steamship Company, the Kaiping Mines, the Chinese Telegraph Authority, the Tianjin Customs Office, and the Tianjin Arsenal. These were designed to assist Korean efforts to establish a customs service, purchase armaments and military equipment, and establish telegraph lines in Korea. In addition, Qing government and self-strengthening institutions as well as important treaty-port companies loaned smaller amounts of money to assist in the establishment of a Korean legation in Tianjin, to defray the living expenses of Korean students at the Tianjin Arsenal, and for other purposes.

These loans demonstrate the intersection of several strands of thought. The influence of officials such as Li Hongzhang and Ma Jianzhong is clear. All these loans were for purposes that Ma would approve: self-strengthening and modernization. In addition, they were properly negotiated, had relatively reasonable terms, and came from trustworthy sources. The influence and, indeed, direct involvement of Chinese advocates of an informal empire are also present. Tang Tingshu and the China Merchants Steamship Company and the Kaiping Mines played prominent roles in loan negotiations and the ultimate provision of funds to Korea. As noted above, the initial proposal for a loan to establish the Korean Customs Service was far more ambitious in amount (500,000 taels) and scope (Tang Tingshu wanted solid Qing government guarantees for the loan and wanted to establish restrictive conditions on how Korea might spend the money) than the 200,000-tael loan ultimately negotiated. The original proposal demonstrates the ambition of China's treaty-port elite; the compromise arranged by Li Hongzhang and Moellendorff demonstrates the restraining influence of those who had more cautious views toward foreign loans.

———

end of the Sino-Japanese War, one Japanese report put Korea's total indebtedness to the Chinese government and Chinese merchants at 422,500 taels (*NGB* 28, no. 1, 336). A Chinese newspaper quoted a different Japanese estimate, which placed the amount at nearly three times that number; see "Gaoli guozhai," *Xianggang huazi ribao*, Mar. 13, 1895 (GX 21.2.17), *JDZH*, 10.

Table 1
Chinese Loans to Korea, 1882–93

Date	Amount (taels)	Interest rate (%)	Term	Source	Purpose
1882	200,000	8	7 years	China Merchants Steamship Co.; Kaiping Mines	Establish customs service
1884	200,540			Tianjin Customs and Arsenal	Armaments, etc.
1885	100,000	0	25 years	Chinese Telegraph Authority	Telegraph
1892	100,000	6	80 months	Tongshuntai	Repay Myer & Co. loan
1892	100,000	6	100 months	Tongshuntai	Repay Japanese and Townsend loan
1893	35,000			Chinese Board of Admiralty	Pay first install-ment of Japanese indemnity for "bean export controversy"

SOURCES: *NGB*, 28, no. 1, 336; Young Ick Lew, "Yuan Shih-k'ai's Residency," 97.

Moreover, an additional factor also restrained and influenced Qing loans to Korea. The rhetoric used in the loan negotiations and in the actual provisioning of funds generally fit well within traditional depictions of relations between Korea and China. The Qing Empire, the suzerain, offered loans in an effort to "show benevolence" to its tributary. Even the fiscally conservative Weng Tonghe once suggested using no-interest loans to demonstrate the Qing Empire's magnanimous intentions toward Korea.[75] Whatever the ulterior profit-seeking motives of Tang Tingshu and the treaty-port elite, the official rhetoric described the loans as altruistic attempts to aid a younger brother. Although it might be easy to dismiss such rhetoric, the interest rates for the loans offered during this period were lower than those offered by other foreign creditors.[76] The telegraph loan

---

75. Tsiang, "Sino-Japanese Diplomatic Relations, 1870–1894," 103–4.

76. This generosity apparently extended to include Qing-appointed foreign advisers to the Chosŏn government. Owen Denny received a personal loan of 2,000 taels from Zhou Fu, the Tianjin Customs *daotai*. When Denny sought to repay the loan in 1888, he was informed that, "as the loan was on friendly terms," interest was not required (Denny to Zhou Fu, June 6, 1888, Kuksa p'yŏnch'an wiwŏnhoe, *Deni munsŏ*, 33–34). Given that

agreement contained no provision for charging interest at all. In addition, Qing officials were not terribly aggressive in pushing for prompt payment of the loans. In fact, in the late 1880s, Yuan Shikai actually proposed that Korea postpone repayment of a loan from the China Merchants Steamship Company in order to alleviate Korea's dire financial straits. Korea seemed more than willing to follow this advice in this and other cases and often never fully repaid the loans it received from Chinese sources.[77] Such "benevolence" had practical advantages as well, as was recognized by Japanese Foreign Minister Inoue Kaoru. In 1895, when Japanese bankers wanted to loan money to Korea at rates of 10 percent or higher, Inoue was "appalled," stating that "since the Chinese government had not asked for any interest at all on their loans to the Korean government, a 10 percent interest rate would be inconsistent with our apparently paternal declaration to help this poor nation."[78]

A second wave of Chinese loans to Korea took place in the early 1890s. In response to Korea's desperate financial situation and its inability to obtain loans from other sources, an inability due in part to Qing interference, Qing officials such as Yuan Shikai called for Qing government support for additional loans to Korea. These loans demonstrate the influence of China's treaty-port community. To be sure, the proposals for loaning money to Korea were still described in terms of the suzerain's benevolent concern for its vassal. Li noted that because of the extreme poverty of the Chosŏn Kingdom, to merely bind Korea to China without devising alternative means for fiscal succor would result in the Koreans' losing faith in "the Imperial Court's kindness to the weak."[79] However, there also was the growing recognition that loans served as an effective means of enhancing Qing control of Korea. In an essay on loans to Korea, Yuan Shikai listed several reasons

---

Denny became an implacable enemy of Yuan Shikai and many Qing policies in Korea, one wonders whether Zhou Fu ever regretted his generosity.

77. In pushing for loans to Korea in the early 1880s, Li Hongzhang emphasized China's role as the suzerain and the need to "shelter humaneness and be kind to the weak" (Sigel, "Ch'ing Foreign Policy and the Modern Commercial Community," 80). Chinese officials were still pushing for repayment of the telegraph line at least as late as 1900; see Xu Shoupeng to Pak Che-sun, Nov. 29, 1900 (KM 4.11.29), *Ch'ŏngan*, 2: 473. Korea apparently never repaid the loan from the China Merchants Steamship Company (Feuerwerker, *China's Early Industrialization*, 159, 286n36).

78. Duus, *Abacus and the Sword*, 93.

79. Li Hongzhang memorial, Nov. 4, 1892 (GX 18.9.15), *WJSL*, 86: 11.

for lending to Korea, including the fact that additional loans would "make China's dominance of Korea more clear, Korea's dependency on China more firm."[80] Loans were also seen as a way of enhancing commercial opportunities for Chinese businesses in Korea. During this period, the Chinese firm Tongshuntai financed two loans of 100,000 taels each and received valuable shipping concessions in return.[81]

In addition to providing funds directly to Korea, the Qing Empire also took an active interest in Korean attempts to borrow money from other sources. In at least one case, the 1885 attempt of the Chosŏn government to borrow money from the German firm Myer and Company, Yuan Shikai interjected himself in the loan negotiations and secured a lower interest rate and less onerous concessions than had been originally negotiated by the Chosŏn government alone.[82] In a report on the negotiations, Yuan noted that Korea's financial difficulties meant that *any* loan was like "cutting a piece of flesh from one part of the body to patch a sore elsewhere." Nevertheless, Yuan reported that he had labored to ensure the best possible arrangement for Korea and the Chinese merchants working in Korea.[83] As a general rule, loans of a suitable size that were sought for what was perceived to be legitimate purposes, as opposed to "extravagance" (*langfei*), did not meet with Qing resistance. Hence, the Korean government was able to arrange several loans from Myer and Company in the period 1885–89. Korea also borrowed money from the Yokohama Specie Bank, Walter Townsend's American Trading Company, and other sources. The result, as summarized in a report by Yuan Shikai, was a not inconsequential amount of debt owed to a wide variety of sources:

––––

80. For Chinese proposals to loan more money to Korea, see Zongli yamen memorial, Dec. 7, 1890 (GX 16.8.24), *WJSL*, 83: 17–18; Li Hongzhang memorial, Nov. 4, 1892 (GX 18.9.15), *WJSL*, 86: 10–12, Li Hongzhang memorial, Dec. 12, 1892 (GX 18.10.24), *WJSL*, 86: 15–16; see also *JSSL*, 12: 5–7; "Yi Chaoxian jiekuan," Aug. 18, 1889 (GX 15.7.22), *YSHG*, 19: 35–36. For Yuan's essay on loans, see Lin Mingde, *Yuan Shikai yu Chaoxian*, 219–20.

81. For text of the loan agreements, see Tongshuntai, "Tongshuntaihao jiekuan hedong."

82. For a documentary account of the negotiations between Myer and Company and the Korean court, see *Togan*, 1: 126–41. For an assessment of the impact of Myer and Company on Korea, see Kim Chŏng-gi, "Chosŏn chongbuŭi Togil ch'agwan toip (1883–1894)."

83. Li Hongzhang to Zongli yamen, Jan. 30, 1886 (GX 11.12.26), *ZRHGX*, 1999–2001.

The King, the Queen, various officials and bureaus had all borrowed. From 1884, Korea had successively borrowed from a German merchant [Myer and Company] to the total sum of two hundred thousand taels; from 1882 on, she had borrowed from Japanese merchants three hundred thousand with interest ranging from ten to twenty percent. The Americans lent no money but had sold goods on credit; Americans in government service had some back pay due to them: altogether the indebtedness to Americans was about one hundred thousand. The sum owed to Britishers was only twenty thousand. Besides these loans there must be others which could not be ascertained.[84]

Qing Opposition to Korean Borrowing

On the other hand, when Chosŏn Korea sought large-scale loans from non-Chinese sources, particularly in the late 1880s and early 1890s, Qing resistance was much more forceful. Qing officials recognized that excessive indebtedness, particularly to a single source, was a fateful step toward undue foreign influence in Korea. The Qing Empire's own experience with foreign debt and its observations of the strategies and tactics of foreign imperialists more generally gave Qing officials a healthy concern about borrowing from abroad. The Qing Empire was not alone in learning lessons from the case of Egypt: specifically citing the case of the British occupation of Egypt, Japanese Foreign Minister Inoue Kaoru wrote: "I firmly believe that if we wish to solidify our position in Korea and establish a pretext for intervention in its internal affairs, we must obtain real interests there, whether through railroad or through loans."[85] The fact that many foreign creditors sought to use the Customs Service, widely regarded as the only reliable source of revenue in Korea, as a guarantee for the loans they proposed also worried Qing officials. The Qing tactics toward these troubling developments reflected the fine line that Li Hongzhang sought to walk: while frequently seeking to discourage Korea from borrowing from abroad, Li also eschewed taking direct control or responsibility for Chosŏn Korea's fiscal affairs.

In 1889, Chosŏn Korea sought two million taels from France in order to repay a number of previous loans as well as for other projects denounced by Yuan Shikai as "extravagances" (*langfei*).[86] Yuan cited the increasing

---

84. Tsiang, "Sino-Japanese Diplomatic Relations, 1870–1894," 103. See also Bonnie B. C. Oh, "The Background of Chinese Policy Formation in the Sino-Japanese War," 153.

85. Duus, *Abacus and the Sword*, 92.

86. Li Hongzhang to Zongli yamen, June 28, 1889 (GX 15.6.1), *WJSL*, 81: 7–8. Yuan later learned that much of the 700,000 taels was to be used for opening mines and de-

French domination of Indochina "as a warning" to the Koreans of what the future might hold if the loan were completed. He also urged an official at the Korean Foreign Office, Cho Pyong-jik, to convince the Korean king that the loan must be stopped, warning that "it is impossible to use putrid meat to relieve hunger; further calamities will inevitably follow such a loan."[87] The issue was finally resolved when members of the Korean court used the "French worker incident"—in which the French consul refused to hand over to Korean authorities a French worker who had publicly humiliated and beaten a member of the Korean gentry—to convince King Kojong to suspend the loan negotiations. Yuan reported that they had convinced the king that if the loan were completed, he could expect only an increase in such unreasonable behavior on the part of the French.[88]

Soon thereafter, Li Hongzhang received a memorandum from Robert Hart, the Inspector General of the Imperial Maritime Customs Service, outlining how Korea's borrowing might be halted. Hart suggested that the Qing Empire should use its claims of suzerainty over Korea to state

---

veloping railroads. This apparently did not change his opinion regarding the "extravagant" nature of the project. He declared that Korea would probably appoint incompetent managers to oversee such projects, which would result in increased indebtedness without even the slightest benefit for Korea; see Li Hongzhang to Zongli yamen, July 27, 1889 (GX 15.6.22). *ZRHGX*, 2624. Yuan's skepticism was, perhaps, not entirely misplaced. Owen Denny was harshly critical of one "Mr. Pierce," a Korean-appointed American mining "expert." Denny noted that Pierce's telegraphed request for a "mill, machinist, and for assistant John Stinner" led to the dispatch of four assistants, all of whom claimed salaries paid by the Chosŏn government. Denny angrily concluded: "So we now have upon our heads a quartz mill and five miners, headed by a stupid man for an expert, all to do nothing except to worry over the payment of their salaries." See Denny to Kennedy, July 21, 1889, Kuksa p'yŏnch'an wiwŏnhoe, *Deni munsŏ*, 47–48.

87. Li Hongzhang to Zongli yamen, June 28, 1889 (GX 15.6.1), *WJSL*, 81: 7–8. See also Yuan Shikai's telegram to Li Hongzhang, June 28, 1889 (GX 15.6.1), *JSSL*, 11: 12–13. Yuan's use of Cho Pyong-jik is indicative of his *modus operandi*. On many occasions, rather than directly addressing the Korean court, he preferred to make his opinions known through sympathetic Korean officials. This behind-the-scenes approach can find precedence in Li Hongzhang's earlier communications with Yi Yu-wŏn. This method may have been expedient and convenient for Li and Yuan, but it makes tracing their actual influence on events a difficult task for the historian.

88. For more details of this "French worker incident," see Li Hongzhang to Zongli yamen, June 15, 1889 (GX 15.5.17), *WJSL*, 81: 6; Yuan Shikai telegram to Li Hongzhang, June 28, 1889 (GX 15.6.1), *JSSL*, 11: 12; and Li Hongzhang to Zongli yamen, July 27, 1889 (GX 15.6.22), *ZRHGX*, 2623–24.

unequivocally that all foreign nations were forbidden to loan money to Korea without Qing approval. In addition, the Qing Empire should assume all of Korea's outstanding loans to foreigners. This suggestion was supported by the Tianjin commissioner of customs, Gustav Detring. He confidently declared that if the Qing were to take control of Korean customs receipts, it could pay off all loans in ten years. Li Hongzhang had doubts about this proposal. He thought Detring's estimate of potential customs receipts was overly optimistic. Furthermore, he feared the reaction of Japan and Russia to such an overt statement of responsibility. Finally, he worried that Hart and Detring's proposal was an attempt to increase the power and influence of the Chinese Customs Service, a result that could not help but diminish Li's own power.[89]

Although Li rejected the proposal, the Qing Empire was later to adopt a somewhat similar but less ambitious measure. In 1890, the Zongli yamen issued a warning to foreign powers regarding loans to Korea: "Such a step [is] unwise and likely to involve those who participate in such loans in serious trouble and financial losses." The warning noted the Korea was poor and unable to repay loans; for example, Korea had been unable to repay the Qing loans made in the early 1880s. Furthermore, the Qing Empire would not guarantee repayment of any loans and would not allow customs revenues to be used for repayment.[90] A subsequent Zongli yamen report indicated that the United States, France, Great Britain, and Russia had agreed (both publicly and privately) to stop lending money to Korea. Only Japan declared that loans were a matter to be settled between autonomous nations. Despite the apparent success of the warning, the report also acknowledged that private agreements might still continue; thus, the halting of Korea's excessive borrowing was likely to be only temporary.[91]

The predictions of the Zongli yamen report were fulfilled in part by Korea's vigorous attempts to obtain loans in the following few years. The Korean king sought loans from American financiers with the help of the American missionary-diplomat Horace Allen and the American adviser to the king, Owen Denny.[92] He also dispatched the French-born American

---

89. Li Hongzhang to Zongli yamen, July 27, 1889 (GX 15.6.22), *ZRHGX*, 2622; Dalchoong Kim, "Korea's Quest for Reform and Diplomacy in the 1880s," 488–89.

90. Tsui Kwo Yin to U.S. Secretary of State, May 6, 1890, *KAR*, 2: 19–20.

91. Zongli yamen memorial, Oct. 7, 1890 (GX 16.8.24), *WJSL*, 83: 17–18.

92. For more on Allen's efforts to secure loans for Korea, see Harrington, *God, Mammon, and the Japanese*, 133–40; and Kim Wŏn-mo, ed., *Allen ŭi ilgi*, 519–37.

Charles LeGendre to seek a loan from a variety of sources including Japanese, British, and American companies.[93] However, despite the generous concessions offered by the Korean government (the very type of concessions warned against by Ma Jianzhong), Allen, Denny, and LeGendre all came up empty. The failure of these attempts is usually blamed on Qing intervention.[94] For example, Owen Denny was quick to castigate Qing officials for "their persistent and unscrupulous efforts . . . to stifle development and progress here by intrigue and falsehood in order to further, as they think, their political designs upon this country."[95] However, in his own efforts to facilitate a foreign loan for Korea, he discovered several other obstacles as well, including "the fact that very little is yet known of the resources and natural worth of Korea" and the "callous indifference" of the Korean government.[96] He also blamed competing offers pursued by LeGendre.[97]

In the end, the Qing Empire probably played a significant role in preventing Chosŏn Korea from borrowing large sums of money from abroad, although some of the sums sought by the Chosŏn government were so large that it is doubtful that any foreign creditor would have been willing to make such a loan. Despite their conservative rhetoric, Qing officials generally seemed less concerned about small-scale borrowing from abroad (a route Chosŏn Korea apparently pursued with vigor) and even encouraged fairly significant borrowing from Chinese sources. The amalgamation of dozens of small loans from a variety of foreign sources echoes the larger Qing acceptance and encouragement of multilateral imperialism in Korea. But Yuan Shikai and Li Hongzhang sought to create a climate in which the Qing Empire was the creditor of first and last resort.

---

93. For more on LeGendre's attempts, see Li Hongzhang telegram to Yuan Shikai, May 1, 1890 (GX 16.3.13), *Diangao*, 12: 18; Li Hongzhang telegram to Nie, May 2, 1890 (GX 16.3.14), *Diangao*, 12: 18; Li Hongzhang telegram to Yuan Shikai, May 3, 1890 (GX 16.3.15), *Diangao*, 12: 18–19; Jiang Tingfu, *Jindai Zhongguo waijiaoshi ziliao jiyao*, 2: 472–74; and Kwŏn Sŏk-pong, "Yi Sŏn-dŭk ŭi p'a-Il kwa ch'ŏngch'ŭk kaeip."

94. Young Ick Lew, "Yuan Shih-k'ai's Residency," 94; Dalchoong Kim, "Korea's Quest for Reform and Diplomacy in the 1800s," 487; Harrington, *God, Mammon, and the Japanese*, 136–37.

95. Denny to Frazar, Dec. 23, 1889, Kuksa p'yŏnch'an wiwŏnhoe, *Deni munsŏ*, 166–67.

96. Denny to Frazar, Mar. 22, 1890, Kuksa p'yŏnch'an wiwŏnhoe, *Deni munsŏ*, 182.

97. Denny to Lindsley, May 3, 1890, Kuksa p'yŏnch'an wiwŏnhoe, *Deni munsŏ*, 199.

Qing Imperialism and Korean Modernity

The Qing's efforts to construct and dominate the Korean peninsula's tele-communications infrastructure, its establishment of the Korean Customs Service, and its multifaceted role vis-à-vis Chosŏn Korea's attempts to bor-row from abroad demonstrate the unprecedented Qing involvement in the affairs of its putative vassal. They also show how differing groups and in-terests within the Qing Empire itself sometimes complemented and some-times worked at cross-purposes in the articulation and execution of Qing imperial policy in Korea. In addition, they further demonstrate the "nor-malcy" of Qing imperial policy and practice in Korea in a way that a focus on Qing policy as the "restoration" or "reassertion" of long-claimed ritual suzerainty does not. This is not to argue that imperialism, formal or infor-mal, should be considered as an undifferentiated homogenous whole wher-ever and whenever it may found across the globe. But it does highlight the fact that seeking control over telecommunications, institutionalizing the way in which foreign trade is calculated and regulated, and attempting to exert influence if not control over domestic attempts to borrow from abroad have far more analogues among the imperialist practices of puta-tively modern (or modernizing) powers such as Great Britain and Japan than they do with previous Qing or Chinese practices.[98] Writing in the preface to Li Gui's account of circumnavigating the globe, *Huan you diqiu xin lu*, Li Hongzhang forcefully articulated his vision of the Qing Empire's utilizing the latest tools of imperialism:

The various Western nations have daily exerted their intelligence and power and contended with one another. In all their plans for wealth and power, i.e., railroads, electric telegraph wires, warships, and arms, all of them copy each other, all seeking the newest [things]. Regarding commercial matters, this point is especially worth

---

98. For more on the integral role played by telecommunications in nineteenth-century imperialism, see Headrick, *Tools of Empire*; and idem, *The Invisible Weapon*, 50–72 *passim*. For an exploration of the role of the telegraph in Japanese imperial expansion, see Daqing Yang, *Technology of Empire*. The Qing Empire was not the only imperial power interested in discouraging Chosŏn Korea from borrowing from abroad, particu-larly if customs revenue were pledged as collateral. Harrington (*God, Mammon, and the Japanese*, 306) notes a case in 1899 when "Japanese and British envoys worked as part-ners, opposing repeated Russian efforts to oust adviser Brown, heading off a Franco-Russian loan involving a twenty-five year pledge of Chosen's customs."

reflecting upon. A nation that disregards this fact cannot stand on its own feet, and now [such competition] influences even diplomacy.[99]

Qing imperial policy regarding the telegraph, the Customs Service, and foreign loans also prompts a reassessment of a prominent strand of Korean historiography that emphasizes the role of Qing intervention in obstructing Korean reform efforts. This is the argument that the Qing Empire in general and Yuan Shikai in particular constitute significant reasons why Chosŏn Korea was unable to reform and modernize and, therefore, avoid colonial rule.[100] Evaluating the influence of the Qing Empire in Korea, the American Minister Hugh Dinsmore concluded: "But for Chinese interference all would go well and smoothly here, and the country would advance rapidly in prosperity and enterprise. But every step forward is opposed by the Chinese Minister."[101] Many among later generations of Korean scholars agreed. Yuan Shikai, according to one, "emerged as a strong foe to all who advocated the modernization and independence of Korea, making himself a curse to the interests of Korea and its people."[102] Opines another, "Yuan Shih-k'ai repressed every effort Korea made toward progress."[103]

The relationship between imperialism and the "progress"—both economic and otherwise—experienced by the colonized has been the subject of intense and largely unresolved debate. Arrayed against the colonizers' own claims of the civilizing and modernizing benefits of colonial rule are the arguments that imperialism, by virtue either of conscious imperial pol-

---

99. Desnoyers, "Toward 'One Enlightened and Progressive Civilization,'" 151.

100. Many scholars point to a variety of other factors or causes for Chosŏn Korea's "failure" to avoid colonization by Japan. Yi Tŏk-ju (*Chosŏnŭn wae Ilbon ŭi sikminjiga doeonŭnga?* 47–75) considers the role of influential individuals including King Kojong, the Taewŏn'gun, and Yi Wan-yong; the impact of Confucianism and factionalism; the influence of Western imperialism; and Korean attitudes toward Western science (among others) in seeking to answer the question "Why did Chosŏn become a Japanese colony?" Yi also devotes a chapter (and more) to considering the role of the "suzerain Qing" (*Chongjuguk Ch'ŏngguk*); see ibid., 77–107.

101. Cited in Chay, *Diplomacy of Asymmetry*, 79. The American Augustine Heard concurred: "Briefly, Corea can never become prosperous, so long as She is held down and expansion prohibited by China. With that oppression removed She would have a chance of reform and progress" (Heard to U.S. Secretary of State, Oct. 21, 1890, *KAR*, 2: 28). See also Gilmore, *Korea from Its Capital*, 82.

102. Yur-Bok Lee, *West Goes East*, 168.

103. Seung, *The Russo-Japanese Rivalry over Korea, 1876–1904*, 83. See also Ku Sŏn-hŭi, *Han'guk kŭndae taeQing chŏngch'aeksa yŏn'gu*, 11, 17.

icy or of the inherent structure of core-periphery relations, retards progress and development in the colony.[104] For many, the case of Korea represents an interesting divergence from the larger debates between modernization and oppression, both strands of which presume that the imperial power is in some significant way more "modern" than the colonized and it is by virtue of this asymmetry in modernity that reforms and progress in the periphery are either facilitated or stymied. By contrast, Qing imperialism in Korea is believed to have blocked Korean modernization precisely because Qing imperialism was *not* modern in its motivation and execution. Thus, according to Young-ick Lew, "Ch'ing China's *anachronistic* policy of intervention toward her tributary state . . . constituted the primary cause for the hiatus in the Korean reform movement."[105] For Yur-Bok Lee, "The main problem with Yuan was that, unlike many contemporary leaders, he was ignorant of contemporary world affairs and was unable to perceive the spirit and trend of his time in universal terms."[106] To Ku Sŏn-hŭi, the Qing

----

104. For a discussion of how the "modernization argument" and the "oppression argument" have been applied to the case of China, see Osterhammel, "Semi-Colonialism and Informal Empire in Twentieth-Century China," 292–93. For a more general discussion of the role of imperialism in development and/or underdevelopment, see Kiernan, *Imperialism and Its Contradictions*, 45–76. For case studies in sub-Saharan Africa, see Gann and Duignan, *Burden of Empire*.

105. Young Ick Lew, "Yuan Shih-k'ai's Residency," 63; emphasis added.

106. Yur-Bok Lee, *West Goes East*, 172. Expressions of the sentiment that it is largely the backward-looking, premodern nature of the Qing outlook and policies that accounts for Qing and Korean failures are legion. A few more examples include: "The historical relations between China and Korea had no relevance in the modern age. It was because Li and the [Zongli] Yamen thought too much of the historical relations that they failed to make the needed adjustment" (Tsiang, "Sino-Japanese Diplomatic Relations, 1870–1894," 99); "China's Korea policy as expressed through either the Tsungli Yamen or Li Hung-chang, or Ho and Huang, was not only self-serving but also contained from the beginning the seeds of inevitable failure with disastrous effects for Korea as well as herself. Her premises were based in wishful thinking, and an anachronistic, self-centered, and self-serving view of power politics" (Woong Joe Kang, *The Korean Struggle for International Identity*, 102); "It might have been better for Yuan, and for Li himself, and above all for China, if Li had recalled Yuan from Korea in 1886 and sent him to the Chinese legation in the United States or in some European country. Who knows but what, in Western countries, Yuan might have been able to open his eyes and become a far-sighted and visionary statesman capable of seeing China's interests and security issues in a context of both short-term and long-term goals?" (Yur-Bok Lee, *West Goes East*, 173); "To a great extent, the Ching court was suffering from a lack of both political foresight and courage to face reality and rearrange priorities accordingly, a

Empire was insufficiently advanced to be a real imperialist in its own right. Its policies, although they resembled imperialism, only mimicked those of more advanced Western nations. Hence, the Qing Empire was an obstacle to social progress in Korea and the source of Chosŏn Korea's failure to modernize as well as of its ultimate fall into colonial rule.[107] To Chŏn In-yŏng, the Qing Empire's increasing involvement and interference in Korean affairs are signs of its traditional suzerainty, rooted in "premodern exclusivism" (*chŏn'gŭndaejŏkin pat'ajuŭi*),[108] a state of affairs that, according to Pak Su-i, shows that the open-port period was, despite signs of progress, a period of retrogression and decline.[109]

The actual relationship of the Qing Empire to Korean reform efforts is much more ambiguous and complex than the simple assertion that China, apparently by virtue of its inherent pre- or antimodernity, dragged Korea down.[110] Certain aspects of Qing imperial policy and practice may indeed be seen as opposed to the interests of individual Korean reformers and their plans for Korea. But it is more difficult to conceive how connecting the Korean peninsula to the global telegraph network or establishing a Customs Service that functioned as one of the only truly reliable sources of

---

problem the Japanese had successfully handled through the Meiji Restoration. Instead, China pursued an unrealistic obsession—through Yuan's often irrational and childish interference—to attach Korea to the disintegrating Middle Kingdom. The Ching court's desperate attempts to gain an international recognition for its dominating influence in Korea were not that much different from its traditional preoccupation to dominate Korea. Even with thousands of years of intercourse, the Chinese had utterly failed to understand the Korean reality" (Jung, *Nation Building*, 164–65).

107. Ku Sŏn-hŭi, *Han'guk kŭndae daeQing chŏngch'aeksa yŏn'gu*, 20, 17.

108. Chŏn In-yŏng, "Chung-Il kabo chŏnjaeng chŏnhu," 65.

109. Pak Su-i, "Kaehanggi Han'guk muyŏk chabon e kwanhan yŏn'gu," 17. Vipan Chandra (*Imperialism, Resistance, and Reform in Late Nineteenth-Century Korea*, 52) characterizes the period 1885–94 as "the decade of Yuan Shih-k'ai," and the authors of *Korea Old and New* conclude that this period was "a dark age for the Korean enlightenment movement" (Eckert et al., *Korea Old and New*, 213).

110. This tendency is not limited to certain scholars who write about Korea. Writing of those who explore imperialism in China, both of the "modernization" and the "oppressionist" schools, Jürgen Osterhammel ("Semi-Colonialism and Informal Empire in Twentieth-Century China," 295) concludes: "Causal connections—or non-connections—between these two sets of data are more often than not asserted rather than proven. What remains to be shown is *where, when, how* and to what *effect* did *which* extraneous forces impinge upon the indigenous socio-economic system? Through what *mechanisms* were world market influences transmitted to the Chinese economy and so on?"

revenue for the impoverished Chosŏn government (and whose revenue was often used for modernizing reform projects) can be seen as an impediment to reform, progress, or modernization (however one chooses to define such protean terms). Even the Qing Empire's role in the Chosŏn court's attempts to borrow from abroad was more ambiguous than a casual look might imply. To be sure, the Qing Empire played a role in discouraging some foreign entities from making large-scale loans to Korea; moreover, the Chosŏn court might indeed have used the money to fund more sweeping and ambitious reform efforts than it was able to accomplish. However, given the role that foreign loans have played in facilitating even greater imperialist inroads and control in many informal colonies across the world, there may very well have been worse fates for the Chosŏn Kingdom than avoiding "becoming an 'Egypt of Asia.'"[111] And although the advice of Yuan Shikai (and Weng Tonghe) on financial and fiscal matters and their emphasis on agriculture and reducing waste and extravagance do, indeed, reflect a certain precapitalist sensibility, the advice of Ma Jianzhong to Korea regarding loans is much more pragmatic and aware of both the pitfalls and the possible benefits of properly conducted loans.

The arguments of some Korean scholars who consider the Qing an impediment to Korean reform and modernity utilize either implicitly or explicitly the case of Japan as a possible model to emulate in terms of successful modernization and the avoidance of becoming a colony. Young Ick Lew is, perhaps, most explicit about this:

Had it not been for the paternalistic protection China provided through Yuan's residency, the vibrant nationalism and enthusiasm for reform exhibited by the Korean leaders of the enlightenment movement indicate that Korea could have succeeded in achieving sufficient modern wealth and power to preserve its national independence, if not to rival modern Japan in economic and military terms, had Korea not been subjected to China's oppressive control.[112]

———

111. Young Ick Lew, "Yuan Shih-k'ai's Residency," 96–97. Lew's critique of Qing imperialism in Korea is interesting in that it is at times critical of Yuan Shikai for his excessive and unwarranted intervention in Chosŏn affairs, and at other times critical of Yuan for not intervening strongly enough, particularly in the arenas of education and military reform. In this, Lew appears to in some ways echo the lament of Ronaldo Munck ("Dependency and Imperialism in Latin America," 149) that "if there is one thing worse than exploitation it is not being exploited at all."

112. Young Ick Lew, "Yuan Shih-k'ai's Residency," 106. Yur-Bok Lee (*West Goes East*, 173) also contrasts Japanese success with Korea's premodern Qing-induced failure:

Proving or disproving such a counterfactual proposition is, of course, impossible. But it bears noting that Meiji Japan (along with the Qing Empire, Siam, Ethiopia, and a handful of other countries) was truly an exception in an age of high imperialism, which resulted in the colonization of the vast bulk of the earth's land surface.

"as a whole, their [Japanese leaders] outlook toward the world and for the future of Japan became much more enlightened, broad, and far-sighted than that of Yuan, who partly because of ignorance of the rapidly changing world and of his parochialism, precipitated for Korea the tragedies of the late 1880's and the early 1890's, ultimately for China itself those of the early 1900's."

SIX

Suzerainty, Sovereignty,
and Ritual

In 1888, Owen Nickerson Denny, an American adviser to King Kojong, published a tract entitled *China and Korea*. This was, in Denny's own words, an attempt to "turn the Corean tiger loose on the Chinese policy in the peninsula." Denny hoped to "not only prick the vassalage bubble, but expose the criminal conduct as well as injustice she [the Qing Empire] has been guilty of towards this little kingdom."[1] In *China and Korea*, Denny cataloged what he saw as the "petty schemes, criminality, injustice and brutality" of Yuan Shikai.[2] He noted that his efforts to steer Chosŏn Korea toward independence and progress were invariably opposed by "Chinese sources."[3] He also attempted to make the legal case for regarding Chosŏn Korea not as a Qing vassal but as a sovereign and independent member of the family of nations. He based his arguments on the "code of international jurisprudence which has guided those nations so well in the past in their intercourse with each other."[4]

Denny's influential work and those of like-minded observers of nineteenth-century East Asia have greatly influenced subsequent generations' understanding of Qing-Chosŏn relations. In some respects, Denny's observations were an accurate depiction of events of the day. Yuan Shikai was indeed involved in a number of schemes and intrigues during his time

---

1. Denny to Mitchell, Feb. 6, 1888, Kuksa p'yŏnch'an wiwŏnhoe, *Deni munsŏ*, 96.
2. Denny, *China and Korea*, 32.
3. Ibid., 3.
4. Ibid., 24–25.

in Korea, although perhaps not quite as many as Denny imagined. But the fact that few of Yuan's plans seemed to bear fruit is significant. Despite support for Yuan's actions among Purist Party officials in China, Li Hongzhang was generally able to restrain his "man on the spot" in Korea. Moreover, Denny's declaration that the Qing had decided on a policy of the "absorption, gradual or otherwise,"[5] of Korea may have reflected the aspirations of Yuan and his Purist Party allies, but it was sharply at odds with Li Hongzhang's determination to aggressively assert an informal empire in Korea but assiduously avoid any entangling formal responsibilities on the peninsula.

More generally, Denny's description of the world as being divided between "sovereign and independent" states, on one hand, and "semi-independent or dependent" ones, on the other, reflects a certain lawyerly precision that does not match Korean reality. Chosŏn Korea was both a sovereign independent state and a vassal of the Qing Empire, and to varying degrees most of the powers involved in Korea at the time acknowledged this state of affairs.[6] Denny was quick to criticize and dismiss the "usual mystification and vagueness . . . that characterizes all of China's intercourse with the peninsular Kingdom."[7] In doing so, he joined the chorus of those who sought to dismiss the "romance and hyperbole"[8] of the traditional, ritual-based Sino-Korean relations and argued for replacing them with new, Western-style relations. But Western-style relations also contained a healthy dose of ritual, if not romance and hyperbole. Chosŏn officials as well as their Qing counterparts might be excused for suffering some "mystification" of their own when confronted with the ritual protocol, not to mention the unwritten social codes, of relations among the "family of nations." Equally mystifying is the ability of Denny and like-

---

5. Ibid., 13.

6. Ibid., 5–6. Denny noted that "The unerring test . . . of a sovereign and independent state, is its right to negotiate, to conclude treaties of friendship, navigation and commerce, to exchange public ministers, and to declare war and peace with other sovereign and independent powers. These are rights and conditions compatible and consistent with sovereignty which, when possessed by a state, place it in the great family of independent nations; while states which do not possess such powers, must be ranked as semi-independent or dependent according to the terms of the agreement."

7. Ibid., 11.

8. John Russell Young, quoted in M. F. Nelson, *Korea and the Old Orders in Eastern Asia*, 162.

minded commentators to write, seemingly with a straight face, of the sacrosanct nature of treaty- and legation-guaranteed sovereignty in an era of unequal treaties and extraterritoriality in which the powerful dominated and, increasingly, annexed and absorbed the weak at will. The reaction of the international community to the British occupation of Kŏmundo (Port Hamilton), Chosŏn Korea's attempts to establish a legation in the United States, and the Qing Empire's attempts to assert special privilege in Korea illustrate the ways in which the reality of power politics did not live up to the high ideals of the world as a family of sovereign and equal nations.

Schemes and Intrigues

Owen Denny and others repeatedly accused Yuan Shikai of plotting and scheming to oust Chosŏn officials who opposed Yuan's policies in Korea. Many of Yuan's plots were said to include ousting the king and queen as well as effecting the annexation of the Chosŏn Kingdom by the Qing Empire. Some characterizations of Yuan and his actions demonstrate the influence of the Orientalist stereotype of the scheming Chinaman. Two of the more prominent and significant imbroglios were Yuan's part in the furor over a secret Korean request for a Russo-Korean alliance in 1886, and Yuan's role (if any) in the so-called baby riots of 1888. These and other instances demonstrate a willingness on Yuan Shikai's part to entertain the idea of taking forceful and often radical action to safeguard what he saw as Qing prerogatives and interests in Korea; they have, therefore, earned Yuan the ire of generations of Korean scholars. What is equally significant about these events is the fact that, for the most part, they failed. Because of Li Hongzhang's careful management of Qing-Chosŏn relations, Chosŏn Korea did *not* follow the global trend of "man-on-the-spotism," the tendency for imperial home governments to be drawn into greater involvement, sometimes even to the point of direct annexation of territory, by the actions of their officials, soldiers, merchants, or others on the ground in the periphery.[9]

On August 5, 1886, Yuan Shikai, worried about the threat of growing Russian influence in Korea and the apparent willingness of King Kojong to invite such influence, proposed what was in essence a coup against the Korean king. He recommended to Li Hongzhang that the Qing Empire

---

9. Curtin, *The World and the West*, 48–49.

send a fleet of gunboats and thousands of troops to Korea and, in concert
with the Taewŏn'gun, oust Kojong and replace him with another member
of the royal family, presumably one less inclined to look to Russia for
help.[10] Eight days later Yuan claimed to have received from Min Yŏng-ik,
the queen's nephew and a close confidant of the Chosŏn court, a copy of a
secret Korean request for Russian protection. Armed with this apparent
proof of Kojong's perfidy, Yuan swiftly informed his superiors that his
fears were well founded and insisted that forceful action be taken. He went
so far as to read the contents of a telegram to Kojong, claiming that "sev-
enty-two battalions of the Chinese army boarded ships this noon and are
coming to Seoul for an investigation."[11]

Yuan's behavior and his insistent invitation of greater Qing intervention
in Korea are characteristic of a frequently cited phenomenon in the annals
of nineteenth-century imperialism. In an age when many imperial powers
had adopted an official policy of nonexpansionism, many empires nevertheless grew because the actions of aggressive officials on the ground entangled the home governments in the acquisition of power or territory, often against the expressed intentions of the home government. In an
analysis of the role of the "turbulent frontier" in imperial expansion, John
Galbraith highlights the role of the man on the spot in British expansion in
India, Malaya, and South Africa.[12] Philip Curtin points to the examples of
the British acquisition of a significant portion of Burma after the 1852
Anglo-Burmese War and the increasing British involvement in Malaya during the 1870s as examples of this tendency.[13] In the case of Korea, the 1882
imo mutiny was instrumental in bringing Qing troops to Korea; absent this
direct threat to the stability of Korea and to its Qing-approved monarch, it
is hard to imagine the cautious Li Hongzhang consenting to the dispatch
of troops to Korea. Similarly, Yuan Shikai's forceful action in quelling the
1884 *kapsin* coup attempt resulted in the Convention of Tianjin and
prompted Li to seek other means to maintain Qing interests in Korea. In

---

10. Lin Mingde, *Yuan Shikai yu Chaoxian*, 262; Kuksa p'yŏnch'an wiwŏnhoe, *Kojong
sidaesa*, Aug. 16, 1886; Swartout, *Mandarins, Gunboats, and Power Politics*, 82.

11. Swartout, *Mandarins, Gunboats, and Power Politics*, 83.

12. Galbraith, "The 'Turbulent Frontier' as a Factor in British Expansion." See also
Aziz, *The British in India*, 23–24; and Long, *The Man on the Spot*. For an in-depth exploration of the expansion of British activity in South Africa in the face of the metropole's
preference for retrenchment, see Galbraith, *Reluctant Empire*.

13. Curtin, *The World and the West*, 42–48.

1886, Yuan was merely continuing this strategy of inviting further Qing intervention by taking advantage of (or creating) promising conditions in Korea. He was doubtless cheered on by Purist Party members, who frequently criticized Li Hongzhang's cautious policies as appeasement.

Some scholars have concluded that Yuan Shikai manufactured a pretext that allowed him to call for Kojong's ouster and another Qing military occupation of Seoul. Denny demanded to see the copy of the Korean request for Russian protection that Yuan claimed to possess, and when Yuan refused to produce it, Denny denounced it as a forgery either of Yuan's own making or of the British consul-general, E. C. Baber.[14] Russian sources, however, reveal that a secret request for protection was sent, but once the furor erupted, both the Chosŏn court and the Russian government found it expedient to deny any knowledge of it.[15] Some have also argued that the telegram Yuan showed to Kojong declaring that the Qing army and navy were on their way to Korea was also a forgery.[16] Whether Yuan was simply presenting a version of his August 5 request for Qing intervention in an attempt to bully the Korean king or attempting to force Li Hongzhang's hand, hoping that his public declaration would make the actual dispatch of gunboats and troops to Korea a *fait accompli*, or whether, perhaps, foreigners like Denny misinterpreted the precise meaning of Yuan's declarations is not clear.

What is clear is that Li Hongzhang was far more cautious than his subordinate in Korea. Upon hearing of the secret Korean request for Russian protection, Li instructed Qing diplomats in St. Petersburg to discourage the Russians from acceding to the Korean request. He also dispatched Chen Yunyi, the former superintendent of the Chinese-administered tele-

---

14. Jerome Ch'en, *Yuan Shih-k'ai*, 21; Denny to Frazar, Nov. 14, 1886, Kuksa p'yŏnch'an wiwŏnhoe, *Deni munsŏ*, 88. See also Swartout, *Mandarins, Gunboats and Power Politics*, 83; and Lin Mingde, *Yuan Shikai yu Chaoxian*, 262.

15. "In point of fact, the note had been genuine, though the king had later alleged to Yuan that it had been sent without his authorization. It had been written by Premier Shen Shun-tsa [Shim Sun-t'aek] and had appealed for Russian naval support in the event China continued to thwart Korean efforts at independence. Receipt of the note was publicly denied by Russia at the time, but was mentioned *en passant* in a joint statement prepared for the meeting of the Special Committee on Korea on May 8, 1888" (Lensen, *Balance of Intrigue*, 75). For Kojong's denial of knowledge of the request (as well as confirming denial from Russian diplomats), see King Kojong to Zongli yamen, Sept. 23, 1886 (GX 12.8.26), *ZRHGX*, 2137–38.

16. Swartout, *Mandarins, Gunboats, and Power Politics*, 83.

graph bureau in Korea, to Seoul to investigate the affair and ordered Qing naval forces to prepare to go to Korea.[17] Several Qing gunboats did show up in Inch'ŏn harbor, but so did, at the urgent request of Owen Denny, the American warship *Ossipee*. In the end, both the Russian consul-general, Karl Ivanovich Waeber, and his superiors in St. Petersburg denied all knowledge of the Korean request, and the entire affair eventually died down.[18] Yuan Shikai was unable to oust Kojong, but he did manage to use the incident to secure the removal of several pro-Russian Chosŏn officials including Kim Hak-u, Cho Chŏn-du, Kim Yang-muk, and Kim Ka-jin. Yuan also pushed for the pro-Chinese official Kim Yun-sik to be reappointed head of the Foreign Office.[19]

Although this particular incident was settled without serious consequences, Denny claimed to have uncovered many other plots hatched by Yuan Shikai. Indeed, according to Denny, "the very air seems to breed intrigues and conspiracies."[20] In letters and conversations with others, Denny recounted plots and intrigues taking place in 1887, early 1888, June 1888, and in 1889.[21] Some, most notably Henry Merrill, the Qing-appointed commissioner of the Korean Customs Service, were skeptical of Denny's claims. Merrill noted that the mere mention of Yuan's name put Denny "in a rage." Writing elsewhere, he noted that "the winter has passed without any political complications save such as have originated in the brains of busy bodies and disappointed beings who write for the newspapers."[22] Whether the assessment of Denny or that of Merrill is closer to the truth, one important characteristic shared by all the schemes Denny accused Yuan Shikai of instigating is that they failed. If the case of the secret Russo-Korean negotiations is any guide, Li Hongzhang's unwillingness to

---

17. Ibid., 82.

18. Lensen, *Balance of Intrigue*, 76.

19. The pro-Russian Korean officials were initially sentenced to death, but Denny convinced the Korean king to commute their sentences to banishment (Swartout, *Mandarins, Gunboats, and Power Politics*, 84–85, 87).

20. Ibid., 87.

21. Ibid., 91. Swartout notes that "Denny also mentions the 1887 plot in his *China and Korea* (pp. 34–36), which many writers have mistakenly cited as the August 1886 plot" (Swartout, *Mandarins, Gunboats, and Power Politics*, 101n51; Merrill to Hart, May 23, 1888, and Merrill to Hart, July 3, 1888 [no. 48], "Merrill's Letterbooks"; Denny to Lindsley, Dec. 8, 1889, Kuksa p'yŏnch'an wiwŏnhoe, *Deni munsŏ*, 165).

22. Merrill to Hart, May 23, 1888, and Merrill to Hart, June 12, 1888 (no. 45), "Merrill's Letterbooks."

allow his man on the spot to dictate Qing policy is a large reason for their failure. Critical to Li's ability to do so was the nearly instant communications afforded by the Qing telegraph lines.

Another case in which Yuan was implicated in domestic intrigue was the so-called baby riots of 1888. In June of that year, rumors swirled around Seoul that mysterious foreigners were kidnapping Korean children and infants. The shadowy foreigners were said to have gouged out their victims' eyes to use as camera lenses; employed their livers and hearts as ingredients in nefarious potions; and, the most frequently repeated and most heinous version, eaten the children. The rumors implicated Japanese, Americans, British, French, and Germans living in Korea. Large groups of Koreans gathered outside foreign-run hospitals, schools, and churches and muttered darkly about the "baby-snatchers" inside. Many in the foreign community made preparations to flee to their respective legations or to leave Korea altogether. [23] Their diplomatic representatives in Korea demanded that the Chosŏn government publicly denounce and repudiate the rumors as false. The Chosŏn government did so, albeit after some foot-dragging (there is strong evidence that many, even government officials, considered the idea of foreigners eating "roast baby" for dinner not entirely implausible).[24] After American, French, and Russian gunboats were called and marines came ashore to protect various foreign legations, the rumors slowly died down.

At the time, the source of the rumors was far from clear. Accusing fingers pointed in a variety of directions—"some person or persons, with malicious intent," [25] "Catholic zeal, Catholic arrogance, Catholic treach-

---

23. Accounts of the events of June 1888 can be found in *KS*, June 19, 1888 (KJ 25.5.10); Kuksa p'yŏnch'an wiwŏnhoe, *Kojong sidaesa*, June 20, 1888 (KJ 25.5.11); Hwang Hyŏn, *Maech'ŏn yarok*, 146; Li Hongzhang to Zongli yamen, July 14, 1888 (GX 14.6.6), *ZRHGX*, 2485–89; Kuksa p'yŏnch'an wiwŏnhoe, *Yun Ch'i-Ho's Diary*, 1: 319; Underwood, *Fifteen Years Among the Top-Knots*, 15–17; Hulbert, *History of Korea*, 2: 245; Allen, *Things Korean*, 226–27; Chaille-Long, *My Life in Four Continents*, 2: 349; Gilmore, *Korea from Its Capital*, 82–85; *North China Herald*, June 29, 1888, 834; and *New York Times*, June 28, 1888, 1.

24. *KS*, June 19, 1888 (KJ 25.5.10). For the allegation that various foreigners enjoyed "roast baby," see Allen, *Things Korean*, 226–27. For the dissatisfaction of foreigners who objected to official Korean proclamations that "baby-butchers" of whatever nationality will be caught and apprehended, see Underwood, *Fifteen Years Among the Top-Knots*, 16–17; see also Chaille-Long, *My Life in Four Continents*, 349–50; Dinsmore to U.S. Secretary of State, July 1, 1888, and Dinsmore to Secretary of State, June 18, 1888, *KAR*, 2: 213, 216.

25. Underwood, *Fifteen Years Among the Top-Knots*, 15.

ery," [26] anti-Christian forces, [27] "enemies of the Queen," [28] or the Tae-wŏn'gun. [29] On reflection, however, many Westerners concluded that the rumors came from China. Many in the foreign community in Korea had already spent time in China and were familiar with the antiforeign invective that circulated through the countryside and led to outbreaks such as the Tianjin Massacre of 1870. [30] They were quick to point to similarities between the rumors in Korea in 1888 and those they remembered hearing in China earlier. [31] Some, not satisfied with the conclusion that the rumors were the result of idle chat on the docks in Inch'ŏn or in a Chinese silk shop in Seoul, concluded that the rumors were *deliberately* spread by Yuan Shikai. [32] Denny related to Merrill his belief that Yuan had started the rumors in order to foment disorder and provide a pretext for Qing military intervention and the removal of King Kojong. [33] Some scholars have subsequently argued that Yuan wished to discourage foreigners from loaning money to Korea. [34] Others were less certain. After considering the available evidence, including a story told by a colleague in whom he had "entire confidence" about how the colleague's interpreter had spoken to someone

---

26. Harrington, *God, Mammon, and the Japanese*, 89–90.

27. Davies, *The Life and Thought of Henry Gerhard Appenzeller*, 300–301.

28. Underwood, *Underwood of Korea*, 74–75. Note that Underwood provides two different explanations for the rumors' origins in her two works.

29. Chaille-Long, *My Life in Four Continents*, 2: 349.

30. For a discussion of antiforeign rumors in China, see Paul Cohen, *China and Christianity*.

31. It should be noted that although some strands of the rumors—eye gouging and using of hearts and livers for creating medicines and potions—did have analogues in China, the allegation that foreigners ate children as a matter of routine dietary choice appears to have been a purely Korean notion; see Larsen, "Cannibals, Cameras, and Chinese."

32. In an addendum to *China and Korea*, Denny wrote: "There does not seem to be any doubt in the minds of intelligent foreigners in Seoul, who have closely observed events for the past two years, as to whose dastardly hand is at the bottom of this business" (Park Il-keun, ed., *Anglo-American and Chinese Diplomatic Materials Relating to Korea*, 1073).

33. Merrill to Hart, July 3, 1888 (no. 48), "Merrill's Letterbooks."

34. Young Ick Lew, "Yuan Shih-k'ai's Residency," 94. In his account of the activities of Horace Allen in Korea, Fred Harrington (*God, Mammon, and the Japanese*, 136–37) writes, "There was little violence, and excitement soon died down; but Wall Street financiers who heard of the episode concluded that Korea must be a completely unenlightened land."

who confessed to having been paid by Yuan to spread antiforeign rumors, the American diplomat Hugh Dinsmore cautiously concluded, "we cannot point out the guilty principals or agents. It may possibly be accidental."[35] Subsequent historians have not been as cautious as Dinsmore: virtually every English-language historical work that mentions the "baby riots" unequivocally invokes the "China connection" to explain the event.[36]

If Yuan were indeed responsible for spreading the antiforeign rumors (something that Yuan emphatically denied to Li Hongzhang), this would appear to constitute another case of an official on the periphery attempting to drag the home government into greater intervention and involvement.[37] As was the case in other instances of Yuan Shikai–fomented intrigues and troubles in Korea, this attempt failed; the Qing government did not send troops or approve the ousting of the Korean king. If the rumors stemmed from other sources, then the allegations that Yuan was responsible are a sign of how quickly some observers (and subsequent scholars) were to conclude that Yuan Shikai was responsible for all of Korea's troubles. As Merrill once quipped, "Yuan has had plenty of mischief here; but I think if an earthquake should topple over half the homes in Seoul, Denny would trace the disaster to Yuan."[38]

---

35. Dinsmore to Secretary of State, July 1, 1888, *KAR*, 2: 214–15. Dinsmore's caution would be praised by those who study contemporary "urban legends." One of the hallmarks of the urban legend is that the source of the story is never an eyewitness but invariably a FOAF (friend of a friend); see Brunvand, *The Vanishing Hitchhiker*, 4.

36. Harrington, *God, Mammon, and the Japanese*, 89; Paik, *The History of Protestant Missions in Korea*, 156; Young Ick Lew, "Yuan Shih-k'ai's Residency," 94; Dalchoong Kim, "Korea's Quest for Reform and Diplomacy in the 1880s," 487. A few Korean-language works mention the incident in passing but do not seek to explain how and why the rumors arose when and where they did. Rather, they point to the rumors and the resulting unrest as yet another sign of the uneasy and troubled times; see Pak Wan, *Sillok Han-guk kidokkyo 100 nyŏn*, 261–63; Kim Kyo-yŏng, *Kaehwagi ŭi Kim Ch'ongni*, 167–69; and Yi Sŏn-gŭn, *Han'guksa*, 953–54.

37. For Yuan's denial, see Li Hongzhang to Zongli yamen, July 14, 1888 (GX 14.6.6), *ZRHGX*, 2486.

38. Merrill to Hart, Mar. 20, 1888, "Merrill's Letterbooks." The former head of the Korean Customs Service, Paul Georg Moellendorff, expressed a similar sentiment about Denny. Writing of Denny's criticism of Yuan Shikai's plots against King Kojong, Moellendorff argued that "the whole story seems to rest on Mr. D's too vivid imagination and his too great animosity towards Yuen [Yuan]" (cited in Yur-Bok Lee, *West Goes East*, 184). Lee (ibid., 184) concludes that Moellendorff made this statement "without investigating or knowing all the facts."

Even if all of the allegations of Denny and like-minded critics of Yuan Shikai were accurate, it is still worth noting that Yuan's schemes to oust the Korean king failed. An excessive focus on Yuan's aims and activities—which may very well have been representative of the aspirations and tactics of some Purist Party members—ignores the fact that Yuan represented only one strand of Qing imperial strategy in Chosŏn Korea, and often not the most influential one at that. Li Hongzhang's insistence on multilateral imperialism and avoidance of excessive Qing responsibility for and entanglement in Korea usually restrained the Qing Resident and carried the day.

It is also interesting and useful to contrast Yuan's failure to oust the Korean king (whatever Yuan's desires may have been) with the fact that Japanese, Japanese-affiliated, and domestic Korean groups were seeking to oust Kojong with varying but greater degrees of success. The soldiers who mutinied in 1882 successfully returned the Taewŏn'gun to power until Qing troops quelled the mutiny and took the Taewŏn'gun to China and returned Kojong to the throne. In 1884, the *kapsin* coup plotters worked closely with the Japanese Minister Takezoe Shin'ichirō (who withdrew his support at the last minute after receiving orders from Tokyo) and were frustrated in their attempts to control the king only by the swift action of Yuan Shikai and Qing and Qing-trained troops. The Qing would again respond to threats to Kojong's security in 1894 by sending troops to help quell the Tonghak Rebellion. In the days leading up to the outbreak of the Sino-Japanese War, Japanese troops surrounded the royal palace and brought the Taewŏn'gun back into power yet again. Equally as plausible as a narrative of Qing intervention and "petty schemes" aimed at the Korean king is a narrative of the Qing Empire as the only power that stood between Kojong and ruin.

The Kŏmundo (Port Hamilton) Affair

On May 12, 1885, British forces occupied Kŏmundo (which they called Port Hamilton), a small group of islands off the southern coast of Korea. Their occupation of the islands would last until February 27, 1887. The British decision to do so had little to do with Korea *per se*; rather, it was part of the British global strategy of countering Russian advances and designs. In fact, absent Russian interest in Korea, there is little indication that the British would have paid attention to the peninsula. In 1881 one British diplomat quipped, "My interest in that wretched country has subsided since the departure of the Russian fleet."[39] But the Russians *did* demonstrate an interest in Korea and established commercial and diplomatic relations with the Chosŏn Kingdom in July 1884.[40] Consequently, the British Empire from time to time considered moves designed to impede Russia's progress.

The occupation of Kŏmundo had at least two motivations. First, it was hoped that the British presence astride the strategic sea-lanes south of Korea and the possibility of a British blockade of Russia's Vladivostok-based Pacific fleet would discourage Russian adventurism, particularly in Afghanistan. The British viceroy of India described this strategy as seeking to "make the dog drop his bone by squeezing his throat." Second, the British hoped to pre-empt a Russian occupation of a Korean harbor such as Port Lazareff, near the Korean town of Wŏnsan.[41]

The British move can be seen as a challenge to the Qing-mediated system of multilateral imperialism in Korea. Port Hamilton was not considered a treaty port, open to all those who had signed and ratified diplomatic and commercial treaties with the Chosŏn Kingdom. Rather, the British asserted exclusive privileges in an effort to maintain their geopolitical interests in the region. And the British action threatened to establish a precedent that other powers could point to in their own acquisition of coveted pieces of Korean territory. Most prominent in this category were the Russians, who had long expressed an interest in a part of Yŏnghŭng Bay that they had christened Port Lazareff. In fact, some Japanese believed that Moellendorff had promised Port Lazareff to the Russians as part of his secret negotiations with Russia. By occupying Kŏmundo, the British were merely engaging, in the words of Hilary Conroy, in "a sort of beat-them-to-it retaliation for Russia's intended taking up of a leasehold at Wŏnsan."[42] But Russia raised the ante when Alexis de Speyer, the Russian envoy, arrived in Seoul and all but announced that he had "instructions to take steps for the annexation of ten times as much [Korean] territory as had been occupied by Great Britain unless the latter withdraws from Port Hamilton."[43]

Concerned about a potential scramble for territory in Korea, Li Hongzhang informed Chosŏn Korea of the dangers of allowing Britain to lease

---

39. Kiernan, *British Diplomacy in China*, 79.

40. For the text of the treaty, see *KS,* July 7, 1884 (KJ 21.5*.15). The treaty uses the Chosŏn, Qing, and Western calendars to date its ratification.

41. Lensen, *Balance of Intrigue*, 55.

42. Conroy, *The Japanese Seizure of Korea*, 210.

43. Deuchler, *Confucian Gentlemen and Barbarian Envoys*, 215.

the islands (citing Hong Kong as an illustrative precedent)[44] and sent Moellendorff and Ding Ruchang to Kŏmundo aboard a Qing gunboat to evaluate the situation.[45] They then traveled to Japan where they met with the British Far East naval commander, W. M. Dowell.[46] In the ensuing months, Li Hongzhang sent out feelers to Britain, Russia, and Japan concerning a potential bilateral or multilateral guarantee of Korea's security and territorial integrity.[47] Li failed to obtain a British promise to announce that the British Empire would protect the territorial integrity of Korea in return for a long-term lease of the islands, but he was finally able to secure a Russian promise not to seek any territory on the peninsula. Satisfied with this assurance and finding the islets a "poor harbour, difficult to defend and with strong currents which tore away both defensive booms and submarine cables," the British withdrew from Kŏmundo in early 1887.[48] A grateful Kojong dispatched a mission to China to express his thanks for intervening on behalf of Korea and for regarding Korea as if it were part of the inner realm (*neifu*).[49]

Not only was Li Hongzhang able to fend off this challenge to the system of multilateral imperialism in Korea, but in doing so he was also able to bolster Qing claims to suzerainty. The British acknowledged Qing claims to a special position in Korea by negotiating directly with the Qing Empire over Port Hamilton. Other nations criticized the British occupation, but did little to hinder a Sino-British resolution of the issue. Japan, while expressing official concern over the British move, did nothing to prevent hundreds of Japanese workers from being hired by the British to construct fortifications on the islands.[50] The Americans also protested the

---

44. *KS*, May 4, 1885 (KJ 22.3.20). The Japanese diplomat Kondō Motosuke sent a similar warning to the Chosŏn court. See *KS*, May 13, 1885 (KJ 22.3.29).

45. *KS*, May 16, 1885 (KJ 22.4.3); *KS*, May 21, 1885 (KJ 22.4.8).

46. Lensen, *Balance of Intrigue*, 37; Chien, *The Opening of Korea*, 172.

47. Chien, *The Opening of Korea*, 174; Lensen, *Balance of Intrigue*, 62, 65–67; Deuchler, *Confucian Gentlemen and Barbarian Envoys*, 215.

48. Pratt et al., *Korea: A Historical and Cultural Dictionary*, 228. The British maintain a lease on a small plot of land on Kŏmundo to this day at the site of a graveyard that dates back to the 1885–87 occupation. Two graves are still visible there (Hoare, *Embassies in the East*, 172).

49. *KS*, May 9, 1887 (KJ 24.4.17).

50. Lensen, *Balance of Intrigue*, 58. The British *chargé d'affaires* in China, Nicholas-Roderick O'Conor, claimed that Itō Hirobumi "preferred a British presence in Port Hamilton 'for the English occupation would be temporary, a Russian one permanent'" (Lensen, *Balance of Intrigue*, 55).

move, but explored a possible U.S. lease of the islands if the British could be convinced to leave.[51] The response of many foreign powers to the Kŏmundo incident is indicative of most foreign powers' willingness to acknowledge some form of special Qing-Chosŏn relationship. This tendency was also evident among the diplomats stationed in Korea.[52]

The Kŏmundo incident did little to resolve Chosŏn Korea's anomalous status in the eyes of the outside world. But it did serve to reinforce the utility of Li Hongzhang's chosen strategy of promoting multilateral imperialism in Korea while seeking to maintain and enhance Qing suzerainty and special privileges but eschewing direct responsibility for Korea's security. On the other hand, it also demonstrated how ineffective informal multilateral imperialism might prove to be in the face of determined attempts at territorial annexation. In the 1880s, the world stood on the brink of a wave of "beat-them-to-it" acquisitions of territory that would hardly be slowed, let alone halted, by treaties and multilateral arrangements.

Permanent Legations: Suzerainty vs. Independence

In 1887, years after Chosŏn Korea had signed and ratified treaties with Japan, the United States, and various European powers, the Chosŏn court sought to establish permanent legations abroad.[53] This issue became a serious point

---

51. Rockhill to U.S. Secretary of State, Jan. 13, 1887, *KAR*, 2: 240.

52. According to Tyler Dennett (*Americans in Eastern Asia*, 475): "Great Britain then showed the trend of its policy by appointing as a diplomatic representative a consul-general who was made responsible to the British minister in Peking. Thus England was supporting the Chinese claim to suzerainty over Korea by making the diplomatic establishment in the peninsula an appendage of the British Legation in China. Germany was represented by a consul who reported directly to Berlin; France by a *"Commissaire"* reporting directly to Paris; and Japan by a *Charge*, Minister, or Ambassador Plenipotentiary, as suited the situation. In 1884 Congress reduced the post at Seoul to that of Minister Resident, equal in rank to that at Bankok [*sic*]." In the case of Great Britain, the British Treasury argued that "so long as the consular establishment in Corea is only a provisional detachment from China and Japan, without any distinct organization or recognition in the Parliamentary Estimates, My Lords [i.e., the Treasury] think it inexpedient to ask Parliament to provide for the erection of permanent Consular buildings in that country of the expensive nature indicated in your report" (Hoare, *Embassies in the East*, 178).

53. Yi Min-sik ("Pak Chŏng-yang ŭi chae-Mi hwaldong e kwanhan yŏn'gu," 426) argues that it was Chosŏn Korea's inexperience with foreign relations that accounts for the long delay between treaty ratification (and the 1883 dispatch of Min Yŏng-ik on a

of contention among the Qing Empire, Yuan Shikai, King Kojong and the Chosŏn court, and a number of American diplomats and advisers to the King. Both Owen Denny and Horace Allen credited themselves with initiating the idea of setting up embassies in foreign countries.[54] To Denny, establishing permanent legations was "the only practical way that presented itself in order to cause China if possible to change her course before it became too late." He concluded that if his suggestion "had the desired effect, it will be the best possible service I could render both countries."[55]

The perceived need for Chosŏn Korea to establish permanent legations abroad hinged on their symbolic and diplomatic significance. Legations headed by properly credentialed representatives of sufficient rank were taken as signs of full participation in the "family" of sovereign and equal nations.[56] Thus, for many contemporary observers and subsequent historians alike, the Korean declaration of its intention to establish legations is taken as a sign of the desire of the Chosŏn Kingdom to shake off the yoke of China and to enter into Western-style, "modern" relations with the rest of the world.[57] Many of the same observers and historians argue that the

---

special observation mission to the United States) and the establishment of permanent legations.

54. For Allen's claim to have originated the idea, see Yur-Bok Lee, "Establishment of a Korean Legation," 6; and Harrington, *God, Mammon, and the Japanese*, 226. Yur-Bok Lee ("Establishment of a Korean Legation," 6) notes that Min Yŏng-ik also encouraged Kojong to establish legations in the United States and Europe. Hilary Conroy (*The Japanese Seizure of Korea*, 188) also credits the American minister in Seoul, Hugh Dinsmore, with encouraging Kojong to establish a legation.

55. Swartout, *Mandarins, Gunboats, and Power Politics*, 90.

56. Regarding the treaty-guaranteed right to exchange diplomats and establish legations, U.S. Secretary of State Thomas Francis Bayard wrote, "The reciprocal sending and receiving of diplomatic and consular officers is provided for in the treaty between the United States and Corea. No act of national sovereignty is more express and decided than this" (Yur-Bok Lee, "Establishment of a Korean Legation," 13).

57. Young Ick Lew ("Yuan Shih-k'ai's Residency," 88) contends that Kojong's "motive was to bolster Korean claims to independence by strengthening her ties with the treaty powers, particularly in light of Yuan's plot to depose the king the previous year." Yur-Bok Lee (*West Goes East*, 183) concludes that "Denny, together with Dr. Horace Allen and Min Yŏng-ik (former vice minister of the Korean Foreign Office and a new enemy of Resident Yuan), had persuaded King Kojong to establish permanent legations in the United States and Europe in order to show the world that Korea was, after all, a sovereign and independent kingdom." Hilary Conroy (*The Japanese Seizure of Korea*, 188) equates "a new Korean mission to the United States" with "another plan to cut into Chinese influence." Yi Min-sik ("Pak Chŏng-yang ŭi chae-Mi hwaltong e kwanhan

Qing Empire sought to block the Korean attempts to establish legations abroad, a sign of the Qing commitment to its traditional suzerainty.[58]

These conclusions both reveal and conceal. Kojong and the Chosŏn court did indeed seek to set up a permanent diplomatic presence abroad and did confront obstacles thrown up by the Qing Empire. However, the fact that King Kojong heeded the advice of his American advisers does not necessarily indicate an appreciation of or longing for Western-style independence. Kojong had plenty of "traditional" reasons and precedents for defending Korea's "autonomy" (*chaju*) in the face of Yuan Shikai's interference. And he seemed in no hurry to end the ritual practices and conventions that had long animated Qing-Chosŏn relations. Those who perceive a Korean longing to participate in Western-style relations often emphasize Qing pressure and coercion as the main reasons why Kojong's actions did not always appear to demonstrate an unequivocal support for independence. However, they neglect to consider the role of Western coercion in the initiation and execution of the plan to set up legations abroad. Moreover, although Yuan Shikai undeniably sought to block the dispatch of Korean diplomats abroad, he was frequently overruled by his superiors in Tianjin (and in the Zongli yamen), who had fewer objections to the Korean enterprise. In the end, the Qing Resident was again restrained by the metropole. Finally, it is clear that whatever the hopes of Denny, Allen, and Kojong, the successful establishment of a Chosŏn legation in Washington, DC, did little to aid the cause of Korean independence or to clarify the nature of what was, to many Westerners, the perennially confusing Qing-Chosŏn relationship.

On July 6, 1887, Kojong dispatched Min Yŏng-jun to serve as Chosŏn Korea's resident minister (*p'alli taesin*) to Tokyo.[59] The official notice of this act, recorded in the *Kojong sillok*, makes no mention of a Korean desire

---

yŏn'gu," 426) argues that the main purpose of setting up a legation in the United States was to borrow the strength of a third power (the United States) to cast off the dependency relationship with the Qing Empire. Therefore, Pak's going alone to present his credentials was the natural act of an independent power. See also Yur-Bok Lee, "Establishment of a Korean Legation in the United States"; Kim Wŏn-mo, *Kaehwagi Han-Mi kyosŏp kwangyesa*, 615; and Chŏn In-yŏng, "Chungil kabo chŏnjaeng chŏnhu," 69–71.

58. See sources in previous note. See also Harrington, *God, Mammon, and the Japanese*, 229; and Hulbert, *History of Korea*, 244.

59. *KS*, July 6, 1887 (KJ 24.5.16). Min was to be assisted in Japan by Kim Ka-jin. See also Li Hongzhang to Zongli yamen, Sept. 13, 1887 (GX 13.7.26), *ZRHGX*, 2342.

to achieve independence or to counter Chinese claims to suzerainty. Rather, it notes the need to rectify Korea's failure to send a diplomat to Japan in order to improve friendly relations with its neighbor.[60] Denny, however, saw the dispatch of Min to Japan, particularly the Chosŏn court's decision to inform the Qing Empire of the action only after the fact, as an important test case to gauge the Qing reaction to the establishment of legations in nations with which the Chosŏn Kingdom enjoyed treaty relations.[61] Both Li Hongzhang and Yuan Shikai grumbled about the delay in being informed, but neither took any immediate action regarding the matter.[62]

Therefore, on August 18, 1887, the Chosŏn Kingdom announced its intention to dispatch Pak Chŏng-yang as envoy extraordinary and minister plenipotentiary and as the head of a Chosŏn legation to Washington, DC, and Sim Sang-hak as the head of a legation in Europe (Sim was shortly replaced by Cho Sin-hŭi).[63] As was the case with the dispatch of Min to Japan, the official announcement made no mention of a desire for independence; rather, the intent was to improve friendly relations (and, in the case of the United States, the need to respond to an American invitation to send a diplomat to Washington).[64]

Yuan Shikai reported these developments to Li Hongzhang, noting that the legations would probably not be dispatched immediately because of lack of funds and conveying the warnings of foreign diplomats in Seoul that the Chosŏn Kingdom's move might damage Qing claims of suzerainty in Korea.[65] Li Hongzhang responded with guarded approval of the establishment of legations abroad, provided that the Chosŏn Kingdom remembered its status as a Qing dependency and that it adhered to the rules of proper etiquette and protocol that emphasized this status.[66] Yuan, however, disregarded his orders and proceeded to convey strong Qing disapproval of the entire venture; he criticized the king for not notifying the Qing prior

---

60. *KS*, July 6, 1887 (KJ 24.5.16).

61. Swartout, *Mandarins, Gunboats, and Power Politics*, 90.

62. Ibid., 90; Yur-Bok Lee, "Establishment of a Korean Legation," 6.

63. For acknowledgment of Cho Sin-hŭi being dispatched in the stead of Sim Sang-hak, as well as some royal exasperation due to Cho's failure to depart on his mission in a timely manner, see *KS*, Sept. 16, 1887 (KJ 24.7.29).

64. *KS*, Aug. 18, 1887 (KJ 24.6.29).

65. Tsiang, "Sino-Japanese Diplomatic Relations, 1870–1894," 100; Young Ick Lew, "Yuan Shih-k'ai's Residency," 88.

66. Li Hongzhang to Zongli yamen, Sept. 14, 1887 (GX 13.7.27), *ZRHGX*, 2343.

to announcing the dispatch of envoys abroad and expressed concerns about the financial burden of establishing and operating legations.[67]

Despite Yuan's objections, Kojong ordered Pak Chŏng-yang to depart for his post on September 23, 1887. Pak left Seoul, but that evening Li Hongzhang cabled a demand that the Chosŏn court ask Qing permission before dispatching Pak. Yuan Shikai used this to accuse Kojong of committing a "triple crime" against the Qing and sent Chinese officials to stop Pak outside the walls of Seoul.[68] A heated debate in the Chosŏn court ensued, with Denny and Allen insisting that Kojong must assert his autonomy by not seeking Qing permission. The American diplomats Hugh Dinsmore and Charles Denby also registered protests with Qing officials in Seoul and Beijing.[69] Despite the encouragement and support of Western advisers and diplomats, Kojong eventually decided to send Yun Kyo-sŏp as a special envoy to China to present an official request for permission.[70] The request, which was filled with the requisite declarations of Korean humility in the face of the suzerain's benevolence and splendor, was published in the Tianjin newspaper, *Shibao.*[71] Thus, the Chosŏn delegations traveled under the same ambiguous cloud that had shadowed Korea's first treaties with Western powers: the Chosŏn Kingdom was apparently seeking to adhere to the forms of Western-style international relations while acknowledging Qing suzerainty over Korea.

Satisfied with Kojong's declaration of vassalage, the Qing Empire granted Korea permission to establish legations, provided that Korean diplomats abided by three rules (which came to be known as the "three protocols"):

1. Before the first official visit to the host government, the Korean envoy would call on the Qing legation and request the assistance of the Qing

---

67. Yur-Bok Lee, "Establishment of a Korean Legation," 8–9; Young Ick Lew, "Yuan Shih-k'ai's Residency," 88. In an earlier letter to Kojong, Yuan Shikai had expressed a concern about Chosŏn Korea's finances and urged the Korean Court to be frugal; see *KS*, Aug. 28, 1886 (KJ 23.7.29).

68. Yur-Bok Lee, "Establishment of a Korean Legation," 9. See also Hugh Dinsmore to Secretary of State, Sept. 30, 1887, *KAR*, 2: 101–4.

69. Yur-Bok Lee, "Establishment of a Korean Legation," 11.

70. Ibid., 12.

71. For the full text of King Kojong's request, see Li Hongzhang to Zongli yamen, Oct. 6, 1887 (GX 13.8.20), *ZRHGX*, 2364. See also Harrington, *God, Mammon, and the Japanese*, 233; and Charles Denby to Secretary of State, Dec. 9, 1887, *KAR*, 2: 109–12.

minister, who would accompany the Korean envoy on his first visit to the host government (after which the Korean envoy could visit freely with or without his Qing counterpart);

2. In official gatherings, banquets, and other functions, the Korean representative must always take a lower position than his Qing counterpart;

3. The Korean envoy should consult with the Qing legation on matters of significance or importance.[72]

King Kojong apparently did not inform Horace Allen, the American entrusted with the task of escorting the Korean mission to Washington, that he had sought Qing permission before officially establishing a legation. As a result, Allen was under the impression that the mission constituted a clear and unequivocal declaration of Korean sovereignty and independence. He was, therefore, rather frustrated when the Korean envoy, Pak Chŏng-yang, declared his intention to abide by the Qing Empire's "three protocols" even though no mention of the rules was included in Pak's official instructions.[73] Exasperated that "what little wit the envoy had possessed had deserted him when he left his native soil," Allen threatened to resign his advisory post if Pak even sent his card, let alone met with Qing officials, before presenting his credentials to the Americans. Allen also stated that should his warnings not be heeded, "the King would surely decapitate him [Pak]. I mean cut off his physical head."[74] Pak succumbed to Allen's pressure and refused to visit the Qing legation before calling on the U.S. State Department and President Grover Cleveland.

Qing protests at Pak's behavior resulted in Kojong and the Chosŏn Foreign Office officially disavowing Pak's conduct, claiming that Pak had acted on his own. They dragged their feet in the face of Qing demands for Pak's recall, a move that took place in 1888 ostensibly for reasons of ill health, and refused to punish Pak for his alleged insubordination.[75]

---

72. Tsiang, "Sino-Japanese Diplomatic Relations, 1870–1894," 100; Li Hongzhang to Zongli yamen, Nov. 11, 1887 (GX 13.9.26), *ZRHGX*, 2379–82; Swartout, *Mandarins, Gunboats, and Power Politics*, 94.

73. Although Pak's official instructions did not explicitly mention the "three protocols," they did include an injunction to work amicably with all foreign ambassadors and consuls beginning with the Chinese minister (Kim Wŏn-mo, *Kaehwagi Han-Mi kyosŏp kwan'gyesa*, 618).

74. Harrington, *God, Mammon, and the Japanese*, 236–37.

75. Yur-Bok Lee, "Establishment of a Korean Legation," 23–24.

The establishment of Chosŏn legations in Tokyo and Washington, DC, would seem to constitute additional evidence of Korea's independence and sovereignty. The fact that Pak Chŏng-yang's official instructions not only did not include the "three protocols" but also used the Chosŏn rather than the Qing calendar are taken as signs of Kojong's desire to be free of Qing suzerainty.[76] Pak's reception with full courtesy by President Grover Cleveland and the U.S. State Department would seem to be evidence that the United States recognized Korea's claims to independence. [77]

But a closer look at the process by which the foreign legations were established as well as international reaction to the process raises more questions than answers. Did Kojong and the Chosŏn government actually desire Western-style sovereignty and participation in the international family of nations, especially if this meant the wholesale repudiation of Korea's special relationship with the Qing Empire? Those who conclude in the affirmative can point to Korea's declaration of its intention to establish legations abroad, the dispatch of Pak Chŏng-yang to Washington (in the face of criticism and pressure from Yuan Shikai), Pak's refusal to follow the "three protocols," Kojong's foot-dragging in the face of Qing demands for Pak's recall, and Kojong's refusal to seriously punish Pak as signs that the Korean monarch wished for full independence from the Qing Empire and desired that Korea be a member of the modern "family of nations."[78]

And yet this conclusion ignores a series of events and incidents that would seem to imply Kojong's commitment to ending Korea's special relationship with China was less than complete. First and foremost is the fact that Kojong heeded the Imperial Qing command to request Qing permission before dispatching Pak to the United States. Upon receiving the impe-

---

76. See, e.g., Mun Il-p'yŏng, *Han-Mi osimnyŏnsa*, 147–80, as cited in Sukhee Han, "Beyond the Celestial Sinic Sphere," 261–62.

77. For the text of Pak's credentials and Grover Cleveland's reply, see *KAR*, 2: 112–13.

78. According to Hugh Dinsmore, Pak was promoted following his return to Korea (Dinsmore to Secretary of State, Dec. 10, 1889, *KAR*, 2: 115). However, two weeks later, Dinsmore reported that "by order of the King Mr. Pak has been reduced to the rank which he held prior to his late promotion" (Dinsmore to Secretary of State, Dec. 24, 1889, *KAR*, 2: 116). This, however, appears to have been a temporary setback at most, since Pak was, in ensuing years, promoted to a variety of positions including minister of justice and of finance. The Qing Empire ultimately dropped its objections to Pak's promotions, "in order to show the 'generous attitude of a suzerain power to its dependent state'" (Yur-Bok Lee, "Establishment of a Korean Legation," 24–25). For Kojong's interview with Pak upon Pak's return to Korea, see *KS*, July 29, 1889 (KJ 26.7.24).

rial permission, Kojong, according to Yur-Bok Lee, sent a letter of thanks to the Qing, which "contained full acknowledgment of Korea's dependent status, his acceptance of the Chinese rules concerning the proposed legations, and assurance that his envoys were duly instructed."[79] Also relevant are Kojong's disavowal of Pak's ignoring of the "three protocols" and Kojong's eventual recall of Pak. Perhaps even more significant, the establishment of a Chosŏn legation in Washington, DC, did not affect Korea's dispatch of tribute missions to China or its use of the customary language of suzerain and vassal in its communications with the Qing Empire.

In an attempt to make sense of this seemingly contradictory set of statements and actions, some historians make much of the issue of coercion. Kojong, so the line of thinking goes, sincerely and unequivocally desired full sovereignty and independence. Any action or statement to the contrary was taken or made under duress. Yur-Bok Lee succinctly summarizes this thinking by stating, "All of these circumstances seem to indicate that the King wanted to behave with as much sovereignty and independence as he possibly could, conceding to Chinese demands as little as possible and only when he was absolutely forced to do so, something which a truly dependent king would hardly do to a true suzerain."[80] The idea of coercion also figures prominently in a growing body of literature, spearheaded by Korean scholars, that denounces the later Japanese Protectorate and annexation of Korea as illegal, largely (though not exclusively) because the agreements and treaties surrendering Korean sovereignty were coerced.[81]

Although there is doubtlessly a certain logic to this conclusion, it is somewhat selective in its acknowledgment of pressure and coercion. One can, upon examining the historical record, quite easily craft a narrative in which coercion from a different source figures prominently: of *Westerners*

---

79. Yur-Bok Lee, "Establishment of a Korean Legation," 18.

80. Ibid. Denny (*China and Korea,* 31) concurred: "If anything has been admitted by any official of the Government at any time which even implies vassalage, it is without authority and void. . . . Even if dependent relations could be created by admissions, and the King, under the threatening, violent and criminal treatment of China for two and a-half years past, were to admit vassalage in the most abject way, it should not be binding upon his Government, for admissions under duress are not admissions." Writing elsewhere, Yur-Bok Lee (*West Goes East,* 183) makes the interesting distinction that the events proved Kojong to be "half-sovereign," while "his kingdom had become independent and sovereign according to modern diplomatic and international rules."

81. See, e.g., Yi T'ae-jin, *Sŏuldae Yi T'aejin kyosu ŭi Tonggyŏngdaesaengdŭl ege dŭllyŏjun Han'guksa,* 210–41; idem et al., *Han'guk pyŏnghap ŭi pulpŏbpsŏng yŏn'gu.*

coercing Chosŏn Korea to adopt a system and series of practices of international relations that Koreans may not have otherwise sought or embraced.

After all, if their own accounts are to be trusted, it was the Americans Horace Allen and Owen Denny who pushed the idea of establishing a legation in Washington in the first place.[82] Moreover, on more than one occasion when Pak Chŏng-yang displayed reluctance to follow the advice of the Americans, he was coerced into cooperation and compliance. According to one American observer, Pak had to be "seized and carried by force over the ship's side and locked in his cabin" to get him off Korean soil in the first place.[83] And when, in Washington, DC, Pak declared his intention to abide by the Qing-mandated "three protocols," Allen resorted to utilizing the threat of impending decapitation to convince Pak to follow Allen's lead in ignoring the Qing demands.[84]

Did Kojong genuinely desire to establish a permanent legation in the United States? His actions, whatever their underlying motivations, would seem to confirm that he did. However, it is far from clear that he saw either the Korean assertion of the right to establish a permanent legation abroad or the actual act of doing so as unequivocal and irrevocable rejections of Qing suzerainty in Korea. According to Horace Allen, the conversation with Kojong that led to the idea of setting up an embassy was prompted by Kojong's intense desire to attract American capital and secure a loan from American sources.[85] Moreover, his formal request for Qing permission to send legations abroad expresses what had been the quite consistent Korean view about Chosŏn Korea's relations with the Qing Empire and the kingdom's relations with other nations. In short, he accepted that Chosŏn Korea was and remained a dependency or vassal of China, but it was one that was autonomous (*chaju*; C. *zizhu*) in both its domestic politics and international affairs.[86] Kojong surely resented the threat to Korean autonomy, both domestic and foreign, posed by the ever-

---

82. For Denny's claim of originating the idea, see Swartout, *Mandarins, Gunboats, and Power Politics*, 90. For Allen's claim, see Yur-Bok Lee, "Establishment of a Korean Legation," 6. See also Harrington's (*God, Mammon, and the Japanese*, 226) conclusion that "the legation action, like the others, was largely Allen's doing."

83. Chaille-Long, *My Life in Four Continents*, 348.

84. Harrington, *God, Mammon, and the Japanese*, 236.

85. Ibid., 226–27.

86. Li Hongzhang to Zongli yamen, Oct. 6, 1887 (GX 13.8.20), *ZRHGX*, 2364.

meddling Yuan Shikai and his Purist Party backers. But this did not mean that he rejected out of hand the idea that Korea had a special relationship with the Qing Empire. It was only in the days immediately before the Sino-Japanese War when Kojong would, at gunpoint, agree to suspend the dispatch of tribute missions to Beijing and to end the use of the Qing calendar and all other indications of Qing suzerainty.

Did the Qing Empire oppose Korea's establishment of permanent legations abroad, as many Korean historians claim? Yuan Shikai clearly did. But his superiors in Tianjin and in the Zongli yamen thought otherwise. In the end, the Qing granted Chosŏn Korea the right to establish legations as long as some gesture to the traditional suzerain-vassal relationship were made. In addition, one wonders what might have happened had Korea agreed to abide by the "three protocols" demanded by the Qing Empire. Precedence in the order of official visits and seating arrangements at banquets appear to be the very type of empty ceremony and ritual that foreign diplomats had been ignoring in the case of Qing-Chosŏn relations for several years. Shufeldt disregarded the letter attached to the 1882 Korean-American treaty. Foreign diplomats apparently paid no attention to the claims that the Chosŏn Kingdom was a Chinese vassal in the 1882 Regulations for Maritime and Overland Trade Between Chinese and Korean Subjects. Why not simply let Pak visit the Qing legation first, sit in a lower position at banquets, and, with these inconsequential ritual niceties out of the way, move on to more substantive issues of diplomatic and commercial import? The fact is that ritual was as important to modern Americans as it was to the supposedly less than modern Koreans or Chinese. What really mattered was which particular rituals were to be held in the highest regard. At stake was less whether Korea was a partially or fully independent power and more which powers—the Qing Empire or the West—could claim control of the rules and norms of international relations.

Did the establishment of legations in Tokyo and Washington change the way in which foreign powers regarded Chosŏn Korea and its status? Alexis Dudden writes that "by definition, international law is a performative discourse in which representatives, acting at the behest of sovereign states, negotiate with similarly entitled foreign envoys. In this relationship, the representatives mutually define one another in a politics of display."[87]

---

87. Dudden, *Japan's Colonization of Korea*, 29.

How was the "display" of Chosŏn Korea's attempt to establish legations received? The reports in American print media of the Chosŏn legation and its activities in Washington support the argument that whatever the intentions of the Korean government and whatever the significance of questions of ritual protocol, the legation did little to help Chosŏn Korea's international standing in American eyes. Even properly conducted rituals were insufficient to overcome the barriers of American condescension, racism, and apathy. The arrival of the legation prompted a flurry of stories in New York and Washington papers and journals. A *New York Times* story argued that the legation amounted to "a practical assertion of complete independence from China." But another article wondered about the significance of the report that King Kojong had "humbly begged" for permission before sending the legation.[88]

The number of media reports discussing Chosŏn Korea's international status was dwarfed by those concerned with the appearance, dress, accoutrements, and behavior of Pak and his entourage. Articles describing in vivid exotic detail the "Corean dress, the Corean glide, the peculiar Corean hat, and the Corean countenance" distracted attention away from substantive diplomatic matters and focused on the appearance of "the Curious Coreans."[89] A description of the all-important first visit to President Cleveland (sans Chinese diplomatic accompaniment) seemed more interested in what the Koreans were wearing than in what they were doing; they "were in full dress, their silks richer, and more voluminous, their smiles more serene and their hats odder and taller than ever."[90]

Even stories that hailed the diplomatic significance of the legation often couched that significance in terms that made their praise of Korea backhanded at best. The Washington *Evening Star* reported that "The embassy . . . is attracting attention from all sides. Their coming is regarded as important from the fact that this act on the part of the Corean government indicates a new step in the direction of advanced civilization by the Mon-

---

88. "Ambassadors Sent to the United States"; "Embassy to the United States Not Subject to China's Control." I am indebted for these references (and the discussion of American media depictions of the legation more generally) to Christine Tanner, "Failures and Legacies of the Print Media."

89. "A Picturesque Embassy"; See also *Evening Star* (Washington, DC), Jan. 17, 1888; *Harper's Weekly* 32: 1623 (Jan. 1888); and "The Curious Coreans."

90. "The Corean Embassy."

golian race, of which the Coreans are a branch."[91] The unspoken assumption was, of course, that Koreans had many more steps to take before being admitted to the ranks of "advanced civilization." Other accounts highlighted Korean violations of American ritual courtesy, as when Pak and company apparently crashed a "fashionable tea party," arriving "gorgeously appareled" but uninvited. In the end, the Korean presence in Washington did little more than highlight the idea that Koreans with "their peculiar notions" were "far behind the Japanese in Society Ways."[92]

Moreover, the fact that Westerners such as Owen Denny and Horace Allen took credit for the initiation and execution of the Korean efforts to set up legations, implicitly reinforced the widely held notion that Korea was unfit for full sovereignty absent a good deal of Western assistance and tutelage. Allen's own account of the mission stresses the fact that although he "was only the Secretary of the mission, in reality he was in change of all important matters except ordering meals for the Korean diplomats. According to Allen, minister Pak, whom Allen adopted as 'father' to please the aging plenipotentiary, was merely a figurehead."[93] This type of description could hardly have enhanced the perception of Korean sovereignty and agency in the eyes of Allen's readership.[94] Little wonder, then, that the

---

91. *Evening Star* (Washington, DC), Jan. 14, 1888. See also "Corea Acts for Herself," which states that "Japanese have already gone beyond far ahead of their neighbors, and now Coreans propose to learn from European and American nations the ways and means of advancement."

92. The hostess of the tea party complained that "from what I understand they can go into any house where they see there is a reception in progress" ("The Curious Coreans"). Alexis Dudden (*Japan's Colonization of Korea*, 16) argues that this "discourse of enlightened exploitation" was prominent in Western newspapers' descriptions of Korea and their contrasting of Korea and Japan.

93. Yur-Bok Lee, "Establishment of a Korean Legation," 19. In addition, upon Pak Chŏng-yang's return to Korea, Allen gave Pak "a document in which I [Allen] took all the responsibility for the course pursued" (Allen, *Things Korean*, 164).

94. In his own diary correspondence, Allen was even more scathing and condescending in his descriptions of Pak and his entourage. " 'The minister is a weak imbecile of a fellow,' wrote Allen while he and his Korean colleagues were en route to the United States, 'the regular interpreter is an idiot and cannot speak English.' Another member of the party was a 'snoop' and all were 'filthy beyond endurance.' More specifically, 'they persist in standing upon the closet seats which they keep dirtied all the time and have severely marked with their hob nailed shoes. They smell of dung continually, persist in smoking in their rooms which smell horribly of unwashed bodies, dung, stale wine, Korean food, smoke, etc. The ship's people are very kind but will be

U.S. State Department, while officially supporting the establishment of a Chosŏn legation in Washington, warned American diplomats, "The agitation of the subject of Corea's complete independence of China, by representatives of the United States is neither desirable nor beneficial."[95]

Several conclusions emerge from the debate over the attempt to establish a legation in Washington, DC. First, the motivations of key actors, particularly King Kojong, are shrouded in ambiguity. The easy confidence with which Kojong's American advisers and subsequent generations of Korean scholars speak and write of Kojong's (and, by extension, the Chosŏn Kingdom's) desire for full independence and an assumed concomitant desire to reject Qing suzerainty is belied by the monarch's behavior at critical moments. The inability of Denny, Allen, and others to even entertain the notion that Kojong's conception of autonomy (a conception probably shared at least in part by Li Hongzhang but not by Yuan Shikai and the Purist Party) was not coterminous with Western conceptions of full independence likely owes more to their insistence that Western norms of international relations were the only conceivable let alone proper ones than to an actual appreciation of Korean (and Qing) attitudes. Second, the influence and effectiveness of establishing legations abroad are rather overstated by legation supporters. Even a fully functioning legation staffed by properly credentialed and properly behaving officials was only a first step in a long series of actions required to signal, to a skeptical and condescending Western world, Korea's worthiness of full independence and participation in the civilized family of nations. Third, the promise of independence was, more generally, an increasingly hollow one in the late nineteenth century. Even if Chosŏn independence had been fully and unequivocally

---

exceedingly grateful to be rid of them, as I will myself" (Harrington, *God, Mammon, and the Japanese*, 228).

95. Swartout, *Mandarins, Gunboats, and Power Politics*, 93. Japan adopted a similar course. "Kondō was sympathetic to the American effort. . . . However, when Kondō sought instructions from the Japanese Foreign Office as to what course he should take, he was told to 'refrain from becoming entangled in this case; but if Japanese treaty rights or merchants are in danger you should inquire for further instructions.' The Japanese Foreign Office, like the American State Department, was avoiding diplomatic embroilment in Korea" (Conroy, *The Japanese Seizure of Korea*, 188). Homer Hulbert (*History of Korea*, 244) describes the events and their outcome as follows: "He was received in Washington with all the punctiliousness due to a minister from any sovereign power. This helped in a certain way to forward Korea's claim to independence but America's well-known policy of non-interference in foreign matters largely neutralized its effect."

declared and accepted by the international community, it is far from clear that this alone would have allowed Korea to avoid falling under colonial rule in the era of high imperialism.

The Chosŏn legation in Washington limped on after Pak Chŏng-yang returned to Korea. But it was often understaffed. When the Korean reformer Yun Ch'i-ho attempted to visit the legation in August 1893, he found no one there to receive him.[96] The Chosŏn legation in Tokyo was similarly understaffed. The proposed legation in Europe was not sent until after 1895.

Ritual vs. Substance

An event in late 1890 highlights the complexity and ambiguity of Chosŏn Korea's position at the intersection of competing imperialisms and systems of international relations. On June 4, 1890, Queen Dowager Cho died.[97] It was customary for Korea to inform the Qing Empire of such events and for the Qing to dispatch an envoy bearing ceremonial condolences to Korea.[98] In this case, King Kojong procrastinated before finally officially sending the news to China along with a plea that the Qing Empire forgo the traditional envoy because of the considerable expenses of receiving him.[99] Members of the Qing Board of Rites refused to relinquish this opportunity to reaffirm the continuity of ritual-based relations between the Qing Empire and Chosŏn Korea and insisted on sending a full mission, which resulted in a 2,000-strong procession of Qing officials and Korean hosts.[100] They did, however, make one concession to the changing times: the condolences mission traveled to Korea by sea on board Chinese gunboats, the first time a ceremonial mission did not use the traditional overland route.[101] An American diplomat described the scene when the Qing procession reached Seoul:

---

96. Kuksa p'yŏnch'an wiwŏnhoe, *Yun Ch'i-ho's Diary*, Aug. 14, 1893, 3: 146–47.

97. *KS*, June 4, 1890 (KJ 27.4.17). For an official announcement/consolation to the Korean people, see *KS*, July 6, 1890 (KJ 27.5.20).

98. For official notification of Yuan Shikai in Seoul, see Min Chong-muk to Yuan Shikai, June 4, 1890 (KJ 27.4.17), *Ch'ŏngan*, 1: 690.

99. Kun'gang et al. (Board of Rites) to Zongli yamen, Oct. 13, 1890 (GX 16.8.30), *ZRHGX*, 2826–27.

100. For the number in the retinue, see China, Imperial Chinese Mission to Korea, *Notes on the Imperial Chinese Mission to Corea, 1890*, 25.

101. Grand Secretariat to Zongli yamen, Oct. 13, 1890 (GX 16.8.30), *ZRHGX*, 2827–28. In addition to dispatching the condolences mission by sea, the imperial commissioners also suggested that they forgo the customary "banquets, music and jugglery"

The envoys were preceded by three Small [*sic*] palanquins—[the] first containing the funeral presents: the second Vases for the libation, and the third, which was closed with Yellow curtains, the Imperial decree conferring on the deceased Queen the grade of Wife of President of the Board of War, or the 1st grade of the Second class, and the Imperial invocation or prayer to be read before the tablet of the deceased and afterwards burned. As the palanquin was borne before the King, the yellow curtains were drawn aside, and he is supposed to have prostrated himself in the interior of the tent.[102]

The procession then moved to "the Hall of the Tablets" where Kojong "knelt twice and prostrated himself eight times" in front of the Imperial letter and remained on his knees as the letter was read aloud.[103]

This would appear to be fairly unequivocal evidence of Chosŏn Korea's continued acceptance of Qing suzerainty despite its participation in modern diplomatic and commercial relations with other powers. Foreign observers responded by attempting to square the circle in two ways. First, they emphasized the rumors that Kojong, while adhering strictly to the proper forms of the required rituals, used body language or other subtle cues to signal his disapproval of the present state of Qing-Chosŏn relations.[104] Augustine Heard, the American minister, went a step further, speculating that Kojong was accepting the current state of affairs because of apocalyptic concerns surrounding the approaching 500th anniversary of the founding of the Chosŏn Kingdom and hoped that "once launched upon a New Year, he will commence a new era of greater self-confidence and independent action."[105] His hopes were dashed as the Chosŏn Kingdom continued to send annual tribute missions and special envoys to the Qing Empire for the next several years.[106]

---

while in Korea. According to the official report of the Qing Board of Rites, "Their motive for this suggestion was to show their consideration for Corean impecuniosity" (China, Imperial Chinese Mission to Korea, *Notes on the Imperial Chinese Mission to Corea, 1890*, 24).

102. Heard to U.S. Secretary of State, Nov. 17, 1890, *KAR*, 2: 31.

103. Ibid. For an exhaustive recounting of the seemingly numberless bows, visits, inquiries into health, and other rituals and ceremonies, see China, Imperial Chinese Mission to Korea, *Notes on the Imperial Chinese Mission to Corea, 1890*.

104. Heard to U.S. Secretary of State, Nov. 17, 1890, *KAR*, 2: 32

105. Heard to U.S. Secretary of State, Nov. 19, 1890, *KAR*, 2: 36.

106. For example, in mid-1891, the Chosŏn Kingdom sent a ceremonial mission to congratulate the Qing emperor on reaching the twentieth year of his reign; see Allen to U.S. Secretary of State, May 22, 1891, *KAR*, 2: 40.

The second way in which some sought to solve the incongruence of a nominally independent and sovereign kingdom declaring its vassalage to another power was more familiar: the traditional rituals were dismissed as meaningless. Although no one disputed that Kojong knelt and prostrated himself before the imperial decree, one observer noted: "but it should not be forgotten that the Act was Oriental between Orientals, and must not be judged by the Western standard." Korea's declaration of vassalage carried no more meaning than the Spaniard's ritual statement to guests that his house and everything in it are theirs or the traditional closing statement in letters declaring the letter writer to be "Your most obedient, humble servant."[107]

This was a neat rhetorical and conceptual trick. But the Korean or Chinese of the time might be excused for failing to recognize why the ritual prostration of Korean kings should be dismissed as an empty ritual while seating arrangements at banquet halls, the rank of sedan-chair passengers, or the protocol of who should present cards to whom were matters of significant diplomatic importance. Heard and other Western diplomats failed to call on the Qing ceremonial envoys during their stay in Seoul, citing confusion over their actual rank: "If they were not Ambassadors, it was their duty to call upon us; if they were, they should have sent their cards." But these empty rituals were perhaps not so empty after all: "Although this may seem a trivial matter, nothing that concerns etiquette is trivial with the Chinese. With them especially it is mandatory to guard against the slightest concession, as it is invariably made a stepping stone to something more."[108]

The Sedan Chair Affair

Another illustration of the conflict between Qing claims of special privilege and Western claims of most-favored-nation concessions was the so-called sedan chair issue. For years, Western diplomats had grumbled at the fact that when they paid official visits to King Kojong, they had to walk between the outer gates of the palace compound and the audience hall, a distance sometimes of several hundred yards. While these complaints might be written off as a minor annoyance, the fact that Yuan Shikai insisted on riding up to the doors of the audience hall in a sedan chair rankled many.

---

107. Heard to U.S. Secretary of State, Nov. 19, 1890, *KAR*, 2: 35.
108. Heard to U.S. Secretary of State, Nov. 18, 1890, *KAR*, 2: 34.

Yuan justified his behavior by asserting that the Qing Empire enjoyed a special relationship with its Korean vassal, and, in light of that relationship, he was not simply another foreign diplomat in Korea.[109] American and other diplomats occasionally contested this assertion of special privilege, but as a general rule their complaints fell on deaf ears. Their superiors in their home governments seemed unconcerned about this matter and its significance. For example, U.S. Secretary of State William Wharton instructed Augustine Heard to "assert and obtain the same ceremonial rights as the Diplomatic body in Seoul have secured or may hereafter enjoy," but not if this meant that "if by so doing you should appear to lend yourself to the provocation of a question concerning the exceptional relation of Corea to China, and the special treatment, growing out of that relation which may be conceded to the Chinese Commissioner."[110]

The issue simmered under the surface throughout the late 1880s and early 1890s but erupted again in 1893 when Yuan Shikai's assistant Tang Shaoyi visited Kojong in the stead of his ill superior and insisted on the same privilege of riding in a sedan chair to the doors of the audience chamber. The American Horace Allen portrays the anger and humiliation of the foreign diplomatic community:

The day was a very rainy one and we were all mortified to find ourselves wading through mud and rain while the Chinese Consul rode past us right up to the door of the reception room. Our Chairs had been, as is the custom, left at the Palace Gates some distance away. We have been informed on several occasions of the fact that Mr. Yuan rides into the Palace as only the members of the Royal Family can do. But while we all knew of this Custom of his, it had never been forced to our notice as on this occasion, which was made doubly humiliating by the rain, our bedraggled condition, and the fact that even the Consul of China could ride dry, where we walked wet.[111]

---

109. According to Sukhee Han ("Beyond the Celestial Sinic Sphere," 241), "Yuan also demonstrated this disrespectful behavior at a banquet given at the Chinese legation in Seoul. Yuan often seated the president of the Korean Foreign Office below all the foreign representatives on the excuse that the Korean official was not a guest but a member of the family of China. From time to time, Yuan also refused to attend conferences of the foreign representatives in Seoul by stating that he was not a member of the regular diplomatic corps."

110. William F. Wharton to Augustine Heard, Aug. 25, 1890, *KAR*, 2: 92–93.

111. Horace Allen to U.S. Secretary of State, Oct. 6, 1893, *KAR*, 2: 94.

Incensed, the foreign diplomats organized a boycott of diplomatic visits to the Korean court until all were granted the privilege of riding to the doors in their sedan chairs. In terms of the Western-style diplomatic rankings of the day, the foreign representatives did not approach this issue from the highest of standing.[112] But Allen felt "I would be justified in uniting with my colleagues in asking that at least equal privileges with the *Consul* of China" be granted to all foreign diplomats in Seoul.[113]

The Korean Home Office procrastinated, made excuses, and ultimately offered a compromise: the Chosŏn government would "build a closed gallery from the nearest Palace Gate to the Reception Hall, through which we might walk, protected from the weather. This compromise was accepted by all and seems quite satisfactory."[114] The proposed walkway was never completed. But complaints from the foreign diplomatic community ceased because in August 1894 the Chosŏn government announced that all foreign diplomats would be allowed to ride as far as they wished in sedan chairs. Commenting on the change, American diplomat John Sill remarked: "This is doubtless the result of Japanese dictation"—a reference to the beginning of the Sino-Japanese War and the occupation of Seoul by Japanese troops. Sill ruefully concluded:

The combined efforts of all the Foreign Representatives except the Chinese, could not secure permission to ride from the outer gates of the palace enclosure to the waiting room. Chinese influence prevailed against all opposition. A Chinese representative might so ride and so might the Chinese Consul and even the telegraph Superintendent, but not the other Foreign Representatives. Within one year a hint from Japan accomplishes all that was vainly sought in '93.[115]

---

112. Allen observed, "England, Japan and Germany are with China on the Korean question. England is represented by a Vice-Consul, who acts as 'Acting Consul General.' Japan has a Minister Plenipotentiary to China and Korea, who will shortly leave his Consul in charge. Germany has a Consul. In the case of the Governments which recognize the independence of Korea, and have agents who correspond direct with the Home Governments, Russia has a Charge d'Affaires, and France a Commissaire. Fortunately this episode occurred while we have but a Charge d'Affaires here, but a new minister should insist on receiving due courtesy, otherwise we "lose face" and have little influence" (*KAR*, 2: 97).

113. Horace Allen to U.S. Secretary of State, Nov. 4, 1893, *KAR*, 2: 95; emphasis in original.

114. Horace Allen to U.S. Secretary of State, Feb. 12, 1894, *KAR*, 2: 99.

115. John M. B. Sill to U.S. Secretary of State, Aug. 24, 1894, *KAR*, 2: 99.

In subsequent years, all foreign diplomats enjoyed the privilege of riding directly to court in sedan chairs, even when the distance between gate and door was less than twenty yards.[116]

This incident and its outcome, I believe, lead to several important conclusions. First, as was the case with the Qing assertion of special commercial privileges in 1882, the reaction of the international community (as represented by foreign diplomats in Korea) was not to criticize the assertion of special privilege *per se* or to point out that such an assertion would seem to violate basic principles of Korea's national sovereignty and dignity, but to insist on the same special privileges for themselves. The "law of nations" was invoked less to protect Korean sovereignty than to secure equal access by all outsiders. Second, as was the case in the debate over the "three protocols," ritual propriety clearly still mattered. But at the same time it would be naïve not to conclude that had not the sedan chair issue directly and personally inconvenienced (and humiliated) foreign diplomats, the same diplomats would have spent far less energy and spilled far less ink over the issue. Third, although ritual protocol may have served as a useful mask for more personal concerns, in the end, treaties, laws, and diplomatic etiquette proved far less effective than the blunt instrument of Japanese military force.

Subsequent generations of historians have often depicted Chosŏn Korea's attempts to declare its sovereignty in terms recognizable to Owen Denny and like-minded Westerners as an unequivocal case of a Korean yearning for autonomy, progress, and modernity being stifled by an obstinately premodern China. Such accounts demonstrate both the advantages of hindsight and the limitations of teleology. Since we know that the "tribute system" was indeed supplanted by a Western-style international order, it is tempting to focus on the handful of progressives who embraced this new order. But to do so overshadows the intense ambivalence that Korea's putative sovereign felt toward the Qing Empire and China. What is one to conclude about Korean yearnings for "sovereignty" when the Chosŏn Kingdom's own sovereign so frequently demonstrated his willingness to remain a vassal? Kojong was not alone in his ambivalence toward China. Min Yŏng-hwan, a royal in-law whose career and suicide are regarded by many Koreans as the height of patriotism, wrote that Li Hongzhang and

---

116. Sands, *Undiplomatic Memories*, 59.

Yuan Shikai "did their best to care for our country and protect it."[117] Young Ick Lew, certainly no admirer of Yuan Shikai, notes that what might be regarded as popular opinion in Korea seemed to concur:

The Korean people tolerated the overbearing attitude of Resident Yuan and the accompanying Chinese economic exploitation of Korea without major protest. The majority of the Korean people, both the educated yangban elite and the illiterate masses, seem to have accepted Chinese oppression in Korea at this time as a matter of course, undoubtedly as a result of having become inured to the age-old tradition of Sino-Korean tributary relations and cultural borrowing. No conscious nationalistic movement, analogous to the anti-Western and anti-Japanese movement to repudiate heterodoxy and defense [*sic*] orthodoxy of the early 1880s, broke out against the Chinese among the yangban literati during the years 1885 to 1894. The Tonghak peasant insurgents who were emphatic in denouncing Japanese and Western imperialism raised no voice of protest against Resident Yuan and the Chinese policy during their uprisings in 1893 and 1894.[118]

The American diplomat Augustine Heard agreed, finding that "there is throughout the Kingdom a sentiment of affection, of clanship, for China, and one only of dread for Russia." Heard also noted that since Western diplomats in Beijing seemed willing to abide by the rules of ritual protocol established by the Qing Empire, it was no surprise that Kojong, too, would wish to do the same.[119]

Those who argue that the telos of modernization requires that Chosŏn Korea should have, nevertheless, plunged ahead toward participation in a Western-style political order are unduly Panglossian about the opportunities and possibilities that awaited Korea at the end of the nineteenth century. The "family of nations" was concerned far more with global geopolitics and securing access to whatever commercial privileges Korea might provide than it was with helping Korea along the path to joining the

---

117. Finch, *Min Yŏng-Hwan*, 47.

118. Young Ick Lew, "Yuan Shih-k'ai's Residency," 77–78.

119. Heard wrote, "Then there is all the traditional glamour, which surrounds the 'Son of Heaven'; if he be tempted at any time to feel confidence in the power and friendship of Western Nations, he is shown their Representatives at Peking, content to wait on the outer circle, and supplicate for a glance from the Imperial throne, which they cannot have. Indeed, their humiliation in submitting at the close of the 19th century to the pretensions of China in refusing an Audience of the Emperor goes very far to excusing the alleged want of dignity in the King of Corea" (Heard to U.S. Secretary of State, Nov. 19, 1890, *KAR*, 2: 36).

family as an equal. The world of imperialism was not kind to nascent nation-states. Yuan Shikai himself was well aware of this fact, as is evident in his surprisingly cogent analysis of the various powers interested in Korea:

Great Britain and France covet the territory of others; seeking help from them is like asking a tiger into your room, no one lives to tell about it. . . . Germany is powerfully militarily and the United States is a prosperous nation, but neither likes to create "incidents" and thus they seldom help others. They are good at protecting their own, but do not think much of far away places. . . . [Seeking help from Russia] is like leaving the door open and allowing the thief to enter . . . if Russia does not have territorial designs on Korea, who does? . . . [And] while the Japanese are developing along Western lines and appear to be strong . . . deep down they are cunning and think only of themselves; one can establish amicable ties with them, but one can not trust them. If Korea were a populous and prosperous nation, it might expect to develop into a strong one by itself, but given its current state of disunity, weakness and poverty, what strong power can it depend upon besides China?[120]

---

120. *KS*, Aug. 28, 1886 (KJ 23.7.29).

SEVEN

Yuan Shikai and 'Commercial Warfare' in Korea

Despite the fact that Yuan Shikai's official title during his residency in Korea was "commissioner of trade of the third rank," most studies of his tenure in Korea focus on the political aspects, with particular emphasis on his attempts to maintain Chinese ritual suzerainty and the numerous cases of his interference and meddling in Korean domestic affairs. Even those actions that arguably have an economic or commercial component have, more often than not, been understood primarily through the lens of their political significance. Thus, to Dalchoong Kim, the 1882 Regulations for Maritime and Overland Trade Between Chinese and Korean Subjects functioned first and foremost as "a political tool for tightening Chinese control over Korea" despite the Regulations' commercial emphasis.[1] Martina Deuchler, writing of Qing support for shipping lines between China and Korea, argues: "From the outset, the establishment of the line was motivated by politics rather than by commercial interest. It was a Chinese attempt to impress her suzerain rights on Korea."[2] To Yur-Bok Lee, the Qing Empire's policies toward Korea's attempts to borrow from abroad reflected the domination of "politics over economics."[3]

---

1. Dalchoong Kim, "Chinese Imperialism in Korea," 107. Ch'oe Mun-hyŏng (*Han'guk ŭl tullŏssan chegukchuŭi yŏlgang ŭi kakch'uk,* 46) concludes that the Regulations amounted to the "proof of suzerainty" (*chongsok ŭi minjŭng*). Lin Mingde ("Li Hung-Chang's Suzerain Policy Toward Korea," 183) argues that the negotiations leading to the 1882 Regulations "shed more light on politics than on economics." See also Deuchler, *Confucian Gentlemen and Barbarian Envoys,* 141; and Chien, *The Opening of Korea,* 197.

2. Deuchler, *Confucian Gentlemen and Barbarian Envoys,* 186.

3. Yur-Bok Lee, "Politics over Economics."

Although few scholarly works on the Residency of Yuan Shikai completely ignore the economic and commercial aspects of Sino-Korean relations during this period, most do not go beyond the simple recognition of the rapid growth of Chinese commerce during this period and the generally unsupported assertion that this growth was due, at least in part, to Qing political power and influence in Korea during this time. The specific ways in which Yuan Shikai promoted Chinese commercial interests are listed in a cursory fashion at best; more often they are simply assumed. Some mention Yuan's tacit if not outright support for Chinese smuggling, his attempts to reintroduce Chinese shipping ventures in Korea, or his efforts to protect Chinese shops from theft and arson by the establishment of Chinese police forces. However, the full extent of official support for Chinese commercial activity in Korea has yet to be explored.[4]

This relative neglect is unfortunate because it masks the significance of commerce in Qing imperial policies in Chosŏn Korea. The contours of Qing informal imperialism in Korea owed as much to the desires and actions of the Chinese treaty-port elite and their concept of "commercial warfare" (*shangzhan*) as it did to the insistence of Purist Party supporters that the traditional tribute missions continue unabated. Late nineteenth-century Chosŏn Korea indeed constitutes one of the first cases in which the Qing Empire proactively established a diplomatic and consular presence in part to promote Chinese commercial interests abroad. A Qing diplomatic presence had been established in other nations such as Britain, Japan, and the United States a few years earlier, but nearly every other earlier

----

4. The tendency to assume the relationship between political power and commercial success is reflected in C. I. Eugene Kim and Han-Kyo Kim's (*Korea and the Politics of Imperialism*, 70) statement "Chinese political influence in Korea reached its zenith in the years 1885–1894, thus spurring Chinese economic activities." For other similar examples, see Yur-Bok Lee, *West Goes East*, 171; Sigel, "The Sino-Japanese Quest for Korean Markets, 1885–1894," 115; and Pak Kyŏng-yong, *Kaehwagi Hansŏngbu yŏn'gu*, 117–18. For examples of cursory lists of ways in which China supported its merchants in Korea, see Yur-Bok Lee, "The Sino-Japanese Economic Warfare over Korea, 1876–1894," 130–31; Jerome Ch'en, *Yuan Shih-k'ai*, 23–24; and Young Ick Lew, "Yuan Shih-k'ai's Residency," 76–78, 97. Lew, in what is otherwise an extremely careful work, mistakenly includes China's "exclusive privileges" guaranteed in the 1882 Sino-Korean trade regulations, such as the right to travel to the interior and set up shop in Seoul, among his list of reasons for Chinese commercial success during this period. By the time Yuan Shikai took up his position as the Qing Resident, these privileges were not exclusive to the Qing Empire but guaranteed to all treaty powers by virtue of most-favored-nation provisions.

case was motivated by the need either to protect Chinese "coolie" laborers or to deal more ably with bilateral diplomatic issues.[5] In the case of Korea, the diplomatic representation came first and served as a foundation and invitation for Chinese commercial activity. An appreciation of the importance of commercial concerns to the Qing Empire serves to correct the mistaken impression that traditional suzerainty dominated the thinking of Qing policy makers.

Yuan Shikai had close ties to influential Purist Party officials in the Qing Empire, and many of his actions in Korea indeed reflect the Purist Party concern with maintaining the forms of Qing ritual suzerainty. However, even Yuan recognized the importance of promoting Chinese commerce. His style of administration differed significantly from that of Chen Shutang. Although Yuan sometimes devoted considerable attention and energy to issues he felt important, he seldom bothered with the day-to-day minutiae of his duties in the commercial sphere. Absent in the correspondence between Yuan and the Korean Foreign Office are reports of the acquisition of property by Chinese in Korea. Rare are reports of theft and demands for reparations. Rather than submitting individual requests for passports for travel to the interior, as was the practice of Chen Shutang, Yuan usually asked for books of blank passport forms to distribute to Chinese merchants and travelers at his convenience.

However, although apparently not as involved in some of the mundane details of Chinese commercial activity, Yuan Shikai went to great lengths to support Chinese business in Korea. His activities can generally be classified into two categories. On one hand, he worked to expand the legacy of Chen Shutang by enhancing Chinese influence within the treaty-port system. Efforts in this category include support for expansion of Chinese settlements in the treaty ports, the growth of Chinese activity in Seoul and its environs, and the promotion of Chinese shipping ventures. However, Yuan also encouraged Chinese commercial efforts outside the purview of the treaty-port system. His actions in this second category include support for smuggling and resistance to the efforts of the Korean government and the Customs Service to expand the scope of their operations to the northwest coast of Korea. In general, Yuan was successful in building on the foundation laid by

---

5. Biggerstaff, "The Establishment of Permanent Chinese Diplomatic Missions Abroad."

the introduction of the treaty-port system to Korea and by the efforts of Chen Shutang.

One significant result of the Qing establishment of diplomatic and consular representation in Korea was the dramatic increase in the numbers of Chinese merchants in Korea. They quickly proved to be worthy competitors to their Japanese counterparts both in traditional trade goods and in modern manufactures, reaching a point in the early 1890s of near parity in terms of Chosŏn Korea's aggregate imports. Their strength and competitiveness were greatest in areas in which the norms and institutions of multilateral imperialism were strongest.

Expansion of the Chinese Treaty-Port Presence

By the time Yuan Shikai assumed office as the Qing Resident in Korea, Chinese merchants already enjoyed the privileges and protection offered by Chinese settlements in Inch'ŏn and Pusan. This was largely the result of the efforts of Chen Shutang and the Qing commissioners of trade in the treaty ports. However, Yuan Shikai was soon confronted by the need for a Chinese settlement in Wŏnsan and the expansion of the settlement in Inch'ŏn. In addition, proposals for revision or modification of existing settlement agreements often occupied the attention of Yuan and his assistants. Yuan's overriding goal regarding Chinese settlements was to secure protection for Chinese merchants and to ensure that the Chinese enjoyed all the privileges available to other foreign powers in the Korean treaty ports.

As Chinese merchants poured into Korea, it soon became clear that the initial Chinese settlements in the treaty ports were too small to hold their growing numbers. This was especially the case in Inch'ŏn, where nearly all the land designated for the Chinese settlement was purchased at the first auction. The settlement agreement allowed for Chinese merchants to purchase land and conduct business within the limits of the much larger "general foreign settlement," and many Chinese merchants took this course. However, the lack of suitable property combined with an apparent preference for gathering in a single location prompted prominent Chinese merchants to importune Yuan Shikai to arrange for an additional Chinese settlement. Yuan relayed this request to the Korean Foreign Office on May 28, 1886, and received the reply that arrangements should be reached with the local Inch'ŏn authorities. The proceedings of the negotiations between the Qing commissioner of trade and the Inch'ŏn *kamni* as well as the agreement they reached cannot be found in the extant documents. It is

clear, however, that some sort of pact was made; numerous Chinese acquired property and set up shop at Samnich'ae (also known as Sarich'ae),
an area on the outskirts of Inch'ŏn straddling the main road to Seoul. The
settlement soon contained a number of shops selling Western textiles and
Chinese silk, as well as several Chinese restaurants, barbershops, and vege-
table stands. Although the number of Chinese in this second settlement is
difficult to determine, there were sufficient numbers by 1888 to justify
Yuan Shikai's calls for police protection.[6]

In the same year, Yuan also deputed his assistant Tang Shaoyi to represent Chinese interests in the negotiations surrounding the Korean government's attempt to modify property prices and rental rates in the general
foreign settlement.[7] Two years later, Yuan personally participated in similar
negotiations as well as in disputes over the exact boundaries of the Chinese
settlements and over settlement maintenance fees.[8] Yuan was also involved

---

6. For Yuan's request to expand to Samnich'ae and the Korean reply, see Yuan Shikai to Sŏ Sang-u, May 28, 1886 (KJ 23.4.25), *Ch'ŏngan*, 1: 305–6; Sŏ Sang-u to Yuan
Shikai, May 30, 1886 (KJ 23.4.27), *Ch'ŏngan*, 1: 305–6. A Japanese consul described the
area as follows: "Although in the so-called Sarich'ae Chinese Commercial Area the Chinese people live somehow in groups, forming thus a sort of settlement, the quarter is
not at all a settlement recognized by treaty" (Son Chŏng-mok, *Han'guk kaehanggi tosi
pyŏnhwa kwajŏng yŏn'gu*, 150). Yuan Shikai claimed that an official agreement was reached
between Chinese officials and the Inch'ŏn *kamni* Ŏm Se-yong in "the summer of 1886,"
and that stone markers were erected at that time; see Yuan Shikai to Min Chong-muk,
Apr. 6, 1890 (KJ 27.2*.17), *Ch'ŏngan*, 1: 671. In 1891 Yuan also complained that Koreans
were constructing thatch-roofed buildings that blocked passage along the "public road"
running through Samnich'ae (Yuan Shikai to Min Chong-muk, June 2, 1891 [KJ 28.4.26],
Ch'ŏngan, 2: 35–36; Min Chong-muk to Yuan Shikai, July 25, 1891 [KJ 28.6.20], *Ch'ŏngan*,
2: 48). For more on the Samnich'ae "settlement," see Pak Kwang-song, "Inch'ŏnhang
ŭi chogye e taehayŏ," 301–2.
7. Yuan Shikai to Cho Pyŏng-jik, Nov. 8, 1888 (KJ 25.10.5), *Ch'ŏngan*, 1: 492–93; Cho
Pyŏng-jik to Yuan Shikai, Nov. 9, 1888 (KJ 25.10.6), *Ch'ŏngan*, 1: 493; Cho Pyŏng-jik to
Yuan Shikai, Nov. 18, 1888 (KJ 25.10.15), *Ch'ŏngan*, 1: 498.
8. Yuan Shikai to Min Chong-muk, Jan. 29, 1890 (KJ 27.1.19), *Ch'ŏngan*, 1: 648–50;
Yuan Shikai to Min Chong-muk, Apr. 6, 1890 (KJ 27.2*.17), *Ch'ŏngan*, 1: 671–72; Min
Chong-muk to Yuan Shikai, Apr. 8, 1890 (KJ 27.2*.19); Min Chong-muk to Yuan Shikai,
Apr. 11, 1890 (KJ 27.2*.22), *Ch'ŏngan*, 1: 674; Yuan Shikai to Min Chong-muk, June 2,
1891 (KJ 28.4.26), *Ch'ŏngan*, 2: 35–36; Yuan Shikai to Min Chong-muk, June 5, 1891 (KJ
28.4.29), *Ch'ŏngan*, 2: 37–38; Min Chong-muk to Yuan Shikai, July 25, 1891 (KJ 28.6.20),
Ch'ŏngan, 2: 48; Yuan Shikai to Min Chong-muk, Sept. 26, 1891 (KJ 28.8.24), *Ch'ŏngan*, 2:
62; Min Chong-muk to Yuan Shikai, Oct. 2, 1891 (KJ 28.8.30), *Ch'ŏngan*, 2: 64; Tang

in the creation and expansion of the Wŏnsan Chinese settlement, a move necessitated by the sudden Japanese decision to expel foreigners from the Wŏnsan Japanese concession. As was the case in Samnich'ae, the negotiations appear to have been carried out between Qing and local Korean officials in Wŏnsan. No settlement agreement has been found in the official records of the Korean government. Nevertheless, nearly all the Chinese in Wŏnsan had moved to the new settlement by 1890.[9] Yuan and his deputies were also active in proposals to expand the tiny settlement in Pusan.[10]

Calls for both the Japanese and the Chosŏn governments to respect Qing treaty privileges in Korea fill the Qing diplomatic correspondence of the next decade. Qing officials also became adept at demanding reparations for perceived financial and other losses, as, for example, in 1888 when three merchants of the Sanhexing firm were killed in a fire believed to have been deliberately set, or in 1890 when the itinerant merchant Sun Guanzhen was injured in Ch'ungch'ŏng Province.[11] Qing diplomats also demanded and received the right to establish police patrols to protect areas in which large

---

Shaoyi to Min Chong-muk, Nov. 29, 1891 (KJ 28.10.28), *Ch'ŏngan*, 2: 75; Tang Shaoyi to Min Chong-muk, Jan. 14, 1892 (KJ 28.12.15), *Ch'ŏngan*, 2: 81.

9. For Chinese activity in Wŏnsan, see Son Chŏng-mok, *Han'guk kaehanggi tosi pyŏnhwa kwajŏng yŏn'gu*, 121–23; Yuan Shikai to Kim Yun-sik, Apr. 11, 1887 (KJ 24.3.18), *Ch'ŏngan*, 1: 346–47; Yuan Shikai to Cho Pyŏng-sik, Apr. 22, 1888 (KJ 25.3.12), *Ch'ŏngan*, 1: 442; Cho Pyŏng-sik to Yuan Shikai, May 30, 1888 (KJ 25.4.20), *Ch'ŏngan*, 1: 448; Yuan Shikai to Cho Pyŏng-jik, Apr. 17, 1889 (KJ 26.3.18), *Ch'ŏngan*, 1: 536–37; Yuan Shikai to Cho Pyŏng-jik, June 8, 1889 (KJ 26.5.10), *Ch'ŏngan*, 1: 551–52; Min Chong-muk to Yuan Shikai, Aug. 17, 1889 (KJ 26.7.21), *Ch'ŏngan*, 1: 581–82; and Yuan Shikai to Cho Pyŏng-jik, Apr. 17, 1893 (KJ 30.3.2), *Ch'ŏngan*, 2: 187–88.

10. For Chinese activity in Pusan, see Yuan Shikai to Kim Yun-sik, Sept. 14, 1886 (KJ 23.8.17), *Ch'ŏngan*, 1: 320; Yuan Shikai to Min Chong-muk, June 19, 1892 (KJ 29.5.25), *Ch'ŏngan*, 2: 103; Yuan Shikai to Min Chong-muk, July 10, 1892 (KJ 29.6.17), *Ch'ŏngan*, 2: 113; and Min Chong-muk to Yuan Shikai, July 11, 1892 (KJ 29.6.18), *Ch'ŏngan*, 2: 114.

11. For correspondence on the Sanhexing arson, see Yuan Shikai to Cho Pyŏng-jik, Jan. 14, 1888 (KJ 24.12.2), *Ch'ŏngan*, 1: 397; Cho Pyŏng-jik to Yuan Shikai, May 30, 1890 (KJ 25.4.20), *Ch'ŏngan*, 1: 447–48; Yuan Shikai to Yi Chung-ch'il, Oct. 8, 1888 (KJ 25.9.4), *Ch'ŏngan*, 1: 484–85; Cho Pyŏng-jik to Yuan Shikai, Nov. 12, 1888 (KJ 25.10.9), *Ch'ŏngan*, 1: 495; and Yuan Shikai to Cho Pyŏng-jik, June 10, 1889 (KJ 26.5.12), *Ch'ŏngan*, 1: 553. For the request for action concerning the injury of Sun Guanzhen, see Yuan Shikai to Min Chong-muk, May 19, 1890 (KJ 27.4.1), *Ch'ŏngan*, 1: 687–88; Min Chong-muk to Yuan Shikai, June 13, 1890 (KJ 27.4.26), *Ch'ŏngan*, 1: 698–99; and Yuan Shikai to Min Chong-muk, June 23, 1890 (KJ 27.5.7), *Ch'ŏngan*, 1: 699–70.

numbers of Chinese lived and worked.[12] Chinese police patrols were, by some accounts, so effective that even the general foreign settlement in Inch'ŏn availed itself of their services.[13]

Promotion of Chinese Activities in Seoul and Its Environs

The Residency of Yuan Shikai saw the growth of Chinese commercial activity in Seoul and its environs. This expansion was increasingly troublesome to Korean merchants, especially those working in the traditional government monopolies. Clashes between Korean and Chinese merchants and repeated protests and boycotts by Korean merchants were frequent. Despite these difficulties, Chinese merchants continued to reside and thrive in Seoul. Yuan was also instrumental in the establishment of a Chinese presence in outlying areas such as Yongsan and Map'o.

By the time Yuan Shikai assumed office, any foreigner whose government had signed a treaty with Korea could reside and do business in Seoul. The growing influx of foreign merchants was disturbing to local Korean merchants, many of whom were members of one of the six government-licensed monopolies. Worried about their livelihoods, many merchants protested to the Korean government and demanded the expulsion of foreign merchants from the capital. The first of these demands came in December 1885 and January 1886, soon after Yuan Shikai assumed office. The Korean Foreign Office duly forwarded the merchants' protests to Yuan and, noting that thefts, brawls, and other "incidents" between Chinese and Koreans were on the rise, wondered if it wouldn't be better if the Chinese (and other foreigners) left Seoul and set up shop in nearby Yongsan or

———

12. For Qing police patrols of Map'o, see Yuan Shikai to Cho Pyŏng-jik, Apr. 30, 1889 (KJ 26.4.1), *Ch'ŏngan*, 1: 541–42; Cho Pyŏng-jik to Yuan Shikai, June 2, 1889 (KJ 26.5.4), *Ch'ŏngan*, 1: 547–48; and Yuan Shikai to Cho Pyŏng-jik, June 20, 1889 (KJ 26.5.22), *Ch'ŏngan*, 1: 558. For Qing patrols of Seoul, see Yuan Shikai to Cho Pyŏng-jik, June 12, 1889 (KJ 26.5.14), *Ch'ŏngan*, 1: 553–54; Cho Pyŏng-jik to Yuan Shikai, June 17, 1889 (KJ 26.5.19), *Ch'ŏngan*, 1: 557; Yuan Shikai to Cho Pyŏng-jik, June 18, 1889 (KJ 26.5.20), *Ch'ŏngan*, 1: 557–58; Cho Pyŏng-jik to Yuan Shikai, June 25, 1889 (KJ 26.5.27), *Ch'ŏngan*, 1: 560–61; and Yuan Shikai to Cho Pyŏng-jik, June 25, 1889 (KJ 26.5.27), *Ch'ŏngan*, 1: 562.

13. For an account of the effectiveness of one particular Chinese night watchman in Inch'ŏn, see Sands, *Undiplomatic Memories*, 84–85.

Yanghwajin. Yuan replied that since the number of Chinese merchants in the capital was not terribly large, he had no objection to the move. However, the proposal foundered on Japanese opposition and demands for extravagant reparations for Japanese merchants if they were forced out of Seoul.[14]

Protests, strikes, and boycotts by Korean merchants grew in size and sophistication. However, attempts by Korean merchants in 1887 and 1889 to oust foreign competition were repressed by the Korean government. Perhaps the greatest challenge to foreign merchants came in January 1890 when thousands of Korean merchants closed their shops and engaged in a weeklong sit-in in front of the Chosŏn Foreign Office and the royal palace. For the first time, the merchants' demands included treaty revision and the holding of direct talks with Li Hongzhang over the issue of Chinese commerce in Korea. After several days of closed shops and demonstrations had convinced the Chosŏn government and Yuan Shikai of the resolve of the merchants, it was agreed to send a Korean envoy to Tianjin to consult with Li Hongzhang. Concurrent negotiations with Japanese officials resulted in a Japanese declaration of willingness to move to Yongsan as long as all foreigners agreed to leave Seoul. They would, however, demand reparations for the move. This time resistance to the move came largely from the Qing Empire. Both Yuan Shikai and Li Hongzhang accused the Chosŏn government of complicity with the strikes and protests. Pyŏn Sŏk-un, the Korean official sent to Tianjin, received a tongue-lashing from Li Hongzhang. Li accused the Korean government of instigating the protests, demanded heavy reparations, and generally avoided discussing the issue of a Chinese removal to Yongsan. The result was a continuation of business as usual in the capital and growing resentment by Korean merchants. Chinese merchants were in Seoul to stay.[15]

---

14. Kim Chŏng-gi, "1890 nyŏn Sŏul sangin," 81.

15. The animus of the Korean commercial community was not directed exclusively, or even primarily, at the Chinese. Rather, Korean merchants demanded that all foreigners be expelled from the capital. For a blow-by-blow account of the 1890 Seoul shopkeepers' strike, see Kim Chŏng-gi, "1890 nyŏn Sŏul sangin," 78–80. See also King Kojong to the Qing Commissioner of the Northern Fleet (Li Hongzhang), Feb. 20, 1890 (KJ 27.2.2), *Ch'ŏngan*, 1: 653; Li Hongzhang to Zongli yamen, Mar. 7, 1890 (GX 26.2.17), *ZRHGX*, 2734–40; and Li Hongzhang to Zongli yamen, Mar. 5, 1892 (GX 18.2.27), *ZRHGX*, 2942–44.

The unwillingness of the Chinese to agree to a wholesale relocation to Yongsan or Yanghwajin should not be taken as a sign that there was no Chinese activity in these areas. The efforts of Chen Shutang to facilitate Chinese shipping up the Han River as far as Map'o have been considered in a previous chapter. Chinese merchants were apparently also active slightly upriver at Yongsan. An 1884 description of the area notes the presence of a "Chinese jetty" at Yongsan, three Korean *li* upriver from Map'o.

Chen Shutang and Moellendorff were also active in negotiations for the selection of a site for a foreign settlement outside Seoul. Initially interested in Yanghwajin or Map'o, their attention soon shifted to Yongsan. Preliminary arrangements for a foreign settlement were made in October 1884, but the *kapsin* coup attempt and the subsequent death or transfer of all the leading foreign figures involved in the negotiations resulted in no official action being taken. In the absence of official sanction for a foreign settlement, Chinese and other foreign merchants took advantage of treaty provisions allowing foreign businesses within 100 *li* of treaty ports to begin operating at Yongsan.[16]

Intrepid Chinese attempted to buy land in Yongsan as early as 1884.[17] In July 1886, Yuan Shikai dispatched Li Yinwu to oversee Chinese commercial activity there.[18] The area became increasingly important as a transshipment point for grain coming into the capital and for beans and other goods leaving Korea. Chinese brick makers established kilns in Yongsan; their bricks were used to construct the famous Myŏng-dong Catholic Cathedral as well as the British Legation.[19] Japanese complaints in the early 1890s of Chinese dominance of the area and demands for equal access to Yongsan indicate the extent of Chinese activity there.[20]

———

16. Yongsan'gu, *Yongsan'guji*, 80–89.

17. For the initial Chinese land purchase in Yongsan, see Chen Shutang to Kim Yun-sik, Sept. 1, 1884 (KJ 21.7.12), *Ch'ŏngan*, 1: 163; and Kim Yun-sik to Chen Shutang, Sept. 17, 1884 (KJ 21.7.28), *Ch'ŏngan*, 1: 170. For a general overview of foreign activity in Yongsan, see Yongsangu, *Yongsanguji*, 74–91, 462–63.

18. For Li Yinwu and other Chinese commercial officials in Yongsan, see Yuan Shikai to Sŏ Sang-u, July 3, 1886 (KJ 23.6.2), *Ch'ŏngan*, 1: 307–8; Yuan Shikai to Cho Pyŏng-jik, Nov. 6, 1887 (KJ 24.9.21), *Ch'ŏngan*, 1: 382–83; and Cho Pyŏng-jik to Yuan Shikai, Nov. 9, 1887 (KJ 24.9.24), *Ch'ŏngan*, 1: 384–85.

19. J. E. Hoare (*Embassies in the East*, 180) recounts: "A contract was signed in Seoul for the delivery of 300,000 red bricks, described as 'of excellent quality,' by 31 Dec. 1889. The contractor was a Chinese resident in Korea."

20. Yongsan'gu, *Yongsan'guji*, 74–91, 462–63.

The visible and growing presence of Chinese merchants in Seoul, Yong-san, and Map'o, as well as in the treaty ports, fueled antiforeign resentment among many Koreans. Anti-Chinese sentiment among Koreans was never as strong as the Korean animus toward the Japanese. The Chinese emerged completely unscathed in the antiforeign riots that attended the *imo* mutiny of 1882 and the *kapsin* coup of 1884. However, as Chinese merchants became increasingly successful competitors to their Korean and Japanese counterparts, a growing number of conflicts and incidents revealed anti-Chinese sentiment among at least some Koreans. Concerned about attacks on Chinese merchants, especially a spate of arson attacks in late 1887 that left three merchants dead and four shops burned to the ground, Yuan Shikai demanded that the Korean government increase its efforts to safeguard Chinese merchants. Yuan ultimately concluded that the Korean government was unable (or unwilling) to take the needed measures, and he worked to establish Chinese police patrols in Seoul, Map'o, and Inch'ŏn. Reminiscent of foreigners' insistence on controlling the police in Chinese treaty ports, this move was apparently effective, since the number of complaints about attacks and arson declined dramatically.[21]

Official Support for Shipping Ventures

One of the advantages most anticipated by Chinese merchants in Korea was proximity. Noting that Japanese merchants were purchasing Western goods in Shanghai and Hong Kong, shipping them to Japanese ports such as Nagasaki and Osaka, and then reshipping them to Korea, Chinese merchants predicted that they could compete on favorable terms with the Japanese in Korea by avoiding the additional costs incurred by transshipping goods via Japan. However, the lack of a regular steamship line between China and Korea at least partially negated this potential advantage. Observing that the Japanese government subsidized Japanese shipping lines to Korea, Chinese merchants and officials were quick to call for similar action from China. As a result of this pressure, Article VII of the 1882 Sino-Korean Regulations for Maritime and Overland Trade included a provision calling for the "China Merchants' Company steamer to make

---

21. For Yuan's complaints about the 1887 arson attacks, see Yuan Shikai to Cho Pyŏng-jik, Nov. 22, 1887 (KJ 24.10.8), *Ch'ŏngan*, 1: 387–88; Yuan Shikai to Cho Pyŏng-jik, Jan. 14, 1888 (KJ 24.12.2), *Ch'ŏngan*, 1: 397; and Yuan Shikai to Cho Pyŏng-jik, Jan. 17, 1888 (KJ 24.12.5), *Ch'ŏngan*, 1: 404–5.

trips to Corea and return to China at a fixed date every month, the Corean Government to assist in defraying the expenses thereof."[22] The services of one of the most prominent institutions of China's treaty-port elite were thus put to use in Korea.[23] An agreement regarding the specific details of a Shanghai–Inch'ŏn service run by the China Merchants Steamship Company was reached a year later, in November 1883.[24]

The venture was, however, short-lived. The first ship to make the trip, the *Fuyou*, arrived in Korea in mid-December 1883. After arriving in Inch'ŏn, it was impressed into the service of Moellendorff and Chen Shutang, who took it to Pusan to investigate the Dexinghao incident and to explore the prospects of a Chinese settlement in the port. While on board, Moellendorff and Chen proposed that the Shanghai–Inch'ŏn route be expanded to include stops at Yantai, Pusan, Nagasaki, and possibly Wŏnsan. The length of this route, however, made accurate prediction of sailing schedules extremely difficult, a fact that significantly reduced its utility. Also troublesome were conflicts between the captains of the steamships and Korean Customs authorities and disagreements with the Korean government over the amount of their subsidy.[25]

The largest problem faced by the line was the nature of the trade between China and Korea. Although Chinese merchants found a ready market for a wide range of goods, including British and Chinese textiles, there was little in Korea to entice consumers in China. The only "goods" that traveled from Korea to China in any large amounts were specie (usually gold dust) and ginseng. Since both of these items were generally carried in the personal luggage of passengers, the Chinese steamships were virtually empty on their return trips to China. Frustrated by the failure to resolve conflicts with the Korean Customs Service and government and less than sanguine about the potential for profit of a route that carried cargo only

---

22. China, Imperial Maritime Customs, *Treaties, Conventions, Etc., Between China and Foreign States*, 2: 852.

23. For more on the China Merchants Steamship Company and its role in "commercial warfare," see Hao, *The Commercial Revolution in Nineteenth-Century China*, 167, 202–11.

24. Kuksa p'yŏnch'an wiwŏnhoe, *Kojong sidaesa*, Nov. 2, 1883 (KJ 20.10.3).

25. Chen Shutang to Min Yŏng-mok, Nov. 1, 1883 (KJ 20.10.2), *Ch'ŏngan*, 1: 5–7; Chen Shutang to Min Yŏng-mok, Jan. 11, 1884 (KJ 20.12.14), *Ch'ŏngan*, 1: 18–20; Chen Shutang to Kim Hong-jip, Mar. 23, 1884 (KJ 21.2.26), *Ch'ŏngan*, 1: 57–58; Chen Shutang to Kim Pyŏng-si, Apr. 19, 1884 (KJ 21.3.24), *Ch'ŏngan*, 1: 72–73.

one way, the China Merchants Steamship Company abandoned the venture after only three trips.

A Chinese-run steamship line between China and Korea resumed in 1888. This was done at the insistence of Chinese merchants in Seoul and Inch'ŏn, who furnished a monthly subsidy of $1,200. However, as before, complaints about profitability, especially on the return trips, and irregularity hampered the effectiveness of the service. Still, it carried on for a few years. By 1892, China Merchants Steamship Company officials were more than happy to welcome a Korean proposal for a Korean-run service between Inch'ŏn and Yantai. However, mismanagement and financial troubles plagued the Korean line. Throughout the 1880s and 1890s Japanese companies dominated the shipping trade to Korea.[26]

Chinese merchants, with the assistance and encouragement of Yuan Shikai, also made several attempts to establish a regular line between Inch'ŏn and Seoul (or, more precisely, between Inch'ŏn and Map'o or Yongsan). The need for such a line was apparent to all involved, and competition was fierce. Japanese, Korean, American, and Chinese ventures braved the often treacherous sandbar-filled Han River in order to gain a share of the lucrative carrying trade. Yuan Shikai encouraged Chinese ventures and increased the Qing presence at Map'o by establishing a police force there in 1892. A year later, Yuan orchestrated the establishment of two transport companies by Chinese merchants. The first transported goods overland via large teams of oxen. The second purchased a 100-ton steamship christened the *Hanyang* (a name for Seoul). Patterned after Yangzi river steamers, the *Hanyang* was capable of carrying up to 100 passengers and prodigious amounts of cargo. It was far and away the largest and finest ship on the river and regularly ran between Inch'ŏn and Yongsan, which was determined to be a more suitable landing spot than Map'o. The *Hanyang* successfully dominated the river carrying trade until the Sino-Japanese War, when it was seized by the Japanese and used to transport troops.[27]

Assessing the significance of official Chinese support for shipping ventures is a difficult task. The perceived commercial value of such enterprises is indicated by the repeated calls for them from Chinese merchants and by

---

26. For more on this venture, see *British Consular Reports*, 1888, 1–2. For Japanese government subsidies to Japanese shipping lines in Korea, see Duus, *Abacus and the Sword*, 250.

27. Yongsan'gu, *Yongsan'guji*, 462–63; *British Consular Reports*, 1892, 2.

the willingness of some merchants to back their requests with money. The period of greatest Chinese shipping activity (1888–94) coincides with some of the greatest advances in Chinese commercial activity. However, the severe imbalance between Chinese exports to and imports from Korea posed a structural obstacle that even the most enterprising shipping venture could not long ignore. Chinese merchants were willing to utilize the obvious advantages afforded by the presence of Chinese (or any non-Japanese for that matter) shipping lines as long as such lines existed. Otherwise, they carried on as best they could.

Irrespective of the commercial utility of official support for shipping lines, some observers see considerable significance in this support. But while the official support for shipping ventures may have had some symbolic or political significance, including its influence as "a Chinese attempt to impress her suzerain rights on Korea," it is clear that the line foundered on issues that were far more commercial than political.[28] The China Merchants Steamship Company was willing to aid the effort to "impress" China's suzerain rights only if it could make a profit.

Yuan Shikai, Henry Merrill, and Chinese Smuggling

The intersection of the Qing imperial strategy of pursuing special privileges and profits in Korea, on one hand, and the equal-access imperatives inherent in the "multilateral imperialism" introduced to Korea largely at the Qing Empire's behest, on the other, is well illustrated in the establishment and functioning of the Korean Maritime Customs Service. Contemporary observers and subsequent generations of scholars alike have dismissed the Korean Customs Service as a mere appendage of Qing imperial ambitions and policies in Korea. However, an examination of the day-to-day operations of the Customs Service reveals that its officials, particularly Chief Commissioner of Customs Henry F. Merrill, worked far more enthusiastically to enforce the norms of equality under the existing law than they did to promote Qing commercial interests in Korea. Merrill also sought to expand the scope of the treaty-port system to include areas of Chinese activity that fell outside the purview of the customs service.

Conflicts between the Korean Customs Service and Chinese merchants began long before Merrill took up his post. Some began literally as soon as

---

28. Deuchler, *Confucian Gentlemen and Barbarian Envoys*, 186.

the Customs Service was established. Among the first issues of contention were Chinese complaints about Inch'ŏn Customs officials blocking Chinese ships seeking to travel up the Han River and claims that Chinese merchants had suffered unequal treatment at the hands of customs inspectors. It is important to highlight the fact that Qing officials such as Chen Shutang had to petition the Chosŏn Foreign Office in such cases. Many contemporary observers as well as some later historians have concluded that Moellendorff was a Qing agent and that the Korean Customs Service, being closely related to the Chinese Imperial Maritime Customs Service, served Chinese commercial interests in Korea. If this had been the case, Chen would have had no reason to work through the Korean government; rather, he would have simply dealt with Customs Service officials directly. Moreover, if the Korean Customs Service had simply been a pawn of its Chinese counterpart, Chen and the Chinese merchants should have had little cause for complaint; rather than accommodating Chinese commercial interests, however, the Korean Customs Service genuinely tried to treat all merchants in Korea equally.[29]

The efforts of Chen Shutang, officials in the Chosŏn Foreign Office, and Korean Customs officials sometimes addressed the proximate causes of conflicts between Chinese merchants and Customs officials, but they did little to reduce the ill feelings of both parties. This underlying unresolved tension reached the boiling point in early 1886 when one Lu Yusheng, a would-be merchant newly arrived from China, was detained on the street in Inch'ŏn by two Korean patrolmen apparently employed by the Inch'ŏn Customs Office. They proceeded to examine Lu and the bedroll he was carrying. Although they found no evidence that Lu possessed any smuggled goods, they forcibly took Lu to the Inch'ŏn Customs Office, where he was harangued by a foreign employee. Hearing of Lu's fate, a crowd of Chinese merchants soon gathered outside the Customs Office and, claiming to hear sounds of torture and mayhem coming from inside, proceeded to storm the office, breaking several windows and destroying a

---

29. Yur-Bok Lee (*West Goes East*, 53), hardly an apologist for Qing imperialism in Korea, concludes that Moellendorff "made every effort to manage the Korean Customs Service independently of the Chinese Maritime Customs and its influence—which annoyed Viceroy Li thoroughly. Chinese merchants would receive no preferential treatment, despite the Trade Regulations of 1882 between China and Korea, which required such preference."

good deal of property in the process. A brawl ensued that left several Chinese merchants injured.[30]

Those Chinese involved in the incident quickly traveled to Seoul, where they lodged complaints of maltreatment by foreign employees of the Customs Service. They also complained of repeated cases of unequal treatment at the hands of the same foreign employees, arguing that customs officials often resorted to unreasonable searches of Chinese luggage and belongings (whereas merchants from the foreigners' own country were allowed to enter Korea without undergoing an inspection) and arbitrary valuations of Chinese goods (even assessing two different values to the same goods at the same time). At the Qing legation in Seoul, these complaints initially fell on sympathetic ears.[31]

Henry Merrill sent a telegram to China reporting the incident. He noted that the swift arrival of British and Chinese gunboats in Inch'ŏn had calmed the town considerably but complained that the "Chinese response [was] insufficient," that local Chinese officials had "sympathize[d] with rioters" and "arrested nobody." A few days later, however, Yuan Shikai personally interrogated several of the Chinese involved and found them to be at fault. He proceeded to deport several of the chief culprits and ordered the director of the Chinese Merchants Association in Inch'ŏn, Dong Weixin, to pay restitution and reparations to the Inch'ŏn Customs Office.[32]

Merrill declared this settlement "very satisfactory" but noted that two underlying issues remained unresolved. First was the tension between the Chinese community and the Korean Customs Service. Indeed, the complaints of the Chinese merchants involved in the incident are remarkable for their sense of outrage and injustice. Merrill had little sympathy for these claims and called for "adequate punishment [to be] dealt out to those who thought they could, with impunity, defy the authority of the Customs, because it was a Chinese institution, and they were the subjects of the Shang

---

30. Kim Yun-sik to Yuan Shikai, Jan. 27, 1886 (KJ 22.12.23), *Ch'ŏngan*, 1: 287–88; Li Hongzhang to Zongli yamen, Feb. 27, 1886 (GX 12.1.24), *ZRHGX*, 2036–40.

31. Kim Yun-sik to Yuan Shikai, Jan. 27, 1886 (KJ 22.12.23), *Ch'ŏngan*, 1: 287–88; Yuan Shikai to Kim Yun-sik, Jan. 29, 1886 (KJ 22.12.25), *Ch'ŏngan*, 1: 288–89; Kim Yun-sik to Yuan Shikai, Jan. 30, 1886 (KJ 22.12.26), *Ch'ŏngan*, 1: 289.

32. Yuan Shikai to Kim Yun-sik, Jan. 29, 1886 (KJ 22.12.25), *Ch'ŏngan*, 1: 288–89; Kim Yun-sik to Yuan Shikai, Jan. 30, 1886 (KJ 22.12.26), *Ch'ŏngan*, 1: 289; *Haegwanan*, 10; Merrill to Yuan Shikai, Jan. 30, 1886, Merrill to Hart, Feb. 3, 1886, and Merrill to Detring, Feb. 5, 1886, "Merrill's Letterbooks."

Kuo [suzerain]." Still, he feared future conflicts and the disruption they would bring to the administration of the Customs Service.[33]

The second issue was the suspicion of widespread Chinese smuggling, especially of ginseng, and of official Qing collusion with the smugglers. In correspondence with Yuan Shikai, Merrill pointed to the "troublesome question of ginseng smuggling," not only as a cause of this particular incident but also as "a serious menace to the pleasant relations existing between China and Korea." Merrill wrote to Gustav Detring "that it is a matter of common report here, that the Chinese representatives high and low, do a good shake of business in ginseng smuggling; and information was given to the Commissioner at Jenchuan [Inch'ŏn] that several [catties] of ginseng were seen lying in the Chinese Consulate at the time of the riot."[34]

Sold only by government monopoly and assessed a 15 percent duty upon its export from Korea, ginseng was an exceptionally important element in Korean government finances. The fact that Chinese merchants, sailors, and officials smuggled ever-greater amounts of ginseng with apparent impunity never ceased to bother Korean Customs officials and other foreign observers. Attempts by customs officials to examine the luggage of Chinese officials and others, especially when they arrived via Chinese gunboats, were usually rebuffed. Complaints against the Customs Service by the local Qing commissioner of trade to Yuan Shikai usually resulted in Yuan requesting and receiving permission from the Korean Foreign Office to avoid inspection and the assessment of duties. Merrill was adamant in his contention that "China's representatives in Corea should not be dealers in ginseng and silk-piece goods; and China's gunboats should not be the medium of their smuggling operations," but ultimately his efforts to regulate this not-so-clandestine trade were less than successful.[35] The twin Qing

---

33. Merrill to Hart, Feb. 3, 1886, "Merrill's Letterbooks."

34. Merrill to Detring Feb. 5, 1886, "Merrill's Letterbooks."

35. References to smuggling, especially of ginseng, are too many to list here. There appear to have been at least two types of "smuggling." In some cases, ginseng and other dutiable goods were excused from duty by an official notice from the Korean Foreign Office. It was an open secret that the Foreign Office wrote such notices at the behest of Yuan Shikai and other Chinese officials. However, Japanese, other foreign, and even Korean officials sometimes availed themselves of this method of avoiding customs duties. Nevertheless, Merrill and Denny (among others) often complained of the practice. The second type is what might be thought of as smuggling in the traditional sense: the attempt to land or export goods without notifying the Customs Service.

strategy of introducing multilateral imperialism and establishing institutions to enforce its norms such as the Korean Customs Service while seeking to circumvent the restrictions imposed by those very same norms and institutions for exclusive Chinese benefit is hardly an anomalous one in East Asia. For decades, the Qing Empire had witnessed at first hand British efforts to impose open-door free-trade institutions and practices on China while generally ignoring the fact that one of the most significant British imports into China was the illegal drug opium.

Merrill was also less than successful in his efforts to expand the scope of Customs Service oversight to include another area of significant Chinese commercial activity: the northwest coast of Korea, especially the area near the city of P'yŏngyang. Soon after his arrival in Korea, Merrill noted the commercial potential of Korea's northwest coast and the area surrounding P'yŏngyang in particular. However, his proposals to open the port were deflected by Qing and Japanese opposition. Merrill speculated that the Japanese opposed opening P'yŏngyang because they feared that its proximity to China would only enhance China's growing commercial presence in Korea. However, he could "not see what possible harm the opening of Ping An [P'yŏngyang] can do to China."[36] When Owen Denny brought the matter up in an interview with Li Hongzhang, he was informed that P'yŏngyang's proximity to the Chinese port of Niuzhuang meant that opening the Korean port would threaten trade in China.[37] Equally compelling but not acknowledged was the existence of a considerable amount of Chinese trade at P'yŏngyang, a trade outside the purview and control of the Korean Customs Service.[38] Despite Merrill's strong support for opening the port and despite Denny's public airing of the issue in his tract *China and Korea*, P'yŏngyang remained officially closed until 1899.

Precise estimates of the extent of smuggling are hard to come by, but it is clear that both Chinese and Japanese merchants were heavily involved in smuggling operations.

36. For Merrill's opinion on the opening of P'yŏngyang and Chinese opposition, see Merrill to Hart, Oct. 4, 1887, and Merrill to Hart, Mar. 20, 1888, "Merrill's Letterbooks"; for Denny's assessment of the situation, see *China and Korea*, 40–41. For an estimate of the amount of illegal Chinese trade taking place at P'yŏngyang, see note 38 to this chapter.

37. Denny, *China and Korea*, 40–41.

38. For an estimate of the volume of the illegal Chinese trade at P'yŏngyang, see *Haegwanan*, 1: 54–55; see also *British Consular Reports*, 1889, 3, 5; *British Consular Reports*, 1892, 6; Dinsmore to U.S. Secretary of State, Nov. 11, 1887, *KAR*, 2: 107; Heard to U.S. Secretary of State, Nov. 19, 1890, *KAR*, 2: 38.

The operation of the Korean Customs Service illustrates the sometimes-contradictory impulses of the various Qing imperial strategies in Chosŏn Korea. It was an institution established with Qing encouragement, financial assistance, and personnel and reflected Li Hongzhang's strategy of using multilateral imperialism to counterbalance perceived Russian and Japanese threats and his desire to foster Korean self-strengthening efforts. Yet its operations served to undermine Qing attempts to use its claims of suzerainty to promote Chinese commercial interests in Korea aggressively. Merrill's failure to stop Chinese smuggling or to extend the reach of the Korean Customs Service to the northwestern coast of Korea should not distract attention from the fact that he attempted to do so. Merrill had fond feelings for China and often sought to convince Yuan Shikai and other Qing officials that adherence to treaty provisions and cooperation with the Customs Service were in the Qing Empire's best interests. However, he was not afraid to clash with Yuan if he perceived a threat to the autonomy or efficiency of his office.[39]

Chinese Commerce in Korea, 1885–94

The number of Chinese merchants coming to and doing business in Korea grew steadily during the Residency of Yuan Shikai. Although they hailed from all parts of the Qing Empire, as time went on, migrants and merchants from nearby Shandong increased to the point where they outnumbered their compatriots from all other parts of China combined. Taken together, Chinese merchants, laborers, adventurers, and officials were the foot soldiers who were to carry out Qing imperial strategies in Korea. Encouraged by the strong foundation laid by Chen Shutang and heartened by the continuing support of Yuan Shikai, Chinese merchants poured into Korea in ever-growing numbers throughout the period 1885–94. As such, they were the personification of the designs and desires of China's treaty-port elite, who saw the aggressive promotion of commercial interests as an integral part of the larger Qing imperial strategy of economic development and modernization at home and the projection of power abroad. Japanese

---

39. Moreover, Merrill occasionally criticized Yuan for political affairs unconnected to the Customs Service. For example, in 1886 he joined Denny and American diplomats in denouncing Yuan's alleged fabrication of a secret Korean-Russian agreement; see Foulk to U.S. Secretary of State, Oct. 14, 1886, *KAR*, 1: 155.

merchants quickly found them to be strong competitors in a variety of markets. Like their counterparts in other colonial contexts, Chinese merchants in Korea sought and benefited from official support and encouragement, but a number of other factors help explain Chinese commercial success in Korea. Chinese merchants expanded traditional networks and trading patterns such as the exchange of ginseng for silk; sought new goods in Korea, most prominently gold; and aggressively moved to wrest the carrying trade in Western manufactured goods, particularly machine-woven cotton textiles, from the Japanese.

EXPANDING TRADITIONAL NETWORKS:
EXCHANGING GINSENG FOR SILK

Throughout the Chosŏn period, Koreans and Chinese traded a diverse range of goods via tribute missions and along the Sino-Korean border. A significant component of this trade was the exchange of Korean (or sometimes Japanese) silver and ginseng for Chinese silks. As noted above, the opening of Korea to maritime trade had the effect of gradually diminishing the significance of the tribute and border trades. However, once Chinese merchants began to travel to and do business within Korea itself, some of them moved quickly to re-establish and expand the long-established exchange of ginseng for silk via maritime rather than land routes.

The ginseng trade between China and Korea existed long before 1876. The demand for the root, prized in China for its medicinal qualities, was large and consistent. Recognizing this demand, the Korean government regularly imposed taxes on the sale of ginseng and attempted to limit the amounts cultivated and exported in any given year. Such attempts to regulate ginseng cultivation and trade began at least as early as the twenty-first year of the reign of King Chŏngjo (1797). By the time of Kojong's reign, royal control of ginseng exports accounted for a significant portion of royal (not to be confused with government) revenue.[40]

---

40. For a history of the attempts of the Chosŏn government to control and profit from ginseng, see Yang Sang-hyŏn, "Tae-Han chaegukki Naejangwŏn ch'aejŏng kawlli yŏn'gu," 15–86. Although exporting Korean ginseng to China is a practice that dates back centuries, it was only in the eighteenth century that ginseng was cultivated (as opposed to gathered from the wild) on any significant scale. For a detailed examination of the various types of ginseng and the process of ginseng cultivation, see Collyer, "The Culture and Preparation of Ginseng in Korea," 18–30.

Exports of ginseng continued after Korean ports were opened to foreign trade. Although it is difficult to measure the amount of ginseng still taken into China via the traditional overland tribute route, reports from the Korean Customs Service show a steady outflow of ginseng from Inch'ŏn, a trend that continued throughout the open-port period. A British consul concluded in 1888 that ginseng was one of "the two most valuable products of the kingdom."[41] Even a cursory glance at annual trade reports would seem to indicate otherwise, since the value of Korean exports of ginseng seldom exceeded that of gold, rice, or beans. However, ginseng was compact, portable, and worth far more per pound than Korea's agricultural or marine exports. These qualities rendered ginseng extremely susceptible to smuggling. In fact, ginseng smuggling was so rampant that customs officials did not even attempt to estimate the actual amount of ginseng that left Korea in any given year. Chinese, Japanese, and Koreans participated in the lucrative if illicit trade.[42]

Korea had also imported silk from China long before 1876. The demand for silk among Korean elites was largely met through the tribute trade. Some quantities of silk may have continued to enter Korea via the traditional overland route (at least until tribute missions were abolished in 1894), but soon after the opening of Inch'ŏn, enterprising Chinese merchants began to import large amounts of silk by sea. The demand for Chinese silks, much of which came from the court, was fairly constant. Periods of official mourning, for Queen Dowager Cho in the early 1890s, for example, temporarily reduced demand, but substantial increases in imports usually followed the end of such periods.[43]

Chinese producers and merchants paid close attention to an exacting and ever-changing Korean market. One British observer noted:

The silk for the Corean market is specially manufactured in the neighborhood of Chinkiang [Zhenjiang], and are quite different from anything worn in China. Coreans like bright and fancy colors, children especially appearing on holidays in

---

41. *British Consular Reports*, 1888, 3.

42. For just a few of the many examples of ginseng smuggling, see Merrill to Detring, Feb. 5, 1886, "Merrill's Letterbooks"; *Korea Review* 1903, 503, 507; *Korea Review*, 1906, 354.

43. For the official announcement of mourning rules and restrictions, see *KS*, June 9, 1890 (KJ 27.4.22); for an assessment of the impact on Chinese silk imports, see *British Consular Reports*, 1892, 5.

clothes of the most dazzling hues. It is amusing in this remote part of the world to hear the Chinese purveyor complaining of the impossibility of keeping pace with the ever-changing fashions of the Coreans.[44]

With the exception of the Japanese stronghold in Pusan, Chinese silks quickly overwhelmed and surpassed those of their Japanese counterparts. In some cases, Japanese merchants chose to market Chinese silks, which had greater appeal for Korean customers, rather than Japanese silks.[45]

Hemp textiles, usually rendered in English as "grasscloth," were also imported into Korea in considerable quantities. The lightweight fabric was especially sought after for summer clothing. As such, grasscloth competed directly with light textiles from the West such as lawns and muslins. The fact that the more expensive Chinese grasscloth crowded out similar Western cotton textiles was puzzling to some observers. The Chinese cloth was, however, more durable and better withstood the abuse entailed in traditional Korean laundry methods, a fact that perhaps made it cost effective in the long run.[46] Whatever the case, Chinese merchants did a brisk business in grasscloth, their imports of the fabric often rivaling and occasionally exceeding those of silk.

GOLD

One of the challenges facing Chinese merchants in Korea was the relative lack of Korean goods that could be exchanged for Chinese imports into Korea. Ginseng was valuable and sought after, but the amount of ginseng available for export was restricted by the size of the crop and the desire of the Chosŏn government to regulate the ginseng trade. Silver was traditionally an important Korean export to China, but much of this originated in Japan, and the overall amount of silver flowing from both Japan and Korea to China diminished considerably throughout the seventeenth and eighteenth centuries.[47] After their arrival in Korea, Chinese merchants

---

44. *British Consular Reports*, 1897, 11.

45. For Japanese imports of Chinese silks, see *TSIS*, 10: 367. In the years 1889–1900, even in the Japanese stronghold of Pusan, the only silk imported was Chinese; see *British Consular Reports*, 1900, 23.

46. See *British Consular Reports*, 1901, 6; and 1910, 5.

47. John Lee, "Trade and Economy in Preindustrial East Asia."

quickly discovered a Korean resource that compensated for this shortfall: gold.[48]

Exports of gold are often omitted in calculations of Korea's foreign trade during the open-port period. Gold's function as a currency in many parts of the world renders problematic the consideration of the precious metal as a simple product like rice or textiles. However, it is clear that in Korea, at least until 1897 (the year Japan adopted the gold standard), gold did not serve as a medium of exchange. The stores of gold held by the Korean government were infinitesimal, even when compared to its nearly empty coffers of silver and copper. A wide variety of materials—iron, copper, silver, paper, hemp cloth, and rice—circulated as media of exchange at various times during the Chosŏn period, but gold was never widely used.[49]

The fact that customs officials did not list gold as an item of export did not mean that they did not regard gold as such. Writing in 1894, W. Osborne, the acting commissioner of customs in Inch'ŏn, noted that in Korea "there is no generally established currency," a fact that made gold "more of the nature of merchandise" than of currency.[50] If one considers gold "merchandise," it becomes clear that gold was one of Chosŏn Korea's chief exports during much of the open-port period. Gold exports become all the more significant when one realizes that the customs returns and other reports recorded only a fraction of the actual gold exports. It was an open secret that foreign merchants routinely carried considerable amounts of gold on their persons or in their personal luggage so as to avoid the export duty. A British report noted in 1888 that "amongst the Chinese and Japanese passengers outwards by every steamer there are always some who take gold, in greater or lesser quantities, on their persons which is never re-

---

48. Much of the gold dust exported was extracted through small-scale surface mining and/or panning. The area around Wŏnsan was particularly known for this. Later in the open-port period, these small-scale ventures were joined by larger, foreign-financed and -operated mining operations.

49. For a discussion of currency during the Chosŏn period, see Palais, *Politics and Policy in Traditional Korea*, 160–67. In 1875, the Korean government treasury held 144 *yang* of gold, 126,848 *yang* of silver, and 108,424 *yang* of copper (ibid., 206). The Korean *yang* was originally a unit of weight equivalent to the Chinese tael (*liang*), 1.3 ounces. However, according to James Palais (*Confucian Statecraft and Korean Institutions,* 857), by the mid- to late Chosŏn period, the *yang* functioned not as a unit of weight but as a "unit of account."

50. *CSR*, 1893, 637.

ported to the customs."[51] In addition, an 1892 report noted, "only a small proportion of the gold exported is shipped as freight, while a large quantity is taken away by junks and fishing vessels that visit the non-treaty ports."[52] Estimates of the amount of gold that illicitly left Korea each year vary. One observer concluded that 90 percent of the gold exported left the country without being reported. However, the consensus seems to have been that it was safe to at least double the amount declared to the Customs Service.[53]

Regarding gold as an item of export rather than as currency significantly alters our understanding of Korea's foreign trade during the open-port period. Most important, the inclusion of gold as an export item helps explain Korea's chronic and otherwise inexplicable trade and payments imbalances. The fact that the Chosŏn Kingdom routinely imported more goods than it exported was noted by many observers. Given the considerable and steadily growing appeal of the wide range of foreign manufactured goods available to Koreans, as well as the relative lack of Korean goods available for exchange, the presence of a trade deficit in terms of goods (as traditionally defined) should not be surprising. What puzzled foreign observers, officials in the Korean Customs Service, for example, was the apparent deficit in terms of payments. Chosŏn Korea had virtually no overseas assets. Therefore, every item imported into Korea had of necessity to be paid for by "money or money's worth obtained within the limits of the kingdom." And yet, the tables and charts painstakingly compiled by customs officials did not add up; rather, they revealed persistent deficits. Including declared gold exports in calculations of Korea's total exports narrowed but did not entirely close the gap between imports and exports. Customs officials concluded that "the excess of imports represents partly the value of the [Korean] produce sent abroad, across the land frontier legitimately or from the seaboard illicitly, and partly the value of the Gold Dust taken out of the country without previous declaration at the Custom House."[54]

---

51. *British Consular Reports*, 1888, 4.

52. Ibid., 1892, 5.

53. Ibid., 1891, 7; see also the volumes for 1885, 1888, 1896, and 1898 *passim*. See also *CSR*, 1884–93 *passim*.

54. *CSR*, 1893, 620–21.

CHINA'S ROLE IN KOREAN GOLD EXPORTS

The export of gold from Korea was of particular importance in the Sino-Korean trade. For much of the open-port period, gold was Korea's primary export to the Qing Empire. The fact that gold was generally cheaper in Korea than in China meant that the Chinese merchant who received gold in exchange for goods found the transaction doubly profitable. In addition, with the exception of ginseng, there was little Chinese demand for other major Korean exports such as rice, beans, animal hides, and marine products. Gold was, by default, one of the only goods Chinese merchants deemed worthwhile to export to China. The depreciation of silver in China made Korean gold all the more valuable, becoming in the words of one British observer, "practically the only Corean produce that can be sent to China for the purchase of Manchester goods [British cotton goods]."[55] Moreover, like ginseng, the compact and portable nature of gold made smuggling a relatively simple task. It was far easier to hide a few bags of gold dust on one's person or in one's luggage than other export items of comparable worth. Gold quickly became the chief means for Koreans to purchase goods imported by Chinese merchants.

Customs officials and other observers of Korea's trade were quick to note that once Chinese merchants entered Korea in earnest, exports of gold to China grew rapidly. J. C. Johnston, the commissioner of customs in Inch'ŏn, noted in 1891: "In former years nearly all the gold exported went to Japan, but most of the precious metal now goes to China."[56] China's strong showing in Korean gold exports before the turn of the century was taken by some to be an indication of "the strengthening role of China in Korean trade at Japan's expense."[57] China's dominance in this arena is all the more remarkable, since the overwhelming majority of Korea's total exports went to Japan. However, whether mercantilist assumptions about the desirability of specie relative to commodities held true in late nineteenth-century Northeast Asia is an open question. It is not entirely clear whether the different dynamics that dominated Korea's trade with Japan and China (i.e., the Koreans being forced to resort to gold to pay for Chinese imports, whereas Japanese demand for Korean goods such as beans and rice

---

55. *British Consular Reports*, 1897, 8.
56. *CSR*, 1891, 633.
57. Sigel, "The Sino-Japanese Quest for Korean Markets," 115.

financed a good portion of Japanese imports) are a sign of Chinese strength or merely a sign of difference.

Certain elements and consequences of the gold-for-goods trade that dominated Sino-Korean trade before the turn of the century were clearly disadvantageous to China's long-term commercial position in Korea. Gold's portability made it easy to smuggle but sharply reduced the profitability of Chinese shipping ventures; even with state subsidies, Chinese steamship lines had difficulty competing with their Japanese counterparts because their boats often returned to China relatively empty whereas Japanese steamers returned to Japan laden with goods. Trading goods for gold may have lacked the risks inherent in the rice trade, but it also lacked the potential for fantastic profit.

IMPORTS OF FOREIGN MANUFACTURED GOODS

In many respects, the Chinese inroads into Korean markets represented an expansion of traditional networks and patterns. When this trade is mapped onto the geography of the Korean peninsula and the distribution of the Chosŏn Kingdom's first three treaty ports—Pusan, Wŏnsan, and Inch'ŏn—it is clear that different dynamics were present in different parts of Korea. Most of Korea's exports of ginseng left for China via Inch'ŏn. A disproportionate amount of Korea's gold was exported via Wŏnsan. In both cases, gold-seeking Chinese merchants often traded silk and hemp textiles for gold. In Pusan, however, the primary dynamic was Japanese demand for rice, a fact that tended to squeeze out other potential competitors. With the exception of some rice shipped by the Qing Empire to Korea in times of dearth on the peninsula, Chinese merchants generally did not participate in the lively and growing agricultural sector, which was dominated by Japanese merchants.[58]

Not all of Korea's growing trade with the outside world was an amplification of previous trading patterns. The treaty ports, particularly Inch'ŏn,

---

58. In 1894, some 340,000 piculs of rice were imported from China. Observers noted, however, that Japanese rice merchants bought much of this rice, mixed it with Korean rice, and exported it to Japan; see *British Consular Reports*, 1894, 4. An 1890 British report pointed out that Korean rice, cleaned and polished by Japanese mills in Korean treaty ports, was often mixed with Japanese rice in Japan where it "finds its way eventually to Europe in increasing quantities" (ibid., 1890, 3).

were also locations for new sectors and patterns of trade. The vast majority of these were centered around the growing demand for various foreign manufactured goods, chief among them cotton textiles. In addition, the growth of foreign communities brought a growing demand for a variety of goods and services. In both of these arenas, Chinese and Japanese merchants competed head to head. Most observers conclude that Chinese merchants got the better of the conflict during the period 1885–94. Still, imports of foreign manufactured goods were hardly monolithic or one-dimensional.

ENCLAVE TRADING: PROVIDING FOR
FOREIGNERS IN KOREAN TREATY PORTS

A large and consistently growing portion of the imports into Korea meticulously recorded by Customs Service officials were placed in the "sundries" category. For example, well over a hundred such items are listed in the 1893 Customs Service report for Inch'ŏn. Among them were cigarettes, "braid, llama," fireworks, iron safes, needles, pomatum, watches, and "worm tablets, in bottles."[59] A good proportion of these sundry goods was imported to meet the demand of the growing foreign community in Korea. Diplomats, missionaries, adventurers, advisers, and merchants from abroad generally seemed to prefer confectioneries, their haberdasheries, and soaps (among other things) from home over the Korean equivalents (if they existed).

Determining which good was imported by which merchant for the use of which foreigner (or Korean) is an always difficult and often impossible task. But the general pattern appears to have been what one might expect: Japanese merchants imported Japanese goods for the use of the growing Japanese communities in Korean treaty ports. Chinese merchants imported goods for their own compatriots; however, they also seemed to have provided for the needs of many Westerners. Isabella Bird Bishop noted that the Chinese "had nearly a monopoly of the foreign 'custom,' their large 'houses' in Chemulpo had branches in Seoul, and if there were any foreign requirement which they could not meet, they procured the article from

---

59. *CSR*, 1893, 640–43.

Shanghai without loss of time."[60] Chinese merchants also served the needs
of Western visitors and travelers in Korea, particularly in Inch'ŏn. Bishop
noted that when she arrived at Inch'ŏn, she stayed "at a Chinese inn,
known as 'Steward's,' kept by Itai, an honest and helpful man who does all
he can to make his guests comfortable, and partially succeeds." Itai may
have only "partially" succeeded in meeting the needs of Westerners, but
he, along with his countryman "Ah Wong," managed to secure virtually all
the business of foreigners (Japanese excepted) entering Inch'ŏn.[61] "Steward's," described by an observer around the turn of the century as a firm
"with an American name and a thoroughly progressive spirit," was also active in importing large quantities of goods largely to meet the tastes of
Westerners in Korea.[62]

Chinese firms were also active in the distribution of goods from the
treaty ports to Seoul and to points in the interior. A British report made
around the turn of the century noted that some Chinese firms imported
British textiles from Shanghai, but others bought them in Inch'ŏn, "which
is the headquarters of both Chinese and foreign merchants and the distrib-
uting center of European and American products for the whole country."
From Inch'ŏn, goods were either sold directly to Korean merchants or, as
was often the case, "repacked for transport into the interior, where they are
distributed amongst the Chinese branch houses, and hawked round the villages by Chinese peddlers."[63]

Despite official restrictions on travel to the interior, Chinese peddlers
were a common sight in many parts of Korea. Sometimes, these intrepid
individuals brought a bag of goods from Yantai or another part of Shandong and traveled through Korea until the goods were gone, whereupon
they returned to China. More often, they were agents of Chinese wholesale
or retail firms operating in Seoul or one of the treaty ports. In 1893 a Japanese report complained that Chinese peddlers were succeeding in wresting
the market for daily necessities from Japanese merchants, in part because
they invariably supplied goods that were urgently needed. The extent of

---

60. Isabella Bird Bishop, *Korea and Her Neighbours*, 31.

61. Ibid., 31.

62. *Korea Review*, 1901, 13. For more on the Steward Hotel and its Japanese competitors, see Ch'oe Sŏng-yŏn, *Kaehang kwa yanggwan yŏkjŏng*, 105–7. See also Carles, *Life in
Corea*, 20; and Tan Que, "Tongshuntai yu jiu Han jiehuan," 27.

63. *British Consular Reports*, 1899, 10.

their success was indicated in the fact that Japanese merchants who sold sundry goods often merely resold goods they had bought from the Chinese.[64]

COTTON TEXTILES: THE TRANSIT TRADE

Although Chinese merchants in Korea found a steady market for Chinese silks and grasscloth, the majority of Koreans wore cotton clothing. The traditional cotton garb was worn (with additional wadding) even in the wintertime. As a consequence, the British hopes of selling large quantities of woolen goods in Korea were never realized. However, the Korean demand for foreign cotton textiles was huge and limited primarily not by a lack of demand but by a lack of purchasing power. Western, particularly British, cotton goods were a significant and permanent feature in Korea's imports during the open-port period. For most of the period, however, British merchants did not attempt to do business in Korea. British textiles found their way to the peninsula through Japanese and Chinese merchants. The competition in this transit trade was fierce, but the advantages possessed by Chinese merchants meant that they eventually gained the upper hand.

That British producers and merchants would shy away from becoming directly involved in imports of British textiles into Korea is not surprising. Many British observers were less than sanguine about Korea's commercial potential, especially compared to the much larger and more developed markets in Japan and China. Moreover, the British had long been accustomed to using "established indigenous merchants within the treaty port system" to market British textiles in both China and Japan.[65] It is apparent that British textiles traveled between China and Japan via indigenous trade networks largely dominated by Chinese merchants. British observers in Japan in the 1870s noted that "the trade in all kinds of shirtings is now entirely in the hands of Chinese merchants, with whom foreigners cannot compete"; Japanese merchants similarly "complained that they had to buy almost all the foreign goods bound for Korea from Chinese houses in Nagasaki."[66] In short, most if not all of the British textiles marketed by

---

64. Qin Yuguang, *Lü Han liushinian jianwenlu*, 20.
65. Sugiyama, "Textile Marketing in East Asia, 1860–1914," 282.
66. Furuta, "Shanghai: The East Asian Emporium for Lancashire Goods," 3, 11.

Japanese in Korea passed through at least one pair of Chinese hands before reaching Korea.

This pattern changed with the establishment of maritime commercial relations between China and Korea in 1882. Chinese merchants based in Japan observed that Japanese merchants were merely transshipping goods from Hong Kong and Shanghai to Korea and concluded that, if they had official protection in Korean treaty ports, they could do the same.[67] The first Japan-based Chinese merchants to attempt to trade in Korea met with significant opposition from the local Japanese community in Pusan (see the discussion of the Dexinghao incident in Chapter 4). Chinese merchants in Wŏnsan were more successful, and those who went to Inch'ŏn after it opened in 1883 were more successful still.

The transformation in the trade in British textiles in Korea is encapsulated in two statements made by British observers. One noted in 1885: "English merchants have avoided entering the country, being content to allow the Japanese to act for them and control the trade." Another concluded in 1899 that the trade of British textiles "is almost entirely in the hands of Chinese merchants."[68] Within a handful of years, Chinese merchants had wrested control of the Korean market for British textiles from the Japanese and would retain their hold for most of the open-port period.[69]

Chinese merchants possessed several advantages over their Japanese counterparts. First was simple geography: Inch'ŏn, the chief port of the Korea trade, especially in imports, was closer to Shanghai, the main distribution center of British textiles, and closer still to Tianjin, an important regional distribution center, than was any port in Japan. The savings in transportation costs alone allowed Chinese merchants to sell British cotton goods at cheaper prices. One estimate made in the 1880s noted that the lower distribution costs meant that Chinese could import cotton goods for half the cost incurred by a Japanese merchant.[70]

---

67. Li Hongzhang to Zongli yamen, Mar. 29, 1884 (GX 10.3.3), *ZRHGX*, 1349.

68. *British Consular Reports*, 1885, 2–3; 1899, 10.

69. As late as 1910, a British observer noted that "the import of British cotton goods is almost entirely in the hands of Shanghai merchants, who import on consignment from stocks held by large importers in Shanghai" (ibid., 1910, 4). See also Pak Su-i, "Kaehanggi Han'guk muyŏk chabon e kwanhan yŏn'gu," 144.

70. Duus, *Abacus and the Sword*, 257.

Second was their proximity to and greater experience with the Shanghai textiles market. Chinese merchants were able to react more swiftly to fluctuations in exchange rates, prices, supply, and demand.[71] Third, most Chinese merchants who imported British textiles had larger amounts of capital than their Japanese counterparts, many of whom were small-scale merchants trying to make the rice trade pay by importing Manchester gray shirtings or T-cloths.[72] This capital allowed them to buy in bulk and to weather short-term fluctuations that were often disastrous for the Japanese merchants. Fourth, and more generally, the widespread Korean antipathy toward Japan meant that Korean consumers generally preferred Chinese merchants to Japanese (all else being equal).[73]

Available trade figures support the contention that Chinese merchants came to dominate the transit trade in cotton textiles. As early as 1885, nearly 90 percent of all British cotton goods imported into Korea came from China. By 1893, fully 99.5 percent of all British cotton textile goods passed through Chinese hands at some point before being sold in Korea.[74] However, the Chinese dominance in the area of British textiles came to mean less over time because British cotton goods would gradually lose their market share in the face of aggressive and determined Japanese competition.

Competing Imperialisms

Chinese expansion of the traditional ginseng, silk, and grasscloth trades; the introduction of gold as the chief Chinese export to Korea; and the Chinese success in providing goods and services for Chinese, foreigners, and Koreans alike combined to the point that by 1892 Chinese merchants handled some 45 percent of all of Korea's imports. Japanese merchants handled nearly all of the remaining 55 percent.[75] In the eyes of many, Chi-

---

71. Furuta, "Shanghai: The East Asian Emporium for Lancashire Goods," 15.

72. A T-cloth is a "coarse, plain weave cotton cloth made with approximately the same number of ends and picks per square inch and heavily sized" (McField, *Resil's Textile Dictionary*). The name derives from the "T" mark used by the original British exporters of the cloth.

73. Pak Kyŏng-yong, *Kaehwagi Hansŏngbu yŏn'gu*, 118. For Chinese merchants' aggressive attempts to secure the best spots in Korean markets, see ibid., 121.

74. Pak Su-i, "Kaehanggi Han'guk muyŏk ch'abon e kwanhan yŏn'gu," 144.

75. Sigel, "The Sino-Japanese Quest for Korean Markets, 1885–1894"; Yur-Bok Lee, "The Sino-Japanese Economic Warfare over Korea, 1876–1894." These figures are most

nese commercial successes were mirroring Qing triumphs in the political realm. The Chinese commercial achievements caused much soul-searching in Japan, with some blaming the poor quality of Japanese manufactured goods and the tendency of Japanese merchants to treat customers poorly or market counterfeit goods as reasons for the Japanese decline and Chinese ascent.[76]

Differences in the quality and the nature of sales and distribution surely account for at least some of the dramatic shift in Chinese and Japanese shares of the Korean market. However, this process is complicated but ultimately more fully explained by other factors. First, although customs officials, consuls, observers, and scholars frequently resort to the national shorthand of "Chinese" or "Japanese" to describe and categorize foreign merchants in Korea, scratching below the surface reveals a diversity that belies the generic national labels. "Chinese" merchants hailed from all parts of China. As was the case in other parts of the world, Chinese migrants and merchants in Korea generally lived and worked with others from their own home region or province; they also formed their own native-place organizations. In Seoul, a Shandong-dominated "Northern League" (Beibang) was most active in and around the Sup'yo Bridge district. Merchants and migrants from Zhejiang and nearby provinces established a "Southern League" (Nanbang) in the western part of Seoul (present-day Sŏsomun). Numerically inferior but commercially significant merchants from Guangdong set up their own "Guangdong League" (Guangdongbang) as well as a lodge (*huiguan*) in the present-day Sogong district.[77] A similar division was observed in Inch'ŏn: members of the "Northern League" hailed largely from neighboring Shandong and accounted for the largest number of merchants in Inch'ŏn. A "Guangdong League" did a brisk trade in textiles as well as tobacco, liquor, canned goods, foodstuffs, and various sundries. A

---

likely derived from materials originally found in Shiokawa Ichitarō, *Chōsen tsūshō jijō*, 56–65, which, in turn, were drawn from Korean Customs Service reports. The exact correspondence of Shiokawa's figures to those found in the Korean Customs Service Reports as well as the fact that Shiokawa lists his figures in Mexican dollars leaves no doubt as to the original source of his data. Reproductions or other use of his charts can be found in Han'guk muyŏk hyŏphoe, *Han'guk muyŏksa*, 115, 134; Lee Ki-baik, *A New History of Korea*, 288; Conroy, *The Japanese Seizure of Korea*, 460; and Yi Sŏn-gŭn, *Han'guksa*, 668.

76. Pak Su-i, "Kaehanggi Han'guk muyŏk chabon e kwanhan yŏn'gu." 139–41.

77. Pak Kyŏng-yong, *Kaehwagi Hansŏngbu yŏn'gu*, 122.

"Southern League" made up of merchants from Jiangsu, Zhejiang, and Jiangxi dealt mostly in piece goods and silk.[78] In addition, the Chinese seizure of the transshipment trade in British textiles in Inch'ŏn came not so much at the expense of Japanese merchants but of the Chinese Nagasaki-based "Zhejiang clique."[79]

Second, as noted above, some of the differences in the success of various merchants were related in part to the location and resource endowment of each individual Korean treaty port and its environs. Pusan was the port closest to the most productive agricultural regions of Korea as well as the closest open port to Japan, and was, therefore, the main base of operations for Japanese rice merchants. Trade in this port was largely export-driven, with the Japanese demand for rice being the key determinant of the level of trade and the profits available. Since there was little demand in China for Korean rice, it is not surprising to find that Chinese merchants found little business in Pusan. Wŏnsan, by contrast, was too far north to be a productive rice-growing region; in fact, the port often imported rice and other foodstuffs from the south. On the other hand, Wŏnsan was close to considerable quantities of easily accessible gold. This fact alone attracted Chinese merchants, who, although considerably outnumbered by their Japanese competitors, managed to seize the upper hand in the port's trade. In 1892, one observer concluded that "the import trade is almost entirely in the hands of the Chinese, who have now five firms established there, all of which made money in 1892, though it was considered to be an unprofitable year."[80] Inch'ŏn was different still. The port's proximity to Seoul meant that it served as the chief conduit for foreign imports into Korea. The success of import-oriented Chinese merchants in Inch'ŏn derives at least partially from this fact. Observers at the time, such as Isabella Bird Bishop, were more willing to credit Chinese pluck and hard work; describing the Chinese settlement in Inch'ŏn, she noted:

Busy and noisy with the continual letting off of crackers and beating of drums and gongs, the Chinese were obviously far ahead of the Japanese in trade. . . . Late into the night they were at work, and they used the roadway for drying hides and storing kerosene tins and packing cases. Scarcely did the noise of night cease when the

---

78. Tang Entong, "Hanguo Renchuan shangwu qingxing," 13. See also Du Shupu, *Renchuan huaqiao jiaoyu bainianshi*, 17–22.

79. Furuta, "Inchon Trade."

80. Hillier, *Report on the Commercial Condition of the Ports of Fusan and Wŏnsan*, 7.

din of morning began. To these hard-working and money-making people rest seemed a superfluity.[81]

However, one would have to conclude that the Chinese in Pusan were less hard-working than their Inch'ŏn counterparts for this perceived ethnic characteristic to be the sole explanatory factor for commercial success.

Third, although the structural differences between treaty ports in Korea are significant, in the end, they were not the sole determinants. Equally as significant was the backdrop of the competing imperialist systems of Meiji Japan and the Qing Empire in Chosŏn Korea. As noted in previous chapters, Meiji Japan used the tools of gunboat diplomacy and modern international law to force Chosŏn Korea to increase its relations with the outside world. However, the type of relations favored by Japan were those of exclusive Japanese privilege in Korea with a minimum of regulatory or other obstacles to the expansion of Japanese trade on the peninsula. This unilateral but informal imperialism was challenged by Qing mediation of Chosŏn Korea's treaties with other powers, by the establishment of Sino-Korean trade regulations, and by the subsequent establishment of tariffs and a Korean Customs Service. All these developments encouraged the arrival of a number of powers, both political and commercial, in Korea. And they signaled the end of Japan's exclusive, monopolistic claims in Korea.

Even after the promulgation of treaties guaranteeing the opening of Chosŏn Korea to multilateral yet informal imperialism spearheaded by the Qing Empire, Meiji Japan sought to continue to defend its traditional monopolistic privileges in Pusan, as the Dexinghao merchants discovered to their regret. The swift action of Chen Shutang and other Qing officials forced a grudging Japanese admission that Pusan was indeed open to non-Japanese residents and merchants. But it is apparent that it did little to cause the Japanese to make the port more accommodating for would-be competitors. The anomalous situation of Pusan in the period 1882–94 is somewhat analogous to Chosŏn Korea's diplomatic status during the same period. Chosŏn Korea was both a sovereign member of the international family of nations and a vassal of the Qing Empire. Pusan was both an open port and a place of monopolistic Japanese privilege. Open-port-era Pusan, according to Peter Duus, even *appeared* Japanese:

---

81. Isabella Bird Bishop, *Korea and Her Neighbours*, 31.

The town looked comfortingly Japanese, not all that different from a port town at home. A cluster of Japanese inns, some of them three stories high, were [*sic*] visible from the docks, and several dozen large Japanese-style shops lined the downtown streets. In the center of town not a single Korean-style dwelling was to be seen. Only the white-garbed Koreans on the dock and in the street revealed the unfamiliar. In fact, the new arrival did not have to deal with Koreans at all, except to get his bags to the inn.[82]

Contrast this depiction with contemporary descriptions of Inch'ŏn with its Chinese, Japanese, and general foreign settlements, its foreigner-dominated municipal council, and its multinational population of people from Japan, China, Russia, the Philippines, Great Britain, France, Germany, Belgium, Switzerland, Austria-Hungary, the Netherlands, Turkey, Egypt, and the United States.[83] Inch'ŏn was clearly more open to multilateral imperialism, a context introduced to Korea by the Qing Empire and a context in which Chinese merchants could avail themselves of their geographical, organizational, and tactical advantages to compete and thrive.

The Chinese commercial achievements in Korea constitute the first successful case of the vigorous promotion of commercial interests abroad by the Qing Empire. Some of this success was surely owing to the aggressive assertion of Qing power and exclusive privilege in Korea. However, even after the obliteration of Qing claims to suzerainty by the 1894–95 Sino-Japanese War, Chinese merchants remained an important and surprisingly competitive element in Chosŏn Korea's foreign trade. In the end, the treaty-port system and attendant institutions of multilateral informal imperialism were more significant factors in explaining Chinese commercial success.

---

82. Duus, *Abacus and the Sword*, 328–29. For other descriptions of the port, see Isabella Bird Bishop, *Korea and Her Neighbors*, 23–30; and Sakurai, "Chōsen jiji."

83. Inch'ŏn chikhalshisa p'yŏnch'an wiwŏnhoe, *Inch'ŏnsisa*, 1239–40.

EIGHT

Defending Multilateral Privilege at Suzerainty's End

The Sino-Japanese War and Its Aftermath

The Sino-Japanese War is a significant watershed in East Asian history. It marks the beginning of an increasingly aggressive Japanese imperial expansion onto the Asian mainland. For many, it also marks the beginning of the end of the Qing Empire, as the demoralizing defeat on the battlefield was followed by increasing foreign inroads into the Qing Empire as outside powers sought to "carve the Chinese melon." Qing attempts at reform, some surprisingly ambitious in scope, would prove to be insufficient to stave off the ultimate collapse of the Manchu dynasty in 1912. In the study of Sino-Korean relations, the intersection of Japanese advance and Qing decline creates a tendency to assume that the Chinese defeat signaled the end of a significant Chinese presence in Korea.

To be sure, the war and its aftermath brought the permanent cessation of tribute missions, abandonment of the Qing calendar, and other indications of the end of Qing suzerainty. But the system of multilateral imperialism introduced by the Qing proved to be remarkably resilient in the face of Japanese attempts to reintroduce a system of monopolistic privilege reminiscent of the immediate post–Treaty of Kanghwa period. Within the comforting confines of the treaty-port system, Qing diplomats and Chinese merchants returned to Korea and continued to prosper for much of the next decade. Their continued success is a strong indication that factors other than political dominance and the assertion of suzerainty were primarily responsible for Chinese commercial accomplishments. The prerogatives of multilateral imperialism and the institutions and practices of the over-seas Chinese (*huaqiao*) in Korea are two of the most important of these.

The proximate cause of the Sino-Japanese War was the Qing decision to heed the calls of King Kojong for military assistance in quashing the Tonghak Rebellion. Since 1892, followers of the banned Tonghak (Eastern Learning) religion had been importuning Chosŏn officials to lift the official prohibition on the sect and to posthumously rehabilitate its founder, Ch'oe Che-u (1824–64). Increasingly frustrated with official procrastination on this issue, Tonghak followers, joined by peasants aggravated by local corruption and the ever more obvious foreign inroads into Korea, took up bamboo spears against local government forces in southwestern Korea. The movement rapidly gained momentum, and government troops appeared entirely unable to cope with the military threat. After the rebels took Chŏnju, the capital of Chŏlla province (and the ancestral seat of the Chosŏn dynasty's founder, Yi Sŏng-gye) in May 1894, King Kojong asked the Qing Empire for help.[1]

After some debate, the Qing Empire declared its willingness to assist its vassal. The official June 7 statement announcing the dispatch of troops mentioned the need "to restore the peace of our tributary state, and to dispel the anxiety of every nation residing in Korea for commercial purposes" as the primary justifications for the Qing intervention.[2] Japanese diplomats in Seoul assured Yuan Shikai that Japan would not oppose the dispatch of troops; rather, it would welcome the stability they would presumably bring. When Li Hongzhang and Yuan Shikai learned that Japan, invoking the 1885 Convention of Tianjin, was also dispatching troops, they expressed alarm and dismay to their Japanese counterparts but were repeatedly assured that Japan had "no other designs" but to quash the rebellion and that "she

---

1. See *KS*, May 24, 1894 (KJ 31.5.1). Kojong had discussed the possibility of inviting Qing troops to Korea to help quell the Tonghak rebellion as early as May 1893. At that time, Kojong's advisers agreed that utilizing Qing troops was better than inviting troops from another foreign nation, but they noted that the cost of supplying such troops would be significant and concluded that foreign troops were not necessary to suppress the rebellion (*KS*, May 10, 1893 [KJ 30.3.25]).

2. Conroy, *The Japanese Seizure of Korea*, 245. For a discussion of the debate in the Qing, see Bonnie B. C. Oh, "The Leadership Crisis in China on the Eve of the Sino-Japanese War of 1894–1895." For the official notification to Japan (as required by the Convention of Tianjin), see Zongli yamen to Komura, June 9, 1894 (GX 20.5.6), *ZRHGX*, 3311.

would withdraw her men as soon as the rebellion was quelled and peace and order were restored."[3]

Aghast that their antiforeign crusade had resulted in a much greater and more menacing foreign presence on Korean soil, Tonghak leaders such as Chŏn Pong-jun negotiated an agreement with the Chosŏn government that temporarily ended the hostilities. Li Hongzhang swiftly expressed his willingness to leave Korea, but his Japanese counterparts refused to reciprocate. Li, ever eager to avoid conflict, asked for foreign assistance in reaching a diplomatic resolution, but Japan rejected a British-French-German-American proposal for the withdrawal of both Qing and Japanese troops from Korea. Japanese Foreign Minister Mutsu Munemitsu observed that this failure to achieve a diplomatic resolution of the standoff "gave my country a free hand and personally I was pleased."[4]

Japan then declared its agenda to include not only the quelling of the Tonghak Rebellion but also the implementation of a sweeping reform program for Korea. Using the customary language of noninterference, the Qing Empire rejected a Japanese proposal for a jointly sponsored reform program: "The idea may be excellent, but the measures of improvement must be left to Korea herself. Even China herself would not interfere with the internal administration of Korea, and Japan, having from the very first recognized the independence of Korea, cannot have the right to interfere with the same."[5]

Critics of Li Hongzhang's attempts to find a diplomatic solution, many of whom hailed from the Purist Party, suddenly declared themselves Korea experts and proceeded to lambaste Li's "appeasement" and to call for war against Japan.[6] Yuan Shikai added his voice to the prowar group. His behavior in Korea, however, implies that he had serious doubts about the outcome of such a conflict. He requested permission to leave Korea in late

---

3. Jerome Ch'en, *Yuan Shih-k'ai*, 26. Yuan Shikai and Ōtori Keisuke, the Japanese minister in Korea, actually agreed to a substantial mutual troop reduction on June 15. But Ōtori was overruled by Japanese legation and military officials (Duus, *Abacus and the Sword*, 68).

4. Jerome Ch'en, *Yuan Shih-k'ai*, 27. See also Mutsu, *Kenkenroku*, 47.

5. Paine, *The Sino-Japanese War*, 119; Mutsu, *Kenkenroku*, 24.

6. Bonnie B. C. Oh, "The Leadership Crisis in China on the Eve of the Sino-Japanese War of 1894–1895," 81. According to Jerome Ch'en (*Yuan Shih-k'ai*, 27), Weng Tonghe and other members of the Grand Council were highly critical of Li Hongzhang's "bungling appeasement."

June, but the permission was slow in coming, and on July 19, 1894, Yuan fled Seoul disguised as a servant.[7]

Unable to secure Qing acquiescence to its reform plans, Japan proceeded to take unilateral action to see that its goals were accomplished. On July 23, 1894, Japanese troops surrounded the royal palace, taking King Kojong prisoner.[8] Japanese troops also disarmed Korean military units in Seoul. On the same day, Kojong's father, the Taewŏn'gun, was brought back to power. Many members of Queen Min's family were promptly banished, and the Chosŏn Kingdom renounced all tributary ties and repudiated all the treaties it had signed with the Qing Empire.[9] War was officially declared on August 1. On August 22, 1894, the Chosŏn government announced an alliance with Japan aimed at expelling the Qing from Korea.[10]

For the Qing Empire, the outcome of the Sino-Japanese War was an unequivocal defeat on both land and sea. This result was surprising to many, not least many Qing officials. Some close observers of the Qing military had noted a number of foreboding problems and deficiencies. These ranged from a tendency to adhere rigidly to battle plans regardless of actual circumstances in the field to severe political and organizational fragmentation (the Sino-Japanese War might more properly be labeled the "Li Hongzhang–Japanese War"). Still, the conventional wisdom was that

---

7. Paine, *The Sino-Japanese War*, 113–15.

8. *KS*, July 23, 1894 (KJ 31.6.21).

9. *KS*, July 30, 1894 (KJ 31.6.28).

10. *KS*, Aug. 22, 1894 (KJ 31.7.22). The alliance agreement declared the two nations' goals to be the expulsion of the Qing from Korea and the firm establishment of Korean. independence (*tongnip*) and autonomy (*chaju*). This agreement and a provisional agreement promulgated two days earlier constitute the first time that the term "independence" (*tongnip*) was used to describe Chosŏn Korea in the *Kojong sillok*. The agreement also stipulated that it was to be abrogated once the Qing was expelled and a peace agreement signed. Speaking of the conditions that led to the promulgation of the alliance, Hilary Conroy (*The Japanese Seizure of Korea*, 266–67) writes, "Behind it lay the simple facts of power, the Japanese seizure of the palace on July 23 and promises extracted by Ōtori from the king on July 25." British Acting Consul-General Gardner concurred on the issue of coercion. He reported that "on the 28th instant, at 4:30 pm., Messrs. Otori and Sugimura went to the Foreign Office, and forced the Minister of Foreign Affairs, an aged and infirm man, by threats of killing him—they drew their swords on him—to sign another Treaty, copy of which I enclose. The Treaty states that, on the 26th July, Corea requested Japan to drive the Chinese out of Korea in order to maintain Corean independence" (Gardner to O'Conor, Aug. 28, 1894, in *ACDM*, 407).

the Qing Empire's massive resources would eventually carry the day. In short, "China was big, therefore it would win."[11]

The dramatic Japanese victories were, therefore, a significant shock to many in the Qing Empire. Some Purist Party adherents continued to advocate aggressive measures, including a joint Korean-Qing invasion of Japan proper.[12] The view that such a course was even remotely feasible may have been due to claims of continuous Qing victories in Chinese newspapers; few Chinese were fully aware of the extent of the Qing defeats. For others, however, the Qing defeat signaled the end of Li Hongzhang's self-strengthening campaign as a viable reform agenda and ushered in an era of deeper soul-searching and calls for ever more fundamental reforms. Li Hongzhang himself was stripped of the "Order of the Yellow Riding Jacket" but was kept in command of Qing forces and was later forced to negotiate on the Qing's behalf with the Japanese.[13]

The Qing defeat also spelled the permanent end of Korean tribute missions to China. After being returned to power by the Japanese, the Taewŏn'gun soon turned on his new benefactors and plotted to use Tonghak rebels against Japanese forces in Korea and to place his favorite grandson on the throne. As a result, the newly arrived Japanese diplomat Inoue Kaoru forced the old regent back into retirement and returned Kojong to power. In January 1895, Kojong, accompanied by a large contingent of Japanese troops, visited the royal ancestral shrine and made a "fourteen-point oath" which called for wide-ranging reforms and promised that "all thought of dependence on China shall be cut away, and a firm foundation for independence (*chajudongnip*; C. *zizhuduli*) shall be secured."[14] The repudiation of earlier forms of relations with the Qing Empire, the ratification of the Chosŏn-Meiji anti-Chinese alliance, and the fourteen-point oath (along with similar declarations of Korean independence)[15] were accomplished within

---

11. Paine, *The Sino-Japanese War*, 156. For a somewhat dissenting view on Qing military capabilities, see Fung, "Testing the Self-strengthening."

12. Bonnie B. C. Oh, "The Leadership Crisis in China on the Eve of the Sino-Japanese War of 1894–1895," 83.

13. Paine, *The Sino-Japanese War*, 162.

14. *KS*, Jan. 7, 1895 (KJ 31.12.12). For an English translation of the fourteen-point oath, see Yŏngho Ch'oe et al., *Sources of Korean Tradition*, 2: 275–76. Conroy (*The Japanese Seizure of Korea*, 276) observes, "The whole procedure is reminiscent of the Meiji Emperor's Charter Oath, which very likely was in the back of Inoue's mind."

15. See, e.g., Kojong's royal proclamation in *KS*, Jan. 8, 1895 (KJ 31.12.13).

the context of a massive Japanese military presence and strong pressure from Japanese diplomats. Thus, whether they can be seen as evidence of the sovereign will of Chosŏn Korea, either in the narrow sense of the actual wishes of Korea's sovereign, Kojong, or in the broader but more difficult to measure sense of the will of "Korea" or the Korean people, remains an open question.[16] What is not in question is that they ended the practice of sending tribute missions to Beijing, using the Chinese calendar, and other trappings of the centuries-old ritual-based relationship.

Equally significant, although perhaps less appreciable at the time, was that the Sino-Japanese War signaled the beginning of a dramatic shift in imperial strategies in East Asia. Meiji Japan's decision to resort to force of arms against the Qing Empire was reached at least in part because of its growing concern about Russian expansion into East Asia. Japanese policy makers were well aware of Russian designs in the region and knew that completion of the Trans-Siberian Railroad would greatly facilitate the Russians' ability to achieve their designs. In the words of S. C. M. Paine, "Once the Russian government had announced its intention to build the Trans-Siberian Railway, Japanese leaders knew that they had approximately one decade to resolve matters in Korea before the completion of the railway would irrevocably alter the balance of power in the Far East and preclude Japanese influence in Korea."[17] The Meiji oligarchs knew that the treaty-

---

16. At the time, the British Consul-General Walter Hillier dismissed the significance of the official Korean declarations of alliance with Japan and opposition to China: "The refusal to extend this privilege to myself as custodian of Chinese interests is justified by Count Inouye, I am informed by the Minister of Foreign affairs, on the ground that China and Corea are at war. This has never been admitted by the Corean Government, who are careful to explain that the Treaty of the 26th Aug. and every subsequent act of apparent hostility against China has been forced on them against their will" (Hillier to O'Conor, Dec. 3, 1894, *ACDM*, 489). The parallels between this allegation of coerced expressions of cooperation with Japan and the conclusions of some Westerners that any action Kojong or the Chosŏn court took in the mid- to late 1880s that was indicative of a desire to maintain the traditional relationship with China was a result of Qing coercion are obvious.

17. Paine, *The Sino-Japanese War*, 102–3. One "Baron von Siebold" who was "of the Japanese Legation," expressed the following about the geo-strategic situation in East Asia: "Under the present regime there is no doubt that Corea is perfectly helpless against any aggression from Russia, and any pressure brought to bear from that quarter would surely lead to a loss of territory, if not to the establishment of a Russian Protectorate. If this has not yet happened so far, it is simply due to the fact that Russia cannot afford yet to develop its political programme in Eastern Asia, because the trans-Siberian

port system in the Korean peninsula and Chosŏn Korea's numerous treaties with foreign powers would likely be unable to withstand a concerted
Russian attempt to dominate if not annex Korea—hence, their astound-
ingly successful use of military power to project Japanese interests in the
region.

Multilateral Imperialism
vs. Japanese Unilateral Demands

Japan's dramatic victories against the Qing Empire demonstrated to all that
Japan was a rising power. They were also a manifestation of the shift toward "high imperialism" and the scramble for territory the world over.
However, the treaty-port system, international law, and the strategy of multilateral imperialism more generally did not immediately disappear from
Korea. Rather, they served to stymie some of Meiji Japan's more ambitious
designs as well as create a space in which Qing commercial and, to a much
lesser extent, political interests in Korea could recover. An alliance of
European powers used threatening diplomacy to restrain Japan's territorial
ambitions in the region, and the British Empire played a prominent role in
maintaining multilateral imperialism in Korea.

With little standing in the way of Japanese armies should they be ordered to take Beijing, the Qing Empire was forced to sue for peace and
grant a series of onerous concessions and indemnities to the Japanese. The
Treaty of Shimonoseki (April 17, 1895) would have been even harsher on
the Qing Empire than it was if a young Japanese had not attempted to assassinate Li Hongzhang. Refusing to return to China, Li Hongzhang sto-
ically continued the negotiations with a bullet lodged in his cheek, a behavior that earned him the grudging admiration of many Japanese. From the
Qing Empire's perspective, the terms were bad enough: a sizable indemnity, Japanese access to Shanghai and the Yangzi River, and the cession to

---

Railway is not finished. But according to the accelerated manner in which the works are
now being pushed on—for it is now believed that the line will be completed as soon as
1901, instead of 1904 as previously reported—there is therefore no time to be lost"
("Memorandum by Baron von Siebold on the Question Between China and Japan re:
Corea [Communicated June 29, 1894]," *ACDM*, 15). The Earl of Kimberley, the British
foreign minister, noted that Siebold's conclusions were "generally in the same sense as
those expressed to me by Viscount Aoki [the Japanese ambassador in London]" (Earl
of Kimberley to Mr Paget, June 28, 1894, *ACDM*, 14).

Japan of Taiwan and the Liaodong Peninsula.[18] Most foreign powers regarded nearly all provisions of the treaty as Japan's just desserts for its military victories. Russia, however, was dismayed at Japan's claims to Liaodong because they directly competed with Russia's own territorial designs in the region. Thus, Russia arranged the so-called Triple Intervention, a demand by Russia, France, and Germany that Japan renounce its claim to Liaodong. Seething with anger and humiliation but unwilling to risk war with three European powers, Japan agreed. Multilateral imperialism, it appeared, still had some efficacy, at least when it was backed by a plausible threat of use of force.

Multilateral imperialism also retained some influence in Korea. Meiji Japan claimed to be fighting against the Qing Empire in order to safeguard Korea's independence. And whatever the long-term plans of some Japanese policy makers, Japan made no immediate attempt to include Korea on its list of territorial spoils of war. This did not mean, however, that Japan was content with the status quo in Korea. As noted above, Japan insisted on a change in leadership and on the imposition of a sweeping reform agenda. A significant element of the new Japanese strategy in Korea was the reimposition of its own brand of unilateral but informal empire on the peninsula. In this case it was not France, Russia, and Germany but Great Britain that utilized treaties, international law, and the institutions of the treaty-port system in general to successfully resist many of Japan's attempts to assert monopolistic privileges.

Both the presence of large numbers of Japanese troops in Korea and the willingness of Japanese diplomats to use them to force a reform program on the Chosŏn government were signs of a dramatic change in the balance of power in Korea. Inoue Kaoru, the newly dispatched Japanese proconsul in Korea, wasted no time claiming the same prerogatives Yuan Shikai had enjoyed; according to Peter Duus, he "insisted on being treated

---

18. For the text of the treaty, see China, Imperial Maritime Customs, *Treaties, Conventions, Etc., Between China and Foreign States*, 2: 590–96 (English and Chinese), 707–13 (Japanese). In order to further emphasize the complete abolition of tributary ties, the first article of the treaty begins with the declaration that "China recognizes definitively the full and complete independence and autonomy [*dulizizhu*, K. *tongnipjaju*] of Corea, and, in consequence, the payment of tribute and performance of ceremonies and formalities by Corea to China, in derogation of such independence and autonomy, shall wholly cease for the future" (ibid., 590).

differently from other foreign representatives in Seoul, and he demanded immediate audiences with the king whenever he wished."[19]

Not satisfied with merely terminating the trappings of the traditional Qing-Chosŏn relationship, Japanese officials moved quickly to curtail Chinese commercial and legal privileges and prerogatives in Korea and to seek exclusive Japanese ones in their stead.[20] Significant among their activities and proposals were plans to sever relations between the Korean and the Chinese customs services and to take over administration of the Korean Customs Service; proposals to confiscate Chinese property in Inch'ŏn; and reforms designed to sharply restrict Chinese residence, travel, and business in Korea as well as to eliminate Chinese extraterritorial privileges. In addition to these legal or quasi-legal measures, Japanese merchants and soldiers repeatedly harassed those Chinese who remained in Korea. In the absence of official Qing representation, British officials took on the burden of protecting Chinese interests.

When Tang Shaoyi fled the Qing legation in July 1894, he left Korea, "leaving the interests of the Chinese subjects who still remained in Corea," in the words of the British consul-general in Seoul, Walter Hillier, "in the hands of Mr. Gardner, the Acting British Consul-General. In this arrangement the Corean Government and the Japanese minister acquiesced." King Kojong had also sent a message to Hillier "asking me to do all I could to ameliorate the condition of the Chinese in this country, in whose welfare he took a warm interest."[21] This was the beginning of a period in which Great Britain actively undertook to protect Chinese citizens and interests in Korea.

---

19. Duus, *Abacus and the Sword*, 84.

20. Even before the outbreak of the Sino-Japanese War (and before it was entirely clear that war was inevitable), the Japanese statesman Mutsu Munemitsu advocated that Japan "take advantage of this opportunity to demand cessions of telegraph lines between Pusan and Seoul, abolition of taxes on Japanese in the interior . . . and the like" (Conroy, *The Japanese Seizure of Korea*, 247; see also Mutsu, *Kenkenroku*, 100, 266).

21. Hillier to O'Conor, Nov. 17, 1894, *ACDM*, 474. See also Hillier to O'Conor, Oct. 17, 1894, *ACDM*, 437–38. Although the British government did not officially move to protect telegraph cables, H. J. Muhlensteth, the longtime engineer for the Great Northern Telegraph Company and the Imperial Chinese Telegraph Administration, traveled to Korea to "look after as much as possible the property belonging to the Imperial Chinese Telegraph Administration." However, he was captured by the Japanese and was forced to stay away from Korea for the duration of the war; see Suyematsu to Munemitsu, Aug. 10, 1894, *ACDM*, 313–14.

British officials paid close attention to the status of the Korean Customs Service, then managed by the British citizen John McLeavy Brown. Japanese designs on the customs were obvious and clearly stated: they wanted any and all connections between the Korean and Chinese customs services severed. This included the ouster of current officials, especially those who had served in and were appointed by the Chinese Imperial Maritime Customs Service.[22] These officials were to be replaced by Japanese nationals, who were to dominate the important positions in the Customs Service with perhaps a few minor posts reserved for Koreans or foreigners. Noting that "British subjects . . . have a certain vested interest in the existence of the Corean Customs Service" as it was then constituted, British officials in Korea resisted these measures.[23] They agreed in principle to the need to end the Chinese Customs Service's subsidizing of the salaries of Korean customs officials. However, they fought hard to prevent the replacement of Brown and the foreign staff. Working closely with Korean Minister of Foreign Affairs (the new designation for the post formerly known as president of the Foreign Office) Kim Yun-sik, British officials were able to propose the ending of the Chinese subsidy but the retention of the current staff, their salaries now to be paid by the Korean government. In addition, Brown was to serve "conjointly" both in the Customs Service and in the Korean Finance Department. As a result, the Korean Customs Service was to exercise more influence on the Korean economy and finances than ever before.[24]

British support for the status quo as far as the Korean Customs Service was concerned was based on a calculation of the interests of British subjects and the conclusion that "it would be impossible to find a more com-

---

22. O'Conor to the Earl of Kimberley, Sept. 19, 1894, *ACDM*, 413; Hillier to O'Conor, Oct. 1, 1894, *ACDM*, 419; Woo, " The Historical Development of Korean Tariff and Customs Administration, 1875–1958," 76–77.

23. O'Conor to Hillier, Oct. 6, 1894, *ACDM*, 420.

24. Woo, "The Historical Development of Korean Tariff and Customs Administration, 1875–1958," 79. Despite the public promise to end the practice of Korean Customs Service officials' salaries being paid by Chinese Imperial Maritime Customs Service, this state of affairs continued for at least several months. Reporting in Feb. 1895, Hillier noted: "As far as the salaries of the Customs employees are concerned, the situation remains as it was at the date of the report; the subsidy from the Chinese Customs continues to be paid, and no notice of the fact is taken by the Corean Government, though they are perfectly aware of it" (Hillier to O'Conor, Feb. 9, 1895, *ACDM*, 506). It is not entirely clear when this practice finally ended.

petent and acceptable Chief Commissioner than Mr. Brown had proved himself to be."[25] The contrast between Brown's efficiency and professional conduct, on one hand, and Japanese officials and merchants who called for "the relaxation of one Customs rule after another on various pretexts, each concession being a gain to the Japanese trader, and offering opportunities for the evasion of the revenue," on the other, was all too clear to Britain's representatives in Korea.[26] They concluded that "Japan has abolished the impalpable suzerainty of China only to replace it by a palpable and selfish domination of her own."[27] Such a course ran counter to what John King Fairbank has described as one of the chief purposes of the foreigner-administered customs services in Asia: "to provide equal terms of competition both among individual traders and among the trading nations."[28]

British resistance to Japanese incursions was not limited to protecting the Customs Service. British officials, aware that the Chinese community in Korea was relatively helpless, worked to secure a minimal degree of security for the Chinese who remained in Korea. The British consul in Inch'ŏn, W. H. Wilkinson, called on all remaining Chinese to register their names, occupations, and ages with him. Over 150 had done so by the middle of September 1894. Wilkinson also declared that until the Japanese officially proclaimed the military occupation of Inch'ŏn, he would exercise jurisdiction over any case of Chinese lawbreaking.[29] By November, nearly 400 Chinese had registered with British officials in Seoul or Inch'ŏn.[30] British officials also worked for the release of Chinese arrested by Japanese soldiers or police. Many of these were traveling peddlers or ginseng buyers who returned from the countryside and learned about the outbreak of war only upon their arrival in Seoul or Inch'ŏn.[31] British officials such as Consul-General Walter Hillier frequently expressed sympathy for this type of merchant: trapped in Korea with little or no capital and, with the cessation of nonmilitary sea transport, little prospect of obtaining additional

---

25. Hillier to O'Conor, Oct. 1, 1894, *ACDM*, 419.
26. Hillier to O'Conor, Dec. 4, 1894, *ACDM*, 484.
27. Hillier to O'Conor, Dec. 4, 1894, *ACDM*, 484.
28. Fairbank, *Trade and Diplomacy on the China Coast*, 463.
29. Wilkinson to O'Conor, Sept. 14, 1894, *ACDM*, 412.
30. Hillier to O'Conor, Nov. 17, 1894, *ACDM*, 472.
31. Hillier to O'Conor, Nov. 17, 1894, *ACDM*, 472–73.

goods to sell. Doing whatever he could for such patient and enduring men was a "pleasure."[32]

Hillier also countered a Japanese demand for "the transfer of the Chinese Settlement to the Japanese."[33] Japanese Minister Ōtori Keisuke reasoned that since Korea had renounced all previous treaties and agreements with the Qing Empire, Korea "was, therefore, at liberty to cede the ground to Japan."[34] Although he claimed no extensive knowledge of international law, Hillier objected to this on the basis of the fact that it would constitute "a grave injustice to the holders of lots in this Settlement to deprive them of property which they have acquired by legal purchase" and concluded that the Japanese were "interfering with rights which it is impossible to ignore."[35] Hillier's objections, backed by his superiors, and especially by consultation with Count Inoue, were sufficient to convince Ōtori to abandon his designs.[36]

British officials also took an active role in influencing the nature of a series of regulations dealing with Chinese activity in Korea. Drafted by Japanese officials and passed to the Korean minister of foreign affairs for promulgation and enforcement, these regulations sought to restrict the ability of Chinese merchants to travel, move, and generally conduct business in Korea.[37] Working to secure "for Chinese the best terms I could," Hillier successfully opposed a measure that would have allowed Japanese police to board and search foreign ships and deny Chinese the right to land and another that gave Japanese police the right to deport any Chinese suspected of disturbing the "peace or welfare of the country."[38] In addition, British officials successfully lobbied for the inclusion of an article that allowed for Chinese travel (with passport) to the interior. They were less

---

32. Hillier to O'Conor, Dec. 3, 1894, *ACDM*, 489–90.

33. Hillier to O'Conor, Oct. 13, 1894, *ACDM*, 440.

34. Ibid., 440–41.

35. Ibid., 441.

36. See Hillier to O'Conor, Nov. 17, 1894, *ACDM*, 474.

37. For the full text of the regulations, see *KS*, Dec. 16, 1894 (KJ 31.11.20). The regulations were described as benevolent attempts to "protect" the lives and livelihoods of Chinese in Korea, but the effect of the regulations was clearly to sharply restrict their ability to live, travel, and do business in Korea. Moreover, the fact that Japanese or Westerners were not afforded the "protections" offered by the regulations is further evidence that they were likely more intended to limit and restrict than to protect.

38. Hillier to O'Conor, Dec. 3, 1894, *ACDM*, 488.

successful in efforts to guarantee that a British official could be present at the adjudication of criminal cases involving Chinese citizens.[39]

British motivations for protecting Chinese interests in Korea are complex. The Zongli yamen officially requested British protection for Chinese nationals on February 1, 1895, months after British officials in Korea had begun working to protect Chinese citizens and privileges in Korea.[40] In addition to the sympathy British officials had for the plight of the Chinese who remained in Korea and the calculation that the maintenance of the Korean Customs Service served British interests, there was a recognition that the Chinese, as the main distributors of British textiles, promoted British commerce in Korea.

Moreover, running through the discourse of British officials—both among themselves and with the Japanese and Koreans—is the British commitment to treaty provisions and the rule of law, in this case the treaties and laws that made up the treaty-port system in Korea. Elements that are specifically mentioned as worthy of defending include the previously mentioned protection of property rights, extraterritorial privileges,[41] most-favored-nation status, and the "principles of justice and equity."[42] In short, although the British had demonstrated in the previous decade that they were not terribly interested in supporting full Korean autonomy or independence vis-à-vis foreign powers, either China or Japan, they remained committed to maintaining the system of multilateral foreign privilege in the face of a concerted Japanese attempt to dismantle it. In the words of Hillier, his goal was to "restore them [the Chinese] to equal rights with those subjects of the other Powers."[43]

---

39. See Hillier to O'Conor, Dec. 3, 1894, *ACDM*, 488–89; and Hillier to O'Conor, Nov. 17, 1894, *ACDM*, 472–74. Many of the restrictions on Chinese merchants' activities in Korea were the subject of discussions in Hong Kong newspapers; see "Chaoxian shanli baohu qingshang guiding jiutiao," *Xianggang huazi ribao*, Mar. 13, 1895 (GX 21.2.17), *JDZH*, 1: 5–6.

40. For acknowledgment and translation of the official Zongli yamen request, see O'Conor to the Earl of Kimberley, Feb. 4, 1895 (received Apr. 1, 1895), *ACDM*, 502. British diplomats had denied the earlier requests made by British companies for protection of Chinese nationals in Japan on the grounds that they had received no official request for such protection (Mr Paget to Consul Enslie, July 12, 1894, *ACDM*, 139).

41. Hillier to O'Conor, Dec. 3, 1894, *ACDM*, 489.

42. Hillier to O'Conor, Dec. 18, 1894, *ACDM*, 515.

43. Hilier to O'Conor, Feb. 11, 1895, *ACDM*, 514, 515.

Examination of British actions during this period and the justifications for them also reveals that whatever opinion the British held of the Chinese generally, it is clear that at least in the Korean context, they considered the Chinese co-participants in the treaty-port system. The British saw a clear contrast between the long-suffering yet well-behaved Chinese and either the corrupt and inefficient Korean courts or those of the Japanese. The British authorities plainly sympathized with the desire of the Chinese to avoid subjection to either the Korean or the Japanese system of law and justice.[44] In the eyes of the British, the Chinese, if not fully civilized, were clearly a level above the Japanese and the Koreans. As such they were worthy participants in a system that maximized advantages to those who sought commercial opportunities in Korea, a system that the Japanese had the audacity to threaten in the months following the Sino-Japanese War. Through deft diplomacy and the ever-present threat of force from what was then arguably the most powerful empire on earth, Great Britain was able to uphold and maintain the treaty-port system and, to a large extent, the Qing Empire's place and privileges within it.[45]

Qing Diplomats Return to Korea

Although both Qing officials and Chinese merchants on the ground in Korea were willing to take advantage of British protection of Qing interests in Korea, they also recognized the utility of returning to a policy of more direct involvement in Korea. With Yuan Shikai in some disrepute, the Qing

---

44. Hillier argued that the "corruption and inefficiency of the Corean Courts of Justice are so notorious that it would, in my opinion, be an act almost of inhumanity to relinquish, and without a struggle, all claims to supervision over Chinese cases, the more that the right of access to Corean Courts where the interests of their own nationals are concerned is granted to the Consular authorities of every Treaty Power." On the other hand, handing jurisdiction in "proceedings where Chinese are concerned" over to Japanese authorities was problematic because Japanese authorities were "insisting on the imposition of heavy penalties, not to mention the barbarous methods of extracting evidence which are not included in the list of reforms that the Corean Government is called upon to carry out" (Hillier to O'Conor, Dec. 3, 1894, *ACDM*, 489).

45. The Chinese expressed their gratitude for British intervention on their behalf by sending £140 to the widow of H. B. Joly, one of the British diplomats who assisted the Chinese in Inch'ŏn. According to J. E. Hoare (*Embassies in the East*, 185), "it was all she got; since her husband had not been a substantive vice-consul she received no pension."

Empire turned to its next Korea expert, Tang Shaoyi. A relative of Tang Tingshu, Tang Shaoyi had been one of the first Chinese students to study in the United States. He attended elementary and high school in New England and enrolled at Columbia University but was recalled to China soon after beginning his university studies. He was recruited by Moellendorff to assist in the establishment and operation of the Korean Customs Service. Tang's cool and courageous behavior during the 1884 *kapsin* coup attempt earned him the praise of Yuan Shikai and Li Hongzhang. Soon thereafter he was appointed an assistant to Yuan and quickly became one the most prominent Qing officials in Korea. It is not surprising, then, that the new commissioner of the northern ports and Zhili governor-general, Wen Wenshao, would commission Tang to go to Korea after the end of the Sino-Japanese War to investigate conditions there and protect and promote Qing interests.[46]

Tang spent five months in Korea in an unofficial capacity. He met with chief representatives of Chinese merchants and heard their complaints about idle ne'er-do-wells, who, according to the director of the Seoul Merchants Association, Chen Deji, were harming the reputation of all upstanding, law-abiding Chinese. Tang proceeded to record and catalog the names and vocations of Chinese in Korea. He used this list to deport a number of soldiers who had been roaming the countryside or lurking in Seoul or the treaty ports since the early days of the war. Tang also dealt with figures such as Wang Shoujing, a Shandong ruffian well known for swindling, gambling, and theft, and the opium smuggler Sun Zhenlin. Tang also redistributed land and other assets that had been seized by the Japanese during the war. The Chinese merchant community in Korea and newspapers back in China both had praise for the young Qing official's efforts.[47]

On the other hand, many observed that Tang's unofficial status hampered his ability to perform his tasks and created conditions in which Koreans and Japanese could harass and humiliate Chinese with relative impunity. Such was the case on January 13, 1896, when Korean soldiers brawled

---

46. For background information on Tang's life, see Hinners, *Tong Shao-Yi and His Family*; and Sigel, "T'ang Shao-yi (1860–1938): The Diplomacy of Chinese Nationalism." For Tang's return to Korea, see "Huashi Tang Shaoquan ru Han," *Xianggang huazi ribao*, Sept. 2, 1895 (GX 21.7.14), *JDZH*, 1: 42.

47. "Zhu Gao lingshi Tang Shaoyi chenxian," *Xianggang huazi ribao*, Oct. 18, 1895 (GX 21.9.1), *JDZH*, 1: 50–51; "Zhu Xian shizhe Tang Shaoquan zhengdun huamin," *Xianggang huazi ribao*, Oct. 18, 1895 (GX21.9.1), *JDZH*, 1: 51–52.

in a restaurant managed by Chinese from Zhejiang, injuring a Chinese waiter in the process. The waiter, one Zhou, was taken to the British consulate and later to a British-run hospital. Although he ultimately recovered, his case and the apparent lack of any official Korean attempt to reduce such abuses of Chinese in Korea were seen as lamentable consequences of the absence of official Qing representation in Korea.[48]

As Tang was attempting to protect Chinese interests in Korea, Korean resistance to the Japanese imposed *kabo* (1894) and *ŭlmi* (1895) reforms was growing. Promulgated by a cabinet filled with pro-Japanese officials, some of whom had participated in the 1884 *kapsin* coup attempt, ambitious and sweeping in scope, and clearly designed to maximize Japanese commercial and other interests on the peninsula, the reforms found vocal opposition in the person of Queen Min. Despite Kojong's promise in his fourteen-point oath to keep his wife out of politics, the queen remained active in her efforts to oust pro-Japanese figures from government and to resist the growing Japanese power in Korea. Inoue Kaoru, although frustrated at the queen's lack of cooperation, had promised "the Japanese Government would not fail to protect the Royal House even by force of arms."[49] However, Inoue's successor in Seoul, Miura Gorō, a figure with little diplomatic experience, announced that his post in Korea was "a fit place to try my own theory of diplomatic methods."[50] This included plotting an anti-Min coup with the Taewŏn'gun and using a combination of Japanese-trained Korean troops, Japanese legation guards, and Japanese civilian ruffians (*soshi*) to storm the palace and assassinate Queen Min on October 18, 1895.[51] Tokyo officially repudiated the actions of its representative in Seoul, but none of those involved was ever convicted.

The assassination of the queen led to increased anti-Japanese fervor in Korea. For many Koreans, this audacious act of the Japanese only added to their anger over elements of the Japanese-imposed reforms, such as the infamous edict that required Korean males to cut their traditional top-knot in the name of modernization. King Kojong felt threatened by popular resistance to pro-Japanese reforms, on one hand, and a Japanese presence in

---

48. "Chaoxian Hancheng xinshe caipansuo," *Xianggang huazi ribao*, Jan. 28, 1896 (GX 21.12.14), *JDZH*, vol. 1, 69–70.

49. Harrington, *God, Mammon, and the Japanese*, 262.

50. Duus, *Abacus and the Sword*, 109.

51. For accounts of the assassination of Queen Min, see ibid., 110–12; and Harrington, *God, Mammon, and the Japanese*, 262–72. See also Critchfield, "Queen Min's Murder."

Korea that had demonstrated a willingness to assassinate even royalty to accomplish its ends, on the other. He turned once again to Russia for help and protection. Karl Waeber heeded the king's pleas, and in February 1896 Kojong fled to the Russian Legation in Seoul. Under Russian protection, Kojong apologized to his subjects for cooperating with the Japanese, repudiated many of the *kabo* and *ŭlmi* reforms (including the top-knot edict), and removed many pro-Japanese officials from office. Russian protection and Korean resistance stopped, for the time being, any Japanese attempts to assert dominance in Korea.

While residing in the Russian Legation, King Kojong explored the possibility of renegotiating a commercial treaty with the Qing Empire and also of sending a Korean envoy to Beijing. Tang Shaoyi, acting as the Qing Empire's unofficial representative in Korea, sought to discourage any Korean attempt to send an envoy to Beijing. He argued that Kojong's presence in the Russian Legation was proof that the king was not fully sovereign and, therefore, was not permitted to send envoys abroad.

If another country's troops are stationed in the capital, then the nation becomes that other country's protectorate. If the King cannot be independent without these troops, he lacks sovereign rights and is dependent upon the other country. He must first be able to found an independent state to have sovereignty, otherwise how is it any different from a border tributary? He is not entitled to send diplomats; it is not permitted by international law. In my opinion, if Korea proceeds with sending an envoy to China, I am afraid he will not be treated with courtesy. I think it would be better to delay.[52]

At the same time, Tang informed his superiors of his opinion that such delaying tactics could not be maintained indefinitely. He called on the Qing Empire to take proactive action by appointing a consul-general in Korea as an attempt to pre-empt the Korean dispatch of an envoy to the Qing capital. He noted that both Britain and Germany had already done so and were enjoying the fruits of diplomatic and consular representation in Korea without the need for exchanging official envoys.[53] Consular and diplomatic representation, Tang concluded, was vital for "preventing a 'loss of national economic rights (*shi liquan*)'" and avoiding "a hindrance to national prestige (*guoti yuai*)."[54]

---

52. Sigel, "Ch'ing Foreign Policy and the Modern Commercial Community," 98.
53. Ibid., 98–100.
54. Ibid., 100–101.

After considerable debate, the Qing Empire agreed in November 1896 to appoint Tang Shaoyi as consul-general. As such, Tang was to continue what he had already been doing in an unofficial capacity: protect and promote Chinese commerce in Korea. He was also tasked with negotiating a new Sino-Korean commercial agreement, preferably one with lower duties on goods such as ginseng and Chinese silk. However, the Qing Empire also announced that Tang would be officially designated consul-general only after a commercial agreement was completed; until then, the British would still be in charge of protecting Chinese persons and interests. Unsurprisingly, this made it extremely difficult for Tang to accomplish his duties.[55]

Tang's anomalous diplomatic status was the result of intense debates and disagreements within the Qing officialdom. Hewing to his usual policy of avoiding conflicts, Li Hongzhang advocated acknowledging Korean independence (as already stipulated in the Treaty of Shimonoseki) and negotiating a new treaty with Korea. Tang Shaoyi concurred and called for the Qing Empire to station a minister resident in Korea rather than a consul-general. Such a move, Tang argued, would allow the Qing to take advantage of the existing international order to assert Qing political and commercial privileges in Korea. Calls for full normalization of Qing-Korean relations also came from Korean progressives such as Sŏ Chae-p'il (Philip Jaisohn) and from Russian officials in Korea, who hoped that Qing acknowledgment of Korean independence and its continued participation in the system of multilateral imperialism in Korea would help forestall Japanese designs on the peninsula.[56]

Opposition to these proposals came from several parts of the Qing Empire. Officials such as acting governor-general of Liangjiang Zhang Zhidong called for repudiating the Treaty of Shimonoseki, particularly the provisions that recognized Korean independence. Prince Gong refused to acknowledge Korean independence and was an influential architect of the ultimate policy of dispatching Tang to negotiate a treaty without the proper diplomatic credentials. Prince Gong would resist the normalization of Qing-Chosŏn relations until his death in 1898.[57] In the end, the Zongli yamen announced

---

55. Sigel, "T'ang Shao-yi (1860–1938): The Diplomacy of Chinese Nationalism," 119–20.

56. Ibid., 121–22.

57. Bonnie B. C. Oh, "The Leadership Crisis in China on the Eve of the Sino-Japanese War of 1894–1895," 87; Sigel, "Chinese Foreign Policy and the Modern Commercial Community," 101–2.

"China will send a consul-general to reside in the Korean capital rather than a minister, in order to preserve the tributary system."[58]

If there still remained those within the Qing Empire that saw preserving the traditional tributary system as feasible, the Chosŏn government sought to disabuse them of this notion by proposing to elevate the status of King Kojong to emperor. Although hobbled by his own uncertain diplomatic status, Tang Shaoyi sought to fend off these attempts. He argued that since Korea and the Qing Empire had yet to negotiate a treaty that recognized Korea's independence, Qing acknowledgment of the Korean king as an emperor was obviously out of the question. Tang also engaged in some characteristic imperialist condescension, noting that "in South America and Africa, there are still small countries of black savages, but the tribal rulers of these states all call themselves King of Kings, Emperor, and all sorts of names, but it is not an indication of these countries' greatness."[59]

The prospect of a nation's putative sovereign elevating his own international status while so obviously relying on an outside power for his very survival proved to be too much for even the most ambitious of Koreans. However, after Kojong felt secure enough to leave the Russian legation in 1897, he heeded the repeated requests of his loyal subjects (following a period of appropriate Confucian procrastination) and announced the end of the Chosŏn period and the beginning of the Great Han Empire (Tae Hancheguk).[60] The name "Han" refers to a group of tribal confederations that occupied the southern portion of the Korean peninsula from the first to third centuries A.D. Their main claim to fame was that they were thought to have been least influenced by the presence of Han Chinese commanderies located in the northern part of the peninsula. Korea was, then, explicitly declaring its independence from and equality with the Qing Empire. Kojong, now properly known as the Kwangmu emperor, proceeded to order the construction of an altar on which he would offer sacrifices to Heaven (Wŏn'gudan) as well as a temple (Hwanggungu) that was reminiscent of the Temple of Heaven in Beijing. These actions were clearly intended to demonstrate Korea's perception of itself as free from its traditional vassalage

---

58. Sigel, "Ching Foreign Policy and the Modern Commercial Community," 101; idem, "T'ang Shao-yi (1860–1938): The Diplomacy of Chinese Nationalism," 120–22.

59. Tang also noted: "My government is certainly disappointed to learn what is happening to the traditional system" (Sigel, "Ching Foreign Policy and the Modern Commercial Community," 104).

60. *KS*, Nov. 7, 1897 (KJ 34.10.13).

and might be taken as one of the final nails in the coffin of Qing suzerainty. One could wonder what Kojong's determination to express Korea's status in terms that surely must qualify as Oriental "romance and hyperbole" reveals about Korea's desire to be a full-fledged participant in the Western-style family of nations. But few could question the fact that Korea no longer accepted its inferior status vis-à-vis China.

Reform-oriented elites in Korea were divided over the issue of Kojong's elevation to emperor. Yun Ch'i-ho dismissed the step as "humbuggery" and wondered "Has the title of emperor been so disgraced as this ever before in the history of the world?"[61] However, Yun and others, particularly members of the Independence Club (Tongnip hyŏphoe), argued that eliminating the vestiges of Chinese suzerainty required far more than simply seeing to it that Yuan Shikai could no longer dominate Seoul. Korea had for far too long, they argued, labored under the yoke of dependency on China and Chinese culture. The *raison d'être* for the founding of the Independence Club was the destruction of the Welcoming Imperial Grace Gate (Yŏngŭnmun), a symbol of the old system of serving the great (*sadae*). The club raised funds for an Independence Gate (Tongnipmun) to be constructed in its stead. Modeled after the Arc de Triomphe, one side of the gate proudly displayed its name in *han'gŭl*, the Korean phonetic alphabet, rather than in Chinese characters. However, on the side of the gate facing north, the direction from which Chinese envoys traditionally approached Seoul, Chinese characters were used, presumably to leave no doubt as to Korean intentions should a sharp-eyed Chinese envoy ever return.[62]

It was only after the death of Prince Gong and after the return of Tang Shaoyi to China that the Qing Empire and Korea successfully negotiated and ratified a new commercial treaty on September 11, 1899.[63] The treaty (sometimes called the Treaty of Seoul), although explicitly commercial in scope, recognized Korea's status as an empire and Kojong's status as its emperor. It also guaranteed to Korea and Koreans in China the same privi-

---

61. Kuksa p'yŏnch'an wiwŏnhoe, *Yun Ch'i-ho's Diary*, 5: 82, 102. Upon hearing of the proposal a few months earlier, Yun wrote: "What will he gain thereby? Nothing but an empty title and a solid contempt" (ibid., 60).

62. According to Hillier, the destruction of the Welcoming Imperial Grace Gate "has been condemned as an act of vandalism by all his colleagues, and has caused grief to the King, but all objections have been ignored" (Hillier to O'Conor, Feb. 11, 1895, *ACDM*, 514).

63. *KS*, Sept. 11, 1899 (KM 3.9.11).

leges accorded to the Qing Empire and Chinese in Korea. In addition, it gave both sides access to any other privileges obtained by other powers via consistent and frequent repetition of the phrase "most favored nation." In short, the 1899 commercial treaty guaranteed to Chinese in Korea the ability to continue to enjoy extraterritoriality; the right to reside, do business, and manage concessions in treaty ports; and the right to travel to and do business in the interior. The same rights and privileges were granted to the rather small number of Koreans in the Qing Empire.[64]

Qing Official Protection and Promotion of Commerce

For many, the Sino-Japanese War was thought to have ended any and all Qing pretensions of suzerainty in Korea. A corollary to this conclusion is that China and the Chinese then disappeared as significant actors from the Korean stage. In the words of an editorialist in the Korean newspaper *The Independent* (*Tongnip sinmun*): "It was a happy day for Korea when the Chinese merchants and coolies decided that things were getting too hot for them here and 'folded their tents like the Arabs and as silently stole away.'"[65] Indeed, a significant majority of secondary works on Sino-Korean relations display a tendency to limit the temporal scope of their analysis to a period that usually ends around the time of the Sino-Japanese War, leaving the obvious implication that post-1895 Sino-Korean relations (if they existed) are not significant or worthy of examination.[66]

Contemporary Chinese newspapers recognized the fact that although most Chinese merchants did indeed flee Korea during the Sino-Japanese

---

64. For the full text of the treaty, see China, Imperial Maritime Customs, *Treaties, Regulations, Etc., Between China and Foreign States*, 2: 864–72. In her analysis of the 1899 treaty, Larisa Zabrovskia ("1899 Treaty and Its Impact on the Development of the Chinese-Korean Trade [1895–1905]," 29) argues that the treaty did not grant most-favored-nation privileges to Chinese in Korea. Given the frequent repetition of the phrases "most favored nation" (*zuiyouzhiguo*; K. *ch'oeujiguk*) and "all the benefits and advantages granted to foreigners," it is difficult for me to see how she reached this conclusion.

65. Independence Club, *The Independent*, Thursday, May 21, 1896.

66. Examples include Kim Chŏng-gi. "Chosŏn chŏngbu ŭi Togil ch'agwan toip"; idem, "Ch'ŏng ŭi Chosŏn chŏngch'aek (1876–1894)"; Yur-Bok Lee, "Politics over Economics"; Young Ick Lew, "Yuan Shih-K'ai's Residency"; Lin Mingde, "Li Hung-Chang's Suzerain Policy Toward Korea"; and Sigel, "The Sino-Japanese Quest for Korean Markets, 1885–1891."

War, many returned after hostilities ended. Still, it was apparent to many that things were not quite what they had been. A Hong Kong newspaper recounted the disappointment of Chinese merchants in Korea who heard rumors that Tang Shaoyi had reopened the Qing yamen in Seoul and rushed to the compound only to find the gates still shut, no dragon flag flying on the flagpole, and no large sign declaring the high office of its occupant.[67] Of course, Tang eventually did reopen the yamen (its abundant flowerbeds were the talk of the town), and normal diplomatic and commercial relations between the Qing Empire and Korea were reestablished.[68] But the consensus appears to have been that the Qing official and commercial presence in Korea was of little consequence. One American diplomat recounted that the Chinese "asked nothing after their great defeat . . . they went about their lawful avocations without politics."[69]

A corollary to this assumption about the disappearance or relative insignificance of the Chinese in Korea after 1895 is the idea that the visibility and much-noted success of the Qing Empire in the earlier, pre-1895, period were primarily results of the Qing assertion of political dominance in general and of its traditional suzerainty in particular. C. I. Eugene Kim and Han-Kyo Kim succinctly summarize this sentiment in their statement that "Chinese political influence in Korea reached its zenith in the years 1885–1894, thus spurring Chinese economic activities."[70] More general examinations of Chosŏn Korea's foreign trade during this period echo this sentiment by their utilization of a periodization that uses 1894–95 to sharply demarcate the period of Sino-Japanese competition and the period of Japanese dominance.[71] In short, in both the political and the commercial

67. "Zhu Han shishu guimo feixi," *Xianggang huazi ribao*, June 29, 1897 (GX 23.5.30), *JDZH*, 1: 84.

68. "Zhu Han lingshi zhaojian Huashang," *Xianggang huazi ribao*, July 24, 1897 (GX 23.6.25), *JDZH*, 1: 88.

69. Sands, *Undiplomatic Memories*, 55.

70. C. I. Eugene Kim and Han-kyo Kim, *Korea and the Politics of Imperialism*, 70. For other similar examples, see Yur-Bok Lee, *West Goes East*, 171; Sigel, "The Sino-Japanese Quest for Korean Markets, 1885–1894," 115; and Pak Kyŏng-yong, *Kaehwagi Hansŏngbu yŏn'gu*, 117–18.

71. Han'guk muyŏk hyŏphoe, *Han'guk muyŏksa*, 102–3; see also Kim Sin, *Muyŏksa*, 393–95. An eerily similar periodization scheme can be found in Ch'oe Song-ho, "Kaehanggi sikminjihwa kwajŏng e issŏsŏ ŭi muyŏk kujo yŏn'gu," 27–30. For a discussion of variations on this theme, see Kim Song-hun, "Han'guk kaehanggi muyŏk ŭi t'ŭkjing

arenas, the Qing defeat in the Sino-Japanese War was thought to have ended the story of China in Korea.

An examination of the activities of Tang Shaoyi and his successors, however, reveals as much continuity as dramatic change. Within the context of multilateral imperialism and the treaty-port system, Qing officials continued to protect and assert Chinese commercial privileges and interests in Korea. This began even before the promulgation of the 1899 Treaty of Seoul. One of the most noteworthy aspects of these efforts is the similarity in motivation and scope to the efforts of their counterparts during the period before the Sino-Japanese War.

During Tang Shaoyi's final tenure in Korea, he reopened the Qing yamen in Seoul, pushed for the opening of branches of Chinese banks in Korean treaty ports, advocated the extension of a telegraph line from Inch'ŏn to Yantai (Chefoo), participated in negotiations to reorganize the Chinese settlement in Inch'ŏn, and explored the possibilities of a Chinese settlement in Seoul. His efforts earned him the praise of the Chinese community in Korea. Tang's successors, beginning with Xu Shoupeng, sought to maximize Chinese merchants' opportunities within the more restricted arena of post–Sino-Japanese War Korea. An examination of the types of issues about which they communicated with the Korean government or their own superiors reveals a striking similarity to those handled by Chen Shutang and Yuan Shikai.

Yuan Shikai's practice of requesting books of blank passports to be filled out at his leisure had ceased with his departure from Korea. However, Qing officials continued to make steady requests for passports for Chinese merchants to travel to the interior. They did so on behalf of the merchant Wang Shixiang in the winter of 1902, the merchant Han Jieshun and his party who sought permission to travel through Kyŏnggi and Hwanghae provinces in the summer of 1905, and in dozens and dozens of other cases each year. As was always the case, the number of Chinese who

---

kwa yŏnghyang," 7–10. This tendency to consider the 1884–94 period and the post-1894 period as distinct and discrete owes much to the fact that nearly every examination of Korea's foreign trade depends on the same set of data provided by the Korean Maritime Customs Service. The Custom Service's annual reports were appended to the annual reports of the Chinese Imperial Maritime Customs Service and were, therefore, available for examination. However, this practice ended with the Sino-Japanese War, causing the task of gathering data on Korea's foreign trade to be much more difficult.

traveled into the interior without permission probably exceeded those who did so legally by a considerable margin.[72]

Like Chen Shutang, Qing officials of the post–Sino-Japanese War period also sought to facilitate the rental of property in Seoul.[73] They sent officials to represent Chinese interests in newly opened treaty ports such as Chinnamp'o and Mokp'o.[74] They demanded reparations in cases of theft and abuse.[75] They mediated in cases of conflicts between Chinese and Koreans, such as the anti-Chinese riot that took place in Seoul in 1901 when Chinese merchants were rumored to have killed and hidden the bodies of

---

72. For Wang Shixiang's request, see Xu Taishen to Pak Che-sun, Jan. 19, 1902 (KM 6.1.19), *Ch'ŏngan*, 2: 529; and Pak Che-sun to Xu Taishen, Jan. 19, 1902 (KM 6.1.19), *Ch'ŏngan*, 2: 529. For Han Jieshun's request, see Zeng Guangquan to Yi Ha-yŏng, Sept. 4, 1905 (KM 9.9.4), *Ch'ŏngan*, 2: 736; and Yi Ha-yŏng to Zeng Guangquan, Sept. 4, 1905 (KM 9.9.4), *Ch'ŏngan*, 2: 737. For other requests, see *Ch'ŏngan*, 2: *passim*.

73. For Qing officials' facilitation of rental contracts in Seoul, see Xu Shoupeng to Pak Che-sun, July 2, 1899 (KM 3.7.2), *Ch'ŏngan*, 2: 350–51; Pak Che-sun to Xu Shoupeng, July 6, 1899 (KM 3.7.6), *Ch'ŏngan*, 2: 353; and Xu Shoupeng to Pak Che-sun, July 10, 1899 (KM 3.7.10), *Ch'ŏngan*, 2: 353–54.

74. For the opening of new treaty ports and the dispatch of Qing officials there, see Xu Taishen to Pak Che-sun, Feb. 24, 1902 (KM 6.2.24), *Ch'ŏngan*, 2: 538; Pak Che-sun to Xu Taishen, Feb. 26, 1902 (KM 6.2.26), *Ch'ŏngan*, 2: 538 (Chinnamp'o); Cho Pyŏng-sik to Xu Taishen, Mar. 23, 1904 (KM 8.3.23), *Ch'ŏngan*, 2: 678; Xu Taishen to Cho Pyŏng-sik, Mar. 26, 1904 (KM 8.3.26), *Ch'ŏngan*, 2: 679 (Yongamp'o); Yi Chi-yong to Xu Taishen, Feb. 25, 1904 (KM 8.2.25), *Ch'ŏngan*, 2: 665; and Xu Taishen to Yi Chi-yong, Feb. 29, 1904 (KM 8.2.29), *Ch'ŏngan*, 2: 665–66 (Ŭiju); *Ch'ŏngan*, 2: *passim*. See also Ma Tingliang, "Hancheng dengchu shanggongye qingxing"; "Yizhou kaifang wenti," *Xianggang huazi ribao*, Aug. 10, 1903 (GX 29.6.18), *JDZH*, 1: 214–15; "Zhongguo jiangshe Pingrang lingshi," *Xianggang huazi ribao*, Nov. 8, 1906 (GX 32.9.22), *JDZH*, 1: 414; and "Jueding sheli Yizhou lingshi," *Xianggang huazi ribao*, Nov. 14, 1906 (GX 32.9.28), *JDZH*, 1: 414–15.

75. For demands for indemnities and punishment of offenses against Chinese in Korea, see Pak Che-sun to Xu Shoupeng, June 5, 1900 (KM 4.6.5), *Ch'ŏngan*, 2: 408–9; Pak Che-sun to Xu Shoupeng, Aug. 7, 1900 (KM 4.8.7), *Ch'ŏngan*, 2: 430–34; Xu Taishen to Sŏ Ki-hwan, June 10, 1902 (KM 6.6.10), *Ch'ŏngan*, 2: 562; and *Ch'ŏngan*, 2: *passim*. See also the case of "a young French mining engineer in youthful and alcoholic exuberance had forced his way into a Chinese wedding, thereby outraging the wedding guests and starting a formidable riot." The Frenchman killed "a Chinese head constable, a man of excellent reputation and discretion, who might have arrested him lawfully, but who in his zeal had gone beyond the boundary of the Chinese quarter and into the general foreign quarter, where his authority ceased." The result was that "the young man was deported and compensation made to the dead constable's family, with some official exculpation to the Chinese authorities" (Sands, *Undiplomatic Memories*, 83).

several Koreans near the Sup'yo Bridge. In this particular case, despite the widespread allegations that Chinese merchants were responsible for the disturbances, Qing officials managed to wrangle a 3,000-*yuan* indemnity from a reluctant Korean government.[76]

As late as 1907, two years after the establishment of Korea as a Japanese protectorate, Qing officials were able to use the principle of equal treatment for all foreigners in Korea to secure the same access to Korea's inland waterways that Japanese boats enjoyed. They also heard the complaints of merchants about the absence of Chinese shipping lines running between China and Korea and oversaw several short-lived attempts to establish such lines as well as the attempts to set up Chinese banks in important Korean cities. Lastly, they called for the introduction of new forms of company organization and the establishment of chambers of commerce to facilitate the adaptation to changing commercial conditions.[77]

In addition to protecting and promoting Chinese commerce in Korea, Qing officials also sought to deal with the legacies of the Sino-Japanese War. For example, the Qing consul in P'yŏngyang arranged for the graves of Chinese war dead to be moved to a single Chinese cemetery.[78] And, as had been the case for Qing officials before the Sino-Japanese War (and still the case for other foreign diplomats in Korea), Qing officials routinely

---

76. For accounts of this incident and its aftermath, see Xu Taishen to Pak Che-sun, June 18, 1901 (KM 5.6.18), *Ch'ŏngan*, 2: 489; Pak Che-sun to Xu Taishen, June 19, 1901 (KM 5.6.19), *Ch'ŏngan*, 2: 489–90; Xu Taishen to Min Chong-muk, Nov. 14, 1901 (KM 5.11.14), *Ch'ŏngan*, 2: 519; Min Chong-muk to Xu Taishen, Nov. 28, 1901 (KM 5.11.28), *Ch'ŏngan*, 2: 521; and Xu Taishen to Min Chong-muk, Nov. 30, 1901, (KM 5.11.30), *Ch'ŏngan*, 2: 521. See also "Huashi qiu Han huang peishang," *Xianggang huazi ribao*, July 29, 1901 (GX 27.6.24), *JDZH*, 1: 136; "Zhong-Han jiaoshe," *Xianggang huazi ribao*, Aug. 6, 1901 (GX 27.6.22), *JDZH*, 1: 137; "Han Hua bingshang xianghong," *Xianggang huazi ribao*, Aug. 9, 1901 (GX 27.6.25), *JDZH*, 1: 138; "Hancheng Huaren yu Hanbing jiufen," *Xianggang huazi ribao*, Oct. 12, 1901 (GX 27.9.1), *JDZH*, 1: 142–43; "Han pei Huan kuan," *Xianggang huazi ribao*, Dec. 19, 1901 (GX 27.11.9), *JDZH*, 1: 149; "Hanren shangkuan," *Xianggang huazi ribao*, Jan. 9, 1902 (GX 27.11.30), *JDZH*, 1: 151; and *Korea Review*, 1901, 268–69, 309, 311, 462–63.

77. For the successful facilitation of water access to the Korean interior, see Ma Tingliang, "Chaoxian Renchuan shangwu qingxing." For official support for other shipping ventures and calls for the establishment of Chinese banks in Korea, see idem, "Hancheng dengchu shanggongye qingxing"; idem, "Chaoxian shangwu qingxing"; and "Zhu Han zonglingshi shenben buwen."

78. "News Calendar," *Korea Review*, 1901, 507.

sought and received permission to move their personal goods in and out of Korea duty-free.[79]

In short, despite the significant setback of the Sino-Japanese War and the concurrent decline in Qing political power and influence in Korea, Qing officials were able to enjoy many of the same privileges and prerogatives that they had before the war. These were largely the same as those enjoyed by the British, French, Americans, and other Westerners in Korea. Only the Japanese efforts to secure special treatment and privileges, efforts that accelerated after 1905, set the Japanese apart from other foreigners in Korea.

Commercial Resurgence

The apparent effectiveness of the efforts of Qing officials is evident in the continuing success of Chinese merchants in the commercial sphere in Korea. In 1891, Chinese merchants in Korea imported just over two million yen worth of goods, a figure that accounted for 38.9 percent of all of Korea's imports that year. Ten years later in 1901, long after Chinese were thought to have abandoned the peninsula, Chinese imports had more than doubled to over 5.5 million yen, a figure that accounted for 38.2 percent of all Korea's imports that year.[80]

Chinese commercial activity continued to follow many of the same patterns established before the Sino-Japanese War. In import-friendly Inch'ŏn, the Chinese share of the port's trade dipped in 1895 when the Sino-Japanese War prompted many Chinese to flee Korea and again in 1900 when the Boxer Rebellion disrupted shipping and trade between China and Korea. Japan's share of the port's trade naturally shows corresponding increases in the same years. However, China's share of the total trade carried out in Inch'ŏn generally hovered around 40 percent until 1906 (averaging 40.9 percent for the period 1887–1905). Chinese merchants continued to seek a significant share of the gold and ginseng that left the port. Moreover,

---

79. For examples, see Min Chong-muk to Xu Taishen, Jan. 8, 1902 (KM 6.1.8), *Ch'ŏngan*, 2: 526; Xu Taishen to Pak Che-sun, Jan. 10, 1902 (KM 6.1.10), *Ch'ŏngan*, 2: 527; Xu Taishen to Cho Pyŏng-sik, Oct. 30, 1902 (KM 6.10.30), *Ch'ŏngan*, 2: 590; Xu Taishen to Pak Che-sun, Nov. 1, 1902 (KM 6.11.1), *Ch'ŏngan*, 2: 591; and Xu Taishen to Cho Pyŏng-sik, Nov. 3, 1902 (KM 6.11.3), *Ch'ŏngan*, 2: 593.

80. Pak Su-i, "Kaehanggi Han'guk muyŏk chabon e kwanhan yŏn'gu," 186–88. For a more thorough exploration of the vagaries of Chosŏn Korea's foreign trade, see Larsen, "From Suzerainty to Commerce," 250–343.

they began participating in regional distribution networks of Korean agricultural exports, particularly soybeans.[81]

In Wŏnsan, Chinese merchants also enjoyed continued commercial prosperity. They continued to exchange British cotton textiles as well as Chinese silks and nankeens for Korean gold. They were dramatically outnumbered by their Japanese counterparts. Around the turn of the century, the Japanese population of Wŏnsan numbered around 1,600, but only 70 Chinese officially resided in the port.[82] However, in the words of Peter Duus, "Even after the Russo-Japanese War the small Chinese merchant community seemed to do as much business as the Japanese."[83] Only in the Japanese stronghold of Pusan did Japanese commercial dominance remain unchallenged, with the brief exception of a flurry of Chinese commercial activity around the turn of the century.[84]

Chinese merchants were also prominent figures in the treaty ports that were newly opened in the years after the Sino-Japanese War: Chinnamp'o—also known as Namp'o—(1897), Mokp'o (1897), Kunsan (1899), Masan (1899), Sŏngjin (1899), Ŭiju (1907), and Chŏngjin (1908).[85] However, the patterns evident in the three original treaty ports—Japanese dominance of regions primarily oriented toward the export of Korean agricultural products and intense Chinese competition in areas oriented toward the import of foreign goods—continued. Chinese merchants were most visible and successful on the west coast, particularly the northwest coast, where they had long carried on clandestine trade before the official opening of ports such as Chinnamp'o and Ŭiju.[86]

Chinese merchants also remained active and prominent in Seoul.[87] There, as well as in the treaty ports, they engaged in currency speculation,

---

81. Larsen, "From Suzerainty to Commerce," 298–309.

82. "Wun-san," *Korea Review*, 1901, 61; Larsen, "From Suzerainty to Commerce," 293–300.

83. Duus, *Abacus and the Sword*, 331.

84. Larsen, "From Suzerainty to Commerce," 292–93.

85. Seoul was also officially designated an open port in 1907. However, given the already substantial foreign commercial presence in the city and its environs, the impact of its official opening (aside from streamlining the collection of customs revenues) was minimal.

86. Hundreds and then thousands of Chinese flocked to ports on the northwest coast after the turn of the century (Hamilton, *Korea*, 202–3, 206).

87. For a detailed description of the locations and nature of Chinese businesses in Hansŏng (Seoul), see Pak Kyŏng-yong, *Kaehwagi Hansŏngbu yŏn'gu*, 122–23.

taking advantage of differences in the price of copper in Korea and China in 1903, for example.[88] Chinese firms also engaged in something of a building boom in the capital as observed in a 1903 "editorial comment" in the *Korea Review*:

In spite of the chaotic state of the monetary system there are evidences that trade has been brisk. Real estate values have appreciated and the hum of commercial life has never been louder. Building operations in Seoul have been on a phenomenal scale. . . . Perhaps the greatest activity has been shown by the Chinese merchants, if building operations are to be taken as an indication. A very large number of Chinese shops, of a substantial character, have been erected.[89]

Foot Soldiers of Informal Empire: The Overseas Chinese in Korea

The significant prosperity of Chinese merchants in Korea after the Sino-Japanese War belies the easy simplicity of assertions that Chinese commercial success resulted from Qing claims of suzerainty or the special privileges obtained by Yuan Shikai. Rather than stemming from exclusive or unilateral privilege in Korea, Chinese commercial fortunes appear to have owed more to the Qing assertion of multilateral privileges, the same type afforded to all foreigners in Korea. Since this system of multilateral imperialism continued in Korea well after the Sino-Japanese War, the continued Chinese commercial activity and success should not be surprising.

However, unequal treaty privileges and the institutional framework of the treaty-port system are only as effective as the flesh-and-blood people who avail themselves of these opportunities. All the imperialist structures in the world are useless without actual imperialists to project and promote the empire's interests. In the case of the Qing Empire and its desire to wage commercial warfare in Korea, these imperialists were what are often known as the Overseas Chinese.

A sizable amount of literature has been devoted to the Chinese diaspora in East and Southeast Asia (and elsewhere) and to chronicling and explaining the commercial success of these "New Asian Emperors," the "Merchant Princes of the East," or the "Lords of the Rim."[90] To some, com-

---

88. "News Calendar," *Korea Review*, 1903, 503.

89. "Editorial Comment," *Korea Review*, 1903, 546.

90. Haley et al., *New Asian Emperors*; Hodder, *Merchant Princes of the East*; Seagrave, *Lords of the Rim*.

Table 2
Overseas Chinese in Korea,
Selected Years, 1883–1910

Year	Number		Year	Number
1883	162		1893	2,182
1884	666		1906	3,661
1885	264		1907	7,902
1886	468		1908	9,978
1891	1,489		1909	9,568
1892	1,805		1910	11,818

SOURCE: Yang Zhaoquan and Sun Yumei, *Chaoxian Huaqiaoshi*, 125.

mercial success is a natural consequence of being Chinese. Almost any-where the Chinese have set foot, it seems, they have succeeded by dint of hard work, frugality, a reliance on family and kin networks, or other "Chinese" traits and practices.[91] More recent works have questioned the use of culture as the chief explanatory factor for Overseas Chinese commercial success and have instead pointed to a variety of increasingly sophisticated theories, contexts, and concepts in their explanations.[92]

In considering how the Chinese in Korea fit within the larger context of Overseas Chinese in Asia, it is important to recognize several key differences. First, the number of Chinese in Korea was relatively small (see Table 2). It pales in contrast with the present-day numbers of Chinese in Indonesia (over seven million), Malaysia (over five million), or even Japan (150,000).[93] Official estimates probably underestimate the total number of Chinese; keeping track of the highly transient portion of this population was rather difficult, as was recording those who had a strong motivation to avoid contact with officials—smugglers, for example. However, even the most generous estimate of the Chinese population in Korea during the

---

91. One of the most widely read explorations of this theme is found in Pan, *Sons of the Yellow Emperor*. For a treatment of Overseas Chinese business with emphasis on the importance of family and clan networks, see Redding, *The Spirit of Chinese Capitalism*.

92. For examples of recent scholarship on the Chinese diaspora in all its complex diversity, see McKeown, "Conceptualizing Chinese Diasporas, 1842–1849"; and Gung-wu Wang, "Greater China and the Chinese Overseas." See also idem, *China and the Chinese Overseas*.

93. For a recent estimate of numbers of Overseas Chinese in various countries, see Poston and Yu, "The Distribution of Overseas Chinese in the Contemporary World."

open-port period ends up with numbers much smaller than those found in other countries or even in Korea in later periods.[94] Second is the fact that, judged by the standard of Chinese in Southeast Asia, the Chinese came relatively late to Korea. Of course, migration of "Chinese" to Korea (or "Koreans" to China for that matter) was nothing new. The present-day inhabitants of the Korean peninsula include those who can, sometimes with considerable pride, count among their ancestors migrants from China during the Tang, Song, and Ming periods. However, official contact between China and Korea was restricted throughout most of the Chosŏn period. Illegal migration, especially along the northern border, surely took place, but the historical record includes no mention of noticeable numbers of Chinese until after 1882.

Behind the general population figures lies another key difference between the Chinese in Korea and those in other parts of Asia. Despite the diversity of "Overseas Chinese," it is still generally valid to state that most, especially those that settled in Asia, came from southern China, to be specific, from Fujian, Guangdong, Hainan, and Zhejiang.[95] Some of Korea's Overseas Chinese population hailed from southern China as well. For, example, Tan Jiesheng (also known as Tan Yishi), founder of Tongshuntai, the largest Chinese firm in Korea, came from Gaoyao prefecture in Guangdong.[96] In the early years of the open-port period, the Chinese population in Korea would include sojourners from Guangdong, Zhejiang, Jiangsu, Jiangxi, Hubei, Hunan, Zhili, Anhui, and Henan, as well as the cities of Shanghai and Tianjin. However, the majority of the Chinese who came to Korea during the last decades of the nineteenth century hailed from nearby Shandong, a place not usually regarded as a large source of emigrants.[97]

Migrants from other parts of China may have come to Korea in search of opportunity. But, at least according to their own explanations of events, those from Shandong more often than not came to Korea because life at home had grown intolerable. The luckless inhabitants of Shandong had to

---

94. The numbers of Chinese in Korea would swell during the period of Japanese colonial rule (1910–45), reaching over 80,000 according to a 1942 official estimate, and topping 100,000 according to unofficial ones; see Eun Kyung Park, "Ethnic Network Among Chinese Small Business in Korea During the Colonial Period," 71.

95. See, e.g., Pan, ed., *The Encyclopedia of the Chinese Overseas*, 19–43.

96. Zhou Nanjing, *Shijie Huaqiao Huaren cidian*, 860.

97. On the other hand, migrants from Shandong were prominent in the mass movement of Chinese to Manchuria; see Gottschang and Lary, *Swallows and Settlers*.

contend with alternating periods of drought and flood (one drought in 1876 was said to have left as many as two million dead) as well as man-made disasters.[98] The Boxer Rebellion of 1900 devastated much of Shandong, for example. Banditry and lawlessness of a lesser sort were common throughout the late nineteenth and early twentieth centuries. One Shandong migrant who first came to Korea in 1910 recalled the abduction of an eight-year-old neighbor girl by bandits. The girl was returned, bereft of both ears, only after fifty sacks of rice had been paid as ransom.[99] These difficult conditions led to the displacement of many inhabitants of Shandong and the establishment of a "pattern of migration and mobility," particularly among villages in the northwestern part of the province.[100] Although many simply moved from place to place within the province or to other parts of the Qing Empire, Korea's proximity to Shandong made it a popular destination for Chinese migrants. As a result, migrants from Shandong ultimately formed the overwhelming majority (more than 90 percent) of all Chinese in Korea, a trend that continues to the present day.[101]

Many observers of the day, as well as the Overseas Chinese in Korea themselves, attribute at least part of their commercial success to specific organizational and business practices. The use of kinship ties (both actual and fictive) in business organization and practice, a reliance on trust in commercial relations, and a relatively high degree of cooperation contributed to the general success of the Chinese commercial community.

Family and native-place ties played a prominent role in facilitating migration as well as in determining the organization of migrant society abroad. In the case of Korea, the pattern of an individual moving to Korea, prospering (at least to some extent), and sending for additional family members was a common one.[102] Fathers and sons, uncles and nephews, and brothers often worked together in the same enterprise. In many cases, however, family members were not available or willing to migrate to Korea. Therefore, many Chinese firms relied on fictive kinship ties between people

---

98. For an account of the difficult circumstances of many who lived in Shandong, see Esherick, *Origins of the Boxer Uprising*, 15–23 *passim*.

99. Qin Yuguang, "Hwagyo."

100. Esherick, *Origins of the Boxer Uprising*, 27.

101. Qin Yuguang, *Lü Han liushinian jianwenlu*, 5–7; Yang Zhaoquan and Sun Yumei, *Chaoxian Huaqiaoshi*, 124–26.

102. Qin Yuguang "Hwagyo"; idem, *Lü Han liushinian jianwenlu*, 22; interviews with Yu Xinzhang, Ni Shiming, and Wang Qingpeng, Jan. 1998.

from the same village, region, or language group. These types of relations were evident not only in commercial firms but also in groups of workers or farmers.[103] Although family participation in business activities undoubtedly had its drawbacks, there are several advantages of such types of organization, such as a high degree of loyalty, a ready supply of inexpensive labor, and a common commitment to commercial success.[104]

Another characteristic generally ascribed to Chinese businesses in Korea is reliance on personal relationships and trust rather than on contracts to secure compliance and cooperation. This tendency, although surely not absolute or universal, had a salutary influence on how Chinese did business. Chinese merchants in Korea generally sold goods on credit, a practice that made them popular among many consumers who often had significant amounts of cash only at harvest time. The practice of settling accounts only once a year allowed many merchants to wait out short-term fluctuations in currency exchange rates or prices. In addition, the Chinese effort to cultivate personal relationships with suppliers, distributors, and consumers compared favorably with the practices of Japanese merchants in Korea, who often had a reputation for cut-throat competition and the sale of counterfeit or shoddy goods. Trust within the Chinese community also allowed for the success of rotating credit (*huiyi*) and traditional lending institutions (*qianzhuang*). Both of these allowed many merchants to start new ventures or to weather difficult times.[105]

Observers of the Chinese community in Korea often noted a high degree of cooperation among Chinese merchants. Some insiders countered that such cooperation was far from universal. For example, Ma Tingliang, the Chinese consul-general in Korea in 1906, complained of the "greed," "deceit," and "trickery" among the Chinese merchant community in Korea.[106] However, many remember substantial cooperation and coordination among merchants, even those from different parts of China. Qing officials worked hard to foster this cooperation by encouraging merchant associations that brought merchants from different groups together. Taken as a whole,

---

103. Eun Kyung Park, "Ethnic Network Among Chinese Small Business in Korea During the Colonial Period," 79.

104. See, e.g., Redding, *The Spirit of Chinese Capitalism*, 7.

105. Qin Yuguang, *Lü Han liushinian jianwenlu*, 22–24; Shim Jae Hoon, "Korea," 341.

106. Ma Tingliang, "Hancheng dengchu shanggongye qingxing."

the Chinese presented a relatively united front in the face of Japanese competition.[107]

Observers of Chinese merchants and businesses in Korea also point to other elements such as the separation of capital (almost invariably located back home in China) and management (in Korea), the tendency to pay close attention to consumer demand, a willingness to sell goods for a smaller profit than competitors, and a long-term vision that allowed merchants and firms to ride out short-term problems. Taken together, these traits and practices help explain the success of many Chinese merchants in Korea.[108]

Tongshuntai: The Premier
Chinese Firm in Korea

Due to a lack of source materials, one can often find only tantalizing anecdotes or scraps of information about Chinese individuals or firms in Korea. Examples range from Wu Litang, a former Chinese diplomat who worked for the Korean Customs Service and built an impressive Victorian house in Inch'ŏn, where he lived with his mysteriously reclusive Spanish wife, to "Old Tang," a figure about whom is known only that he incurred significant debts to the prosperous firm Tongshuntai.[109] Indeed, it is Tongshuntai and its founder, Tan Jiesheng, that are the exceptions to this general rule of little or no specific evidence about Chinese in Korea. One Japanese observer noted that whereas Yuan Shikai controlled the political aspects of Chinese society in Korea, Tan Jiesheng controlled the economic aspects.[110] According to the recollections of Tan's descendants, the twenty-year-old Guangdong native moved to Korea in 1874. Some fifty years later, according to the same recollections, Tan was paying the single largest amount of

---

107. For example, Qin Yuguang (*Lü Han liushinian jianwenlu*, 25–27) recalls stories of two restaurants on the same street in Sinŭiju operated by migrants from Shandong and Guangdong; rather than competing, these establishments worked together and helped each other through difficult or slow times.

108. Duus, *Abacus and the Sword*, 256–57; Qin Yuguang, *Lü Han liushinian jianwenlu*, 20–25; *British Consular Reports*, 1894.

109. For more on Wu Litang, see Ch'oe Song-yŏn, *Kaehang kwa yanggwan yŏkchŏng*. For references to "Old Tang," see Tongshuntai, "Tongtai laixin."

110. Eun Kyung Park, "Ethnic Network Among Chinese Small Business in Korea During the Colonial Period," 76.

taxes of any inhabitant of Seoul.[111] Both claims are difficult to verify, but there is plenty of well-documented evidence to support the claim that Tongshuntai was the premier Chinese trading firm in Korea.

Whether Tan Jiesheng actually arrived in Seoul two years before the signing of the Treaty of Kanghwa may never be known. However, it is clear that by the mid-1880s he had established one of the largest and most profitable trading firms in Korea. Tan's main retail establishments were located in Ch'ŏn'gaech'on (near Tongdaemun, the Great East Gate) and near the Sup'yo Bridge. However, he also operated a sundries shop in Chŏng-dong and two flour mills in the Seoul area. Nor were his commercial activities limited to the capital. Tongshuntai had branch offices in the Korean port cities of Inch'ŏn, Wŏnsan, Pusan, Chinnamp'o, and Kunsan, in the Chinese cities of Shanghai and Guangzhou (Canton), and in Hong Kong and Nagasaki.[112]

Most sources note that Tongshuntai imported and sold primarily Chinese silks, grasscloth, and medicine. However, the firm also imported a wide variety of sundries and even participated in the British cotton textiles trade. In return for these goods, Tongshuntai exported gold and ginseng back to China. Data on specific years are unavailable, but a variety of sources note that the firm often monopolized the purchase of ginseng at official government auctions.[113]

Tongshuntai's prominence and success were quickly recognized among the Chinese community in Korea. It is likely that the establishment of a Guangdong League (*bang*) and the construction of a Guangdong *huiguan* owed much more to Tan Jiesheng's wealth and influence than to the size of the Guangdong community in Korea. Both were active throughout the open-port period, and Tan Jiesheng led both the Guangdong League and the *huiguan* from their inception.[114]

Tan was also active in affairs that affected the Chinese community at large. His name is affixed to the petition made by Chinese merchants to merge the Inch'ŏn Chinese settlement with the general foreign settlement

---

111. Qin Yuguang, *Lü Han liushinian jianwenlu*, 2.

112. Zhou Nanjing, *Shijie Huaqiao Huaren cidian*, 254; Pak Kyŏng-yong, *Kaehwagi Han-sŏngbu yŏn'gu*, 122–23.

113. See, e.g., Zabrovskaia, "1899 Treaty and Its Impact on the Development of the Chinese-Korean Trade," 35.

114. Pak Kyŏng-yong, *Kaehwagi Hansŏngbu yŏn'gu*, 122.

in the chaotic period following the Sino-Japanese War.[115] He also led the Chinese Merchants Association (Zhonghua shangwu zonghui), an umbrella organization established in 1901, and was active in this and other umbrella organizations for at least the next two decades.[116]

Tongshuntai was at the forefront of Chinese real estate acquisitions. Unlike the treaty ports, where Chinese businesses and residences were generally restricted to designated concessions or settlements, Chinese merchants were active in all parts of Seoul. In fact, the aggressive pursuit of property had the effect of driving up real estate prices throughout the city. An 1892 proclamation made by Hansŏng (Seoul) authorities complained that since the number of sales of property and buildings to Chinese merchants had increased, "the dwelling-places of our own people are gradually becoming narrower and more inadequate." Attempts to restrict and regulate the sale of real estate to Chinese merchants were not sufficient to overcome the potential for considerable profit in such transactions, since buildings were sold for as much as three times their real value.[117]

In addition, the firm apparently participated in a particularly speculative type of real estate purchasing and construction. In 1901, the firm constructed a three-story building on ground purchased just outside the wall of one of the royal palaces. The height of the building allowed residents on the third story to look into the palace grounds, a fact not lost on its builders, who apparently hoped to force the purchase of the building by royal authorities. Western observers were critical of this attempt at "blackmail," and the Qing consul ultimately ordered Tongshuntai to remove the offending third story. The Korean government later officially requested that all foreign nationals limit construction near the palace to two-story buildings.[118]

The wealth and reputation of Tongshuntai was such that the firm issued banknotes in 1903. The abysmally chaotic state of Korean currency throughout the entire open-port period was noted and lamented by nearly every foreign observer. Currency fluctuations ruined many a small merchant. Gallant but often ill-advised attempts by the Korean government to mint new coins only added to the confusion. Growing Japanese activity in the Korean economy led to the circulation of the yen as the *de facto*

---

115. Wang Wenshao to Zongli yamen, Sept. 11, 1895 (GX 21.7.23), *ZRHGX*, 4431–34.

116. Yang Zhaoquan and Sun Yumei, *Chaoxian Huaqiaoshi*, 138.

117. "Edicts, Proclamations etc." *Korean Repository*, 1: 34; Keijōfu, *Keijōfushi*, 615.

118. "News Calendar," *Korea Review*, 1901, 461, 558.

currency of Korea. Still, the Korean government doggedly continued to attempt to develop and circulate a Korean currency, a move motivated as much by a desire to hold on to a rapidly shrinking sovereignty as by economic or commercial concerns. When Tongshuntai issued private banknotes in 1903, the move was accepted by many Koreans and Japanese in Seoul, who were happy to use a medium of currency that was more reliable and stable than Korean coins. The Korean government, however, was swift to protest the move, claiming that "no one has a right to issue notes for circulation in Korea without its consent." The Korean government had earlier protested a similar move made by the Japanese Dai Ichi Bank. In both cases, the printing of the offending banknotes was suspended.[119]

Differing Perceptions of the Chinese

Although Chinese sojourners in Korea have largely disappeared from many present-day considerations of Korea during the open-port period, they were significant and highly visible to observers of the day. A multitude of opinions concerning the Chinese presence in Korea and the reasons for Chinese commercial success were offered by a variety of observers—Korean, Japanese, and Western.

Perhaps the most accessible Korean views on the Chinese in Korea as well as on China in general can be found in the writings of Korean "progressives." Increasingly committed to the idea of a world of social Darwinistic competition between civilized and enlightened nations and uncivilized ones, many progressives saw China as being firmly in the latter camp and as having exerted a strong retarding influence on Korea's own efforts at reform. They often spoke of the need to shake off the shackles of the "serve the great" (*sadae*) mentality and practices. The comparisons between uncivilized China and the civilized West as well as Japan (which was, in the eyes of some, civilizing if not civilized) carried over into perceptions of the Chinese living and doing business in Korea. An 1896 editorial in *The Independent* is indicative of the tenor of these perceptions. It noted the ubiquity of Chinese merchants in trade and distribution in Korea, stating that "as merchants they sold silks and velvets and clocks to fat-pursed officials or

---

119. Yang Zhaoquan and Sun Yumei, *Chaoxian Huaqiaoshi*, 143; "News Calendar," *Korea Review*, 1903, 30; Yi Sŏn-gŭn, *Han'guksa*, 693; Cho Pyŏng-jik to Xu Taishen, Jan. 13, 1903 (KM 7.1.13), *Ch'ongan* 2, 606; Xu Taishen to Cho Pyŏng-jik, Jan. 15, 1903 (KM 7.1.15), *Ch'ŏngan*, 2: 607.

else they peddled thread, matches and pipe mouth-pieces on the street," but concluded that "in neither of these capacities did they serve any large end or bring much good to the country." Equally obnoxious to the writer was the growing influx of Chinese workers:

We are sorry to see a tendency on the part of the Chinese to come in here for their coming will have the same influence only in less degree that it did in America. He will underbid the Korean laborer and drive him to the wall. The reason is evident. He will wear clothes, the ordinary Chinese coolie, which no Korean would wear even though he had to go naked. For abject and irredeemable filth commend us to the Chinese coolie. He will eat anything that any creature will eat and grow fat on absolute garbage. Some people call this economy, frugality, thrift and commend the Chinese for it, but we believe this condition is the result of a collapse toward barbarity rather than an evolution toward enlightenment.

The editorial also complained that Chinese were introducing opium to Korea and concluded that "it was a happy day for Korea when the Chinese merchants and coolies decided that things were getting too hot for them here and 'folded their tents like the Arabs and as silently stole away.' It is safe to say that Korea never missed them; that neither the commercial, social, nor moral interests of the country suffered a bit because of their departure."[120] The editors of *The Independent* must have been disappointed when many Chinese returned after the cessation of hostilities between China and Japan. The descriptions of China's backwardness both at home and in Korea continued to fill many of the editorials of the day, and those who praised the glories of China in the traditional *sadae* fashion were roundly ridiculed.[121]

The Sinophobia of many "progressives" and their grudging admiration for Japan were apparently not reflected in the economic behavior of the average Korean consumer, who often seemed to prefer doing business with the Chinese to dealing with Japanese merchants. The Korean

---

120. Independence Club, *The Independent*, Thursday, May 21, 1896, 1.

121. See, e.g., editorial comment on the publication of "Yu Hak Kyung Wi, 'The Confucianist Scholar's Handbook of Latitudes and Longitudes'" in *The Independent*, Tuesday, Sept. 29, 1896. For an insightful and detailed explication of the attitudes of progressives in Korea toward China, see Schmid, "Constructing Independence," esp. 149–63. For more examples of the thought of "progressives" on China, see Kuksa p'yŏnch'an wiwŏnhoe, *Yun Ch'i-ho's Diary*, 2: 18–19, 40, etc.; see also Kuksa p'yŏnch'an wiwŏnhoe, *The Collected Letters of Yun Tchi Ho*, 5–6, 82, 90, *passim*; Schmid, *Korea Between Empires*, 55–60.

consumer was motivated primarily by price considerations; however, it is clear that, price and quality being roughly equal, anti-Japanese sentiment moved many Koreans to deal with the Chinese. This fact was not lost on Japanese merchants, officials, and writers. Many viewed the Chinese not only as worthy competitors in the commercial realm but also as a useful foil for highlighting problems among the Japanese community in Korea. If Japanese consuls complained that their own countrymen were too concerned with short-term profits and "were often cold and brutal in their dealings with the Koreans," the Chinese were "cordial and ingratiating, cultivating their customers and doing their best to accommodate them."[122] Some also noted the greater Chinese willingness to travel to and do business in the interior. One 1893 report noted that there was hardly a spot in Korea with commercial potential where the Chinese could not be found and concluded that, unless measures were taken, the Chinese would likely dominate the interior trade in all eight Korean provinces.[123] Some measures were taken, and many Japanese merchants took advantage of the sudden Chinese exodus during the Sino-Japanese War to begin their own trade in the interior. Still, the continued Chinese commercial presence throughout Korea meant that Japanese merchants and officials had to continually maintain vigilance against the sale of shoddy goods and other poor business practices for fear of losing the market.[124]

Many Westerners regarded the Chinese they encountered in China as something less than civilized. Although the same general mindset undoubtedly held sway in Korea, it is apparent that when compared to either Japanese or Koreans, the Chinese rose somewhat in the estimation of at least some Westerners. Whereas one observer described the Japanese in Korea as "unscrupulous adventurers, bullies, and the scum of all the ruffiandom of Japan . . . a poor recommendation of the new civilization of which they boasted," the Chinese were "law observing, peaceable and scrupulously honest in all of their transactions—were living certificates of the morality engendered by a faithful observance of the old."[125]

---

122. Duus, *Abacus and the Sword*, 256–57. See also Yongsangu, *Yongsanguji*, 112.

123. Yi Pyŏng-ch'ŏn, "Kaehanggi oeguksangin ŭi ch'imip kwa Han'guksangin ŭi taeŭng," 130.

124. See, e.g., the anxious musings of Inoue Kaoru recounted in Longford, *The Story of Korea*, 337–38.

125. Ibid., 328. Christian missionaries, on the other hand, had a strong incentive to compare Koreans favorably to Chinese due to the receptivity of many Koreans to the

The Western appreciation if not admiration for the Chinese was particularly strong in the case of the British. This stemmed not only from a perception that the Chinese were somewhat higher on the scale of civilization than either the Japanese or Koreans but also from the very utilitarian consideration that whatever British commercial interests existed in Korea were in the hands of the Chinese. This recognition of a convergence of interests persisted long after the Sino-Japanese War; a British observer in the early twentieth century proclaimed:

I have the honor to state that the Chinaman himself is pleased to represent Manchester and other British products, and, as a sapient middleman dealing at close prices, undersells Osaka. . . . Everywhere in the Far East the Chinaman represents what must be ultimately classed as British interests, and touts for British stuffs and manufactures because having used them he knows that they are durable and worth their price—and more the Far East does not seek to know.[126]

Moreover, many felt that the Chinese possessed a greater degree of experience and competence in a variety of businesses. "The Chinaman makes the better mason, carpenter, bricklayer, tailor, bootmaker," wrote one observer. Chinese merchants are "infinitely better traders than their Japanese rivals, being more energetic and enterprising, as well as content with a smaller margin of profit," concluded another.[127]

Westerners also turned to the Chinese for service in a variety of other areas. Many personal and household servants came from China. The Americans Horace Allen, Owen Denny, Lucius Foote, and William Franklin Sands, to name a few, all employed Chinese servants, often in considerable numbers, as did many of their British counterparts. Describing life among foreigners in Korea, Sands concluded that "one kept far too many servants, according to the custom everywhere in the East. There must be a head boy and a second boy and a coolie for the housework even in a bungalow of four rooms. The first two must be Chinese; the coolie might be a native. . . . A Chinese cook and scullion were necessary even for the needs of one bachelor who only dined at home when people dine with him."[128]

Christian message and the subsequent proclamations of P'yŏngyang as the "Jerusalem of the East."

126. Weale, *The Re-shaping of the Far East*, 19–20.

127. H. B. Drake, *Korea of the Japanese*, 114–15; *British Consular Reports*, 1895.

128. Sands, *Undiplomatic Memories*, 99–100. When Owen Denny's wife, Gertrude, joined him in Korea, she brought with her four servants: "an Amah, a boy, a tailor, and

Chinese servants often performed menial tasks but some were entrusted with considerable responsibility; Horace Allen, for example, left his Chinese steward in charge of his household affairs whenever he and his family traveled abroad.[129] Western households often became training grounds for Chinese apprentices, especially in the kitchen. Sands noted that if one entertained with any frequency, "innumerable young Chinese fill your kitchen, who pay your cook a monthly sum for the privilege of learning under him." The result is that when the head cook decides to return to China, there is always a "number two," usually a junior family member, ready to replace him.[130]

In addition to serving the needs of Westerners in Korea, Chinese were also involved in many areas in the service sector aimed at a more general audience. One present-day informant recalled that many of the Chinese in Korea found work using one of the "three knives": wielding a razor to cut hair, using scissors to make clothing (usually Western-style), or handling knives to cut food (i.e., running a restaurant).[131] This description probably more closely describes conditions during the period of Japanese rule, but it is clear that the origins of Chinese participation in these occupations can be found in the open-port period. The Chinese settlement at Samnich'ae (Sarich'ae) on the road between Inch'ŏn and Seoul boasted several barbershops, taverns, and restaurants as well as shops that sold textiles or sundries.[132] Seoul also had its share of Chinese-run taverns, barbershops, tailors, and restaurants. Chinese restaurants were popular among both Chinese and Koreans. They ranged from large-scale operations to street vendors who sold *hottŏk*, a Chinese-style stuffed pancake.

The continued presence and relative significance and success of the Chinese commercial community in Korea for a decade after the Sino-Japanese War is an indication of how little such presence and success relied on the suzerainty-based Qing assertion of exclusive privilege in Korea. Far

---

a washman" (Swartout, "Journey to Old Korea," 42). For other references to the employment of Chinese servants in Korea, see Carles, *Life in Corea*, 65, 81; Foote to U.S. Secy of State, Dec. 17, 1884, *KAR*, 1: 99; Kim Wŏn-mo, ed., *Allen ŭi ilgi*, 401, 404, 415, 458; Sands, *Undiplomatic Memories*, 160.

129. Kim Wŏn-mo, ed., *Allen ŭi ilgi*, Oct. 11, 1884, 403.

130. Sands, *Undiplomatic Memories*, 101–2.

131. Interview with Yu Xinzhang, Jan. 1998. A similar pattern prevailed in Japan; see Syukushin Kyo, "Japan," 337–38.

132. Qin Yuguang, *Lü Han liushinian jianwenlu*, 15.

more significant was the support afforded by the system of multilateral but informal imperialism introduced to Chosŏn Korea by the Qing Empire, aided by the traditions and practices of the Chinese community in Korea. Neither of these, however, would prove to be strong enough to resist the concerted Japanese attempt to dismantle multilateral imperialism and assert formal colonial control in Korea.

NINE

Endings, Echoes, and Legacies

The Russo-Japanese War (1904–5) and the establishment of Korea as a Japanese protectorate in November 1905 marked the beginning of the end of multilateral imperialism in Korea. As was happening with increasing frequency all over the world, competition between imperialist powers was settled either on the battlefield or by direct annexation of territory. However, just as both Qing suzerainty and Chosŏn Korea's status as a sovereign member of the family of nations coexisted nearly two decades after the first ostensible declaration of Korea's independence in the Treaty of Kanghwa, growing Japanese formal rule and the imperatives of the treaty-port system overlapped for a number of years. Moreover, the idea of suzerainty and its cultural connotations continued to influence how Chinese, Japanese, and Koreans viewed themselves and their relations with others for decades to come.

In 1894, Meiji Japan had declared war on the Qing Empire in large part to secure Korea and forestall Russian expansion. However, the Triple Intervention and Russia's continued push into its Maritime Province as well as Manchuria signaled to Japan that the competition for survival and dominance in Asia was far from over. In the Russo-Japanese War, Japanese troops landed in Korea in large numbers and used the peninsula as a base for their operations on both land and sea. Many observers expected the much larger Russia to prevail in the conflict. However, after a series of dramatic Japanese victories, Russia—beset by internal chaos—sued for peace. Japan claimed the southern half of Sakhalin (Karafuto) Island as well as Port Arthur and its environs as spoils of war. It also insisted on an acknowledgment of a Japanese sphere of influence in Korea.

Unlike 1894–95, there was no Triple Intervention or other European attempt to contest the Japanese claims, especially as they related to Korea.

Great Britain was more than happy to see its Russian foe humbled, and the Anglo-Japanese alliance of 1902 included a British acknowledgment of special Japanese interests in Korea.[1] American President Theodore Roosevelt, eager to broker the end of the Russo-Japanese War, expressed no qualms about giving Japan a free hand in Korea, a position that was certainly not impeded by Japan's similar expression regarding the United States' activities in the Philippines.[2] Many in the Qing Empire resented the passing of Port Arthur from one imperialist power to another, but the Qing, despite last-minute attempts at reform, was in no position to contest the Japanese claims.

Japan attempted to express its now-unchallenged position in Korea in legal terms by declaring Korea a Japanese protectorate.[3] As might be expected, the Koreans were less than cooperative.[4] It was only after Japanese troops surrounded Kojong's quarters for two days that some Korean government officials agreed to sign a document giving Japan the right to "advise" Korea in important diplomatic affairs.[5] A series of additional agreements and protocols over the next five years would increase Japan's presence and power in Korea until ultimately Japan officially and formally annexed Korea in 1910.[6]

Japan encountered little Western opposition to its moves in Korea. At the mere hint from Tokyo that the foreign legations in Seoul should be

---

1. The 1902 Anglo-Japanese treaty included a clause that guaranteed the territorial integrity of Korea. However, the treaty was revised in the summer of 1905, and in the revised treaty the clause was "buried" (Nish, "John McLeavy Brown in Korea," 43–44).

2. Many Koreans today decry the so-called Taft-Katsura memorandum, which they regard as a "secret agreement" between Japan and the United States in which the United States explicitly exchanged approval of Japanese imperial rule in Korea for Japan's approval of the United States' imperial rule in the Philippines. A close analysis of the background to and actual text of the memorandum reveals little support for the conclusion that it was an explicit *quid pro quo*; see Nahm, "The Impact of the Taft-Katsura Memorandum on Korea." Nevertheless, Roosevelt can in no way be seen as a champion of Korean independence.

3. For text of the Protectorate Treaty, see *KS*, Nov. 17, 1905 (KM 9.11.17).

4. Ki-Seok Kim, "Emperor Gwangmu's Diplomatic Struggles to Protect His Sovereignty."

5. The five Korean officials who signed the agreement have come to be known as the "five traitors" (*o jŏk*). Many Korean scholars have contested the legality of the Protectorate Agreement and subsequent legal documents used by Japan to expand its control of Korea; see Yi T'ae-jin, *Tonggyŏngdaesaengdŭl e ge tŭllyŏjun Han'guksa*, 210–41; idem, *Han'guk pyŏnghap sŏngniphajianada*, and idem et al., *Han'guk pyŏnghap ŭi pulbŏpsŏng yŏn'gu*.

6. See *SS*, July 24, 1907 (KM 11.7.24); and Aug. 22, 1910 (YH 4.8.22).

withdrawn, the governments of Russia, Britain, and the United States agreed to recall their ministers and replace them with lower-ranking chargés d'affaires. The United States had already (in 1906) removed "Korea" as a separate category in the official *Record of Foreign Relations*, cataloging all Korea-related materials under the heading "Japan."[7] In the words of Peter Duus, "Far from rallying to the side of the beleaguered Korean monarch or attempting to obstruct the Japanese, these three major powers were ready to abandon the country to the Japanese."[8]

Some Koreans resisted this growing Japanese encroachment. Kojong secretly sent representatives to the 1907 Hague Peace Conference to plead Korea's case (they were ignored).[9] Incensed at this insubordination, Japanese officials forced Kojong to abdicate in favor of his mentally challenged son, Sunjong. Koreans of all stripes took to the hills to form "righteous armies" (*ŭibyŏng*). They were methodically hunted down and imprisoned or killed. Some Koreans resorted to assassination, killing Durham Stevens, an American adviser appointed to Korea by Japan, in 1908 and the former Japanese Resident-General Itō Hirobumi in 1909. Although these actions are remembered with patriotic fondness in Korea today, they did little to stem the Japanese onslaught.

The End of Multilateral Imperialism in Korea

Once Korea was declared a Japanese protectorate, Japan moved to dismantle piece by piece the system of multilateral imperialism introduced to Korea by the Qing Empire some 23 years earlier. Some of the basic structures and institutions of the treaty-port system, such as the treaty ports themselves and foreign concessions within them, would remain in place. However, the sheer weight of the growing Japanese colonial apparatus would serve to crowd out, first, Japan's Chinese competitors and, ultimately, its Western competitors in Korea as well.

Despite the official severing of ties between the Chinese and the Korean Maritime Customs Services following the Sino-Japanese War, the Korean Customs Service had continued to be managed by a foreigner, the British subject John McLeavy Brown. In addition, many of the foreign employees of the Customs Service were veterans of the Chinese Imperial

---

7. Dudden, *Japan's Colonization of Korea*, 23.

8. Duus, *Abacus and the Sword*, 188; Harrington, *God, Mammon, and the Japanese*, 200.

9. Dudden, *Japan's Colonization of Korea*, 7–15.

Maritime Customs Service. However, once Japan declared Korea a protectorate, Brown's days at the head of the Customs Service were numbered. Japanese officials had proposed to take over operation of the Customs Service even before official announcement of the Protectorate. And in contrast to earlier attempts to unseat Brown, this time he had no support from the British Empire or from the foreign community more generally. After the 1902 Anglo-Japanese alliance, British diplomats in Korea were instructed "to refrain from any intervention on the part of the British Government in the Korean Customs."[10]

A more ambitious Japanese proposal to unify the Korean and Japanese Customs made in March 1906 was, in the words of a local observer, not "opposed by any organization of consequence."[11] After Brown's exit, the Chemulp'o commissioner of customs served as the temporary chief commissioner until the arrival of Megata Tanetarō from Japan. This move was quickly followed by a Japanese proposal to eliminate all duties on exports from Korea, a move that hearkens back to the days of duty-free trade for Japan in the period 1876–82. Foreign observers concluded that such a move could only benefit Japanese commercial interests since Japanese merchants controlled the vast bulk of Korea's exports. The *Korea Review* lamented: "The Chief Commissioner of customs readily consented to the proposition to do away with the export duty. We wonder what J. McLeavy Brown would have said if he had been approached with regard to such a scheme."[12] The extent to which the Japanese takeover of the Korean Customs Service served to blatantly promote Japanese commercial interests on the peninsula is seen in the fact that a group of Neo-Confucian scholars from South Hamgyŏng province penned a manifesto that called for, among other things, the return of the Customs Service to British management.[13] Not surprisingly, their calls were not heeded by the Japanese Residency-General in Korea. Qing claims of a special exclusive position in Korea were shattered a decade earlier. Now, the Chosŏn court had to contend with an ever-growing chorus of Japanese claims to similar concessions and privileges.

---

10. Woo, "The Historical Development of Korean Tariff and Customs Administration, 1875–1958," 84.

11. *Korea Review*, 1906, 117.

12. Ibid., 261; see also ibid., 1904, 124; 1906, 117, 118, 259; and Woo, "The Historical Development of Korean Tariff and Customs Administration, 1875–1958," 85.

13. *Korea Review*, 1906, 40.

Other institutional reforms also served to enhance the Japanese commercial dominance in Korea at the expense of Chinese merchants. One Protectorate-era reform required all foreigners wishing to travel to the interior of Korea to apply to the Japanese resident-general for a *laissez-passer* rather than to the Korean Foreign Office.[14] The Japanese resident-general also took measures to wrest the ginseng export market away from the Chinese. By 1907, Chinese consuls were complaining that although the Chinese demand for ginseng continued unabated, Chinese merchants were no longer permitted to purchase ginseng in Korea and could only watch helplessly as a monopoly on export was granted to a Japanese firm.[15] Japanese attempts to facilitate the integration of Korea by railroad, although having the effect of increasing trade generally, were similarly biased toward Japanese commercial interests. According to one observer, Japanese railroad officials used "every possible means" including the manipulation of railroad rates to encourage trade in Pusan at the expense of Inch'ŏn. Merchants in Inch'ŏn also complained that much-needed harbor improvements were deliberately stalled so as to facilitate trade in Japan-dominated Pusan.[16] Moreover, attempts to standardize and regulate Korean currency, culminating in the virtual imposition of the Japanese yen as Korea's currency, also worked to the advantage of Japanese merchants. This was especially evident in direct competition with Chinese merchants, because the lack of Chinese banks in Korea meant that they had to pay additional fees to remit earnings back to China via Japanese banks, a fact that drove up costs and prices.[17]

Equally significant was the transformation of the role of gold in Korea's foreign trade. Formerly a natural resource that Koreans used to trade for desired goods, gold became more of a product of foreign semi-colonial extraction as numerous foreign firms sought and received mining concessions from the Korean government.[18] Moreover, Japan's adoption of the

---

14. Ibid., 79.

15. "Zhu Han zonglingshi shenben buwen."

16. *British Consular Reports*, 1908, 10; see also ibid., 1909, 10.

17. For an example of Chinese complaints about the disadvantages caused by the lack of Chinese banks in Japanese-dominated areas, see Ma Tingliang, "Hancheng dengchu shanggongye qingxing."

18. The most prominent of these was the Oriental Consolidated Mining Company, an American venture that obtained a concession to work mines in the Unsan district of P'yŏngan province in 1897. Employing some seventy Westerners, a similar number of

gold standard and the expansion of Japanese banking in Korea significantly increased the Japanese demand for Korean gold. Japanese proposals to officially promote the extraction and export of Korean gold date at least to 1900. By the Protectorate period, Japanese *de facto* and growing *de jure* control of Korea's banking system and currency exports meant that more and more gold was leaving Korea for Japan rather than China.[19] Chinese merchants were powerless in the face of Japanese steps to monopolize the export of Korean gold. It took time to find markets in China for other Korean goods such as soybeans; in the meantime, the Chinese position in imports slipped relative to that of Japan.

In addition, the Japanese military and administrative expansion into Korea influenced commercial patterns as well. Significant portions of both the Sino-Japanese and the Russo-Japanese wars were fought on Korean soil. As a result, during wartime, Korea saw a huge influx of Japanese soldiers, support staff, matériel, and attendant equipment. Much of this proceeded directly to the front, but significant portions still passed through Korean Customs and were, therefore, duly recorded as trade. Moreover, after the establishment of Korea as a Japanese protectorate in 1905, the amount of imports associated with the Japanese colonial governing apparatus surged. Japanese imports of railroad material, for example, constituted the third single-largest import into Korea for most of the Protectorate period (1905–10).[20] Such imports have a tenuous relationship at best with patterns of Korean consumption or demand. Moreover, if the Japanese colonial experience in Korea is anything like that of most of Japan's imperialist counterparts in other parts of the world, the imperial power's investment in colonial infrastructure and administration constituted a net drain on the metropole, particularly the imperial government (even if individuals and firms profited from colonial expansion). However, at the same time, the

---

Japanese, nearly 700 Chinese, and close to 2,000 Koreans, the company oversaw the most prominent and successful mining venture of the period; in the words of a British observer in 1904, it was the "only mine in Korea which pays" (Harrington, *God, Mammon, and the Japanese*, 166; *British Consular Reports*, 1898, 7). The success of the Unsan mine did not translate into a great deal of economic advantage for Korea. In 1899, the Oriental Consolidated Mining Company bought out King Kojong's share of the venture for $100,000 and the promise of an annual payment of $12,000; see Harrington, *God, Mammon, and the Japanese*, 162.

19. For an early proposal for Japan to buy Korean gold ore, see Duus, *Abacus and the Sword*, 162.

20. Larsen, "From Suzerainty to Commerce," 357.

growing Japanese colonial presence, particularly the increasingly firm commitment to formal colonial rule, created opportunities for Japanese merchants and threw up barriers to their competitors.[21]

The growing formal Japanese colonial presence in Korea served to sharply reduce the share of Korea's foreign trade controlled by Chinese merchants and companies. Chinese peddlers would still be a common sight in the interior for decades to come. And, if family lore is to be believed, Tongshuntai magnate Tan Jiesheng would pay the single largest property tax bill of any resident of Seoul (known after 1910 as Keijō) well into the 1920s.[22] But in aggregate terms, the role and influence of Chinese merchants in many Korean markets declined precipitously after 1905. Chinese migrants, overwhelmingly from Shandong, would continue to move to Korea, but they found themselves increasingly relegated to the service sector of the "three knives"—the barbershop, the tailor shop, and the restaurant.

The Japanese commercial ascent and concomitant Chinese decline owed much to factors that transcended Sino-Japanese competition in Korea. The products of a rapidly industrializing Japan proved increasingly capable of competing with British machine-woven cotton textiles. Since transshipping British goods constituted a significant portion of China's trade with Korea, it is only natural that Chinese commercial fortunes would decline as Japanese cotton textiles entered Korea in ever-greater amounts.

The factors behind the British decline and Japanese ascent are myriad and diverse. Some stress the fact that British producers and merchants simply did not work as hard to discover and meet the tastes of Asian consumers as did their competitors from the Continent, the United States, and Japan.[23] The inability or unwillingness of the British merchant to

---

21. Chinese commercial interests were not the only ones harmed by the growing Japanese colonial presence. The United States, too, felt the squeeze: "As Allen knew, she could make concessionaires 'feel the screws of Japanese oppression . . . until American enterprises were practically crowded out of Korea.' This would be easy after 1905 when Roosevelt withdrew the United States legation from Seoul" (Harrington, *God, Mammon, and the Japanese*, 200).

22. Qin Yuguang, *Lü Han liushinian jianwenlu*, 2.

23. One British consul grumbled that "a communication was recently received bearing this address 'British Consul, Corea, Africa.' Nor is Corea in China, as many appear from their letters to imagine. Business cannot be done in that vague sort of manner" (*British Consular Reports*, 1902, 8–9; see also ibid., 1886, 1–2; 1899, 11, 22; and 1908,

get his hands dirty in the field was taken as emblematic of an empire in decline.[24] Other scholars have stressed more impersonal shifts in factor endowments that gave the comparative advantage to Japan.[25] But in the end it was the combined weight of the Japanese colonial apparatus and the benefits this gave to Japanese merchants that tipped the scales in favor of Japan. Japanese control of the Korean Customs Service and the banking, shipping, railroad, and telegraph systems, not to mention the presence of significant numbers of Japanese soldiers, police, and administrators, all of whom proved willing to promote exclusive Japanese privileges whenever possible, combined to create an inexorable pressure to push Japanese commercial interests to the top. The results were clearly indicated in annual trade reports: Japanese merchants handled 72.2 percent of Korea's total trade in 1910, versus only a meager 10.1 percent for Chinese merchants. The days of fierce Sino-Japanese commercial competition in Korea were over.[26]

---

7). Many of these complaints were echoed by observers in China and elsewhere. A general summary of these complaints noted the "disinclination of British traders to supply a cheaper class of goods, to be content with a small order at first, to study the customer's wishes, to adopt the metric system in calculations of cost, weight, etc., and to grant credit facilities. It also mentioned the scarcity of British commercial travelers, their ignorance of the language of the countries they visited, and the fact that the catalogues they distributed were available only in English" (Sugiyama, "Textile Marketing in East Asia," 295*n*).

24. A more general consideration of how the British middle class adopted upperclass values of rural leisure and abandoned the values and practices responsible for their dramatic worldwide success can be found in Wiener, *English Culture and the Decline of the Industrial Spirit.*

25. For an assessment of the British "entrepreneurial failure" and "comparative advantage" approaches to explaining British decline in Asian textile markets, see Reynolds, "The East Asian 'Textile Cluster' Trade, 1868–1973." For another long-term explication of the "comparative advantage" approach, see Young-il Park and Kym Anderson, "The Experience of Japan in Historical and International Perspective."

26. Larsen, "From Suzerainty to Commerce," 354. Some British observers ruefully observed the passing of multilateral informal empire. Sir Francis Plunkett prophesied "that the days of the 'foreign settlements' and 'enforced tariffs' are rapidly passing away, and that the small profits on which trade must now be carried on will make it every day more and more difficult for the English merchant to compete on the spot with the native, whom education and the telegraph are every day placing more on a par with him" (Lensen, *Balance of Intrigue,* 60).

Dismantling the Treaty-Port System

One reason for Japan's decision to pursue a protectorate in Korea rather than simply annexing the peninsula in 1905 was a concern about the reaction of Western powers to outright annexation. Not wishing to risk the indignity of another Triple Intervention, Japan sought to maximize its commercial and geopolitical interests in Korea without the entanglements and commitments that would accompany formal colonial rule.

However, Japanese officials became increasingly convinced that the intractable Koreans could be subdued and ruled only through direct formal colonization. To their delight, they found that Western powers made little protest at the growing Japanese presence in Korea. Still, even as formal colonial rule loomed closer and closer, Japan moved cautiously to dismantle the treaty-port system in Korea.

In fact, before eliminating the treaty-port system as a whole, Japan first sought to exclude the Qing Empire from participating in it. These attempts date to the Sino-Japanese War, when Japan attempted to seize Chinese properties in the Chinese settlement in Inch'ŏn and elsewhere. As noted above, these earlier attempts were resisted by British diplomats in Korea. However, after the Anglo-Japanese alliance of 1902 and the establishment of Korea as a Japanese protectorate, Britain ceased upholding the treaty-port system or the status of the Qing Empire within it. Japanese officials first sought to abolish the Chinese settlements in Wŏnsan and Pusan. The legal basis for this move was found in the fact that the settlement agreements for both ports had not been reached or ratified at a state-to-state level; rather, they had been negotiated by Qing commissioners of trade and local Korean officials.[27] Then, in 1909, Japanese officials used a proposed new settlement agreement in Inch'ŏn to attempt to sharply reduce the Chinese presence and ability to maneuver in the treaty port. Multilateral imperialism and the treaty-port system made one last gasp as Qing diplomats secured permission to continue fielding a Chinese police force in the Chinese settlement, an accomplishment achieved in part by the Qing diplomats' arguing that recent agreements had allowed for Japanese police forces in Chinese cities such as Suzhou, Hangzhou, and Chongqing. Qing officials also protested language in the new settlement agreement that

---

27. Son Chŏng-mok, *Han'guk kaehanggi tosi pyŏnhwa kwajŏng yŏn'gu*, 404–5.

explicitly referred to the eventual abolition of the Chinese settlement in Inch'ŏn and demanded to know why the Chinese were being singled out. The Japanese replied that their ultimate goal was the complete abolition of all settlements, just as was happening in Japan itself. However, they were forced to admit that there was no clear reason why the Chinese settlement should be explicitly singled out.[28] The system of foreign settlements in Korean ports actually lasted beyond the formal colonization of Korea by Japan, but by 1913 the last vestiges of the old treaty-port system had been swept away.[29]

"The Strong Eat Up the Weak"

The transition from a Qing-introduced treaty-port system to Japanese formal colonial rule is often thought to have been the result of the vastly divergent paces at which Meiji Japan and the Qing Empire embraced Western-style modernization. However, such an account does not seem to explain why the Western powers were equally unable or unwilling to uphold the system of multilateral imperialism in Korea; the Western powers were, after all, the very embodiments of the modernity that Meiji Japan was ostensibly emulating. They would, therefore, presumably have possessed the requisite power to defend their multilateral prerogatives in Korea. And yet, the Western powers were swept out of Korea at the same time as the Qing Empire. The answer to this seeming conundrum is, of course, that the vagaries of imperialism in Korea owed little to the relative degree of modernity of the contestants. Rather, a constellation of geopolitical, military, economic, and other factors influenced each actor in different ways.

---

28. Ibid., 408–10. Although not directly connected to the treaty-port system in Korea, the Qing Empire did engage in one piece of diplomacy with Japan that would have significant ramifications for decades to come. In 1909, Qing and Meiji diplomats signed the Chientao Agreement, which officially recognized the Tumen River as the boundary between China and Korea and, while allowing Koreans who lived north of the Tumen to remain, subjected them to Qing jurisdiction; see *Treaties, Conventions, etc. Between China and Foreign States*, 2: 762–69. Much to the resentment and chagrin of many Koreans, both then and now, this agreement effectively denied the longstanding claims of many Koreans to territorial claims in the Kando/Jiandao region north of the Tumen; see Schmid, *Korea Between Empires*, 199–223.

29. Son Chŏng-mok, *Han'guk kaehanggi tosi pyŏnhwa kwajŏng yŏn'gu*, 427–35. For text of the agreement ending the system of foreign settlements and concessions, see Kukhoe tosŏgwan, Ippŏp chosaguk, *Ku Hanmal choyak hwich'an*, 2: 34–43.

Stepping back and looking at Korea's fall into formal Japanese colonial rule from a global perspective, one finds that the direct annexation of Korea was consistent with global trends. The age of high imperialism had arrived, and imperialist powers the world over were claiming and annexing territory as swiftly as possible. Western powers engaged in the so-called scramble for Africa, with a similar wholesale acquisition of territory taking place in Southeast Asia.[30] This upswing in imperialist expansion saw new powers such as Germany, Belgium, and the United States throw their hats into the ring, as well as the consolidation of control over previously claimed territory in the cases of Russia in Central Asia, Brazil in the Amazon, and the Ottoman Empire in Mesopotamia.[31] In Northeast Asia, various powers moved to stake out spheres of influence in the Qing Empire, the so-called carving of the Chinese melon. But the most significant territorial expansion was Japan's: with the Meiji Empire and its successors claiming Taiwan in 1895, the southern half of Sakhalin (Karafuto) and Port Arthur in 1905, Korea in 1910, the former German possessions in China in 1919, the rest of Sakhalin in 1920, and so on.

Much of this global scramble for territory had little to do with perceived economic or commercial interests in the short term and everything to do with perceived security interests, not to mention the need to pre-empt other powers' attempts at grabbing coveted territory.[32] Seen from this larger global perspective, it would have been more surprising to find Korea

---

30. Bayly, *Birth of the Modern World*, 228. Damodar SarDesai ("British Expansion in Southeast Asia," 7–8) observes that "the term 'scramble' would be an equally appropriate term to describe the new Southeast Asian phase of imperialism in the final decades of the nineteenth century. Between 1860 and 1914, nearly one million square miles of Southeast Asian territory came under Western domination." Included in this Southeast Asian "scramble" are the British conquest of Burma, Malaya, Sarawak, Brunei, and North Borneo; the expansion of Dutch holdings in Indonesia and French holdings in Indochina; and the American annexation of the Philippines.

31. Bayly, *Birth of the Modern World*, 228–29.

32. Ibid., 233; Iriye, "Imperialism in East Asia," 125–26. Norman Angell remarked on the irrationality of territorial expansion for economic reasons in his oft-misunderstood work, *The Great Illusion* (vii): "For a modern nation to add to its territory no more adds to the wealth of the people of such nation than it would add to the wealth of Londoners if the City of London were to annex the county of Hertford." See also ibid., 43–45. What he failed to realize is the importance of other motivations, particularly nationalism and competition, in spurring territorial acquisition, even to the point of resorting to costly military conflict.

not annexed by Japan or some other foreign power. The system of treaties, international law, treaty ports, concessions, settlements, and institutions such as a foreign-managed customs service were far from sufficient to resist the blunt instrument of military power. This fact was not lost on Japanese diplomats even decades before direct colonial rule became a reality. In a telling exchange with Li Hongzhang, the Japanese diplomat Mori Arinori bluntly declared:

Mori: It seems to me that treaties cannot be relied upon.

Li: The peace of nations depends on treaties. How can you say they are not relied upon?

Mori: Treaties would do for ordinary commercial relations. But great national decisions are made according to comparative national strength, not according to treaties.

Li: This is heresy. To rely upon strength and violate treaties is not tolerated by international law.

Mori: International law is also useless.

Li: (pointing to a wine cup) Peace is a spirit; a treaty is something to uphold it. Human hearts are like this wine; the cup keeps them within limits.

Mori: The spirit of peace comes in and goes out by every nook and crevice. How can a cup confine it?[33]

Japanese public opinion, if popular songs are any indication, seemed to agree. One song ran: "There is a Law of Nations, it is true, / but when the moment comes, remember, / the Strong eat up the Weak."[34]

---

33. Tsiang, "Sino-Japanese Diplomatic Relations, 1870–1894," 59. See also the tension between the ideals of international law as expressed in Nakae Chōmin's famous treatise, *A Discourse on Government by Three Drunkards* (1887), in which the protagonist, "Professor Nankai," argues, "Despite the power of survival of the fittest . . . all more or less recognize international law. . . . Moreover, [the four Powers'] duty in maintaining the balance among nations and their agreement to uphold international law secretly binds their limbs," and the reality as aptly summarized by Alexis Dudden (*Japan's Colonization of Korea*, 26), "In practice, however, Japan's engagement with international law afforded the opposite result."

34. Cited in Dower, *Embracing Defeat*, 21. Some Korean newspapers agreed: Andre Schmid (*Korea Between Empires*, 38) observes that "on the question of law—an issue central to *munmyŏng kaehwa* (civilization and enlightenment) as a rational regulator of human society—social Darwinism stressed its use as a tool of the powerful. As one paper had a person in an editorial declare about international law, 'These so-called public laws, righteous principles, alliances and treaties, and morality all are nothing more than words on a piece of paper.'"

Legacies and Implications

The trajectory of Qing imperialism in Korea left legacies and implications that reverberated long after Korea was annexed by Japan. The Qing Empire's defeat in the Sino-Japanese War was described by the Chinese reformer Kang Youwei as "China's 'greatest humiliation in more than two hundred years since the advent of the Qing dynasty.'"[35] Kang and others questioned the premises and execution of Li Hongzhang's foreign policy and domestic self-strengthening reforms. Many went further to question the efficacy of the Qing Empire as a whole. Qing efforts at recentralization and "reimperialization" of power proved to be too little too late, as the Empire crumbled and was replaced by a republic in 1912.[36]

The failure of reform in the late Qing and the demise of the Qing Empire itself have given rise to a powerful consensus that the Qing Empire was a decidedly premodern relic in a rapidly modernizing world. This contrasted sharply with images of a swiftly modernizing Japan. The Japanese thinker Fukuzawa Yukichi wrote of the Sino-Japanese War as "a kind of religious war" between "a country which is trying to develop civilization and a country which disturbs the development of civilization."[37] Japan's success in that war and in the subsequent Russo-Japanese War, along with the Meiji Empire's rapid modernization, took Japan "out of the stagnant life of Asia, to infuse into its veins the life of Europe and America," prompting (as noted in the Introduction) one observer to conclude that the Japanese archipelago had literally been "towed across the Pacific" away from Asia and toward the New World.[38] On the other hand, Qing leaders were thought to be mired in tradition and unable to "perceive the spirit and trend of [the] time."[39] Incapable or unwilling to recognize that the rules of the game had changed, they clung to outmoded ideals and practices and, unsurprisingly, failed. Concludes one scholar, "Even with thousands of years of intercourse, the Chinese had utterly failed to understand the Korean reality."[40] In short, "Yuan's

---

35. Paine, *The Sino-Japanese War*, 269.

36. For late Qing efforts at recentralization and reimperialization, see Rhoads, *Manchus and Han*.

37. Conroy, *The Japanese Seizure of Korea*, 255.

38. Henry M. Field, quoted in Duus, *The Japanese Discovery of America*, 38.

39. Yur-Bok Lee, *West Goes East*, 172.

40. Jung, *Nation Building*, 165.

residency was the gasp of a dying order; Japan's merchants, the cat's feet of a new movement."[41]

For many in Korea, the end of Qing suzerainty and the following decline of multilateral imperialism in Korea were taken as signs that the Western notions of Japan joining the ranks of the civilized and enlightened nations and China becoming the "sick man of Asia" were clarion calls for Korean domestic reform. Not only was it imperative that Korea eschew old tributary ties and reject any Qing claim of special privilege in Korea, it was vital that Korea jettison all aspects of the Korean polity and culture thought to have been corrupted by Chinese influence.

The previously mentioned efforts of the Independence Club to destroy physical symbols of Chinese suzerainty in Korea were only the tip of the iceberg, as generations of Korean reformers took on the less tangible but nonetheless significant signs and symbols, such as the use of Classical Chinese and a still powerful reverence for Confucianism. In addition, Korean historians have gone to great lengths to imagine a history of Korea in which China figured hardly at all. The celebration of Tan'gun as the founder of Korean civilization stresses the indigenous origins of Korea at the expense of the Kija legend, popular during much of the Chosŏn period, which highlighted Korea's long-standing relationship with China.[42] Korean archaeologists have emphasized the significance of artifacts that link Korea to ancient Siberia or Central Asia and have often downplayed the voluminous finds that suggest a strong Chinese presence in Korea during the so-called Han Commanderies period (108 B.C.–A.D. 313).[43] The Koguryŏ General Ŭlchimundŏk, known for his successful repulse of the Chinese Sui armies, was revered by seminal Korean nationalist historians such as Sin Ch'ae-ho and generations of their successors. *Han'gŭl*, the phonetic Korean script developed during the reign of King Sejong (1418–50), has consistently received lavish praise, whereas Chinese characters, essential elements of a vast number of words in the Korean vocabulary, have at times not even been taught in school (especially in North Korea). Shamanism rather than Confucianism has come to be regarded as the quintessentially Korean

----

41. Cumings, *Korea's Place in the Sun*, 206.

42. For more on the Kija legend, see Han Yŏng-u, "Kija Worship in the Koryo and Early Yi Dynasties."

43. For a review of the role of archaeology, myth, and ancient history in the formation of a modern Korea, see Pai, *Constructing "Korean" Origins*.

religion. In short, the effort to imagine a unique Korean nation has meant the virtual erasure of China.

For Korean reformers, eliminating all "Chinese" cultural influences was an ingenious solution to the thorny dilemma that confronted many a would-be nation-builder in the nineteenth and twentieth centuries: how to convince a group of people that they have a shared identity and culture in the name of the nation while persuading them to abandon many if not most elements of their traditional culture—the very elements that bound them together—in the name of modernization. Korean reformers opted to take all the things and ideas that proponents of "civilization and enlightenment" labeled as backward, reactionary, or otherwise detrimental to modernization, put them in a box labeled "Chinese," and expel it (never mind the fact that Koreans had practiced many "Chinese" elements of their culture for centuries if not millennia). Thus, to become more modern was to become more Korean at the same time. The chief drawback to this ingenious approach was that Korean reformers had little rhetorical ammunition to use against the Japanese when they claimed to be colonizing Korea for the purpose of eradicating baleful Chinese influences from the peninsula.

For Japan, too, claimed to be acting in the name of freeing Korea from the Chinese yoke. If Japan, by virtue of its rapid modernization, had drifted across the Pacific to become an archipelago off the coast of California, Korea, a land and people thought to have shared origins with Japan, had "gradually drifted away" in a different direction. "While the Japanese maintained their independence, the Koreans, living in the shadow of a more powerful China, became enmired in that country's conservative cultural tradition, acquiring traits that inhibited progress."[44] The Japanese Chōsen Government-General made no effort to hide the perceived links between Korea's backwardness and Chinese suzerainty, declaring on the first page of its introduction to the history of Korea in a report on "reforms and progress" in Korea: "for many centuries, Chosen was more or less tributary to China, and her people did little towards development as a nation."[45] For 35 years of direct Japanese colonial rule, Koreans had to grapple with the dilemmas posed by the intrusive and oppressive presence of a people whose power and modernity (and ability to shed the shackles of Chinese culture) many admired, but whose brutal tutelage far many more heartily resented.

---

44. Duus, *Abacus and the Sword*, 420.
45. Government-General of Chosen, *Annual Report on Reforms and Progress in Chosen*, 1.

The Qing Empire in the World

In 1887 Zeng Jize, son of the famous Zeng Guofan, published an essay entitled "China: The Sleep and the Awakening." In it, he acknowledged that the
Qing Empire was suffering under the burden of unequal treaties and other
humiliations. But he spoke with confidence of the lessons China was learning and of the future. "China is no longer what she was even five years ago.
Each encounter . . . has, in teaching China her weakness, also discovered to
her her strength."[46] For Zeng, the Qing Empire's newfound strength was
manifested in relations between the Empire and its vassals. These relations
were in the process of being placed "on a less equivocal footing . . . in a sense
more in accordance with the place which China holds as a great Asiatic
Power."[47] He gave notice to the world that the "Warden of the Marches is
now abroad, looking to the security of China's outlying provinces—of Korea, Thibtet, and Chinese Turkestan. Henceforth, any hostile movements
against these countries, or any interference with their affairs, will be viewed
at Peking as a declaration on the part of the Power committing it, of a desire
to discontinue its friendly relations with the Chinese Government."[48] With
the benefit of knowing what happened in the years and decades that came after Zeng penned this piece, it is tempting to dismiss Zeng's bold claims as
hopelessly naïve and misinformed. The Qing Empire had yet to experience
the humiliating defeat of the Sino-Japanese War, the chaos of the Boxer Rebellion and its suppression, and the growing scramble for concessions in
China by foreign powers, all of which would set the stage for the ultimate
demise of the Manchu dynasty in 1912. Moreover, some three decades after
Zeng had declared China to have awakened, prominent May Fourth intellectuals such as Lu Xun and nation builders (both Nationalist and Communist)
were still lamenting the somnolence of the Chinese people.[49] The decades of
"humiliation" would turn into a century before China would finally "stand
up" under CCP rule in 1949.

And yet, a brief examination of the Qing Empire's policies toward the
"outlying provinces" singled out by Zeng provides a good way to assess
the Empire in the late nineteenth century and situate it in larger regional

---

46. Tseng, "China: The Sleep and the Awakening," 148.
47. Ibid., 152.
48. Ibid.
49. See, e.g., Fitzgerald, *Awakening China*, and Mitter, *A Bitter Revolution*.

and global contexts. As noted in Chapter 2, the Qing government held a significant foreign policy debate in 1875 in which it decided to emphasize "frontier defense" (*saifang*) at the expense of maritime defense (*haifang*). For "Chinese Turkestan," this meant a series of aggressive military campaigns led by Zuo Zongtang designed to put down rebels and preclude Russian expansion in the region. Success on the battlefield was followed by reforms designed to integrate the region into the Empire in ways heretofore unimagined. Xinjiang was declared a province in 1884 with its capital renamed Dihua (instead of the traditional Urumchi). Governors (*xunfu*) were appointed, and Chinese-style civil administration complete with circuits, prefectures, and the like were created. New schools were established and, perhaps most significantly, migration of Han Chinese to Xinjiang was encouraged.[50]

The case of Tibet was similar. Britain's attempts to increase its influence in Tibet ultimately culminated in an invasion in 1904. Aided by two Maxim guns (nicknamed "Bubble" and "Squeak"), the British expeditionary force made short work of Tibetan resistance and bloodily and ruthlessly asserted British dominance.[51] Tibet would seem, then, to be yet another case of the technologically superior West asserting its will over the "sick man of Asia." And yet, within two years, the British signed a convention with the Qing Empire promising "not to annex Tibetan territory or to interfere in the administration of Tibet" and essentially "[reaffirming] Tibet's political subordination to China" (an Anglo-Russian agreement the following year would further strengthen the Qing Empire's claims to Tibet).[52] In the ensuing years, the Qing Empire, largely under the leadership of Zhao Erfeng, would intervene to an unprecedented degree in Tibetan affairs (including bloody invasions).[53] Zhao led Qing armies into Lhasa in 1910, putting the

---

50. Millward, *Beyond the Pass,* 250–51.

51. Meyer, *Dust of Empire,* 11.

52. Goldstein, *Snow Lion and the Dragon,* 25–26.

53. Melvin Goldstein (ibid., 26) concludes: "The Qing dynasty, although enfeebled and on the brink of collapse, responded with surprising vigor. Beijing got the British troops to leave Tibetan soil quickly by paying the indemnity to Britain itself and began to take a more active role in day-to-day Tibetan affairs." Cf. Thomas Laird's (*The Story of Tibet,* 234) conclusion: "In an ominous shadow of events to come, not a single country intervened as Chinese troops, under Manchu command, occupied Lhasa and took steps to establish administrative control over Tibet, something which no Chinese or Manchu government had ever accomplished."

Dalai Lama to flight. Local headmen were replaced by Qing-appointed officials, and a Chinese postal service was established with Tibet's first stamps (using both Chinese and Tibetan script) being issued. Only the collapse of the Qing temporarily ended this process of "Tibet's incorporation into China proper."[54]

The decision to emphasize "frontier defense" was understood by Immanuel Hsu to be a sign of how "obsolescent," anachronistic, and "premodern" the Qing Empire policymakers were.[55] If only they had listened to Li Hongzhang and devoted more resources to the Qing navy, then the humiliating defeats of the Sino-Japanese War and perhaps even the subsequent dynastic collapse might have been avoided.[56] Although such counterfactuals are by their nature impossible to prove, Hsu's conclusions may be correct. However, it is also important to consider the implications of the course the Qing Empire chose to take. In an era in which most depictions emphasize Qing weakness and Chinese humiliation, the Empire vigorously and successfully asserted heretofore unprecedented degrees of control over both Xinjiang and Tibet, in the face of competition with two of the world's most powerful empires—the Russian and the British—no less. The Qing Empire, it appears, was also capable of participating in the territorial annexation and consolidation characteristic of the age of high imperialism.[57]

The Qing may very well have demonstrated the influence of "vestiges of the steppe-oriented mentality" of its Manchu founders in making the strategic decision to focus on Xinjiang and Tibet at the expense of the maritime littoral.[58] But seen from the broad view of more than a century's hindsight, this decision may not have been as ill-informed as Hsu has concluded. The Qing Empire, like its Chinese predecessors, displayed many of the characteristics of "the great military and absolutist land empires, often linked to universalist religions, which existed from antiquity to

---

54. Goldstein, *Snow Lion and the Dragon*, 28.

55. Hsu, "Great Policy Debate in China, 1874," 224, 225, 227.

56. Ibid., 228.

57. It should be noted that to argue that the Qing Empire, too, practiced "high" or "new" imperialism is not to say that this was simple mimicry of foreign practices. The Qing Empire had a long and complex tradition of imperial relations and practices toward its frontier upon which to draw as it formed new policies and practices in the nineteenth and early twentieth centuries; see Perdue, *China Marches West*.

58. Hsu, "Great Policy Debate," 224–25, 227.

the twentieth century."[59] In the nineteenth and early twentieth centuries, European maritime empires generally got the better of conflicts with these land empires. But after the dust of decolonization had settled, the striking continuity between the borders of the Qing Empire and the present-day PRC contrasts dramatically with contraction of Japanese, European, and American empires in Asia (and the world over).[60]

The long-term durability of the Qing imperium resulted in part from the strategic decision to focus on contiguous landholdings but also in part from another strategic decision made by the early leaders of the Chinese Republic. One of the slogans of the revolutionaries who brought about the end of the Qing Empire was "overthrow the Qing and restore the Ming." Explicit in their agenda was the notion that the Qing Empire's Manchu rulers were foreign overseers whose removal would enable China to be restored to greatness. The anti-Manchu riots and pogroms that accompanied the Chinese Revolution of 1911–12 attest to the strong feeling among many that Manchus, whatever their actual genetic makeup, were not part of China.[61] And yet early on in the Republic, leaders of the new China made it patently clear that the borders of the new Republic would contain all former Qing possessions, including territory never ruled by an ethnic Han Chinese dynasty. And, from a position of relative weakness, Chinese policy makers, particularly among the Nationalists, displayed a remarkable ability to maintain their territorial claims.[62] Later attempts by the PRC to portray

---

59. Lieven, *Empire*, 25. Lieven contrasts the scholarship on land empires, typified by the work of Samuel Eisenstadt and Maurice Duverger, with the scholarship on "modern European maritime empires" as exemplified by Michael Doyle. It is fair to say that for many Western scholars, the latter has been the dominant strain (for obvious reasons) of imperialism they have chosen to study, so much so that in some cases it appears that European maritime empires were the only kind of empires worth considering in the modern world. See also Maier, *Among Empires*, 32; and Iriye, "Beyond Imperialism," 108–9.

60. The United States presents an interesting case. Akira Iriye ("Beyond Imperialism," 108–9) has argued that the United States might be included on the list of land empires: "It, too, grew as a territorial empire during the nineteenth century, expanding northward, westward, and southward, with the central government establishing its authority over all parts of its territory, at least after the Civil War." But its behavior in the late nineteenth and throughout the twentieth (and into the twenty-first) centuries also displays characteristics of modern maritime empires as well.

61. See Rhoads, *Manchus and Han*.

62. See Kirby, "The Internationalization of China."

China as a multicultural and multiethnic polity welcomed even what few identifiably Manchus remained into the larger Chinese fold. This was part of a larger process of reimagining a Chinese nation that was contiguous with the territory and peoples of the Qing Empire. Although this is still an open-ended and highly contested process, it appears that the Qing/ Chinese empire has been more successful in making the transition from empire to nation than many of the other great land empires, such as the Ottoman, Austro-Hungarian, and, to a lesser extent, Mogul and Russian/Soviet Empires. In the words of Dominic Lieven, "The transition from the old imperial concept of 'one center under heaven' to modern nationalism appears to have been achieved. As a result of this largely successful transition from empire to nation, China is the natural future hegemon in East and South-East Asia."[63]

The Qing failures in Korea, are, then, in part a result of the larger structures and priorities of the Qing Empire. But they are also an indication of the vastly different traditions and strategies that the Qing Empire brought to Korea in the first place. From the beginning, the Qing conceived of and treated Chosŏn Korea in ways quite different from the ways it approached the Empire's growing Inner Asian possessions. The assertion of Qing suzerainty while allowing Korean autonomy, the utility of the systems and institutions of multilateral imperialism, the constraints of the decision to focus on Inner Asia, and the strong Korean sense of identity and jealously guarded autonomy combined to create a situation in which direct territorial annexation (regardless of Purist Party dreams) was neither a viable nor a seriously pursued option.

The new post-Qing China would regard and approach Korea in much the same way that its Qing predecessor had. Jiang Jieshi (Chiang Kaishek) often mentioned the need to support Korea's independence and freedom, sometimes in the same breath as referring to Taiwan. In a speech entitled "Korea and Taiwan Are China's Lifelines" ("Gaoli Taiwan shi Zhongguo shengmingxian"), Jiang stated: "We must enable Korea and Taiwan to restore their independence and freedom, and enable them to solidify the

---

63. Lieven, *Empire*, 83. See also Maier, *Among Empires*, 29. John Schrecker (*Imperialism and Chinese Nationalism*, 250) argues that this transition to nationalism is "one of the most significant features of the Qing response to the imperialist onslaught at the turn of the century, and it is probably a crucial factor in explaining why China as a whole was saved from foreign domination."

national defense of the Republic of China and consolidate the base for peace in East Asia."[64] Although Nationalist and Chinese Communist Party policies would later clarify claims that Taiwan was Chinese territory, they would also maintain that China and Korea shared a special relationship complete with reciprocal obligations. Indeed, one cannot consider the dispatch of hundreds of thousands of Chinese "volunteers" to Korea in 1950 to assist North Korea's efforts to stave off American-led encroachments into North Korean territory without seeing echoes of the Ming troops sent to counter the Hideyoshi Invasions of 1592–98 or the Qing dispatch of troops to Korea in 1882 and 1894.

North Korea has maintained a close but often prickly relationship with its Chinese neighbor. Declarations of alliance and solidarity, based in part on past tradition and in part on shared socialist ideology, were always tempered by a North Korean fear of domination (or abandonment) by the PRC. Present-day DPRK leaders worry greatly about intervention or "strangulation" by the United States or a resurgent Japan, but they also have anxieties about potential intervention from China, particularly in times of political unrest or turmoil.[65]

South Korea, for decades on the other side of the Cold War fence, recognized the Republic of China on Taiwan as the legitimate government of China and avoided direct diplomatic relations with the PRC. However, a result of ROK President Roh Tae Woo's "Nordpolitik," the ROK switched recognition and normalized diplomatic and commercial relations with the PRC in 1992. One interesting result of this policy shift was the resurgence of the Chinatown in Inch'ŏn. For decades a handful of dilapidated buildings and restaurants, the district has recently been refurbished and equipped with Chinese-style gates marking the entrance to a thriving commercial center. A statue of Confucius, donated by a Chinese-Korean friendship association, now looks down the steep stairway that once divided the Chinese and Japanese settlements in Inch'ŏn. Many South Koreans study Mandarin Chinese in private language academies (*hagwŏn*) and growing numbers seek university educations in China. And although some public opinion polls indicate that younger South Koreans appear to regard

---

64. Jiang Jieshi, "Gaoli Taiwan shi Zhongguo de shengmingxian" (Korea and Taiwan are China's lifelines), printed in *Taiwan wenti yanlun ji* (Chongqing, 1943), 1–2; quoted in Phillips, "Retrocession and Sinification," 6–7.

65. See, e.g., Kaplan, "When North Korea Falls."

China as South Korea's most natural ally for the twenty-first century, the PRC's attempt to include the ancient Korean kingdom of Koguryŏ within the umbrella of a far-flung multiethnic Chinese polity has caused at least some to reconsider the ramifications of the PRC's increasingly assertive foreign policy. Although few fear an outright Chinese annexation of Korea, it is plain that Chinese imperialism of some sort may be in Korea's future as well as its past.

Reference Matter

Works Cited

Abernathy, David B. *The Dynamics of Global Dominance: European Overseas Empires, 1415–1980.* New Haven: Yale University Press, 2000.

Academia Sinica. Institute of Modern History, ed. *Qingji Zhong-Ri-Han guanxi shiliao.* 11 vols. Taibei: Academia Sinica, Institute of Modern History, 1972.

Adas, Michael. "Imperialism and Colonialism in Comparative Perspective." *International History Review* 20, no. 2 (1998): 371–88.

———. *Machines as the Measure of Men: Science, Technology, and Ideologies of Western Dominance.* Ithaca: Cornell University Press, 1989.

Ahn, Yonson. "Competing Nationalisms: The Mobilisation of History and Archaeology in the Korea-China Wars over Koguryo/Gaogouli." *Japan Focus*, Feb. 9, 2006. http://www.japanfocus.org/products/details/1837. Accessed Mar. 13, 2007.

Allen, Horace N. *Things Korean: A Collection of Sketches and Anecdotes Missionary and Diplomatic.* New York: Fleming Revell, 1908.

"Ambassadors Sent to the United States." *New York Times*, Feb. 8, 1888: 4.

Anderson, Benedict. "Census, Map, Museum." In *Becoming National: A Reader*, ed. Geoff Eley and Ronald Grigor Suny. New York: Oxford University Press, 1996, 243–58.

Angell, Norman. *The Great Illusion.* London: William Heinemann, 1911.

Aziz, K. Z. *The British in India: A Study in Imperialism.* Islamabad: National Commission on Historical and Cultural Research, 1976.

Bailey, Paul, ed. *Strengthen the Country and Enrich the People: The Reform Writings of Ma Jianzhong (1845–1900).* Richmond, Eng.: Curzon, 1998.

Bastid, Marianne. *Educational Reform in Early 20th-Century China.* Trans. Paul J. Bailey. Ann Arbor: Center for Chinese Studies, University of Michigan, 1988.

Bayly, C. A. *The Birth of the Modern World, 1780–1914.* Malden, MA: Blackwell, 2004.

Beasley, William G. *Japanese Imperialism, 1894–1945.* New York: Oxford University Press, 1987.

Bickers, Robert A. "Introduction." In *Ritual and Diplomacy: The Macartney Mission to China, 1792–1794,* ed. idem. London: British Association for Chinese Studies, 1993, 7–10.

Biggerstaff, Knight. "The Establishment of Permanent Chinese Diplomatic Missions Abroad." *Chinese Social and Political Science Review* 20, no. 1 (1936): 1–41.

Bishop, Donald M. "Shared Failure: American Military Advisors in Korea, 1888–1896." *Transactions of the Korea Branch of the Royal Asiatic Society* 58 (1983): 53–76.

Bishop, Isabella Bird. *Korea and Her Neighbours.* London and Boston: KPI, 1985 [1897].

British Foreign Office. *Diplomatic and Consular Reports on Trade and Finance, 1884–1910.* 1884–1910. Note: later editions in the series are entitled *Diplomatic and Consular Reports.*

Brook, Timothy. *The Confusions of Pleasure: Culture and Commerce in Ming China.* Berkeley: University of California Press, 1998.

Brunvand, Jan. *The Vanishing Hitchhiker: American Urban Legends and Their Meanings.* New York: Norton, 1981.

Cady, John F. *The Roots of French Imperialism in Eastern Asia.* Ithaca: Cornell University Press, 1954.

Cain, P. J., and A. G. Hopkins. *British Imperialism, Innovation and Expansion, 1688–1914.* London: Longman, 1993.

Callahan, William A. "National Insecurities: Humiliation, Salvation, and Chinese Nationalism." *Alternatives* 29 (2004): 199–218.

Carles, William Richard. *Life in Corea.* London and New York: Macmillan, 1888.

Cassel, Par. "Excavating Extraterritoriality: The 'Judicial Sub-prefect' as a Prototype for the Mixed Court in Shanghai." *Late Imperial China* 24, no. 2 (Dec. 2003): 156–82.

Chaille-Long, Charles. *My Life in Four Continents.* London: Hutchinson, 1912.

Chandra, Vipan. *Imperialism, Resistance, and Reform in Late Nineteenth-Century Korea: Enlightenment and the Independence Club.* Berkeley: University of California, Institute of East Asian Studies, and Center for Korean Studies, 1988.

Chay, Jongsuk. *Diplomacy of Asymmetry: Korean-American Relations to 1910.* Honolulu: University of Hawai'i Press, 1990.

Chen Guding, ed. *Zhong-Ri-Han bainian dashiji.* Taibei: Zhonghua, 1972.

Ch'en, Jerome. *Yuan Shih-k'ai.* 2nd ed. Stanford: Stanford University Press, 1972.

Chien, Frederick Foo. *The Opening of Korea: A Study of Chinese Diplomacy, 1876–1885.* Hamden, CT: Shoe String Press, 1967.

Chilcote, Ronald H., ed. *The Political Economy of Imperialism: Critical Appraisals.* Lanham, MD: Rowman and Littlefield, 2000.

China. Imperial Chinese Mission to Korea. *Notes on the Imperial Chinese Mission to Corea, 1890.* Shanghai, 1892.

———. Imperial Maritime Customs. *Returns of Trade and Trade Reports.* Shanghai: Inspector General of Customs, 1885–94.

————. ————. *Treaties, Conventions, Etc., Between China and Foreign States.* Shanghai: Inspector General of Customs, 1917.

————. ————. *Treaties, Regulations, Etc. Between Corea and Other Powers, 1876–1889.* Miscellaneous Series, 19. Shanghai: Inspectorate General of Customs, 1891.

"China's Ancient Koguryŏ Kingdom Site Added to World Heritage List." *People's Daily Online*, July 2, 2004. http://english.peopledaily.com.cn/200407/01/eng20040701_148209.html. Accessed Mar. 13, 2007.

Cho Il-mun, ed. *Chosŏn ch'aengnyak.* Seoul: Kŏn'guk taehakkyo, 1977.

Cho Ki-jun. "The Impact of the Opening of Korea on Its Commerce and Industry." *Korea Journal* 16, no. 2 (1976): 27–44.

Choe, Ching Young. *The Rule of the Taewŏn'gun, 1864–1873: Restoration in Yi Korea.* Cambridge, MA: Harvard University Press, 1972.

Ch'oe Mun-hyŏng. *Han'guk ŭl tullŏssan chegukchuŭi yŏlgang ŭi kakch'uk.* Seoul: Chisiksanŏpsa, 2001.

Ch'oe Song-ho. "Kaehanggi sikminjihwa kwajŏng e issŏsŏ ŭi muyŏk kujo yŏn'gu." Ph.D. diss., Kyŏngnam taehakkyo, 1988.

Ch'oe Song-yŏn. *Kaehang kwa yanggwan yŏkchŏng.* Inch'ŏn: Kyŏnggi munhwasa, 1958.

Ch'oe Sŭng-no. "Ch'oe Sŭngno: On Current Affairs." In *Sourcebook of Korean Civilization*, vol. 1, *From Early Times to the Sixteenth Century*, ed. Peter H Lee. New York: Columbia University Press, 1993, 282–88.

Ch'oe T'ae-ho. "Map'o haegwanbun'guk ŭi sŏlch'i wa hyŏkp'a." *Kyŏngje sahak* 1978: 29–39.

Ch'oe Tŏk-su. "The Dawning of a New World: Korea and the West, Korea and a Changing Asia in 1882." Paper presented at ICKS International Forum on Korean Studies: Current Trends and Future Objectives of Korean Studies, July 14–15, 2005.

Ch'oe, Yong-ho. "The *Kapsin* Coup of 1884: A Reassessment." *Korean Studies* 6 (1982): 105–24.

Ch'oe, Yŏngho, Peter Lee, and Wm. Theodore de Bary, eds. *Sources of Korean Tradition*, vol. 2, *From the Sixteenth to the Twentieth Centuries.* New York: Columbia University Press, 2000.

Choi, Mun-hyung. "Korean-British Amity and Its Historical Significance." *Korea Journal* 24, no. 4 (1984): 9–22.

Chŏn In-yŏng. "Chung-Il kabo chŏnjaeng chŏnhu Chungguk ŭi Chosŏn insik pyŏnhwa." *Kuksagwan nonch'ong* 90 (2000): 41–84.

Chosŏn chŏnsa 13 kŭndae 1. Pyŏngyang: Kwahak paekkwa sajŏn ch'ulp'ansa, 1980.

Chu, Samuel C. *Reformer in Modern China: Chang Chien, 1853–1926.* New York: Columbia University Press, 1965.

Chu, Samuel C., and Kwang-Ching Liu, eds. *Li Hung-Chang and China's Early Modernization.* Armonk, NY: M. E. Sharpe, 1994.

Chun, Hae-jong. "Sino-Korean Tributary Relations in the Ch'ing Period." In *The Chinese World Order*, ed. John K. Fairbank. Cambridge: Harvard University Press, 1968, 90–111.

Chung, Chai-sik. *A Korean Confucian Encounter with the Modern World: Yi Hang-No and the West*. Berkeley: Institute of East Asian Studies, 1995.

Chung, Henry. *Korean Treaties*. New York: Nichols, 1919.

Chung, Lisa. "Somnolent in Korea: Korean-British Trade at the Turn of the 20th Century." Unpublished paper, George Washington University, 2005.

Clark, Donald. "The Ming Connection: Notes on Korea's Experience in the Chinese Tributary System." *Transactions of the Korea Branch of the Royal Asiatic Society* 58 (1983): 77–89.

———. "Sino-Korean Tributary Relations Under the Ming." In *The Cambridge History of China*, vol. 8, *The Ming Dynasty, 1368–1644, Part II*, ed. Denis Twitchett and Frederick W. Mote. Cambridge, Eng.: Cambridge University Press, 1998, 272–300.

Cohen, Paul A. *China and Christianity: The Missionary Movement and the Growth of Chinese Antiforeignism*. Cambridge, MA: Harvard University Press, 1963.

———. *China Unbound: Evolving Perspectives on the Chinese Past*. New York: Routledge, 2003.

———. *Discovering History in China: American Historical Writing on the Recent Chinese Past with a New Preface by the Author*. New York: Columbia University Press, 1986.

Cohen, Warren I. *East Asia at the Center: Four Thousand Years of Engagement with the World*. New York: Columbia University Press, 2000.

Collyer, C. T. "The Culture and Preparation of Ginseng in Korea." *Transactions of the Korea Branch of the Royal Asiatic Society* 3 (1903): 18–30.

Conroy, Francis Hilary. *The Japanese Seizure of Korea, 1868–1910: A Study of Realism and Idealism in International Relations*. Philadelphia: University of Pennsylvania Press, 1960.

Cook, Harold F. *Korea's 1884 Incident: Its Background and Kim Ok-Kyun's Elusive Dream*. Seoul: Royal Asiatic Society, Korea Branch, and Taewon Publishing, 1972.

"Corea Acts for Herself." *Evening Star* (Washington, DC), Jan. 14, 1888.

"The Corean Embassy: They Put on Their Best Robes and Call on the President." *Evening Star* (Washington, DC), Jan. 17, 1888.

Cottrell, Arthur. *East Asia: From Chinese Predominance to the Rise of the Pacific Rim*. New York: Oxford University Press, 1993.

Critchfield, Theodore. "Queen Min's Murder." Ph.D. diss., Indiana University, 1975.

Crossley, Pamela Kyle. *The Manchus*. Cambridge, MA: Blackwell, 1997.

———. *A Translucent Mirror: History and Identity in Qing Imperial Ideology*. Berkeley: University of California Press, 1999.

Cumings, Bruce. *Korea's Place in the Sun: A Modern History*. New York: Norton, 1997.

"The Curious Coreans: Far Behind the Japanese in Society Ways—Their Peculiar Notions." *New York Times*, Jan. 27, 1889.

Curtin, Philip. *The World and the West: The European Challenge and the Overseas Response in the Age of Empire*. Cambridge, Eng.: Cambridge University Press, 2000.

Davies, Daniel M. *The Life and Thought of Henry Gerhard Appenzeller (1858–1902): Missionary to Korea*. Lewiston, NY: Edwin Mellen Press, 1988.

Dennett, Tyler. *Americans in Eastern Asia: A Critical Study of the Policy of the United States with Reference to China, Japan and Korea in the 19th Century*. New York: Barnes & Noble, 1941.

Denny, Owen N. *China and Korea*. Shanghai, 1888.

Desnoyers, Charles. "Toward 'One Enlightened and Progressive Civilization': Discourses of Expansion and Nineteenth-Century Chinese Missions Abroad." *Journal of World History* 8, no. 1 (1997): 135–56.

Deuchler, Martina. *Confucian Gentlemen and Barbarian Envoys: The Opening of Korea, 1875–1885*. Seattle: University of Washington Press, 1977.

———. *The Confucian Transformation of Korea: A Study of Society and Ideology*. Cambridge, MA: Council on East Asian Studies, 1992.

Ding Jinjun. "Yuan Shikai zhujie Chaoxian qijian handu xuanji." *Lishi dang'an* 3 (1992): 56–63.

Dower, John. *Embracing Defeat: Japan in the Wake of World War II*. New York: Norton, 1999.

Doyle, Michael W. *Empires*. Ithaca: Cornell University Press, 1986.

Drake, Frederick C. *The Empire of the Seas: A Biography of Rear Admiral Robert Wilson Shufeldt, USN*. Honolulu: University of Hawai'i Press, 1984.

Drake, Henry Burgess. *Korea of the Japanese*. London: J. Lane, 1930.

Du Shupu, ed. *Renchuan huaqiao jiaoyu bainianshi*. Inch'ŏn: 2001.

Duara, Prasenjit. *Rescuing History from the Nation: Questioning Narratives of Modern China*. Chicago: University of Chicago Press, 1995.

Dudden, Alexis. *Japan's Colonization of Korea: Discourse and Power*. Honolulu: University of Hawai'i Press, 2005.

Duus, Peter. *The Abacus and the Sword: The Japanese Penetration of Korea, 1859–1910*. Berkeley: University of California Press, 1995.

———. *The Japanese Discovery of America: A Brief History with Documents*. New York: Bedford Books, 1997.

Ebrey, Patricia; Anne Walthall; and James Palais. *East Asia: A Cultural, Social and Political History*. Boston: Houghton Mifflin, 2006.

Eckert, Carter J.; Ki-baik Lee; Young Ick Lew; Michael Robinson; and Edward W. Wagner. *Korea Old and New: A History*. Seoul: Ilchogak; Cambridge, MA: Harvard University Press, 1990.

Edney, Matthew H. *Mapping an Empire: The Geographical Construction of British India, 1765–1843*. Chicago: University of Chicago Press, 1999.

Elkins, Caroline, and Susan Pedersen, eds. *Settler Colonialism in the Twentieth Century: Projects, Practices, Legacies*. New York: Routledge, 2005.

Elvin, Mark. *The Retreat of the Elephants: An Environmental History of China.* New Haven: Yale University Press, 2004.

"Embassy to the United States Not Subject to China's Control." *New York Times,* Feb. 2, 1888, 4.

Esherick, Joseph. *Origins of the Boxer Uprising.* Berkeley: University of California Press, 1988.

Evening Star. Washington, DC.

Fairbank, John King. *China: A New History.* Cambridge, MA: Belknap Press of Harvard University Press, 1992.

————. "The Creation of the Treaty System." In *The Cambridge History of China,* vol. 10, *Late Ch'ing, 1800–1911,* ed. idem. Cambridge, Eng.: Cambridge University Press, 1978, 213–63.

————. "The Early Treaty System in the Chinese World Order." In *The Chinese World Order: Traditional China's Foreign Relations,* ed. idem. Cambridge, MA: Harvard University Press, 1968, 257–75.

————. "A Preliminary Framework." In *The Chinese World Order: Traditional China's Foreign Relations,* ed. idem. Cambridge, MA: Harvard University Press, 1968, 1–19.

————. *Trade and Diplomacy on the China Coast 1842–1854.* Cambridge: Harvard University Press, 1951.

Fairbank, John King, ed. *The Chinese World Order: Traditional China's Foreign Relations.* Cambridge, MA: Harvard University Press, 1968.

Fang Chaoying. "Weng T'ung-ho" [Weng Tonghe]. In Arthur Hummel, ed., *Eminent Chinese of the Ch'ing Period.* Washington, DC: U.S. Government Printing Office, 1944, 2: 860–61.

Feuerwerker, Albert. *China's Early Industrialization: Sheng Hsuan-Huai (1844–1916) and Mandarin Enterprise.* Cambridge, Eng.: Harvard University Press, 1958.

Fieldhouse, D. K. *Colonialism, 1870–1945: An Introduction.* London: Weidenfeld and Nicolson, 1981.

————. *Economics and Empire, 1830–1914.* Ithaca: Cornell University Press, 1973.

Finch, Michael. *Min Yŏng-Hwan: A Political Biography.* Honolulu: University of Hawai'i Press, 2002.

Fitzgerald, John. *Awakening China: Politics, Culture, and Class in the Nationalist Revolution.* Stanford: Stanford University Press, 1996.

Frank, Andre Gunder. *ReOrient: Global Economy in the Asian Age.* Berkeley: University of California Press, 1998.

Fukuyama, Francis. "Asian Values and the Asian Crisis." *Commentary* 105, no. 2 (Feb. 1998): 23–27.

Fung, Allen. "Testing the Self-Strengthening: The Chinese Army in the Sino-Japanese War of 1894–1895." *Modern Asian Studies* 30, no. 4 (Oct. 1996): 1007–31.

Furuta, Kazuko. "Inchon Trade: Japanese and Chinese Merchants and the Shanghai Network." In *Commercial Networks in Modern Asia,* ed. Shinya Sugiyama and Linda Grove. Richmond, Eng.: Curzon, 2001, 71–95.

———. "Shanghai: The East Asian Emporium for Lancashire Goods: A Statistical Analysis." Paper presented at the Commercial Networks in Asia: 1850–1930 conference, Atami, Japan, 1994.

Galbraith, John S. *Reluctant Empire: British Policy on the South African Frontier, 1834–1854.* Berkeley: University of California Press, 1963.

———. "The 'Turbulent Frontier' as a Factor in British Expansion." *Comparative Studies in Society and History* 2 (1959–60): 155–68.

Gale, James Scarth, and Richard Rutt. *James Scarth Gale and His History of the Korean People: A New Edition of the History Together with a Biography and Annotated Bibliographies by Richard Rutt.* Seoul: Royal Asiatic Society, 1972.

Gallagher, John, and Ronald Robinson. "The Imperialism of Free Trade." *Economic History Review* 6, no. 1 (1953): 1–15.

Gann, L. H., and Peter Duignan. *Burden of Empire: An Appraisal of Western Colonialism in Africa South of the Sahara.* Stanford: Hoover Institution Press, 1971.

Garver, John W. "More from the 'Say No Club.'" *China Journal,* no. 45 (Jan. 2001): 151–58.

Giersch, C. Pat. "'A Motley Throng': Social Change Along Southwest China's Early Modern Frontier, 1700–1880." *Journal of Asian Studies* 60, no. 1 (2001): 67–94.

Gilmore, George William. *Korea from Its Capital: With a Chapter on Missions.* Philadelphia: Presbyterian Board of Publication and Sabbath-School Work, 1892.

Gold, Thomas. *State and Society in the Taiwan Miracle.* Armonk, NY: M. E. Sharpe, 1984.

Goldstein, Melvin C. *The Snow Lion and the Dragon: China, Tibet, and the Dalai Lama.* Berkeley: University of California Press, 1997.

Gottschang, Thomas R., and Diana Lary. *Swallows and Settlers: The Great Migration from North China to Manchuria.* Ann Arbor: Center for Chinese Studies, University of Michigan, 2000.

Government-General of Chosen, *Annual Report on Reforms and Progress in Chosen (1918–1921).* Keijō: Government-General of Chosen, 1921.

Griffis, William Elliot. *Corea, the Hermit Nation.* 9th ed. New York: C. Scribner's Sons, 1911.

Grove, Linda, and S. Sugiyama. "Introduction." In *Commercial Networks in Modern Asia,* ed. S. Sugiyama and Linda Grove. Richmond, Eng.: Curzon, 2001, 1–14.

Gugong bowuyuan, ed. *Qing Guangxu chao Zhong-Ri jiaoshe shiliao.* Beiping: Gugong bowuyuan, 1932.

Haboush, JaHyun Kim. *The Confucian Kingship in Korea: Yŏngjo and the Politics of Sagacity.* New York: Columbia University Press, 2001.

Haley, George T.; Tan Chin Tiong; and Usha C. V. Haley. *New Asian Emperors: The Overseas Chinese, Their Strategies and Competitive Advantages.* Oxford: Buttterworth-Heinemann, 1998.

Hall, J. C. "A Visit to the West Coast and Capital of Korea." *Transactions of the Asiatic Society of Japan* 11 (1883): 148–61.

Hamashita, Takeshi. "Tribute and Treaties: Maritime Asia and Treaty Port Networks in the Era of Negotiation, 1800–1900." In *The Resurgence of East Asia: 500, 150, and 50 Year Perspectives*, ed. Giovanni Arrighi, Takeshi Hamashita, and Mark Selden. London: Routledge, 2003, 17–50.

Hamilton, Angus. *Korea: Its History, Its People, and Its Commerce*. London: William Heinemann, 1904.

Han, Sukhee. "Beyond the Celestial Sinic Sphere: King Kojong and Korea's Pursuit of Modernization." Ph.D. diss., Tufts University, Fletcher School of Law and Diplomacy, 1998.

Han U-gŭn (Woo-keun Han). *Han'guk kaehanggi ŭi sangŏp yŏn'gu*. Seoul: Ilchogak, 1970.

———. *The History of Korea*. Trans. Lee Kyung-shik. Ed. Grafton K. Mintz. Seoul: Eul-yoo Publishing, 1974.

Han Yŏng-u (Young-woo Han). *Tasi ch'annŭn uri yŏksa*. Seoul: Kyŏngsewŏn, 1997.

———. "Kija Worship in the Koryo and Early Yi Dynasties: A Cultural Symbol in the Relationship Between Korea and China." In *The Rise of Neo-Confucianism in Korea*, ed. Wm. Theodore de Bary and JaHyun Kim Haboush. New York: Columbia University Press, 1985, 349–74.

Han'guk kwanse yŏn'guso. *Han'guk kwansesa*. Seoul: Han'guk kwanse yŏn'guso, 1985.

Han'guk muyŏk hyŏphoe. *Han'guk muyŏksa*. Seoul: Han'guk muyŏk hyŏphoe, 1972.

Hansŏng sunbo. Seoul.

Hao, Yen-p'ing. *The Commercial Revolution in Nineteenth-Century China: The Rise of Sino-Western Mercantile Capitalism*. Berkeley: University of California Press, 1986.

———. *The Comprador in Nineteenth Century China: Bridge Between East and West*. Cambridge, MA: Harvard University Press, 1970.

———. "A Study of the Ch'ing-Liu Tang: 'The Disinterested' Scholar-Official Group (1875–1884)." *Papers on China* (Harvard University) 16 (1962): 40–65.

Hao, Yen-p'ing, and Erh-min Wang. "Changing Chinese Views of Western Relations, 1840–1895." In *The Cambridge History of China*, vol. 11, *Late Ch'ing, 1800–1911, Part 2*, ed. John K. Fairbank and Kwang-Ching Liu. Cambridge, Eng.: Cambridge University Press, 1980, 142–201.

Hara, Takemichi. "Korea, China, and Western Barbarians: Diplomacy in Early Nineteenth-Century Korea." *Modern Asian Studies* 32, no. 2 (1998): 389–430.

Harper's Weekly. New York.

Harrington, Fred Harvey. *God, Mammon, and the Japanese: Dr. Horace N. Allen and Korean-American Relations, 1884–1905*. Madison: University of Wisconsin Press, 1961.

Headrick, Daniel. *The Invisible Weapon: Telecommunications and International Politics, 1851–1945*. New York: Oxford University Press, 1991.

———. *The Tools of Empire: Technology and European Imperialism in the Nineteenth Century*. New York: Oxford University Press, 1981.

Henthorn, William E. *Korea: The Mongol Invasions*. Leiden: E. J. Brill, 1963.

Hevia, James. *Cherishing Men from Afar: Qing Guest Ritual and the Macartney Embassy of 1793*. Durham, NC: Duke University Press, 1995.

————. *English Lessons: The Pedagogy of Imperialism in Nineteenth Century China*. Durham, NC: Duke University Press, 2003.

Hillier, Walter C. *Report on the Commercial Condition of the Ports of Fusan and Wŏnsan*. British Foreign Office, Miscellaneous Series, 318. London, 1894.

Hinners, David G. *Tong Shao-Yi and His Family*. Lanham, MD: University Press of America, 1999.

Ho, Ping-ti. *Studies on the Population of China, 1368–1953*. Cambridge, MA: Harvard University Press, 1959.

Hoare, J. E. *Embassies in the East*. Richmond, Eng.: Curzon, 1999.

Hobson, John. *Imperialism*. Ann Arbor: University of Michigan Press, 1965.

Hodder, Rupert. *Merchant Princes of the East: Cultural Delusions, Economic Success and the Overseas Chinese in Southeast Asia*. Chichester, Eng.: John Wiley and Sons, 1996.

Holcombe, Charles. *The Genesis of East Asia, 221 B.C.–A.D. 907*. Honolulu: Association for Asian Studies and University of Hawai'i Press, 2001.

Hopkirk, Peter. *The Great Game: The Struggle for Empire in Central Asia*. New York: Kodansha International, 1992.

Horowitz, Richard. "International Law and State Transformation in China, Siam, and the Ottoman Empire during the Nineteenth Century." *Journal of World History* 15, no. 4 (Dec. 2004): 445–86.

Hostetler, Laura. *Qing Colonial Enterprise: Ethnography and Cartography in Early Modern China*. Chicago: University of Chicago Press, 2001.

Hou Yijie. *Yuan Shikai quanzhuan*. Beijing: Dangdai Zhongguo chubanshe, 1994.

Howe, Stephen. *Empire: A Very Short Introduction*. Oxford: Oxford University Press, 2002.

Hsu, Immanuel C. Y. "The Great Policy Debate in China, 1874: Maritime Defense Vs. Frontier Defense." *Harvard Journal of Asiatic Studies* 25 (1964–65): 212–28.

Hulbert, Homer B. *History of Korea*. Ed. Clarence Norwood Weems. Richmond, Eng.: Curzon, 1999.

Hummel, Arthur W., ed. *Eminent Chinese of the Ch'ing Period (1644–1912)*. 2 vols. Washington, DC: U.S. Government Printing Office, 1943, 1944.

Hwang Hyŏn. *Maech'ŏn yarok*. Trans. Hŏ Kyŏng-jin. Ed. Hŏ Kyŏng-jin. Hanyang kojŏn sanch'aek, 6. Seoul: Hanyang ch'ulp'an, 1995.

Hwang, Kyung Moon. *Beyond Birth: Social Status in the Emergence of Modern Korea*. Cambridge, MA: Harvard University Asia Center, 2004.

Inch'ŏn chikhalshisa p'yŏnch'an wiwŏnhoe. *Inch'ŏnshisa*. Inch'ŏn: Inch'ŏn chikhalshi, 1993.

Independence Club (Tongnip hyophoe). *The Independent (Tongnip sinmun)*. Seoul: LG Sangnam ŏllon chaedan, 1996.

Iriye, Akira. "Beyond Imperialism: The New Internationalism." *Daedalus* 134, no. 2 (Spring 2005): 108–17.

――――. "Imperialism in East Asia." In *Modern East Asia: Essays in Interpretation*, ed. James B. Crowley. New York: Harcourt, 1970, 122–50.

Jiang Tingfu, ed. *Jindai Zhongguo waijiaoshi ziliao jiyao.* 3 vols. Taibei: Taiwan shangwu yinshuguan, 1959.

Johnston, Alastair Iain. *Cultural Realism: Strategic Culture and Grand Strategy in Chinese History.* Princeton: Princeton University Press, 1998.

Jung, Walter. *Nation Building: The Geopolitical History of Korea.* Lanham, MD: University Press of America, 1998.

Kang, David. "Getting Asia Wrong: The Need for New Analytical Frameworks." *International Security* 27, no. 4 (Spring 2003): 57–85.

――――. "Hierarchy, Balancing, and Empirical Puzzles in Asian International Relations." *International Security* 28, no. 3 (Winter 2003/4): 165–80.

Kang, Etsuko Hai-Jin. *Diplomacy and Ideology in Japanese-Korean Relations: From the Fifteenth to the Eighteenth Century.* New York: St. Martin's, 1997.

Kang Tŏk-sang. "Rishi Chōsen kaikō chokugo ni okeru bōeki no tenkai." *Rekishigaku kenkyū* 265 (1962): 1–18.

Kang, Wi Jo. *Christ and Caesar in Modern Korea. A History of Christianity and Politics.* Albany: State University of New York Press, 1997.

Kang, Woong Joe. *The Korean Struggle for International Identity in the Foreground of the Shufeldt Negotiation, 1866–1882.* Lanham, MD: University Press of America, 2005.

Kaplan, Robert D. "When North Korea Falls." *Atlantic Monthly* 298, no. 3 (Oct. 2006): 64–72.

Keijōfu. *Keijōfushi.* Keijō: Keijōfu, 1934–41.

Kennedy, Dane. "Imperial History and Post-Colonial Theory." *Journal of Imperial and Commonwealth History* 24, no. 3 (Sept. 1996): 345–63.

Kennedy, Paul. *The Rise and Fall of Great Powers.* New York: Random House, 1987.

Kennedy, Thomas L. "Li Hung-Chang and the Kiangnan Arsenal, 1860–1895." In *Li Hung-Chang and China's Early Modernization*, ed. Samuel Chu and Kwang-Ching Liu. Armonk, NY: M. E. Sharpe, 1994, 197–215.

Kiernan, V. G. *British Diplomacy in China, 1880–1885.* Cambridge, Eng.: Cambridge University Press, 1939.

――――. *Imperialism and Its Contradictions.* Ed. and with an introduction by Harvey J. Kaye. New York: Routledge, 1995.

Kim Chŏng-gi. "Ch'ŏng ŭi Chosŏn chŏngch'aek (1876–1894)." In *1894 nyŏn nongmin chŏnjaeng yŏn'gu 3*, ed. Han'guk yŏksa yŏn'guhoe. Seoul: Yŏksa pip'yŏngsa, 1997, 40–67.

――――. "Chosŏn chŏngbu ŭi Togil ch'agwan toip (1883–1894)." *Han'guksa yŏn'gu* 39 (1982): 85–120.

――――. "1876–1894 nyŏn Ch'ŏng ŭi Chosŏn chŏngch'aek yŏn'gu." Ph.D. diss., Seoul National University, 1994.

————. "1890 nyŏn Sŏul sangin ŭi ch'ŏlsi tongmaeng p'aŏp kwa siwi t'ujaeng." *Han'guksa yŏn'gu* 67 (1989): 77–100.

Kim Chŏng-wŏn. "Cho-Chung sangmin suyuk muyŏk changjŏng e taehayo." *Yŏksa hakpo*, no. 32 (1966): 120–69.

Kim, C. I. Eugene, and Han-kyo Kim. *Korea and the Politics of Imperialism, 1876–1910.* Berkeley: University of California Press, 1967.

Kim, Dalchoong. "Chinese Imperialism in Korea: With Special Reference to Sino-Korean Trade Regulations in 1882 and 1883." *Journal of East-West Studies* 2 (1976): 97–110.

————. "Korea's Quest for Reform and Diplomacy in the 1880s: With Special Reference to Chinese Intervention and Control." Ph.D. diss., Tufts University, Fletcher School of Law and Diplomacy, 1972.

Kim, Hak-chun. *Korea's Relations with Her Neighbors in a Changing World.* Elizabeth, NJ: Hollym, 1993.

Kim, Hodong. *Holy War in China: The Muslim Rebellion and State in Chinese Central Asia, 1864–1877.* Stanford: Stanford University Press, 2004.

Kim, Key-hiuk. "The Aims of Li Hung-Chang's Policies Toward Japan and Korea, 1870–1882." In *Li Hung-Chang and China's Early Modernization,* ed. Samuel Chu and Kwang-Ching Liu. Armonk, NY: M. E. Sharpe, 1994.

————. *The Last Phase of the East Asian World Order: Korea, Japan, and the Chinese Empire, 1860–1882.* Berkeley: University of California Press, 1980.

Kim, Ki-Seok. "Emperor Gwangmu's Diplomatic Struggles to Protect His Sovereignty Before and After 1905." *Korea Journal* (Summer 2006): 233–57.

Kim Kyo-yŏng. *Kaehwagi ŭi Kim Ch'ongni.* Seoul: Soul taehakkyo ch'ulp'anbu, 1977.

Kim Kyŏng-t'ae, ed. *T'ongsang hwich'an [tsusho isan]: Han'guk p'yŏn.* 10 vols. Seoul: Yŏgang ch'ulp'ansa, 1987.

Kim, Nan-Tsung. "The Neighbour as Mirror: Images of Korea in Chinese Writings, 1876–1931." Ph.D. diss., University of London, 1999.

Kim Ok-kyun. "*Kapsin* Reform Edict." In *Sources of Korean Tradition,* ed. Yŏngho Ch'oe, Peter Lee, and Wm. Theodore de Bary. New York: Columbia University Press, 2000, 2: 255–56.

Kim Sin. *Muyŏksa.* Seoul: Sokjong, 1995.

Kim Song-hun. "Han'guk kaehanggi muyŏk ŭi t'ŭkching kwa yŏnghyang." M.A. thesis, Ch'angwŏn taehakkyo, 1995.

Kim Sun-dŏk. "1876–1905 nyŏn kwanse chŏngch'aek kwa kwanse ŭi unyong." M.A. thesis, Seoul National University, 1985.

Kim Wŏn-mo. *Han-Mi sugyosa.* Seoul: Ch'ŏlhak kwa hyŏnsilsa, 1999.

————. *Kaehwagi Han-Mi kyosŏp kwangyesa.* Seoul: Tan'guk taehakkyo ch'ulp'anbu, 2003.

Kim Wŏn-mo, ed. *Allen ŭi ilgi* [H. N. Allen's Diary]. Seoul: Dankook University Press, 1991.

Kim, Yongkoo. *The Five Years' Crisis, 1866–1871.* Seoul: Circle, 2001.

Kimura, Mitsuhiko. "Japanese Imperialism and Colonial Economy in Korea and Taiwan: A Study in an International Perspective." *Discussion Paper Series F-079*, Faculty of Economics, Tezukayama University, Japan.

Kirby, William C. "The Internationalization of China: Foreign Relations at Home and Abroad in the Republican Era." *China Quarterly*, no. 150 (June 1997): 433–58.

———. "Traditions of Centrality, Authority, and Management in Modern China's Foreign Relations." In *Chinese Foreign Policy: Theory and Practice*, ed. Thomas W. Robinson and David Shambaugh. New York: Oxford University Press, 1994, 13–29.

Ko, Dorothy. "The Body as Attire: The Shifting Meanings of Footbinding in Seventeenth-Century China." *Journal of Women's History* 8, no. 4 (Winter 1997): 10–26.

Korean Customs Service. *Yunghŭi wŏnnyŏn Han'guk oeguk muyŏk yŏlam*. 1908? Copy at Korean Customs Service Museum, Seoul.

Korean Repository. Seoul: Trilingual Press, 1892–98.

Korea Review. 1900–1906.

Koryŏ taehakkyo, ed. *Ku-Han'guk oegyo kwan'gye pusok munsŏ: Haegwanan*. Seoul: Koryŏ taehakkyo, 1962.

———. *Ku Han'guk oegyo munso: Ch'ŏngan*. 2 vols. Seoul: Koryŏ taehakkyo, 1970.

———. *Ku Han'guk oegyo munso: Tokan*. 2 vols. Seoul: Koryŏ taehakkyo, 1970.

Ku Sŏn-hŭi. *Han'guk kŭndae taeQing chŏngch'aeksa yŏn'gu*. Seoul: Hyean, 1999.

Kuhn, Philip. *Rebellion and Its Enemies in Late Imperial China: Militarization and Social Structure, 1796–1864*. Cambridge, MA: Harvard University Press, 1970.

Kukhoe tosŏgwan. Ippŏp chosaguk. *Ku Hanmal choyak hwich'an*, vol. 2 (*chung*). Seoul: Tonga ch'ulpansa, 1965.

Kuksa p'yŏnch'an wiwŏnhoe, ed. *Ch'ŏlchong sillok*. Accessed at http://sillok.history.go.kr.

———. *The Collected Letters of Yun Tchi Ho*. Seoul: Kuksa p'yŏnch'an wiwŏnhoe, 1980.

———. *Deni munsŏ*. Han'guk saryo, 28. Seoul: Kuksa p'yŏnch'an wiwŏnhoe, 1981.

———. *Kojong sidaesa*. Seoul: Kuksa p'yŏnch'an wiwŏnhoe, 1970.

———. *Kojong sillok*. Accessed at http://sillok.history.go.kr.

———. *Sunjong sillok*. Accessed at http://sillok.history.go.kr.

———. *Yun Ch'i-Ho's Diary*. Seoul: Kuksa p'yŏnch'an wiwŏnhoe, 1971.

Kwŏn Sŏk-pong. "Ch'ŏngjŏng e issŏsŏ ŭi Taewŏn'gun kwa kŭ ŭi hwan'guk." 2 pts. *Tongbang hakchi* 27 (1981): 125–54; 28 (1981): 109–64.

———. "Yi Sŏn-dŏk ŭi p'a-Il kwa ch'ŏngch'ŭk kaeip." *Paeksan hakpo* 8 (1970): 575–628.

Kyo, Syukushin. "Japan." In *Encyclopedia of the Overseas Chinese*, ed. Lynn Pan. Cambridge, MA: Harvard University Press, 1999, 332–40.

Laird, Thomas. *The Story of Tibet: Conversations with the Dalai Lama*. New York: Grove Press, 2006.

Landes, David. *The Wealth and Poverty of Nations*. New York: Norton, 1999.

Larsen, Kirk. "Cannibals, Cameras, and Chinese: Rumor and the Formation of a 'Modern' Korea in the Late 19th Century." Paper presented at the Korean Modernity in Comparative Perspective conference, Georgetown University, May 3–5, 2001.

———. "From Suzerainty to Commerce: Sino-Korean Economic and Business Relations During the Open Port Period (1876–1910)." Ph.D. diss., Harvard University, 2000.

Ledyard, Gari. "Confucianism and War: The Korean Security Crisis of 1598." *Journal of Korean Studies* 6 (1988): 81–119.

———. *The Dutch Come to Korea.* Seoul: Royal Asiatic Society, Korea Branch, 1971.

———. "Hong Taeyong and His 'Peking Memoir.'" *Korean Studies* 6 (1982): 63–103.

Lee, Hyun-hee; Sung-soo Park; and Nae-hyun Yoon. *New History of Korea.* Trans. Gilsang Lee. P'aju: Jinmoondang, 2005.

Lee, John. "Trade and Economy in Preindustrial East Asia, c. 1500–c. 1800: East Asia in the Age of Global Integration." *Journal of Asian Studies* 58, no. 1 (1999): 2–26.

Lee Keun-yeup. "Glory of Ancestors, Contemptible Descendants." *Korea Times*, Feb. 18, 2004. Accessed at http://times.hankooki.com/lpage/opinion/200402/kt2004021817051411390.htm.

Lee Ki-baik. *A New History of Korea.* Trans. Edward W. Wagner, with Edward J. Schultz. Cambridge, MA: Published for the Harvard-Yenching Institute by Harvard University Press, 1983.

Lee, Peter H. *A Korean Storyteller's Miscellany: The* P'aegwan chapki *of Ŏ Sukkwŏn.* Princeton: Princeton University Press, 1989.

Lee, Peter H., ed. *Sourcebook of Korean Civilization,* vol. 1, *From Early Times to the Sixteenth Century.* New York: Columbia University Press, 1993.

Lee, Peter H., and Wm. Theodore de Bary, eds. *Sources of Korean Tradition,* vol. 1, *From Early Times Through the Sixteenth Century.* New York: Columbia University Press, 1997.

Lee, Yur-Bok. "Establishment of a Korean Legation in the United States, 1887–1890: A Study of Conflict Between Confucian World Order and Modern International Relations." *Illinois Papers in Asian Studies* 3 (1983).

———. "Politics over Economics: China's Domination of Korea Through Extension of Financial Loans, 1882–1894." In *Han'guk sahak nonch'ong,* ed. Such'ŏn Pak Yongsŏk kyosu hwagap kinyŏm nonch'ong kanhaeng wiwŏnhoe. Seoul: Such'ŏn Pak Yongsŏk kyosu hwagap kinyŏm nonch'ong kanhaeng wiwŏnhoe, 1982, 1–94.

———. "The Sino-Japanese Economic Warfare over Korea, 1876–1894." *Russia and the Pacific* 1, no. 5 (1994): 122–32.

———. *West Goes East: Paul Georg Von Mollendorff and Great Power Imperialism in Late Yi Korea.* Honolulu: University of Hawai'i Press, 1988.

Leifer, Walter. "Paul-Georg Von Mollendorff and the Opening of Korea." *Asian and Pacific Quarterly of Cultural and Social Affairs* (South Korea) 14, no. 2 (1982): 1–23.

Lenin, V. I. *Imperialism: The Latest Stage in the Development of Capitalism.* Trans. J. T. Kozlowski. Detroit: Marxian Educational Society, 1924.

Lensen, George Alexander. *Balance of Intrigue: International Rivalry in Korea and Manchuria, 1884–1899.* 2 vols. Tallahassee: University Presses of Florida, 1982.

Lew, Young Ick. "Yuan Shih-K'ai's Residency and the Korean Enlightenment Movement, 1885–94." *Journal of Korean Studies* 5 (1984): 63–107.

Li Hongzhang. *Li wenzhong gong quanshu.* Ed. Wu Rulun. 100 vols. Nanjing: Li Family, 1908.

Lieven, Dominic. *Empire: The Russian Empire and Its Rivals.* New Haven: Yale University Press, 2001.

Lin, Mingde (Lin Ming-te). "Li Hung-Chang's Suzerain Policy Toward Korea, 1882–1894." In *Li Hung-Chang and China's Early Modernization*, ed. Samuel C. Chu and Kwang-Ching Liu. Armonk, NY: M. E. Sharpe, 1994.

———. *Yuan Shikai yu Chaoxian.* Taibei: Institute of Modern History, Academia Sinica, 1984.

Lin, T. C. "Li Hung-Chang: His Korea Policies, 1870–1885." *Chinese Social and Political Science Review* 19 (1935): 202–33.

Liu, Kwang-Ching. "The Confucian as Patriot and Pragmatist: Li Hung-chang's Formative Years, 1823–1866." In *Li Hung-chang and China's Early Modernization*, ed. Samuel C. Chu and Kwang-Ching Liu. Armonk, NY: M. E. Sharpe, 1994, 17–48.

Long, Roger, ed. *The Man on the Spot: Essays on British Empire History.* Westport, CT: Greenwood, 1995.

Longford, Joseph H. *The Story of Korea.* London: T. Fisher Unwin, 1911.

Lowell, Percival. *Choson: Land of Morning Calm. A Sketch of Korea.* Boston: Ticknor, 1886.

Lynn, Martin. "British Policy, Trade, and Informal Empire in the Mid-Nineteenth Century." In *The Oxford History of the British Empire*, vol. 3, *The Nineteenth Century*, ed. Andrew Porter. Oxford: Oxford University Press, 1999, 101–21.

Ma Jianzhong. *Dongxing sanlu.* Shanghai: Shanghai shudian, 1982.

———. *Shikezhai jiyan.* Beijing: Zhonghua shuju, 1960.

Ma Tingliang. "Chaoxian Renchuan shangwu qingxing." *Shangwu guanbao*, no. 13 (1907): 15–17.

———. "Chaoxian shangwu qingxing." *Shangwu guanbao*, no. 16 (1908): 14–17.

———. "Hancheng dengchu shanggongye qingxing." *Shangwu guanbao*, no. 27 (1906): 16–18.

MacKinnon, Stephen R. *Power and Politics in Late Imperial China: Yuan Shih-K'ai in Beijing and Tianjin, 1901–1908.* Berkeley: University of California Press, 1980.

Maier, Charles. *Among Empires: American Ascendancy and Its Predecessors.* Cambridge, MA: Harvard University Press, 2006.

Mancall, Mark. *China at the Center: 300 Years of Foreign Relations.* New York: Free Press, 1984.

McField, Vik. *Resil's Textile Dictionary.* http://www.resil.com/otd.htm. Accessed on Aug. 17, 2007.

McKeown, Adam. "Conceptualizing Chinese Diasporas, 1842 to 1949." *Journal of Asian Studies* 58, no. 2 (May 1999): 306–37.

Meng, T. S. *The Tsungli Yamen: Its Organization and Functions.* Cambridge, MA: Harvard University Press, 1962.

Merrill, Henry F. "Merrill's Letterbooks." Houghton Library, Harvard University.

Meyer, Karl Ernest. *The Dust of Empire: The Race for Mastery in the Asian Heartland.* New York: Public Affairs, 2003.

Millward, James. *Beyond the Pass: Economy, Ethnicity, and Empire in Qing Central Asia.* Stanford: Stanford University Press, 1998.

Min, Tu-ki. "The Jehol Diary and the Character of Ch'ing Rule." In idem, *National Polity and Local Power: The Transformation of Late Imperial China,* ed. Philip Kuhn and Timothy Brook. Cambridge, MA: Council on East Asian Studies, Harvard University, 1989, 1–19.

Mitter, Rana. *A Bitter Revolution: China's Struggle with the Modern World.* London: Oxford, 2004.

Morse, Hosea Ballou. *The International Relations of the Chinese Empire.* 3 vols. London: Longmans, Green, 1910.

Munck, Ronaldo. "Dependency and Imperialism in Latin America: New Horizons." In *The Political Economy of Imperialism: New Appraisals,* ed. Ronald H. Chilcote. Lanham, MD: Rowman and Littlefield, 2000, 141–56.

Murphy, Kevin C. *The American Merchant Experience in 19th Century Japan.* London: RoutledgeCurzon, 2003.

Mutsu Munemitsu. *Kenkenroku. A Diplomatic Record of the Sino-Japanese War, 1894–1895.* Ed. and trans. Gordon Mark Berger. Tokyo: Japan Foundation, 1982.

Myers, Ramon, and Mark Peattie, eds. *The Japanese Colonial Empire, 1895–1945.* Princeton: Princeton University Press, 1984.

Nahm, Andrew. "The Impact of the Taft-Katsura Memorandum on Korea: A Reassessment." *Korea Journal,* Oct. 1985: 4–17.

Nelson, Melvin Frederick. *Korea and the Old Orders in Eastern Asia.* Baton Rouge: Louisiana State University Press, 1945.

Nelson, Sarah Milledge. *The Archaeology of Korea.* Cambridge, Eng.: Cambridge University Press, 1993.

New York Times.

Nihon gaikō bunsho. 73 vols. Tokyo: Nihon kokusai rengō kyōkai, 1936–63.

Nish, Ian. "John McLeavy Brown in Korea." *Papers of the British Association for Korean Studies* 2 (1992): 29–50.

Nish, Ian, ed. "Korea, the Ryukyu Islands, and North-East Asia, 1875–1888." In *British Documents on Foreign Affairs: Reports and Papers from the Foreign Office Confi-*

dential Print, ed. idem, Kenneth Bourne, and D. Cameron Watt. Frederick, MD: University Publications of America, 1989–94.

North China Herald. Shanghai.

Oh, Bonnie B. C. "The Background of Chinese Policy Formation in the Sino-Japanese War of 1894–1895." Ph.D. diss., University of Chicago, 1974.

————. "The Leadership Crisis in China on the Eve of the Sino-Japanese War of 1894–1895." *Papers on Far Eastern History*, no. 29 (1984): 67–90.

Osterhammel, Jürgen. "Britain and China, 1842–1914." In *The Oxford History of the British Empire: The Nineteenth Century*, ed. Andrew Porter. Oxford: Oxford University Press, 1999, 146–69.

————. "Semi-Colonialism and Informal Empire in Twentieth-Century China: Towards a Framework of Analysis." In *Imperialism and After: Continuities and Discontinuities*, ed. Wolfgang J. Mommsen and Jürgen Osterhammel. London: Allen and Unwin, 1986, 290–314.

Pai, Hyung-il. *Constructing "Korean" Origins: A Critical Review of Archaeology, Historiography, and Racial Myth in Korean State-Formation Theories.* Cambridge, MA: Harvard University Press, 2000.

Paik, L. George. *The History of Protestant Missions in Korea, 1832–1910.* Seoul: Yonsei University Press, 1980.

Paine, S. C. M. *The Sino-Japanese War of 1894–1895: Perceptions, Power, and Primacy.* Cambridge, Eng.: Cambridge University Press, 2003.

Pak Chega. "On Revering China." In *Sources of Korean Tradition*, vol. 2, *From the Sixteenth to the Twentieth Centuries*, ed. Yŏngho Ch'oe, Peter Lee, and Wm. Theodore de Bary. New York: Columbia University Press, 1996, 101–4.

Pak Kwang-song. "Inch'ŏnhang ŭi chogye e taehayo." *Kijon munhwa yŏn'gu* 20 (1991): 283–312.

Pak Kyŏng-yong. *Kaehwagi Hansŏngbu yŏn'gu.* Seoul: Ilchogak, 1995.

Pak Su-i. "Kaehanggi Han'guk muyŏk chabon e kwanhan yŏn'gu." Ph.D. diss., Tonga University, 1978.

Pak Wan. *Sillok Han'guk kidokkyo 100 nyŏn*, vol. 1, *yomyong ŭi chang.* Seoul: Sŏnmun ch'ulp'ansa, 1971.

Palais, James B. *Confucian Statecraft and Korean Institutions: Yu Hyŏngwŏn and the Late Chosŏn Dynasty.* Seattle: University of Washington Press, 1996.

————. *Politics and Policy in Traditional Korea.* Cambridge, MA: Harvard University Press, 1975.

Palmer, Spencer J., ed. *Korean-American Relations: Documents Pertaining to the Far Eastern Diplomacy of the United States.* Vol. 1, *The Initial Period, 1883–1886.* Vol. 2, *The Period of Growing Influence, 1887–1895.* Berkeley: University of California Press, 1951, 1963.

Pan, Lynn. *Sons of the Yellow Emperor: A History of the Chinese Diaspora.* New York: Kodansha International, 1994.

Pan, Lynn, ed. *The Encyclopedia of the Chinese Overseas.* Cambridge, MA: Harvard University Press, 1999.

Park, Eun Kyung. "Ethnic Network Among Chinese Small Business in Korea During the Colonial Period (1910–1945)." *Journal of Social Sciences and Humanities* 67 (1989): 67–89.

Park, Il-keun. "China's Policy Toward Korea, 1880–1884." *Journal of Social Sciences and Humanities* 53 (1981): 45–78.

Park, Il-Keun, ed. *Anglo-American and Chinese Diplomatic Materials Relating to Korea, 1887–1897.* Pusan: Institute of Chinese Studies, Pusan National University, 1984.

——. *Anglo-American Materials Relating to Korea (1866–1886).* Seoul: Shin Mun Dang, 1982.

Park, Young-Il, and Kym Anderson. "The Experience of Japan in Historical and International Perspective." In *New Silk Roads: East Asia and World Textile Markets,* ed. Kym Anderson, 15–29. Cambridge, Eng.: Cambridge University Press, 1992.

Peattie, Mark. "The Japanese Colonial Empire, 1895–1945." In *The Cambridge History of Japan,* ed. Peter Duus. New York: Cambridge University Press, 1998, 217–70.

Perdue, Peter. *China Marches West: The Qing Conquest of Central Eurasia.* Cambridge, MA: Harvard University Press, 2005.

——. "Comparing Empires: Manchu Colonialism." *International History Review* 20, no. 2 (1998): 255–62.

——. *Exhausting the Earth: State and Peasant in Hunan.* Cambridge, MA: Council on East Asian Studies, Harvard University, 1987.

Peyrefitte, Alain. *The Collision of Two Civilisations: The British Expedition to China in 1792–4.* Trans. Jon Rothschild. London: Harvill, 1993.

——. *The Immobile Empire.* Trans. Jon Rothschild. New York: Knopf, 1992.

Phillips, Steven. "Retrocession and Sinification: The Nationalists and Taiwan, 1941–1945." Paper presented at annual conference of the Association for Asian Studies, Chicago, Mar. 2001.

"A Picturesque Embassy: Unique Appearance of the Corean Officials Now in Washington." *Evening Star* (Washington, DC), 1888.

Pomeranz, Kenneth. *The Great Divergence: China, Europe, and the Making of the Modern World Economy.* Princeton: Princeton University Press, 2000.

Poston, Dudley L., and Yu Mei-yu. "The Distribution of Overseas Chinese in the Contemporary World." *International Migration Review* 24, no. 3 (1990): 480–509.

Pratt, Edward Ewing. "The Attitude of Business Towards Foreign Trade." *Annals of the Academy of Political and Social Science* 59 (May 1915): 291–300.

Pratt, Keith; Richard Rutt; and James Hoare. *Korea: A Historical and Cultural Dictionary.* Surrey, Eng.: Curzon, 1999.

Pusan chikhalsisa p'yŏnch'an wiwŏnhoe. *Pusansisa.* Pusan: Pusan chikhalsisa p'yŏnch'an wiwŏnhoe, 1989.

Qin Yuguang. "Hwagyo." *Chungang ilbo*, Sept. 19, 20, 24, 1979. (Note: Qin had a regular column in this newspaper; it always appeared on p. 5.)

———. *Lü Han liushinian jianwenlu*. Taibei: Zhonghua minguo Hanguo yanjiu xuehui, 1983.

Redding, S. Gordon. *The Spirit of Chinese Capitalism*. New York: Walter De Gruyter, 1993.

Reischauer, Edwin. *Ennin's Travels in Tang China*. New York: Ronald Press, 1955.

Reynolds, Bruce L. "The East Asian 'Textile Cluster' Trade, 1868–1973: A Comparative Advantage Interpretation." In *America's China Trade in Historical Perspective*, ed. John K. Fairbank and Ernest May. Cambridge, MA: Harvard University Press, 1986, 129–50.

Rhoads, Edward J. M. *Manchus and Han: Ethnic Relations and Political Power in Late Qing and Early Republican China, 1861–1928*. Seattle: University of Washington Press, 2000.

Robinson, Kenneth R. "From Raiders to Traders: Border Security and Border Control in Early Chosŏn, 1392–1450." *Korean Studies* 16 (1992): 94–114.

Rossabi, Morris, ed. *China Among Equals: The Middle Kingdom and Its Neighbors*. Berkeley: University of California Press, 1983.

Rowe, William. *Hankow: Commerce and Society in a Chinese City, 1796–1889*. Stanford: Stanford University Press, 1984.

Said, Edward. *Orientalism*. New York: Vintage, 1979.

Sakurai Gunnosuke. "Chōsen jiji." In *Soul e namgyodun kkum*, ed. Han Sang-il. Seoul: Kŏn'guk taehakkyo, 1993, 263–75.

Sands, William Franklin. *Undiplomatic Memories: The Far East, 1896–1904*. London: John Hamilton, 1904.

SarDesai, Damodar R. "British Expansion in Southeast Asia: The Imperialism of Trade in the Nineteenth Century." In *The Man on the Spot: Essays on British Empire History*, ed. Roger D. Long. Westport, CT: Greenwood, 1995, 7–20.

Schmid, Andre. "Colonialism and the 'Korea Problem' in the Historiography of Modern Japan: A Review Article." *Journal of Asian Studies* 59, no. 4 (Nov. 2000): 951–76.

———. "Constructing Independence: Nation and Identity in Korea, 1895–1910." Ph.D. diss., Columbia University, 1996.

———. *Korea Between Empires, 1895–1919*. New York: Columbia University Press, 2002.

Schrecker, John E. *Imperialism and Chinese Nationalism: Germany in Shantung*. Cambridge, MA: Harvard University Press, 1971.

Seagrave, Sterling. *Lords of the Rim: The Invisible Empire of the Overseas Chinese*. New York: Putnam, 1992.

Seeley, John. *The Expansion of England: Two Courses of Lectures*. Boston: Roberts Brothers, 1883.

Seung, Kwon Synn. *The Russo-Japanese Rivalry over Korea, 1876–1904.* Seoul: Yuk Phub Sa, 1981.

Shim Jae Hoon. "Korea." In *Encyclopedia of the Overseas Chinese,* ed. Lynn Pan. Cambridge, MA: Harvard University Press, 1999, 341–43.

Shiokawa Ichitarō. *Chōsen tsūshō jijō.* Tokyo: Hachio shoten, 1895.

Sigel, Louis T. "Business-Government Cooperation in Late Qing Korean Policy." In *To Achieve Security and Wealth: The Qing Imperial State and the Economy, 1644–1911,* ed. Jane Kate Leonard and John R. Watt. Ithaca: Cornell University East Asia Program, 1992, 157–82.

————. "Ch'ing Foreign Policy and the Modern Commercial Community: T'ang Shao-Yi in Korea." *Papers on Far Eastern History* (Canberra), no. 13 (1976): 77–106.

————. "Foreign Policy Interests and Activities of the Treaty-Port Chinese Community." In *Reform in Nineteenth-Century China,* ed. Paul A. Cohen and John E. Schrecker. Cambridge, MA: Harvard University Press, 1976, 272–81.

————. "The Role of Korea in Late Qing Foreign Policy." *Papers on Far Eastern History* (Canberra), no. 21 (1980): 75–98.

————. "The Sino-Japanese Quest for Korean Markets, 1885–1891." *Essays in Economic and Business History* 10 (1992): 104–16.

————. "T'ang Shao-yi (1860–1938): The Diplomacy of Chinese Nationalism." Ph.D. diss., Harvard University, 1972.

Sin Pok-kyŏng and Kim Un-gyŏng, eds. *Moellendorup'u munsŏ.* Seoul: P'yŏngminsa, 1987.

Sluglett, Peter. "Formal and Informal Empire in the Middle East." In *The Oxford History of the British Empire,* vol. 5, *Historiography,* ed. Robin Winks. Oxford: Oxford University Press, 1999, 416–36.

Sohn Pow-Key, Kim Chol-choon, and Hong Yi-sup. *The History of Korea.* Seoul: Korea National Commission for UNESCO, 1970.

Son Chŏng-mok. *Han'guk kaehanggi tosi pyŏnhwa kwajŏng yŏn'gu.* Seoul: Ilchisa, 1982.

Sugiyama, Shinya. "Textile Marketing in East Asia, 1860–1914." *Textile History* 19, no. 2 (1988): 279–98.

Swartout, Robert R. "Journey to Old Korea: The 1886 Diary of Gertrude Hall Denny." *Transactions of the Korea Branch of the Royal Asiatic Society* 61 (1986): 35–68.

————. *Mandarins, Gunboats, and Power Politics: Owen Nickerson Denny and the International Rivalries in Korea.* Honolulu: Asian Studies Program, University of Hawai'i, 1980.

Tan Que. "Tongshuntai yu jiu Han jiehuan." *Hanhua chunqiu* 4 (1964): 26–28.

Tan Yongsheng (Tam Yŏng-sŏng). "Chosŏn malgi ŭi Ch'ŏngguk sangin e kwanhan yŏn'gu." M.A. thesis, Tan'guk University, 1971.

Tang Entong. "Hanguo Renchuan shangwu qingxing." *Shangwu guanbao,* no. 2 (1908): 13–14.

Tang, Yen-Lu. "The Crumbling of Tradition: Ma Chien-Chung and China's Entrance into the Family of Nations." Ph.D. diss., New York University, 1987.

Tanner, Christine. "Failures and Legacies of the Print Media: Korea's First Legation in Washington, D.C. (1888)." Unpublished paper, George Washington University, 2001.

Teng, Emma Jinhua. *Taiwan's Imagined Geography: Chinese Colonial Travel Writing and Pictures, 1683–1895.* Cambridge, MA: Harvard University Asia Center, 2004.

Teng Ssu-yü and John King Fairbank. *China's Response to the West: A Documentary Survey, 1839–1293.* Cambridge, MA: Harvard University Press, 1954.

Thongchai, Winichakul. *Siam Mapped: A History of the Geo-Body of a Nation.* Honolulu: University of Hawai'i Press, 1997.

Tongshuntai. "Tongshuntaihao jiekuan hedong." Kyujanggak #26383, ca. 1892.

———. "Tongtai laixin." Kyujanggak #27584.

Tseng, Marquis (Zeng Jize). "China: The Sleep and the Awakening." *Chinese Recorder and Missionary Journal* 18 (1887): 146–53.

Tsiang, T. F. "Sino-Japanese Diplomatic Relations, 1870–1894." *Chinese Social and Political Science Review* 17 (1933/34): 1–106.

Turnbull, Stephen. *Samurai Invasion: Japan's Korean War, 1592–98.* London: Cassell, 2002.

Underwood, Lillias Horton. *Fifteen Years Among the Top-Knots: or, Life in Korea.* Boston and New York: American Tract Society, 1904.

———. *Underwood of Korea: Being an Intimate Record of the Life and Work of the Rev. H. G. Underwood, D.D., LL.D., for Thirty-one Years a Missionary of the Presbyterian Board in Korea.* Seoul: Yonsei University Press, 1983.

Van de Ven, Hans. "The Onrush of Modern Globalization in China." In *Globalization in World History*, ed. A. G. Hopkins. London: Pimlico, 2002, 177–87.

Varg, Paul A. "The Myth of the China Market, 1890–1914." *American Historical Review* 73, no. 3 (Feb. 1968): 742–58.

von Glahn, Richard. *Fountain of Fortune: Money and Monetary Policy in China, 1000–1700.* Berkeley: University of California Press, 1996.

Wagner, Edward Willett. *The Literati Purges: Political Conflict in Early Yi Korea.* Cambridge, MA: East Asian Research Center, 1974.

Wakeman, Frederic, Jr. *The Great Enterprise: The Manchu Reconstruction of Imperial Order in Seventeenth-Century China.* Berkeley: University of California Press, 1985.

Wang Bogong. *Quanlu suibi.* Taibei: Wenhai chubanshe, 1968.

Wang Erh-min. *Zhongguo jindai sixiang shilun.* Taibei: Huashi chubanshe, 1977.

Wang Gungwu. *China and the Chinese Overseas.* Singapore: Times Academic Press, 1991.

———. "Greater China and the Chinese Overseas." *China Quarterly*, no. 136 (Dec. 1993): 926–48.

Wang Jianlang. *Zhongguo feichu bupingdeng tiaoyue de licheng.* Nanchang: Jiangxi renmin chubanshe, 2000.

Wang Kŏn. "Wang Kŏn: Ten Injunctions." In *Sourcebook of Korean Civilization*, vol. 1, *From Early Times to the Sixteenth Century*, ed. Peter H. Lee. New York: Columbia University Press, 1993, 150–56.

Wang Liang and Wang Yanwei, eds. *Qingji waijiao shiliao*. Taibei: Wenhai chubanshe, 1964.

Wang, Tseng-Tsai. "The Macartney Mission: A Bicentennial Review." In *Ritual and Diplomacy: The Macartney Mission to China, 1792–1794*, ed. Robert Bickers. London: British Association for Chinese Studies, 1993, 43–56.

Weale, Putnam. *The Re-shaping of the Far East*. London: Macmillan, 1905.

Welch, William M. *No Country for a Gentleman: British Rule in Egypt, 1883–1907*. New York: Greenwood Press, 1988.

Wiener, Martin. *English Culture and the Decline of the Industrial Spirit*. Oxford: Oxford University Press, 1981.

Wilson, Andrew. "Ambition and Identity: China and the Chinese in the Colonial Philippines, 1885–1912." Ph.D. diss., Harvard University, 1998.

Wong, R. Bin. *China Transformed: Historical Change and the Limits of European Experience*. Ithaca: Cornell University Press, 1997.

Woo, Philip Myungsup. "The Historical Development of Korean Tariff and Customs Administration, 1875–1958." Ph.D. diss., New York University, 1963.

Wright, Mary C. "The Adaptability of Ch'ing Diplomacy: The Case of Korea." *Journal of Asian Studies* 17 (1958): 363–81.

Yang Daqing. *Technology of Empire: Telecommunications and Japanese Imperialism, 1930–1945*. Cambridge, MA: Harvard University Asia Center, forthcoming.

Yang Sang-hyŏn. "Tae Han chegukki Naejangwŏn chaejŏong kwalli yŏn'gu." Ph.D. diss., Seoul National University, 1997.

Yang Zhaoquan and Sun Yumei. *Chaoxian Huaqiaoshi*. Beijing: Huaqiao chubanshe, 1991.

Yen, Ching-hwang. *Coolies and Mandarins: China's Protection of Overseas Chinese During the Late Ching Period (1851–1911)*. Singapore: Singapore University Press, 1985.

Yi Kwang-nin. "T'ongni kimu amun ŭi chojik kwa kinung." *Yihwa sahak yŏn'gu*, no. 17–18 (1988): 503–7.

Yi Min-sik. "Pak Chŏng-yang ŭi chae-Mi hwaldong e kwanhan yŏn'gu; munhwa kyŏnmunŭl chungsimŭro." *Han'guk sasang kwa munhwa* 1 (1998): 425–48.

Yi Pyŏng-ch'ŏn. "Kaehanggi oeguk sangin ŭi ch'imip kwa Han'guk sangin ŭi tae-ŭng." Ph.D. diss., Seoul National University, 1985.

Yi Sŏn-gŭn. *Han'guksa: ch'oe kŭnse p'yŏn*. Seoul: Chindan hakhoe, 1977.

Yi T'ae-jin. *Han'guk pyŏnghap sŏngnip haji anatta*. Seoul: Taehaksa, 2001.

———. *Sŏuldae Yi T'aejin kyosu ŭi Tonggyŏngdaesaengdŭl ege tŭllyŏjun Han'guksa*. Seoul: Taehaksa, 2005.

Yi T'ae-jin, Kim Ki-sŏk, Paek Ch'ung-hyŏn, Yi Kŭn-gwan, Sin Hyo-suk, and Yi Yong-kwŏn. *Han'guk pyŏnghap ŭi pulpŏpsŏng yŏn'gu*. Seoul: Sŏul taehakkyo ch'ulp'anbu, 2003.

Yi Tŏk-chu. *Chosŏn ŭn wae Ilbon ŭi singminji ga doeŏnnŭn'ga?* Seoul: Edit'ŏ, 2002.

Yi Yang-ja. "Ch'ŏng ŭi tae Chosŏn kyŏngje chŏngch'i wa Wŏn Segae." *Pusan sahak* 8 (1984): 113–54.

Yongsan'gu. *Yongsan'guji.* Seoul: Yongsangu, 1992.

"Yuan Shikai zhujie Chaoxian qijian handu xuanji." *Lishi dang'an* 3 (1992): 56–63.

Zabrovskaia, Larisa V. "1899 Treaty and Its Impact on the Development of the Chinese-Korean Trade (1895–1905)." *Korea Journal* 31, no. 4 (1991): 29–39.

Zhang Cunwu. *Qing-Han zongfan maoyi.* Taibei: Institute of Modern History, 1978.

Zhang Cunwu, ed. *Jindai Zhong-Han guanxishi ziliao huibian.* 12 vols. Taibei: Guoshiguan, 1987.

Zhang Ruogu, ed. *Ma Xiangbo xiansheng nianpu.* Zhangsha: Shangwu yinshiguan, 1939.

Zhang, Shunhong. "Historical Anachronism: The Qing Court's Perception of and Reaction to the Macartney Embassy." In *Ritual and Diplomacy: The Macartney Mission to China, 1792–1794,* ed. Robert Bickers. London: British Association for Chinese Studies, 1993, 31–42.

Zhou Nanjing, ed. *Shijie Huaqiao Huaren cidian.* Beijing: Beijing daxue chupanshe, 1993.

"Zhu Han zonglingshi shenben buwen." *Shangwu guanbao,* no. 11 (1907): 6.

Index

Harvard East Asian Monographs
(*out-of-print)

Harvard East Asian Monographs

Harvard East Asian Monographs

Harvard East Asian Monographs

Harvard East Asian Monographs

Harvard East Asian Monographs

Harvard East Asian Monographs